Conversing with God

Conversing with God

The Conversational Prayers in the Hebrew Bible

Terry Giles

◆PICKWICK *Publications* • Eugene, Oregon

CONVERSING WITH GOD
The Conversational Prayers in the Hebrew Bible

Copyright © 2022 Terry Giles. All rights reserved. Except for brief quotations in critical publications or reviews, no part of this book may be reproduced in any manner without prior written permission from the publisher. Write: Permissions, Wipf and Stock Publishers, 199 W. 8th Ave., Suite 3, Eugene, OR 97401.

Pickwick Publications
An Imprint of Wipf and Stock Publishers
199 W. 8th Ave., Suite 3
Eugene, OR 97401

www.wipfandstock.com

PAPERBACK ISBN: 978-1-7252-8687-0
HARDCOVER ISBN: 978-1-7252-8686-3
EBOOK ISBN: 978-1-7252-8688-7

Cataloguing-in-Publication data:

Names: Giles, Terry, author.

Title: Conversing with God : the conversational prayers in the Hebrew Bible / Terry Giles.

Description: Eugene, OR: Pickwick Publications, 2022. | Includes bibliographical references and index.

Identifiers: ISBN 978-1-7252-8687-0 (paperback). | ISBN 978-1-7252-8686-3 (hardcover). | ISBN 978-1-7252-8688-7 (ebook).

Subjects: LCSH: Bible—Prayers—History and criticism. | Bible. OT—Criticism, interpretation, etc. | Prayer—Biblical teaching.

Classification: BS680.P64 G55 2022 (print). | B680 (ebook).

03/30/22

Except where otherwise noted, Scripture quotations are taken from the New Revised Standard Version Bible, copyright © 1989 by the National Council of the Churches of Christ in the United States. Used by permission. All rights reserved.

Cover art by William J. Doan. Used by permission.

For

*Eli, Ellie, Easton, Rowen,
and Quinton*

May their conversations with God
be pleasant and frequent

Contents

Preface | ix
Abbreviations | x

1. Introduction | 1
2. Conversation Analysis | 13
3. Abraham Cycle | 35
4. Jacob Cycle | 62
5. Moses | 83
6. Balaam, Joshua, the Judges | 140
7. Parallel Prayers: Samuel–Kings, Chronicles, Isaiah | 171
8. Elijah/Elisha Cycle | 209
9. Conversational Prayers Only in Chronicles | 223
10. Prophets | 239
11. General Observations | 254

Postscript: The Last Word | 263
Appendix 1: Genesis 3:9–19; Adam and Eve | 265
Appendix 2: Non-Conversational Prosaic Prayers | 271
Bibliography | 273
Subject Index | 287
Author Index | 289
Ancient Document Index | 293

Preface

This book is about prayer. More, it is about the act of praying and the interpersonal relationship formed with God through prayer. The conversational prayers found in the Hebrew Bible serve as models, guiding our investigation. The investigation of those conversational prayers has led me to an unexpected conclusion. The conversational prayers in the Hebrew Bible are a beginning point, a springboard that must lead us to consider our own conversations with God. The analysis of prayer, for it to be authentic, must give way to the commitment of prayer. The observer must become the participant. I have come to learn that prayer is a journey with no end. On that journey, I welcome your company.

Terry Giles
Spring 2021

Abbreviations

AB	Anchor Bible
AYB	Anchor Yale Bible
BDB	F. Brown, S. R. Driver, and C. A. Briggs, *A Hebrew and English Lexicon of the Old Testament*
BHS	Biblia Hebraica Stuttgartensia
BZAW	Beiträge zur Zeitschrift für die alttestamentliche Wissenschaft
CA	Conversation Analysis
CBQ	*Catholic Biblical Quarterly*
DSS	Dead Sea Scrolls
ESV	English Standard Version
ET	English translations
FOTL	Forms of the Old Testament Literature
GKC	Gesenius–Kautzsch–Cowley, *Gesenius' Hebrew Grammar*
ICC	International Critical Commentary
JBL	*Journal of Biblical Literature*
JHS	*Journal of Hebrew Scriptures*
JSJSup	Journal for the Study of Judaism Supplements
JPS	Jewish Publication Society Tanak
JSOT	*Journal for the Study of the Old Testament*
JSOTSup	Journal for the Study of the Old Testament Supplement Series

LXX	Septuagint
MT	Masoretic Text
NAB	New American Bible
NASB	New American Standard Bible
NIV	New International Version
NRSV	New Revised Standard Version
OTL	Old Testament Library
RSV	Revised Standard Version
SP	Samaritan Pentateuch
v./vv.	verse/verses
VT	*Vetus Testamentum*
VTSup	Vetus Testamentum Supplements
WBC	Word Biblical Commentary
ZAW	*Zeitschrift für die alttestamentliche Wissenschaft*

1

Introduction

"Talk is at the heart of human social life."[1]

IS TALK ALSO AT the heart of the Divine human life together? Is the human relationship to the Divine built on talk? Is it truly possible to engage in conversation with God, to participate in give and take, to listen and be listened to? If so, it's only sensible to understand and be intentional about engaging in these Divine human talks. This book is an investigation into the conversational prayers contained in the Hebrew Bible to see if help can be found for conversing with God.

In 1983, Moshe Greenburg published a small book presenting a series of lectures on non-psalmic prayer he delivered at the University of California during the 1981–82 academic year.[2] In these lectures, Greenburg concluded, "the biblical narrators all portrayed speech between man and God on the analogy of speech between humans." To be sure, Greenburg recognized the "literary shaping" of speech that occurs when embedded in prose, but nevertheless asserted that direct speech patterns are still present among these prayers.[3] In Greenburg's view, human conversation with God is patterned after typical human to human conversation. How we talk with each other provides the structures for how we talk with God.

Greenburg's observation serves as the impetus for this book. If conversational prayers appearing in a prose literary context are structured according to the same speech patterns found in human to human conversation, can Conversation Analysis (CA), the social scientific methodology for the analysis of conversation, assist in understanding the discourse of conversational prayer in the Hebrew Bible, even if those prayers are shaped by the literary concerns of their prose context? It follows that just as the presentation

1. Sidnell, *Conversation Analysis*, 1.
2. Greenburg, *Biblical Prose Prayer*, 36.
3. Greenburg, *Biblical Prose Prayer*, 37.

of inter-human dialogue in literary prose retains some of the characteristics of normal conversation, so, too, conversational prayer (prayer in the form of a dialogue with God), even when appearing in prose, retains some of the characteristics of conversational activity and analysis of those characteristics can help us to understand the human Divine interaction. But this formation of the problem guiding our study has in it two embedded assumptions that must be addressed before we progress any further.

Does the Literary Context of Conversational Prayer Preclude Conversation Analysis?

First, does the prose setting of the prayers invalidate a conversational structural analysis?[4] Has the prose writer altered conversation structure in order to achieve his or her own designs in a manner that makes those conversations hopelessly lost? Others have asked the same question and concluded yes. Samuel Balentine notes, "Whatever the original, spontaneous utterings were, one no longer has the luxury of hearing them directly."[5] And on this point, surely Balentine is correct—the conversational prayers are preserved in texts. That means some of the characteristics we seek most—spontaneity and immediacy, the unfiltered dynamics shared by the conversationalists, have been shrouded in the formalization of prose construction. But does this mean that we are at a methodological impasse? Perhaps not.[6] The conversational prayers embedded in narrative are literary constructions. We are examining literary constructions in conversational form. But does this mean that CA, which has to do with "normal" or naturally occurring conversation,[7] has no contribution to make when applied to the analysis of conversation in texts or other more "institutionalized" settings? No. While differences do exist between conversation appearing in texts and normal conversation, the evidence points to a closer connection rather than a disconnection between the two forms of communication.[8] Even while appearing in texts, conversation is still recognizable

---

4. There are conversation analysts that object to the application of the methodology to texts, but for a reply see Sidnell, *Conversation Analysis*, 20.

5. Balentine, *Prayer in the Hebrew Bible*, 15.

6. Aspects of Conversation Analysis have been utilized by various biblical researchers. See for example: Matthews, *More than Meets the Ears*, 68–69; Person, *In Conversation with Jonah*, 20–23. To a lesser degree, see Mandolfo, *God in the Dock*; Suomala, *Moses and God in Dialogue*.

7. Heritage, "Current Developments," 22.

8. Sacks et al., "Simplest Systematics." For an application of the method to biblical texts, see Person, *In Conversation with Jonah*, 23–30.

as conversation, even if now functioning for a purpose determined by a narrator and not the conversationalists. CA will allow us to compare the literary conversation constructs to normal, direct conversation and allow us to make observations. Those resulting observations can then be used to analyze the prayers as the heart of the Divine human interaction.

Are Conversation Structures Culture Specific?

The second preliminary question we must ask is: Are speech patterns culturally specific so that transference of analysis from one culture to another is misleading if not unattainable altogether? Can modern CA be applied to ancient texts with any sort of plausibility? A great deal of investigation has been conducted on just this question and it is becoming more apparent that the basic structures of conversation are not culturally specific.[9] One of the pioneers of CA, sociologist Erving Goffman, considered face-to-face interaction the foundation of everything else in society and so had at least the potential to illuminate across cultures.[10] That potential is made concrete in a structure commonly used by CA—adjacency pairs. The structure of adjacency pairs, a system of turn-taking[11] among the conversation participants, appears to be a "translinguistic organization."[12] While the turn-taking structure is abstract enough to apply across languages,[13] it is also concrete enough to serve as a means whereby "speakers regulate their own participation in, and through, time with each other, unit by unit."[14] Another leading conversation analyst, Jack Sidnell writes, "the structures that organize conversation are context-free in certain basic and crucial respects, they are at the same time capable of extraordinary context-sensitivity."[15] Conversation utilizes structures and concepts that can be observed across languages, yet the application of those concepts and structures in a particular conversation is context specific. Even within the same cultural and linguistic system, how turn taking is regulated from context to context (for example: courtroom,

9. Moerman, *Talking Culture*, 3–4; Clift, *Conversation Analysis*, 65, 73–76; Stivers et al., "Universals and Cultural Variation," 10587–92.

10. Goffman, "Alienation from Interaction," 57. The foundational nature of turn-taking is also asserted by Sidnell, *Conversation Analysis*, 37, and Levinson, "On the Human Interactional Engine," 39–69.

11. See the seminal paper by Sacks et al., "A Simplest Systematics."

12. Clift, *Conversation Analysis*, 139.

13. Clift describes turn-taking as having "universal validity." Clift, *Conversation Analysis*, 95. See also Person, *In Conversation with Jonah*, 15.

14. Clift, *Conversation Analysis*, 139.

15. Sidnell, *Conversation Analysis*, 6.

interviews, speeches, normal everyday conversation) is governed by social convention. The conversation of prayer presented in the Hebrew Bible illuminates not only the private interaction between the participants of the prayer, but the social expectations and structures governing the verbal exchange that would have been familiar to the reader.

Our examination of the conversational prayers in narrative will be structured around the adjacency pairs of the prayers. The structure of the adjacency pair, and the placement of the components within the pairing system, is a fascinating constituent in understanding the total dynamic of the conversation. Examination of the form of the conversation of prayer, allows us to ask: "Why that now?" a question about the placement of an utterance in conversation that is relevant to understanding the function of the utterance.[16] Understanding *how* something is said will assist us to better understand *what* is said.

Conversational Prayer Defined

Although CA has never been applied to the conversational prayers of the Hebrew Bible, there are predecessors to this present work.[17] Friedrich Heiler published a monumental work in 1918 entitled *Das Gebet: Ein Religionsgeschichtliche und Religionspsychologische Untersuchung*[18] in which he argued forcefully that genuine prayer is a free expression directed by present circumstance and not a formal liturgy prone to repetition and reuse. Conversation analysis of the conversational prayers calls this assessment into question. The very appearance of the prayers in a prose context, suggests that the pattern of exchange between the human and Divine, if not the exact words used, can be modeled and extended beyond the prose context. Just as other verbal forms of human exchange (song, epic, riddle) can be borrowed by prose writers, human to human conversations or human Divine conversations appearing in prose may be borrowed. In the borrowing, the conversational form takes on new functions. Yet, the form of the conversation must still be recognizable as conversational activity for it to be meaningfully inserted into the prose. The compelling nature of

---

16. Sacks and Schegloff, "Opening up Closings," 299.

17. Although not applied to biblical texts, Raymond Person has provided a valuable discussion of oral tradition and Conversation Analysis. Person, *From Conversation to Oral Tradition*. Application of CA to biblical texts can be found in Mali, "Language of Conversation"; C. Miller, "Silence as a Response," 23–43; Moshavi, "Biblical Dialogue"; Moshavi, "Conversation Analysis."

18. Translated into English as *Prayer: A Study in the History and Psychology of Religion*.

the conversational prayers is that they use structures commonly found in human to human conversation.

At this point we must distinguish between different forms of prayer to clearly define the categorical limits of the prayers under consideration. Some researchers (such as Greenburg) have used the term *prose prayer* and defined the group as those prayers in narrative involving speech to or with God. *Conversational prayer* is a bit more nuanced. We will consider conversational prayer as a subset of prose prayer, a subset that includes not speech broadly, but conversation or conversational activity (including consequential action derived from conversation) to, with, or between dialogical partners.[19]

As might be imagined, those who previously examined the prose prayers in the Hebrew Bible have not always agreed on their working definitions of prayer. Consequently, variations in the pool of data admitted (the prayers considered) have led researchers to different conclusions about conversational prayer.[20] The work of four researchers illustrates the predicament.

We'll begin with Moshe Greenburg. He defined prose prayer as "non-psalmic speech to God—less often about God—expressing dependence, subjugation, or obligation."[21] Our second researcher, Samuel Balentine, agreed with parts of Greenburg's definition, particularly in using the content of the address as a distinctive characteristic of prayer. Balentine suggested that prayer be differentiated from oaths, vows, or simple dialogue.[22] Third, Jack W. Corvin investigated prose prayers and noted the "conversational orientation" characteristic of these prayers.[23] Corvin recognized the dialogic nature of the prayer, a question-answer exchange initiated by the human supplicant and designed to come to a resolution or understanding of the apparent absence or misbehavior of God.[24] For Corvin, the structure of the exchange (question-answer) and the presence

---

19. Prose prayers that are judged not to display a minimal amount of conversational activity include: Gen 24:12–24; Judg 16:28–30; 21:3; 1 Sam 1:11–12; 7:6; 12:10–11; 2 Sam 15:31; Ezra 9:6–15; Neh 1:4–11; 4:4–11; 5:19; Jer 4:10 (14:11); 32:16–25; Jonah 1:14; Dan 2:20–23; 9:4–11.

20. Patrick Miller acknowledges this difficulty when writing, "The reader may note the absence of an extended definition of prayer . . . The assumption at work here is that on those occasions when human beings, at their initiative, address God with some sort of need and in hopes of divine response, prayer is in place." P. D. Miller, *They Cried to the Lord*, 4.

21. Sidnell, *Conversation Analysis*, 7.

22. Balentine, "Prayer in the Wilderness Traditions," 53.

23. Corvin, "Stylistic and Functional Study of the Prose Prayers," 159.

24. Corvin, "Stylistic and Functional Study of the Prose Prayers," 169–73.

of a human initiator helped define the conversational exchange as prayer. Finally, Edwin E. Staudt focused on prose prayer in the Deuteronomic literature (Deuteronomy—2 Kings),[25] applying three criteria by which conversational prayer could be identified: (1) explicit communication;[26] (2) initiated by the individual or group; (3) effective in that it elicits a response from God.[27] It can easily be imagined that the different definitions of prose and conversational prayer offered by Greenburg, Balentine, Corvin, and Staudt resulted in different texts admitted for examination and variety in the conclusions about those texts.[28]

In this work, we will consider conversational prayer as:

- Unmediated direct address with God
- Initiated by the human conversational partner,
- And generally presenting a request or objection.[29]

But these three criteria will need to be held loosely. In 2 Sam 24:10–17, David's direct address to God is unmediated, but the Divine response is mediated through Gad, David's seer.[30] In other instances, the human initiated request is preceded by Divine direct address, serving as a necessary introduction to the prayer (Gen 15:1–2). There are times when the conversation is initiated by Deity (Exod 3), or only one speaker gives voice in the conversation (typical of the Jacob Cycle), or when a prayer is included within the context of a pre-existing conversation (Gen 3 and 4). In the end, the criteria put forth serve as guidelines, but are not capable of fully defining conversational prayer.

We will distinguish prayer from normal conversation with God as a participant (e.g., Gen 3:9–20; 4:9–15; 16:7–14; Exod 16:4, 28; 17:14) by

25. Staudt, "Prayer and the People."

26. In our use of conversation analysis, we will include silence as a meaningful component of the dialogic exchange.

27. Staudt, "Prayer and the People," 58.

28. We could add Adolf Wendel to this list of researchers. Wendel examined narratives in Genesis through 2 Kings, applying form critical descriptions to prayers considered apart from their narrative context. Wendel, *Das freie Laiengebet im vorexilischen Israel*.

29. As does Corvin, "A Stylistic and Functional Study of the Prose Prayers," 23, and Imschoot, *Theologie de l'Ancien Testament*," 170. See also Long, *1 Kings*, 255. These same three characteristics are at the heart of Miller's understanding of prayer in P. D. Miller, *They Cried to the Lord*, 4.

30. See also the prophetic mediation in 2 Kgs 19:20 parallel to Isa 37:21; 2 Kgs 20:1–7 parallel to Isa 38:3–8 and 2 Chr 20:15, or the reported response from God in Jer 14:14.

noting that prayer is conversation initiated by the petitioner, be it individual or community.[31] Direct address with God will be understood as conversational prayer when marked by a demonstrated self-awareness of the participants, articulated either directly by the participants in conversation or by the narrator presenting the conversation. This unmediated direct address includes theophanic personages when understood as such by the speaker.[32] Not included are prayers referencing God in the third person (i.e., speech *about* God not *with* God). Further, the dialogue will be considered conversational prayer when it demonstrates "procedural consequentiality."[33] That is, when the consequential actions or results can be seen to be normally considered within the orb of prayer. But even here, there is room for debate and a judgment must be rendered.[34] For example, it seems clear that the Divine human conversations in Genesis 3 and 4 are not intended as prayer (at least in full), but what about the conversation in Gen 17:1–21[35] or Exodus 3? Here, there does seem to be a crisis that prompts a response from God and obligation to obey from the human participant. And, if we consider more closely the Divine human conversation in Genesis 3–4 and Exodus 3–4 it does seem that, on occasion, conversation with God can include elements of prayer as in Cain's conversation with God, initiated by God in Gen 4:9, but resolving into a petition of God (if only implied) and the Divine response in 4:14–15. Likewise, the conversation between God and Moses in Exodus 3–4 is initiated by God but includes requests from Moses that certainly seem prayerful.[36] Consequently, we cannot, with Balentine, limit conversational prayer by form, eliminating any element of oath, vow, or normal conversation with God.

In the analysis of the conversational prayers, we will need to keep in mind the rhetorical function of the prayers as they now appear in prose

---

31. And so many of the prophetic revelations in which the "word of the Lord" comes to a prophet will not be included as this type of prophetic revelation is distinguishable as something other than prayer. See, for example, the many such revelations in Jeremiah (1:11), Ezekiel (1:3), Haggai (2:20), or Zechariah (4:8).

32. The prayer in Dan 9:4–19 is not included for, even though certainly Daniel expresses direct address to God, the response from Gabriel (Dan 9:21–27) refers to the "word [that] went out" presumably voiced by God, in the third person and so not a conversation with God.

33. Schegloff, "Reflections on Talk and Social Structure," 53.

34. See the distinction made between "a conversation" and "conversational activity" in Levinson, *Pragmatics*, 318.

35. See also Numbers 11 in which a conversational prayer is contained within the larger extended dialogue. Other instances of prayer embedded in dialogue will considered.

36. So, too, the conversational activity with Balaam in Numbers 22.

contexts. At times, it is clear that the prayer is being used as an address delivered to the audience present in the narrative (i.e., the Moses speech of Deuteronomy 3, the corporate Israelite prayer of Judges 10, or the Solomon dedication of 1 Kgs 8 and 2 Chr 6). In all instances, the reading audience is present as a rhetorical recipient of the conversational prayer address.[37]

Where Found?

The conversational prayers in the Hebrew Bible are not uniformly present across the span of biblical literature. The informal conversations with the patriarchs and judges give way to a more distant and formal presentation in the monarchy and later. The intimate conversation between supplicant and God gives way to a mediated exchange voiced by court prophet. The immanent God gives way to the transcendent God[38] (but oddly the more emotionally present God).

Further, the structure of those conversational prayers also changes throughout the Hebrew Bible. The dialogical portrayal of prayer found in the Abraham Cycle gives way to a single speaker communication in the Jacob Cycle. The introductory phrases announcing the presence of God in Genesis (*He appeared, He came down, He appeared in a dream*, etc.)[39] are missing in Exodus as Moses simply turns to talk with God.

Unless we assume God becomes suddenly less talkative as we enter the era of the Israelite monarchy, we must conclude that the conversational prayers are intentionally placed, valuable in forming a particular view of God or pattern of Divine human interaction that is not equally applicable in all biblical narrative.

Staudt argues that the conversational prayers are placed strategically in the narratives, appearing between a crisis (often involving a disruption or emergency in the Divine human relationship) and the resolution of the crises, shaping the drama of the narrative.[40] In other words, the prayers are constructed and placed in narrative to accomplish a function in the plot development. And that plot often has an ideological point. As Staudt puts

---

37. See the section titled "Context" in chapter 2.

38. Corvin, "Stylistic and Functional Study of the Prose Prayers," 188–21.

39. Conversation is embodied speech, even when presented (represented) in prose or other literary contexts. Consequently, the person of the conversationalist is an important component of the conversational dynamics. For that reason, when describing the biblical prayers, the gender designations of the participants will be retained. When summary statements are offered or generalized observations are made, inclusive gender descriptions will be used.

40. Staudt, "Prayer and the People," 335–38.

it, "the Deuteronomist explicitly presents prayer as the instrument for the participation of the people with their God in the unfolding history of Israel's covenantal relationship."[41] In at least part of the biblical narrative, conversation in prayer gives voice to a Divine-human partnership active in shaping real events. Implicit in the narrative presentation is an invitation, welcoming the reader to enter that partnership.

Conversation analysts are quick to remind us that any particular conversation or fragment of conversation is "the unique product of multiple, intersecting organizations of practices."[42] That is, conversations form the meeting point of layer upon layer of social interactions, influences, and perceptions that all have a bearing on: the *what-is-said* of the conversation, the *how-its-said* of the conversation, and the *what-it-does* of the conversation. When conversational prayers are placed in narrative, the biblical writers appropriate elements of those layers upon layers of social interactions in order to add power or persuasiveness to the narrative being composed. When examining the conversational prayers of the Hebrew Bible, we are looking through a window upon a vast landscape of Divine human interaction. That landscape of Divine human interaction affords the narrator an opportunity to develop the character of both, the supplicant and God. The conversation of prayer includes motivational elements in both request and response that give the narrator an opportunity to highlight preferred character qualities. Those qualities, both human and Divine, are open for inspection. It is striking that many of the conversational prayers in the Hebrew Bible share a common dilemma: Can God be trusted? In Genesis, the patriarchs often wonder if God will keep his word—will the promises of land and nation made to Abraham really come to fruition? (Is God good?) With Moses and the Judges, the issue is reframed to inquire about the presence of God. Is God effectively present to provide what he has promised (Is God powerful?)? The dialogical exchange of conversational prayer can bring into sharp focus essential questions of a human relationship with God, often by forcing affirmation of the power and presence of God exactly at the moment when both are most fundamentally in doubt.

The Always-More of Conversational Prayer

In the early part of the twentieth century the Israeli philosopher, Martin Buber, argued that religious experience is experience with a personal

---

41. Staudt, "Prayer and the People," 339.
42. Sidnell, *Conversation Analysis*, 258.

subject (a *Thou*) rather than an object or thing (an *It*).[43] Buber provides language that we might profitably borrow in our investigation of conversational prayer. Buber understood that, as human, we exist in two modes: an *I–It* mode of existence (the I acting upon the world around as a thing or it), and an *I–Thou* mode of existence (the I interacting with Persons). Buber's description of human existence is particularly powerful in helping to understand conversational prayer. In conversation, persons interact, establishing and negotiating status relationships, forming an inter-subjectivity or joint understanding, and when required, initiate consequential action to be conducted after the conversation ceases. But, Buber's presentation must also give us pause at the sobering prospect ahead. Conversational prayer (*I–Thou*) is confrontational. It is the moment of encounter between the human heart and the near, yet hidden God. Conversational prayer is relational and uncontrolled by the *I*. Conversational prayer is *I–Thou*.

Buber's construct of the *I–Thou* not only conditions our understanding of the Divine participant in conversational prayer, it conditions how we position ourselves in undertaking this investigation. In Buber's terms, the *I* of the *I–Thou* differs from the *I* of the *I–It*. The *I* may be taken as the sum of its inherent attributes and acts (the *what* I am to others of an *I–It*), or it may be taken as a unitary, whole, irreducible being (the *who* I am to others of an *I–Thou*). The *I* analyzing the conversational prayers (an *It*) in the Hebrew Bible is very different from the *I* engaged in conversation with the *Thou* whose presence is still felt in those conversational prayers. The *I* analyzing the prayers can be distant and aloof, detached, noncommittal, and safe within predetermined expectations. The *I* engaged in conversational prayer is stripped bare, subject to the *Thou*, and open to the expectations of the *Thou*.

When prayer addresses the *Thou*—the *I* of the *I–Thou* is also present. When prayer addresses the *It*, the *I* of the *I–It* is also present. Prayer, articulating an *I–Thou*, can only be uttered with the whole being. But when prayer addresses the *It*, the whole being of the *I* can never be present.[44] Prayer changes the *I*. The *I* of prayer addressing *It* is not the same *I* when addressing the *Thou*. At its most fundamental level, its base and primary expression, conversational prayer demands the *I* of *I–Thou*. That *I* pretends no control. That *I* has no future, expectation, or hope except as found in the *Thou*.

---

43. Portions of this section, as well as the discussions on Hagar, Ezekiel, and Jonah, appeared in an earlier form in Giles, "God Talk," 113–36.

44. Buber, *I and Thou*, 3.

The importance of the *I–Thou* speaks to the need for conversational prayer. "As soon as the relation has been worked out or has been permeated with a means, the *Thou* becomes an object among objects—perhaps the chief, but still one of them."[45] When prayer becomes formalized, rehearsed, and transferable—when I think I control the relationship or am proficient in prayer it becomes a means that unwittingly transforms the *Thou* to *It*.[46] This all too common reduction, (substituting religion for an encounter) allows the *I* of the *I–It* to repress the *I* of the *I–Thou* while masking the *Thou* behind the pretense of the *It*.

The *I–It* exists as monologue, while the *I–Thou* is always dialogue. To perceive the other as an *It* is to take the other as a classified and hence predictable object that can be manipulated and controlled. The *It* exists only as a part of one's own experiences. We begin our investigation of conversational prayer as an *I–It*, but that is only the beginning. The *Thou* participating in the conversational prayers is never so contained. The *Thou* is never reduced to a classification or subsumed under a universal category (Supreme, Deity, Omnipresent, God) but encountered as a wholly unique entity—just as unique as the *I*. The *Thou* of the *I–Thou* relationship is a pure encounter of one unique entity with another. The *It* is exhaustibly known by the experience of the *I*. The *It* never exceeds or exists independently of the *I*, while the *Thou* is never so limited by the experience of the *I*. The *Thou* is always more.

The importance of the *I–Thou* does not deny the necessity of the *I–It*. In the absence of the *It* none of us can live. The *I–It* of prayer is the starting point, the preliminary understanding upon which conversational prayer is built. In conversational prayer we encounter *Thou* without whom *I* am not. When in prayer, the *I* of the *I–Thou* becomes wholly present—the experiences of time are made immediately present to the *Thou* as the *I* stands complete, indivisible, and irreducible. The *I* in conversational prayer is subject with the *Thou*. Conversational prayer is an encounter between the eternal *Thou* and the irreducibly present *I*. Conversational prayer is an *I–Thou* articulating in dialogue. Conversational prayer is not just another form of prayer, comparable to liturgical or institutional forms of prayer, in which the prayer itself can be repeated and applied by different people in different circumstances. In conversational prayer, the *I* of the *I–Thou*

---

45. Buber, *I and Thou*, 17.

46. This is not to say that formalized and liturgical prayer is not valued in the Hebrew Bible. The Psalms reflect a long and vibrant religious tradition and on at least one occasion (Num 14:18) a creedal formula makes its way into the dialogue of conversational prayer as do variations on liturgical pieces (1 Kgs 8:50b–53; 2 Chr 6:40–42).

relationship becomes fully formed in a non-repeatable fashion and the *Thou* becomes fully recognized.[47]

When the *I–Thou* of conversational prayer becomes a reality, it becomes clear that conversational prayer is always an act of grace. The *Thou* meets me, not summoned by me but summoning me. The *Thou* chooses to speak and to listen, but so does the *I*. Conversational prayer is a choice by the *I* and being chosen by the *Thou*. For Buber, "all real living is meeting."[48] All *real living* requires conversation. Conversation is not just the heart of human social life. Conversational prayer is the heart of the Divine-human social life, forcing the *I* to address God with the whole person. Conversational prayer encounters God in a reciprocal relationship—a relationship of engagement between God and human.[49]

As we embark on this journey of discovery, an unavoidable question must now be asked. Will an *I–It* investigation of conversational structures lead to an *I–Thou* of prayer? A sober reflection is required. Are we willing to enter the *I–Thou* of conversational prayer? As we beckon the Divine, it is our hearts that are laid bare. Are we willing to be truly authentic, honest, and unfiltered? Are we willing to enter a partnership with God to shape real events? Are we willing to pray?

---

47. Samuel Balentine expresses a similar idea: "Wherever God is being God and humanity is acting in full accord with its nature, God and people are in dialogue." Balentine, *Prayer in the Hebrew Bible*, 262.

48. Buber, *I and Thou*, 11.

49. Heschel, *The Prophets*, 2:9.

2

Conversation Analysis

IN THIS CHAPTER, WE will survey the CA methodology, highlighting some of the more pertinent features that have direct application to the examination of the conversational prayers in the Hebrew Bible.

Conversation Analysis of Conversational Prayers: The *Who-We-Are-to-God* in Prayer

Conversation involves joint understanding, an "intersubjectivity," that occurs during the process of verbal interaction in a way not possible in monologue or single person address. Conversation allows the participants a joint understanding of a topic and a relational status, a *who-we-are-to-one-another*, between the conversationalists. This relational function of conversation certainly must be given additional significance when one of those conversational partners is Deity.[1]

Attention to the interpersonal status between conversationalists in prayer was anticipated by Jack W. Corvin when he described conversational prayer in terms of various combinations including three elements: God-man-God or man-God-man.[2] The *who-we-are-to-one-another* function of conversation is often expressed, not in the topic of the conversation, but in the structure of the conversation. Very frequently, the conversational

---

1. This is alluded to in Exod 32:11, where conversation between Moses and the LORD is mentioned to illustrate their shared friendship.

2. Corvin, "Stylistic and Functional Study of the Prose Prayers," 157. Corvin considers a subset of conversational prayer—those that he terms "single response" prayers—differing from conversational prayer in that the dialogue is limited to a single request. "On very rare occasions the single response prayers may extend beyond a mere request, but they are not comparable in magnitude to the conversational prayers or to the formal prayers." Corvin, "Stylistic and Functional Study of the Prose Prayers," 181.

prayers of the Hebrew Bible include a question (sometimes implicit) that opens a door to consider the *who-we-are-to-one-another* function of conversation. In these instances, the conversational prayers are predicated upon a disagreement and are designed to resolve that disagreement or controversy. Either, God asks a question designed to uncover human motives and actions or, God is questioned in the midst of an expression of human disappointment or frustration with the Divine.[3] The question can be pertinent to a specific occasion (Gen 15:2), or the question can address a moral issue with repetitive application, such as Abraham's protest against the innocent suffering (Gen 18:23). The questions addressed to God serve multiple rhetorical functions, moving the plot of the narrative and giving voice to issues placed before the reader in a manner designed by the author and leading the reader to a desired outcome.

In a variety of forms, two questions are repeatedly present in the conversational prayers: (1) *Why do the innocent suffer?* (2) *Is God effectively present?* These questions are particularly well suited for conversational prayer, for each implies questions about the moral character of God, Deity's reliable presence, and active concern for those in need. That these concerns are repeatedly present can be, at once, both troubling and reassuring. The questions are troubling in that the answers are not self-evident, easy, or readily accessible, but seem to be a repeated concern of the human heart. The repeated way the human conversationalists press God for answers indicates that these issues are not private to any of us. That these questions find their way into conversational prayer can also be reassuring. No topic is off limits, offensive to God, and never breathed, regardless of how it troubles the human heart. The Divine response may be in the form of a verbal reply to the request, silence, or, more generally, in the consequential action described by the narrator in resolution to the conversation.

In conversational prayer, the dilemma posed by the suffering of the innocents is not addressed by an appeal to a philosophical principle, defining away either the experience of the suffering or the innocence of the plaintive. Neither is there resort to a moral balance sheet adding up cosmic good and evil for a positive sum. No, the cry of the innocent sufferer is given full

---

3. Corvin suggests a rhetorical function of the conversational prayers. "An author was able to transmit information to his readers and involve them in seeking solutions by leading them step by step through a conversational prayer. This style of writing keeps alive in the reader such elements as surprise, anticipation, embarrassment, uncertainty and delight." Corvin, "Stylistic and Functional Study of the Prose Prayers," 158. Corvin suggests the same function is evident in the wisdom writing of Job and Ecclesiastes but not using the medium of conversational prayer.

expression and the pained complaint is made to God—directly in conversation, desperate to discover *who-we-are-to-one-another* with the Divine.

Conversation Analysis—Fundamental Concepts

Generally, CA is conducted with audio or video recordings, allowing extended analysis of "talk-in-interaction."[4] The transcripts used as the data for CA include notation that doesn't just record the words of the conversation, but seeks to describe the manner of delivery, timing, pauses, intensity, interruption (verbal, nonverbal, and vocal laughter, crying, etc.), stumbling and insertions—all of which are part of normal conversation but are absent when only the words of the conversation are preserved. Observations on all these components of conversation are brought to bear on what Jack Sidnell identifies as the focus for CA analysis:[5]

1. Patterns across data samples—Examining patterns that can be observed across conversations conducted in multiple contexts and cultures.

2. Patterns within the data—Are there recurring patterns, within a given conversation, that give structure to the conversation and assist in the meaning of the conversational exchange?

3. Selecting formulations—Why do conversation participants use this articulation and not some other? How do terms, labels, and status identifiers function in the conversation?

4. Selecting formats—Why do the conversationalists choose this question and not another—or why a question and not a statement? How was the conversation structured?

Obviously, we have no such access to live conversations when examining the conversational prayers in the Hebrew Bible and we do not have transcripts preserving the kind of data common in CA. We do have narratives in which conversational prayers are reported, and even admitting that the conversations are literary constructions, molded to fit the design of the narrator, those conversations still allow examination of the patterns, formulations, and formats identified by Sidnell.

---

4. Sidnell, *Conversation Analysis*, 20. In fact, some conversation analysts might well object to the application of the methodology to conversations in literature. Although see the extensions of the methodology in Hutchby and Wooffitt, *Conversation Analysis*, 182–206.

5. Sidnell, *Conversation Analysis*, 30.

Several of the structures common in CA and most helpful in the examination of conversational prayers are now introduced below.

Adjacency Pairs

CA examines the linguistic structure of dialogue through a fundamental organizational concept called "adjacency pairs."[6] An adjacency pair is a pairing of verbal or non-verbal conversational components that are:[7]

- Adjacent
- Contributed by different conversation partners
- Ordered as statement and response
- Constructed so that the second (response) is related to the first as either a preferred or dispreferred response[8]

The conversational prayers in the Hebrew Bible are presented in the form of reported speech. The reported speech may be direct (the narrator quoting the words attributed to the speaker), indirect (the narrator paraphrasing the speaker's words), or the narrator may choose to report the consequential action that functions as a dialogical response, in effect omitting or condensing part of the dialogue as a means of bridging the conversational prayer to the action that follows.

The manner in which the narrator sets up or introduces the adjacency pairs of the conversation can influence the direction or structure of the dialogue. The first part of the dialogue (A) determines the set of potential responses (B) especially as a preferred or dispreferred response and how that response will assist in the narrator's overall goal of: problem solving, character development, or plot advancement. The manner of reporting that response (direct speech, indirect speech, narrated consequence) is a choice made by the narrator not a choice made by the conversation partners—a narrative choice that adds additional structure to the reported conversational prayer.

The basic structure of adjacency pairs is characteristic of dialogue whether in normal conversation, constructed oral narrative, or constructed written narrative. In all three (normal conversation, constructed oral narrative, or constructed written narrative), the same forms of presentation

---

6. Rebecca Clift thinks adjacency pairs are "*the*—fundamental structure in the organization of talk." Clift, *Conversation Analysis*, 65.

7. See Levinson, *Pragmatics*, 303–7; Sidnell, *Conversation Analysis*, 64.

8. For "preferred" or "dispreferred" response, see below.

for the adjacency pairs apply: direct speech, indirect speech, narrated consequence or omission (silence).

The adjacency pair concept is not just intended to describe a general tendency regarding the immediacy of two speech acts in a conversation. In the adjacency pair structure, the first part of the pair establishes an expectation for what is to follow. That expectation is established by the producer of the first part of the adjacency pair. When that expectation is not fulfilled, the conversation takes an unanticipated turn. A new expectation can be established, or a new producer of expectation can be identified. When placed in narrative, an unfulfilled expectation may signify the conversation is being used by the narrator for a purpose other than that shared by the conversation participants—or that the reader may actually have become part of the conversation and the reader's reaction is the fulfillment of the primary's expectation.

Preference

One of the most basic observations made by CA concerns the organization of the adjacency pairs into "preferred" or "dispreferred" linguistic structures.[9] Preference does not refer to the positive or negative affiliation between the conversationalists, but to the structural organization of the conversational exchange. The preference organization is a powerful driver in conversation, a structural force providing "conversation inertia or momentum."[10] Preference propels the progression of the conversation.

Preferred Response

A preferred structure provides a response (generally the second paired part of an adjacency pair) that conforms to the preference of the initial assessment, question, invitation, or command (the first paired part of an adjacency pair). The response in a preferred structure is generally immediate and unmitigated.[11] Preference responses, confirming agreement and contiguity, are more frequent forms of response than are dispreferred responses.[12] In the conversational prayers of the Hebrew Bible, preferred

---

9. Schegloff, "Introduction," ix–lxii.
10. Sidnell, *Conversation Analysis*, 93.
11. Schegloff, *Sequence Organization in Interaction*, 59.
12. Stivers et. al., "Question-Response Sequences in Conversation," 2615–19.

responses tend to be shorter and gravitate toward reporting consequential action rather than forming direct speech.

Dispreferred Response

A dispreferred response does not conform to the preferences of the initial component of the adjacency pair and is generally more complex than a preferred response.[13] A dispreferred response may contain: delay, diversion (including partial agreement before disagreement, compliment, or admiration before refusal), qualifiers, pro forma agreement (*yes, but* . . .), explanation for the dispreferred response, silence, or declination of the initial request assessment, question, or command.[14] Dispreferred responses tend to be longer and more developed than preferred responses. The dispreferred response is often mitigated and indirect. The refusal or disagreement may come after a delay or rationale for the dispreferred response, thereby softening the conflict represented by the dispreferred response. When incorporated into narrative, this delay can become part of the plot of the narrative and so provides the narrator a device to soften the dispreferred response in a way not available to participants in ordinary conversation.[15] In our investigation of conversational prayer we will be specially tuned to this technique, for its use in softening conflict may be particularly important when that conflict is with God.

When conversation appears in narrative, three tendencies emerge that may be at play when structuring the conversational prayers in the Hebrew Bible:[16]

1. First parts of the dialogue tend toward direct speech establishing a set of possibilities for the remaining dialogue to follow.

2. Preferred responses tend toward reported consequential action.

3. Dispreferred responses tend in two directions: (1) they can express in the form of direct speech, especially when followed by additional dialogue, allowing for further exploration of the embedded conflict, or (2) they may tend toward reported consequential action thereby mitigating the conflict embedded in the dispreferred response.

---

13. Levinson, *Pragmatics*, 333. See also Heritage, "Current Developments in Conversation Analysis," 111.

14. Clift, *Conversation Analysis*, 144. See also Sidnell, *Conversation Analysis*, 78–79.

15. Person, *In Conversation with Jonah*, 27.

16. Person, *In Conversation with Jonah*, 28.

Dispreferred responses or the anticipation of a dispreferred response (signaled by partial agreement or delay on the part of the respondent) can be used by the speaker of the first part of the pair to adjust the initial statement by modifying, withdrawing, or adding elements to increase the likelihood of a preferred response. Dispreferred and preferred responses can take several forms, or combinations, either in action or verbal response.[17] The chart below presents several of the more common combinations:

	Preferred Format	Dispreferred Format
Preferred Action	Preferred action in a preferred format	Preferred action in a dispreferred format
Dispreferred Action	Dispreferred action in a preferred format	Dispreferred action in a dispreferred format

This chart indicates that the *what-it-does* (action) of a conversation need not conform to the *what-it-says* (format) of the conversation. CA encourages the analyst to be sensitive to both aspects of conversational activity.

Levinson provides the following table to describe the common format combinations evident in adjacency pairs:[18]

First Part:	request	offer	assessment	question	blame
Second Part (Preferred)	acceptance	acceptance	agreement	expected answer	denial[19]
Second Part (Dispreferred)	refusal	refusal	disagreement	unexpected answer, silence	admission

Expansion

To the above combinations, additional speech elements can be included that; begin the conversation (a summons-answer pre-sequence to the conversation that establishes the attention of the participants and establishes

---

17. Kendrick and Torreira, "Timing and Construction of Preference," 273.

18. Levinson, *Pragmatics*, 336.

19. The denial is articulated in a preferred format, while acceptance (agreeing with the statement of blame) is often accompanied by mitigation, explanations, or deflection—that is, a dispreferred format.

the initiator and the respondent),[20] expand within the conversation (repairing misunderstanding, or restate in an effort to secure a preferred response), or close the conversation (terminating the topic of conversation and confirming the status relationship of the conversational participants). These elements can be considered as expansions upon the established concept of adjacency pairs. The adjacency pairs can be expanded with pre-expansion elements, insert expansion elements, or post-expansion elements.[21]

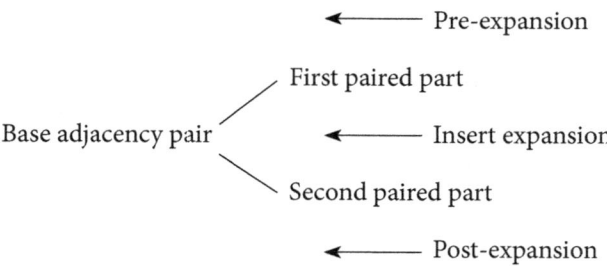

Pre-expansion

A pre-expansion prepares the way for the first base pair (round) in a conversation. The pre-expansion establishes a context, testing the legitimacy of the intended first paired part.[22] There are several functional pre-expansion forms—below are some of the more common.[23]

1. The summons—answer. This pre-expansion establishes the participants in the conversation and the role assumed (at least initially) by each participant: initiator, respondent, etc.
2. Pre-invitation (a statement or declaration of conditions that establish the context for the following invitation)—response.
3. Pre-announcement. "A statement or question designed to determine if the respondent has already received the news to follow, or, in the case of bad news, a way to alert the recipient of the gravity of what is about to come"[24] at times prompting the respondent to guess or verbally an-

---

20. Clift, *Conversation Analysis*, 77.

21. As the adjacency pair seems to be universal structures, so too the expansions have demonstrated cross-cultural validity. Clift, *Conversation Analysis*, 89; Sidnell, *Conversation Analysis*, 95.

22. Sidnell, *Conversation Analysis*, 95.

23. Schegloff, "On Complainability," 449–76.

24. Clift, *Conversation Analysis*, 80.

ticipate the news, diminishing the role of the initiator in relating the bad news.[25]

4. Pre-apology—prepares the recipient for the bad or perceived to be unwelcome news to follow, lessening the potential of personal rejection or conflict by the recipient.

Insert Expansion

An insert expansion separates the two direct addresses of an adjacency pair. Insert expansions are generally introduced by the respondent of an adjacency pair and may be either "post-first" or pre-second."

Post-first Insert Expansion

Inserts are designed to *repair*; that is to repair or clarify a problem in hearing or understanding the preceding talk. The post-first insert, addresses a problem that "may interfere with the production of an appropriate response to it, or even grasping what an appropriate type of response would be."[26] A post-first insertion may function as a pre-dispreferred implicated response, allowing the initiator to rephrase or alter the first and so increase the likelihood of a preferred response. In the conversational prayers of the Hebrew Bible, that expansion may take the form of an editorial insertion. In the conversation between God and Abimelech of Genesis 20, an editorial insertion appears at v. 4. The insertion, "Now Abimelech had not approached her," functions to repair the Divine statement of v. 3, softening the dispreferred response of v. 4b, and making more likely a preferred response to the corrected Divine statement (vv. 6–7). The insert addresses an underlying premise upon which the initial pair is built.

Pre-second Insert Expansion

This kind of insertion is designed to clarify the appropriate response to the initial statement or question by supplying additional information required to make a response. This insertion narrows the range of contingencies available in the formation of the second paired part of the first adjacency pair.

---

25. Pre-invitations and pre-announcements are designed to lessen the likelihood of a dispreferred response.

26. Schegloff, *Sequence Organization in Interaction*, 102.

In the following example of a conversation between a parent and school age child, the inserted question and answer help inform the appropriate response (B^1) to the initial question (A).

> A: May I go out and play?
>
> > B: Did you finish your homework?
> >
> > A^1: Yes.
>
> B^1: Sure, come back in for dinner.

In the following conversational prayer from Genesis 18, the adjacency pairs 1–5 function as inserts seeking to clarify the initial dispreferred response: "Far be it from you to do such a thing . . . !"

> A: [23] Then Abraham came near and said, "Will you indeed sweep away the righteous with the wicked? [24] Suppose there are fifty righteous within the city; will you then sweep away the place and not forgive it for the fifty righteous who are in it? [25] Far be it from you to do such a thing, to slay the righteous with the wicked, so that the righteous fare as the wicked! Far be that from you! Shall not the Judge of all the earth do what is just?"
>
> B: [26] And the Lord said, "If I find at Sodom fifty righteous in the city, I will forgive the whole place for their sake."
>
> A^1: [27] Abraham answered, "Let me take it upon myself to speak to the Lord, I who am but dust and ashes. [28] Suppose five of the fifty righteous are lacking? Will you destroy the whole city for lack of five?"
>
> B^1: And he said, "I will not destroy it if I find forty-five there."
>
> A^2: [29] Again he spoke to him, "Suppose forty are found there."
>
> B^2: He answered, "For the sake of forty I will not do it."
>
> A^3: [30] Then he said, "Oh do not let the Lord be angry if I speak. Suppose thirty are found there."
>
> B^3: He answered, "I will not do it, if I find thirty there."
>
> A^4: [31] He said, "Let me take it upon myself to speak to the Lord. Suppose twenty are found there."
>
> B^4: He answered, "For the sake of twenty I will not destroy it."
>
> A^5: [32] Then he said, "Oh do not let the Lord be angry if I speak just once more. Suppose ten are found there."

B⁵: He answered, "For the sake of ten I will not destroy it."

³³ *And the Lord went his way, when he had finished speaking to Abraham; and Abraham returned to his place.*

The initial dispreferred response by Abraham, objecting to the proposed Divine judgment, becomes ever softened as the negotiation takes place, moving both parties to a more amenable middle ground. The give and take of the conversation is directed by the initial dispreferred response, as both parties attempt to reach a mutual understanding—an intersubjectivity.

Post-expansions

Post-expansions are frequently classified as either (1) Minimal post-expansions or (2) Non-minimal post-expansions. Minimal post-expansions are short, often one word such as: greetings, farewells and closures ("okay . . . good"). The closure brings the conversational sequence to an end, often with a preferred or dispreferred assessment of the sequence. Non-minimal post-expansions are often used to repair or explain a dispreferred response (similar in function to the post-first insertion). We will discover that biblical narrators often use narrated action as a functional way of concluding the dialogue of conversational prayer with a non-minimal expansion, providing either a preferred or dispreferred response in the form of consequential actions.

Turn-Taking

Turn-taking is more than simply not all speaking at once (a common behavior found in pre-schools and presidential debates), but is a social convention that allows participants to speak, listen, and condition what is said based upon the knowledge that other speakers follow.[27] Turn-taking is generally understood as the smallest unit of conversational exchange. It is the turn-taking protocol rather than the content of the first part pairing of the adjacency pair that requires a response (the second part pairing of the adjacency pair). The turn-taking process opens a window onto social organization. Jack Sidnell argues that "some system for turn-taking is a requirement of any coordinated action and thus of human society. It is hard to imagine a society in which people don't organize their conversations this way and, in

---

27. Like many aspects of CA there is good evidence to conclude the cross-cultural applicability of turn taking guidelines. Levinson, *Pragmatics*, 301.

fact, none have been found."[28] Attention to the turn taking process becomes even more important when Deity is one of the conversational participants. CA has identified two components in the process of turn-taking.

1. Turn Construction

Generally, in conversation, one person speaks at a time. Turn-taking is organized to minimize gaps as well as overlaps in conversation. Of course, there are exceptions to this one-person-at-a-time rule. Often, greetings offered to a new participant entering a group are made simultaneously, as is laughter at a joke, or other expressions, primarily emotional instead of cognitively informative. These exceptions to the rule confirm the normally constructed turn taking, highlighting the transition-relevance place—the place at which one speaker ends and another begins—the violation of which is considered rude or inappropriate: the *when* a next speaker makes an utterance. The turn-taking point is identified and anticipated by a number of signals: grammatical, tonal, metrical, prosodic. Participants anticipate turn-taking points, preparing for the response prior to the actual completion of the preceding utterance. While certainly variable to the syntactical norms of a given language, the manner in which an utterance is formed can impact the turn-taking process.[29] If information is front loaded, the respondent is given more opportunity to digest information and form a response while anticipating the point of turn-taking. Conversely, an end heavy information utterance can be used to surprise, confuse, or mollify the respondent—providing less opportunity to form the response while anticipating the turn-taking point.[30] Partners in the conversation project and anticipate the transition relevant place in the conversation. This anticipation can be interrupted or constrained by the manner in which conversation partners construct speech in order to forestall a dispreferred response. The transition-relevance place—the point of turn taking—can be contested and negotiated by the participants in conversation. How these pivotal points in conversation are navigated can communicate just as much as the actual words spoken by the participants. Status, perceived authority, and dominance can be expressed by controlling the transition-relevant place in the conversation. But also, a sense of vulnerability, insecurity, and

---

28. Sidnell, *Conversation Analysis*, 37.

29. Ford and Thompson, "Interactional Units in Conversation," 134–84; Tanaka, "Prosody for Marking Transition Relevance Places," 63–96; Selting, "Construction of Units in Conversational Talk," 477–517.

30. At times, a strategy to prevent a dispreferred response.

fear of a dispreferred response can cause a speaker to disallow the next participant at a turn-relevant place in the conversation. *What* is said in conversation is important, but so is *how* it is said.

2. Turn Allocation

The turn-allocational[31] process relates to *who* should speak next in conversation. There are two basic possibilities for determining who speaks next in conversation: the current speaker selects, or the next speaker self-selects. When the current speaker selects, the selection by the current speaker can be accomplished in a variety of ways through direct address, repair, gaze, and posture.[32] If not specified by the first speaker, a respondent may self-select (the next-speaker select), signaling their intention to enter the conversation by a range of verbal and non-verbal techniques. When no one fills the next speaker slot a void is formed that may signal surprise, astonishment, or discomfort as uncertainty pervades concerning how to respond to the previous direct speech address.

Basic Turn-Taking Guidelines[33]

There are observable patterns for turn taking that help give structure to the conversation encounter. The simplest pattern allows the first speaker (A) to select the next speaker (B) who is obliged to respond at the next turn. Otherwise, any participant may self-select, with the first speaker (A) preferred for entrance in the conversation at the next turn, following (B). Lacking an initial response (B) at the appropriate turn, the initial speaker (A) may choose to continue.

Certainly, this set of base "rules" for turn-taking is upset in normal conversation; punctuated by interruption, over-lap, multiple response (everyone talking at once), that can range in meaning from confirmation (*yes . . . that's right*), to challenge and denial (*un uhh*), delivered both verbally and non-verbally. The departures from the one person at a time turn-taking are intentional and establish connections, not only to the *what* that is being said, but to the *who* that is speaking. Interruption in typical turn-taking can signal strong agreement or disagreement with the content of

---

31. Also termed "turn-distribution" by some analysts. See Hutchby and Wooffitt, *Conversation Analysis*, 49.
32. Goodwin, "Interactive Construction of a Sentence," 97–121.
33. Clift, *Conversation Analysis*, 124.

the speech but also can signal social dominance when "over-speaking" the initial speaker occurs, quite literally drowning out the voice of the original speaker. Moreover, verbal turn-taking may occur simultaneously with non-verbal interruption (for example: turning attention to text messages on a phone during a conversation).

Silence in Turn-Taking

Within a conversation, silence is just as potent as the turn-taking process. A gap or silence at a turn may prompt the initial speaker to continue. And the manner of the continuance is conditioned by how the initial speaker interprets the silence. If the silence is interpreted as a preferred response, the initial speaker may understand tacit agreement, and so press the point or continue the stream of thought. If the silence is perceived as a dispreferred response (denial, objection, refusal), the initial speaker may repair or alter the utterance, seeking to elicit a preferred response. Silence is a powerful component of conversational prayer, often communicating aspects of interpersonal status negotiation more than topical agreement or disagreement.[34]

Agency

Agency is the exercise of influence among the participants of a conversation and consequent action resulting from the conversation.[35] Generally, the initiator of the conversation has agency to which the respondent conforms or resists. The perceived authority relationship among the conversation participants allows the recognition of imperative and declarative components of a conversation. Deontic stance and deontic status[36] (who has power and who communicates power) are usually congruent, but not always: "highly authoritative speakers rarely need to command, while speakers with low authority sometimes can try to inflate their authority with more assertive directives."[37] In conversation, status is not static but may change and that

---

34. Powerfully illustrated in the conversational prayer of 1 Kings 19.

35. Rodney Werline's description of prayer as "a ritual enactment of the power relationships within a society" is particularly relevant in the examination of the conversational prayers. Werline, "Prayer, Politics, and Power in the Hebrew Bible," 16. Samuel Balentine hints at this dynamic as well in *Prayer in the Hebrew Bible*, 50, as does P. D. Miller, *They Cried to the Lord*, 124.

36. That is, the ability to impose obligation, permission, or prohibition on other conversation participants.

37. Stevanovic and Peräkylä, "Three Orders in the Organization of Human Action," 191.

change is reflected in the formation of the utterances.[38] In conversational prayer, status between the conversationalists is often dependent upon the perceived sincerity between the conversation participants. When that sincerity is in doubt, no verbal formulation is, in itself, sufficient to restore personal status. Status between conversational participants is an important dynamic expressing the *who-we-are-to-one-another* of the conversation.

Opening

Openings to a conversation can describe the social standing of the participants in the conversation. Ordinary, introductions to conversations (hello . . . he said . . .)—minus preamble, introductions, or indications of disparate social standing between the participants can indicate the familiarity the conversationalists have with one another.[39] This lack of formality is striking with many of the patriarchal conversational prayers (as well as the Divine human conversations of the patriarchs). The impression is given of familiarity—even when the human partner to the conversation has no previous interaction with the Divine.[40]

Social recognition is an important factor in the way conversations are begun. Familiar participants will address each other quite differently than will participants who have never met or who are unsure of their social footing. The opening to a conversation accomplishes three purposes:[41]

1. Gatekeeping. An opening quickly establishes if a conversation will follow. The initiator of the conversation is not always the one who speaks first in the opening—but the one who initiates the conversation. For example, in a phone conversation—the person who answers with "Hello" may be said to be the first speaker—but is actually the respondent—the ring of the phone an equivalent to the initiator of the conversation. In its simplest form—"a summons-answer" opening establishes if a conversation will follow. The opening of the conversation between God and Moses in Exodus 3 presents the burning bush the functional equivalent to the ring of a telephone.

2. (Re)Constituting the relationship: The opening establishes the participants-in-relationship-to-each-other. The opening acknowledges or establishes the social status between participants. This can be done by;

---

38. A point made by Matthews, *More than Meets the Ear*, 75.
39. Sidnell, *Conversation Analysis*, 198–99.
40. See for example the conversation with Hagar in Genesis 17.
41. Sidnell, *Conversation Analysis*, 199–200.

(1) *Self-identification* where each participant introduces to the other or through, (2) *Recognition* by the other. Recognition by the other reaffirms the relationship between participants in an uncontested manner whereas self-identifying to the other assumes contesting an established relationship even if nothing other than moving from non-recognition to recognition. The preferred response to a greeting is recognition. The way the participants in the conversation constitute the relationship (self-identification, recognition) conditions the way the conversation will be conducted (recipient design). The opening establishes the "who" of the conversation—an affirmation of the participants-in-relationship-to-each-other.

3. Establish the "what" of the conversation: The opening introduces the content of the conversation. Getting to the topic of the conversation is not always immediate or direct in the opening. Having established the participants-in-relationship-to-each-other, an "anchor position,"[42] of social status, the participants are ready to engage a topic.

The familiarity between participants is amplified in the content of the conversation. In the conversational prayers in the Hebrew Bible, God is often subjected to an interrogation by the human participant eliciting a defense of moral action. CA allows for the analysis of conversation structure by asking not only *what* is being said,—but also by asking "What is the speaker doing in saying this and in saying it in this way?"[43] CA investigates *who-we-are-to-one-another* formed and expressed in dialogue. That is, the social relationships and identifications forming the foundation of social life.[44] In conversational prayers the opening can help inform the *who-we-are-to-God*.

Closing

A typical feature of conversation, with an interesting application to the conversational prayers in the Hebrew Bible is a closing. Conversations don't just end—they are brought to a close.[45] The closing must be prepared in a manner that allows for recognition by all parties in the conversation. Conversations can be brought to a closing by a topic-less passing turn followed by a terminal adjacency pair that serves as a signal for ending the conversation

---

42. Sidnell, *Conversation Analysis*, 212.
43. Sidnell, *Conversation Analysis*, 16.
44. Sidnell, *Conversation Analysis*, 15.
45. Sacks and Schegloff, "Opening up Closings," 290.

("bye," "so long," etc.).⁴⁶ The first part of the terminal exchange functions as an invitation to end the conversation that can either be accepted ("bye" from the second speaker) or rejected as the conversation is extended by the second speaker. If the conversation is ended without the agreement of both participants, the status of the participants in relationship to each other is in jeopardy. The participant ending without joint agreement, can appear rude, or can express distain, or can simply choose to ignore the other conversation participants. The closing can (1) signify that a position of understanding concerning the topic has been achieved to the satisfaction of the participants. The closing can (2) signify the status of the participants-in-relationship-to-topic establishing the interest or lack of interest each participant has to the topic. And, the closing can (3) signify the participants in relationship to each other. Frequently, the conversational prayers in the Hebrew Bible have no closing other than the narrated consequent action. This may mean that one or more of the typical functions of the conversational closing is left unfulfilled, supplied in some fashion by the subsequent narrative and so perhaps drawing the reader into the orb of the conversational prayer.

Recipient Design

Recipient design in conversation is "the multitude of respects in which the talk by a party in a conversation is constructed or designed in ways which display an orientation and sensitivity to the particular other(s) who are co-participants."⁴⁷ Speakers tailor their talk to make it appropriate for the person being addressed. This design can include everything from posture, volume or tone of speech, delay or silence, and word selection. This modification can involve a name used—signifying the social relationship the speakers may share (evident when one person in a conversation can be: Mom (to a child), Grandma (to a grandchild), and Rosa (to a friend) all within the same conversation, but spoken by different conversational participants, or word usage and syntax that communicates subtle nuances between the speakers (the use of slang between friends that would not be used when addressing a less familiar conversation partner). Recipient design is part of the mechanism by which the conversation navigates a shared meaning between the participants regarding what is being said and navigates a shared meaning of relationship and status between the participants. The way in which the recipient design changes during a conversation reveals

---

46. Levinson, *Pragmatics*, 317; Sacks and Schegloff, "Opening up Closings," 295.

47. Sacks et al., "Simplest Systematics," 727. See also Hayashi et al., *Conversational Repair and Human Understanding*.

the changing shared understanding of the social interaction represented by the conversation. The recipient design unveils an understanding of the character addressed in the person of the conversation partner.[48] Speakers modify their talk, making it appropriate for the persons with whom they are speaking. One of the fascinating aspects of conversational prayer is to notice the change or lack of change in human address when God is the recipient. Often the way in which recipient design is formulated signals the overarching rhetorical design of the conversation, at times, indicating the reading audience as the primary recipient of the direct address.

Repair

Repair is the process of fixing "problems of speaking, hearing and understanding."[49] It is a movement toward shared understanding between the conversation participants, a "progressivity" in the conversation[50] based upon the "very possibility of a world known in common that transcends the views of the individual actors."[51] On one level, repair can be compared to plot in narrative. It is the movement that carries the dialogue. Repair can certainly fix a problem of understanding, but it can also develop a mutual understanding as preunderstandings become reshaped by the flow of conversation to achieve mutual intersubjective understanding.[52]

Repair can involve the suspension of the normal turn-taking sequence in order to attend to a developing misunderstanding as either the initiator or the recipient can, through the insertion of expansions, introduce and carry out the repair.[53] Repair can be directed by the respondent as well as the initiator in the conversation. In addition to addressing a problem of hearing, speaking, or misunderstanding, repair can be used by either partner of the conversation to direct the progress of the conversation. Through the crafting of a misunderstanding, perhaps intentional, a respondent can direct a conversation partner to attempt a repair and so lead the conversation in a direction not intended or desired by the initiator. Through guided

---

48. This observation has been made by others examining prayers in the Hebrew Bible but has not been developed in terms of conversation analysis. Balentine, *Prayer in the Hebrew Bible*, 48–49. Robert Alter considers this notion in terms of embedded dialogue within narrative. Alter, *Art of Biblical Narrative*, 116.

49. Sidnell, *Conversation Analysis*, 12, 110. See also, Schegloff et al., "Preference for Self-Correction," 361–82.

50. Sidnell, *Conversation Analysis*, 90.

51. Hayashi et al., "Conversational Repair and Human Understanding," 29.

52. Sidnell, *Conversation Analysis*, 91.

53. Hutchby and Wooffitt, *Conversation Analysis*, 60.

repair, a dispreferred response can be avoided by the respondent and yet mutual understanding achieved as control of the conversation is effectively transferred to the respondent. As we have seen, the expansion into the conversation of Genesis 18 is a good example. God tells Abram his design for Sodom and Gomorrah. Abram raises an objection (a problem in achieving mutual intersubjective understanding) and a repair is initiated whereby Abram seeks to establish the moral credibility of God (will not the Judge of all the earth do right?).[54]

Context

Conversation analysts point out the importance of context while attempting to understand "even the seemingly most straightforward utterances."[55] For example, the question, "Can I drive?" posed by a child with a learning permit to her parent has quite a different meaning than the same question posed by a motorist to an auto mechanic immediately after a fender bender. But, the idea of context, when used by conversation analysts goes further. Context also includes the "particular type or kind of interaction the participants understand themselves to be engaged in."[56] That is, our beginning point when determining if a particular dialogue in the Hebrew Bible is a conversational prayer is to ask did the participants in the conversation consider the conversation a prayer, or does the narrator of the episode intend the reader to understand a prayer happening? Often the narrator makes clear how the embedded conversation is to be understood.[57] The Divine human conversation can be introduced by indicating: X prayed saying,[58] or X called upon the name of God, or X assumed a posture associated with prayer, or a crises predicates the conversation that the reader would normally associate with prayer. In all these examples, the prose writer uses conventions to create a context that the assumed reader would associate with prayer. The rhetorical design of the prose writer forms a layer of meaning covering the conversational prayers that must be kept in mind during our investigation.

---

54. Sidnell, *Conversation Analysis*, 111.

55. Sidnell, *Conversation Analysis*, 245.

56. Sidnell, *Conversation Analysis*, 245. The type of interaction understood by the participants should include, "the propositions, describing the beliefs, knowledge, commitments" of the participants in a discourse. See Levinson, *Pragmatics*, 276.

57. Balentine, "Prayer in the Wilderness Traditions," 55.

58. As we will see, this is surprisingly uncommon in the conversational prayers in the Hebrew Bible.

Context is applied by conversation analysts in a second manner that also has application to our investigation. Context also refers to the social place occupied by the conversation. E. A. Schegloff explains this broader application of context: "how does the fact that the talk is being conducted in some setting (say, 'the hospital') issue in any consequences for the shape, form, trajectory, content, or character of the interaction that the parties conduct?"[59] Does the fact that the conversation happens in *this* setting and not *that* setting have any bearing on the participants and does the setting shape the consequences of the talk? An example of the role that context or setting has on the meaning of conversation can be seen in the reactions elicited from the attention given to the audio recording of Donald Trump's "groping" conversation in the summer of 2005.[60] Donald Trump's wife, Melania, excused the conversation by contextualizing it as "locker room talk"[61] even though the conversation did not occur in a locker room and even though, within the talk itself, consequential actions were anticipated by the conversation partners involving a female reporter that was not part of the conversation and certainly went beyond idle but non-actionable statements. The re-contextualizing of the conversation by Mr. Trump's defenders was an effort to recast the meaning of the conversation. If conversation is taken out of context, or re-contextualized, the words can communicate something very different than that intended by the speaker. The importance of setting as context will be seen as especially significant in the conversational prayers of Abraham (Gen 18) and Elijah (1 Kgs 19).

When examining the context of the conversational prayers of the Hebrew Bible, we must consider two levels of context. First, is the structured narrative created by the narrator in which the conversation takes place—the context in which the conversationalists find themselves. The second level of context is the rhetorical design of the narrator—the literary context in which the episode of the conversational prayer finds itself.

Storytelling

Stories function more broadly than to recite past events. Stories can be told in conversation to boast, explain, justify, or to accomplish a host of other participant related functions. The recipient of the story is oriented not just to the formal features of the narrative talk, but to the

---

59. Schegloff, "Reflections on Talk and Social Structure," 53.
60. Fahrenthold, "Trump Recorded."
61. Gajanan, "Melania Trump."

what-is-being-accomplished through the telling of the story.⁶² Sometimes a story is told already known, whole or in part, to the recipient. This joint-telling allows for a preferred disposition to the what-is-being-accomplished through the conversational narrative—an affirmation of the what (the story) contextualizing the preference for the what-is-being-accomplished by the telling of the story.⁶³ This is an important aspect of the conversational prayers in the Hebrew Bible as often the human partner will rehearse for the Deity a story (most of which is already known to the Deity) as a way to introduce a justification for an action or a defense against a moral wrong committed by the Deity. The story provides the context for a presumed change of status between the conversational participants.

Topic

Focus on the topic of conversation is considered problematic by many conversation analysts, and this may constitute an important shift in how we view the conversational prayers in the Hebrew Bible. "A focus on topic may obscure important questions about what the participants were doing in and by talking about whatever it was they were talking about."⁶⁴ In our analysis of the conversational prayers, questions arise concerning how a topic is established, sustained, and changed in conversation. It is common that topic initiation maximizes the probability that additional information is offered as a response to a request rather than volunteered by conversation participants.⁶⁵

An interesting feature of topic transition is a "stepwise transition." A stepwise transition is a feature in conversation that involves connecting or linking the current topic with a new topic even though the topics themselves are quite distinct. "I link up whatever I'm now introducing as a new topic to what we've just been talking about [in such a way that] so far as anybody knows we've never had to start a new topic . . . it flowed."⁶⁶ Topic transitions in conversational prayer provide a window into the movement of the exchange, altering status between participants and guiding the what-is-being-accomplished of the prayer. Often, the initial request beginning a conversational prayer in the Hebrew Bible will be transitioned into a second topic that is more relevant to the interests of the narrator.

62. Sidnell, *Conversation Analysis*, 194.
63. Sacks et al., "Simplest Systematics," 727.
64. Schegloff, "On the Organization of Sequences," 52.
65. Sidnell, *Conversation Analysis*, 233; Button and Casey, "Topic Nomination and Topic Pursuit," 23.
66. Sacks, *Lectures on Conversation*, 2:566.

A Note on Notation

CA has developed an extensive transcription system for the analysis of conversation.[67] In this book the full system is not needed, nor helpful. The conversational prayers under examination will be presented according to the adjacency pairs that give structure to the conversational exchange. Generally, the first paring part of the adjacency pair will be labeled *A*, and the second pairing part labeled *B*. Subsequent rounds or pairings in the conversational exchange will be labeled sequentially by superscript numerals. When narrative expansions appear within the conversational exchange, the text will be presented in *italics*. Likewise, post-expansions functioning as consequential action to the conversational exchange are presented in *italics*.

---

67. See Clift, *Conversation Analysis*, 53–63.

3

Abraham Cycle

THE MIDDLE PART OF Genesis (12–36) is commonly divided into two subdivisions, the Abraham Cycle (12:1—25:19) and the Jacob Cycle (25:20—36:43).[1] In recent years, the origin and early form of these independent units have come under intense scholarly scrutiny[2] with competing paradigms offered to explain some of the literary differences now resident in the stories.[3] Without intending to make comment on the origin of the material, we simply note here that the prayers in the Abraham Cycle are structured differently from the prayers found in the Jacob Cycle. Further, the structure of the prayers within each cycle is consistent enough to conclude that the differences between the cycles are not accidental. Something about the rhetorical function of the conversational prayers in the Abraham Cycle is very different from the rhetorical function of the conversational prayers in the Jacob Cycle.

A clue to the rhetorical design of the conversational prayers in the Abraham Cycle may be found in the reputation Abraham achieved with other biblical authors. Both, 2 Chr 20:7 and Isa 41:8 refer to Abraham as a "friend of God."[4] Since many of the stories about Abraham are also retold in the Jacob Cycle (applied to Jacob), it doesn't seem that Abraham's reputation as God's friend was based upon uniquely shared experiences or even moral

---

1. See the discussion in Westermann, *Genesis 12–36*, 401–3.

2. See Friedman, "Foreword."

3. Insight into the literary history of Genesis has developed significantly in the last several decades, although recognition of the early independence and integrity of the Abraham Cycle and the Jacob Cycle is well established. See Schmid, "Genesis in the Pentateuch," 27–50; Dozeman et al., eds., *Pentateuch*. The performative nature of the oral literature, preceding the Abraham narrative is especially evident in the dialogical material of the narrative. See the important analysis by Polak, "Oral Substratum," 225, 229–30; Polak, "Oral Platform," 429–30.

4. Also Jas 2:23.

character. Rather, it is the conversational prayers in the Abraham Cycle that are distinctive, and it may be that Abraham's friendship with God was forged in conversation.[5]

Genesis 15:1–10: Do Not Be Afraid

A: [1] After these things the word of the LORD came to Abram in a vision, "Do not be afraid, Abram, I am your shield; your reward shall be very great."

B: [2] But Abram said, "O LORD God, what will you give me, for I continue childless, and the heir of my house is Eliezer of Damascus?"

Ba: [3] And Abram said, "You have given me no offspring, and so a slave born in my house is to be my heir."

A^1: [4] But the word of the LORD came to him (saying), "This man shall not be your heir; no one but your very own issue shall be your heir."

A^1a: [5] He brought him outside and said, "Look toward heaven and count the stars, if you are able to count them."

A^1b: Then he said to him, "So shall your descendants be."

B^1: [6] *And he believed the Lord; and the Lord reckoned it to him as righteousness.*

A^2: [7] Then he said to him, "I am the LORD who brought you from Ur of the Chaldeans, to give you this land to possess."

B^2: [8] But he said, "O LORD God, how am I to know that I shall possess it?"

A^3: [9] He said to him, "Bring me a heifer three years old, a female goat three years old, a ram three years old, a turtledove, and a young pigeon."

B^3: [10] *He brought him all these and cut them in two, laying each half over against the other; but he did not cut the birds in two.*

---

5. This is implied similarly in God's friendship with Moses (Exod 33:11; Num 12:8).

Recipient Design

One of the unusual characteristics of the conversational prayer in Genesis 15 is the lack of recipient design.[6] Recipient design is the label given to the idea that speech in conversation is tailored to the recipient. A prominent feature of the principle of recipient design is that, in conversation, a speaker should not tell a "recipient what they already know."[7] This is certainly not the case in the conversation in Genesis 15. Abram is quite aware of his journey from Ur and needs no reminder of it, just as God needed no reminder about his previous promise made to Abram. In fact, except for the metaphors (dust and stars) used to describe the multitude of Abram's promised descendants, most of the conversation of Gen 15:1–6 could be reconstructed from earlier exchanges in Genesis 12–14. The lack of recipient design in the conversation of Gen 15:1–6 makes clear that the primary recipient in the conversation, now placed in a prose context, is the reader (or viewer of a performance). In the conversation, it is the reader whose attention is being drawn to key features of the developing relationship between Abram and God, highlighted by the repetition from earlier conversations and layered over with the addition of new metaphors and symbolic acts (Gen 15:9–21).

Opening

A second observation to be made about this conversational prayer is that there is no opening or closing made by either participant in the conversation. Openings and closings are part of the structural organization of conversation that connects conversations to a larger social network.[8] A greeting, such as that between friends, establishes a mutual recognition of a prior social relationship and an understanding that the conversation to follow will at least begin with that prior relationship in mind. An opening establishing a conversation between two previously unknown participants must establish the willingness of both parties to engage in conversation, minimize the likelihood of rejection by the person addressed, and quickly establish a shared topic and standing between the parties of the conversation. The conversational prayer in Genesis 15 has none of that. Instead, the narrator provides a contextualization for the conversation "after these things" and in "a vision." And, although generally not translated, it is worth noting that the narrator does use the infinitive in v. 4 ("saying") to frame

---

6. Sacks et al., "Simplest Systematics," 727.
7. Sacks, *Lectures on Conversation*, 438.
8. Sidnell, *Conversation Analysis*, 197–98.

the following dialogue, probably indicating the narrator's intent to present a direct address.⁹ The conversation itself is important to the narrator, even if awkwardly conducted.

The narrative opening, "after these things" immediately connects the following conversation to the events of chapter 14. Although some time may have passed, and other events and concerns intruded into the thinking of Abram and God, between the end of chapter 14 and the beginning of chapter 15, no greeting is required to reestablish the topic of the following conversation or to reestablish the status relationship of the conversationalists. The standing of the conversation partners is established by the phrase "in a vision." Visions are venues of unequal status and power, controlled by the Deity and placing the recipient in a contingent position. As readers, we are prepared for the presence of Deity or proxy as Abram enters conversation. Missing, however, is any summons by the Deity, calling Abram to attention. Nor do we find any honorific title or posture of reverence offered by Abram upon God's sudden appearance.

The lack of greeting allows the prayer of chapter 15 immediate connection to where God and Abram left off in the conversation of 13:14–17, the only difference, 15:1–6 is "in a vision" while no such context is established in 13:14. But, if the conversation of chapter 15 is presented as a continuation, why the delay? And why the change of venue? What has changed between the beginning of the conversation in 13:14–16 and the continuation of the conversation in 15:1–5? The intervening episode of Lot's dramatic rescue, the rout of the five-king coalition, blessing by Melchizedek, and Abram's refusal of war booty, establishes for the reader something of Abram's character, hidden when the conversation began in chapter 13. Abram's military prowess and standing among Canaanite leaders will not substitute for his reliance upon the promise made by God. And that reliance is assumed by the opening phrase of the LORD's turn: "Do not be afraid." The conversational context of chapter 15 and the opening sentence at once reaffirms Abram's dependency upon the LORD while offering Abram the freedom to speak, and so permission to articulate the question that will guide the conversation.

---

9. It should be noted that not all direct speech is framed by the לאמר infinitive and so care must be taken to not quickly conclude indirect speech when the infinitive is absent. See C. Miller, *Representation of Speech*, 174.

Standing

The standing between the conversationalists is also framed by the narrative introduction, explaining that the Lord came to Abram in a vision. This mode of conversing establishes that initiative and agency belong to the Lord. Abram has no choice. He cannot refuse the vision or turn away from the conversational partner. As recipient of the vision, Abram is placed in a position of being acted upon. The standing between Abram and the Lord, so begun by the mode of presentation, will be developed further through the dialogue itself. The promise made by God to Abram revolves around offspring that God will make "like the dust of the earth" (13:16). But, Abram protests, "You [the Lord] have given me no offspring" (15:3). The accusation is undeniable. Abram's wording of 15:3 makes the Lord directly responsible for the lack of offspring and questions the veracity of the promise made by God in 13:14–16.[10] And it is Abram's demonstrated loyalty to the Lord in chapter 14 that gives him moral standing for the challenge made in 15:2–3. Abram has earned the right to question the Lord.[11] That moral standing is summarized in v. 6, "He believed the Lord and the Lord reckoned it to him as righteousness."

Abram's initial challenge is met with a variation of the promise delivered in 13:14–16. But there's more. Verses 7 and 8 contain an adjacency pair that will introduce a new dynamic to the dilemma of God's trustworthiness.

> A^2: [7] Then he said to him, "I am the Lord who brought you from Ur of the Chaldeans, to give you this land to possess."
>
> B^2: [8] But he said, "O Lord God, how am I to know that I shall possess it?"

Verse 7, here labeled A^2, continues the response to the initial protestation of v. 3: "You have given me no offspring, and so a slave born in my house is to be my heir." A^2 adds to the response found in A^1, A^{1a}, A^{1b} by reminding Abram (and more the reader) of how this promise began: with a Divine call to leave Ur. Abram's repeated protest in v. 8 implies that the reminder of v. 7 is irrelevant and, in fact, it adds little, if anything, to the topic of conversation. Verse 7 does, however, position the conversation for the consequential activity to follow.

The consequential activity is in the ceremony of vv. 9–11. Animals are slaughtered and butchered into pieces that are then placed in two parallel

---

10. The fulfillment of the promise made by God is the dilemma driving the Abraham narrative. Polak, "Oral Platform and Language Usage," 409–10.
11. See Rogland, "Abram's Persistent Faith," 43–44.

lines, between which partners of an agreement pass in a ceremonial walk, signifying the solemnity with which they understood the promise they are making to each other. Even though the promise between God and Abram involved both parties, in Abram's deep sleep he witnessed only the smoking pot and flaming brand, symbolizing the presence of Deity, pass through the carcasses. Abram's question of v. 8 is met with a final response in which God assumes full and sole responsibility for fulfillment of the promise to Abram of descendants and land. Just as the initiative, calling Abram from Ur was solely God's, so, too, responsibility for the final fulfillment of the promise made to Abram will be God's alone. Having assumed sole agency at the beginning of the conversation by appearing in a vision, reinforcing that agency through the reminder of v. 7, and now concluding the conversation with a ceremonial action designed to retain agency, the LORD reaffirms his fidelity to promises made at the beginning of his relationship with Abram.

Closing

Just as the prayer of chapter 15 has no opening, it has no closing. The conversation is interrupted at the end of 15:9 (when Abram goes to fetch the carcasses and shoo away the birds) and in 15:17 (as the sun has finally gone down and darkness set in) but is able to resume (15:13, 18) without missing a beat. Similar to those interruptions, the conversation simply ends in 15:21 without closure.

Usually, conversations are brought to a close, they don't simply end.[12] A closing to a conversation serves several functions. It can reinforce the standing between the conversation participants, and it can signal that the topic of conversation has been satisfied as conversation partners offer topicless turns (*bye, so long, amen* in prayer). The lack of a closing to the prayer in Genesis 15 suggests that the status of the conversational partners is still dynamic and that the topic of God's promise to Abram (of an heir) is not exhausted. The lack of a closing to the conversational exchange in Genesis 15 strengthens the bond to the following episode in Genesis 16. Specifically, Genesis 16 is bound to the last round of the conversation in Genesis 15, a round that introduces the status of the "other" (the Kenites, Kenizzites, Kadmonites, Hittites, Perizzites, Rephaim, Amorites, Canaanites, Girgashites, and Jebusites) living in the land promised to Abram and his heirs.[13]

---

12. Sidnell, *Conversation Analysis*, 214–15; Levinson, *Pragmatics*, 317.

13. Undoubtedly, also the concern of the editorial notion in Gen 15:16 regarding the moral disposition of the Amorites.

Genesis 17:1–21: Walk before Me and Be Blameless

A: ¹ "I am God Almighty; walk before me, and be blameless. ² And I will make my covenant between me and you, and will make you exceedingly numerous."

B: (Narrated Response): ³ *Then Abram fell on his face;*

A¹: and God said to him (saying), ⁴ "As for me, this is my covenant with you: You shall be the ancestor of a multitude of nations. ⁵ No longer shall your name be Abram, but your name shall be Abraham; for I have made you the ancestor of a multitude of nations. ⁶ I will make you exceedingly fruitful; and I will make nations of you, and kings shall come from you. ⁷ I will establish my covenant between me and you, and your offspring after you throughout their generations, for an everlasting covenant, to be God to you and to your offspring after you. ⁸ And I will give to you, and to your offspring after you, the land where you are now an alien, all the land of Canaan, for a perpetual holding; and I will be their God."

A¹a: ⁹ God said to Abraham, "As for you, you shall keep my covenant, you and your offspring after you throughout their generations. ¹⁰ This is my covenant, which you shall keep, between me and you and your offspring after you: Every male among you shall be circumcised. ¹¹ You shall circumcise the flesh of your foreskins, and it shall be a sign of the covenant between me and you. ¹² Throughout your generations every male among you shall be circumcised when he is eight days old, including the slave born in your house and the one bought with your money from any foreigner who is not of your offspring. ¹³ Both the slave born in your house and the one bought with your money must be circumcised. So shall my covenant be in your flesh an everlasting covenant. ¹⁴ Any uncircumcised male who is not circumcised in the flesh of his foreskin shall be cut off from his people; he has broken my covenant."

A¹b: ¹⁵ God said to Abraham, "As for Sarai your wife, you shall not call her Sarai, but Sarah shall be her name. ¹⁶ I will bless her, and moreover I will give you a son by her. I will bless her, and she shall give rise to nations; kings of peoples shall come from her."

B¹: ¹⁷ *Then Abraham fell on his face and laughed*, and said to himself, "Can a child be born to a man who is a hundred years old? Can Sarah, who is ninety years old, bear a child?"

B¹a: ¹⁸ And Abraham said to God, "O that Ishmael might live in your sight!"

A²: ¹⁹ God said, "No, but your wife Sarah shall bear you a son, and you shall name him Isaac. I will establish my covenant with him as an everlasting covenant for his offspring after him. ²⁰ As for Ishmael, I have heard you; I will bless him and make him fruitful and exceedingly numerous; he shall be the father of twelve princes, and I will make him a great nation. ²¹ But my covenant I will establish with Isaac, whom Sarah shall bear to you at this season next year."

Closure: ²² *And when he had finished talking with him, God went up from Abraham.*

Opening

Unlike the previously recorded conversational prayer between Abram and God,[14] this conversation does begin with an opening. The narrator establishes context for the conversation, telling the reader Abram is now ninety-nine years old and the LORD appears. Perhaps because of the time that has gone by (about twenty-four years since God and Abram last spoke), or perhaps because of the significance of the dialogue and imbedded prayer, this conversation does begin with an opening that establishes the social relationship between the conversation participants. In 17:1 God introduces himself as "God Almighty" (אל שדי), the first time this title is used with Abram. A similar introductory announcement is made in 15:7, in which God self-identifies as LORD (יהוה), the originator of the call to leave Ur and the Deity Abram had come to worship (12:7) and know (13:4).[15] Additional titles are used for Deity in conversation with Melchizedek (God Most High אל עליון, 14:19–22) and in previous conversations with God (LORD God אדני יהוה, 15:8), but this self-identification of God Almighty inserts a new dynamic in the relationship

---

14. For similarities to Gen 15:1–21, see Arnold, "Holiness Redaction," 52–53. Arnold argues that the conversation of Genesis 17 is designed, at least in part, to "move the old priestly agenda beyond the purely cultic interests of P in a more ethical and moral direction" (52). While there can be little doubt that the Genesis 17 conversation post-dates the Genesis 15 conversation, the present literary context assumes that each account will be read in light of the narrative flow connecting the episodes. Even though similarities exist, Genesis 17 is not exactly a parallel account to Genesis 15, but Genesis 17 does not replace Genesis 15. Claus Westermann identifies two major strands woven into this conversational exchange. Westermann, *Genesis 12–36*, 263.

15. See Arnold, "Holiness Redaction," 52.

with Abram for, in response, Abram falls to his face on the ground, also a first for Abram in his relationship with God.

Standing

The standing of the conversational participants is of major importance within this conversation. The repeated use of the "between" formula in first and second person (17:2, 7, 10, 11) emphasizes that the conversation is deeply relational. Bearing in mind that relationship, the use of "God Almighty" in 17:1 adds to the dynamics of the conversation in a manner that gives pause. First, note the relatively few instances when the label appears in the patriarchal narratives,[16] and the only time it is used with Abram. This singular use of the label in conversation with Abram, results in a singular response. This is the only time when, in the presence of God, Abram falls on his face to the ground, an explicit act of worship and contriteness. Second, it is no doubt important to note that the use of the label "God Almighty" is part of a name changing episode, here in 17:5, and again with Jacob in 35:10–11 (the only other time God Almighty is present in first person throughout the patriarchal narratives). The change of name implies an attendant change of status. At least in the patriarchal narratives, the status between conversational partners is up for grabs and likely to be changed when "God Almighty" joins the conversation.

Closing

A closing, too, is implied in this conversation between God and Abram. Although the actual wording of the conversational closing is not reproduced, the narrator signifies a conversational closure in 17:22, "And when he had finished talking with him, God went up from Abraham." In this brief description, both elements of a typical conversation closure are present. The topic of conversation seems to have been exhausted (he had finished talking) and the relationship between conversational partners is established both, through the unusual departure of God Almighty (went up) and the new name given to Abram (Abraham).

---

16. There are only two instances when God Almighty is present (17:1; 35:11). The other uses in the patriarchal narratives reference God Almighty as third person (Gen 28:3; 43:14; 48:3; 49:25 [shortened form]). In fact, the title appears relatively few times in the Hebrew Bible (Ezek 10:5). A notable exception is Job, where a shortened form, "Almighty," is a favorite.

The conversation in Genesis 17 between God and Abram changed both participants. Both, God and Abram received new names, and both assumed a new point of view. Abram begins the conversation with face on the ground and God concludes the conversation going up (עלי). There can be no doubt that the *who-we-are-to-one-another* in this exchange is of prime importance to the narrator and a vital component of the *what-it-does* of this conversational prayer.

Rounds

This conversational exchange is structured into two complete rounds (A, A^1–B^1) followed by a direct response (A^2). The second-round Divine speech (A^1) is segmented by three introductory phrases, separating the Divine speech thematically.

The opening and closing of this conversation are not the only unusual parts of the conversational exchange. Following the opening, the first round between God and Abram is lopsided. God's initial speech extends from v. 4 to v. 14 and includes:

1. Divine commands to "walk before me" and "be blameless"
2. A rehearsal of the Divine promise initially delivered in chapter 12
3. Pronouncement of a name change from Abram to Abraham
4. The introduction of circumcision as a sign of the covenant between God and Abraham (with the threat of consequence for nonconformity)[17]
5. Pronouncement of a name change for Abraham's wife from Sarai to Sarah
6. The announcement of a son given by God to Abraham and Sarah

The first part of the round, the Divine direct address, is framed by the infinitive (saying) followed by an emphatic self-assertion[18] ("Look, I Myself . . ."). Abraham has fallen face to the ground while God Almighty is making abundantly clear his personal involvement in the matters to be discussed. There is no doubt that both conversationalists are committed to the *who-we-are-to-one-another* of this conversational prayer.

---

17. See Thiessen, "Text of Genesis 17:14," 625–42.
18. Muraoka, *Emphatic Words and Structures in Biblical Hebrew*, 95. A similar structure is used in the Jacob conversational prayer of Gen 28:15. See also Arnold, "Holiness Redaction," 55.

The Divine direct address of the round is quite lengthy, interrupted by narrative prefaces at vv. 9 and 15. In a normal conversation, we might suppose that these narrative prefaces marked where God paused to catch his breath or where Abraham attempted to offer a response without success. Certainly, any one of these six topics could merit a response from Abraham, but it is only the last that causes him to once more fall to the ground, this time not out of reverence but beside himself with laughter.

Abraham's response to God's initial pronouncement comes in two parts. First, "he said to himself." Abraham's self-talk expresses incredulity, a dispreferred response that is a direct challenge to God Almighty's veracity. Abraham does not believe what God has told him, and, in fact, thinks it quite ridiculous, literally rolling on the ground with laughter. This direct challenge is softened, yet still formed as a dispreferred response in the second part of Abraham's response, this time directed to God. This part of the response does assume the truthfulness of what God has said but offers a preferred alternative to God's plan: "O that Ishmael might live in your sight!" Abraham's request is that Ishmael might be the channel through which the various other blessings from God might be accomplished.

The insertion of Ishmael into the conversation is unexpected and, in terms of furthering the topic at hand, unnecessary. Abraham's mention of Ishmael does allow a Divine dispreferred response, and so an opportunity to expand the conversation (a stepwise transition) to include the Divine disposition toward other people groups in the near vicinity (continuing the conversation ended in Gen 15:20). Abraham asks that Ishmael might live in God's sight. Abraham's request on behalf of Ishmael is heard (v. 20). In fact, it, too, deserves God Almighty's special notice,[19] nevertheless the request is denied. Yet, Ishmael is not banished, forced to live hidden from the face of God (as is Cain; Gen 4:14). Instead, Ishmael is promised a future that is blessed by God (v. 20), using some of the same rhetoric describing God's creative activity in Genesis 1 (fruitful and exceedingly numerous).[20] Ishmael will be the father of twelve princes and from him will come a great nation. From Sarah, however, and through her offspring, Isaac, will come nations and kings of peoples (v. 16). The comparison between the two seems to favor Sarah's descendants, but the real difference is the divinely established covenant with Isaac (v. 21).

Why does Abraham only respond to the last of God's speech? Is there a building crescendo where the last signifies the whole? This does not seem

---

19. The particle הנה (often translated: *behold*) is used here in a manner similar to its use beginning v. 4.

20. See also Exod 1:7.

to be the case. Presumably, Sarah's remarkable pregnancy would be no less remarkable even if her husband was named Abram. And the threatened punishment of v. 14 presupposes that at least some of Abram's descendants would not "be blameless." No, Abraham seems to be fixated on the possibility of Sarah becoming pregnant and the implied consequence that would have for Ishmael. Abraham's dispreferred response of vv. 17–18 allows an explanation, a more detailed description of the Divine attitude taken not just toward Ishmael, but toward two people groups: of Sarah's child—nations and kings of peoples (v. 16); of Ishmael—twelve princes and a great nation (v. 20). The unexpected insertion of Ishmael into the topic of conversation allows the narrator to define insiders and outsiders, continuing the topic of the unclosed conversation from 15:21. It's not that God doesn't like Ishmael and his descendants, but that something more is being accomplished through the recipients of an everlasting covenant (v. 7). The thrust of the first exchange (vv. 2–18), leading to the third round (vv. 19–21), is to establish who is on the inside and who is on the outside—who is "covenanted" with God in an everlasting covenant (v. 7) and who is not. And more, it is this everlasting covenant that functions as the identifying characteristic, marking those on the inside and those on the outside. Insiders, outsiders, and the morality of God's disposition toward each will again form a topic of conversation between God and Abraham.

An additional name is inserted into the conversation at v. 19—Isaac (צחק: he laughed). The Divine disclosure of Isaac's name is presented as a response to Abraham's untoward response in v. 17. A similar outbreak, this time by Sarah and also motivated by disbelief, is found in Genesis 18:12–15 and a second naming account is found in Genesis 21:6–7, also accompanied by Sarah's laughter, this time not motivated by disbelief but by joy.

At the heart of this conversational prayer is the who-we-are-to-one-another between the conversational participants. Both conversationalists receive new names and new points of view as the conversation progresses toward a shared intersubjectivity—a shared understanding. And like ripples on a pond, the dynamic interpersonal relationship between God and Abraham reaches outward, moving others also. Sarah, Ishmael, Isaac, their descendants, and a multitude of the unnamed will all have their destinies changed because of Abraham's conversational prayer with God.

Genesis 18:23–32: Will the Judge of All the Earth Do What Is Just?

A: ²³ Then Abraham came near and said, "Will you indeed sweep away the righteous with the wicked? ²⁴ Suppose there are fifty righteous within the city; will you then sweep away the place and not forgive it for the fifty righteous who are in it? ²⁵ Far be it from you to do such a thing, to slay the righteous with the wicked, so that the righteous fare as the wicked! Far be that from you! Shall not the Judge of all the earth do what is just?"

B: ²⁶ And the Lord said, "If I find at Sodom fifty righteous in the city, I will forgive the whole place for their sake."

A¹: ²⁷ Abraham answered, "Let me take it upon myself to speak to the Lord, I who am but dust and ashes. ²⁸ Suppose five of the fifty righteous are lacking? Will you destroy the whole city for lack of five?"

B¹: And he said, "I will not destroy it if I find forty-five there."

A²: ²⁹ Again he spoke to him, "Suppose forty are found there."

B²: He answered, "For the sake of forty I will not do it."

A³: ³⁰ Then he said, "Oh do not let the Lord be angry if I speak. Suppose thirty are found there."

B³: He answered, "I will not do it, if I find thirty there."

A⁴: ³¹ He said, "Let me take it upon myself to speak to the Lord. Suppose twenty are found there."

B⁴: He answered, "For the sake of twenty I will not destroy it."

A⁵: ³² Then he said, "Oh do not let the Lord be angry if I speak just once more. Suppose ten are found there."

B⁵: He answered, "For the sake of ten I will not destroy it."

³³ *And the Lord went his way, when he had finished speaking to Abraham; and Abraham returned to his place.*

Context

The narrative set up for this conversational prayer is unusual. The Lord (earlier in the form of three "men" [18:1–2] but now accompanied by three "men") and Abraham have ended a meal together during which a child is promised to Sarah. The Divine guests take their leave and begin the journey toward Sodom. Abraham walks with his companions a short while, setting them on their way. During this short walk, the Lord either, thinks to himself, or wonders out loud, in the hearing of the "men" accompanying him, but in a manner preventing Abraham from overhearing, whether or not he should share his plans for Sodom with Abraham since:

1. He (Abraham) shall become a great and mighty nation and all the nations of the earth shall be blessed by him
2. The Lord has chosen him that he may charge his household and children to keep the way of the Lord by doing righteousness and justice

Apparently concluding the Divine deliberation, the Lord then speaks, this time loud enough for all, including Abraham, to hear his intention of visiting Sodom and Gomorrah in order to see if the residents are as bad as he has heard. The three "men" head off toward Sodom, while the Lord and Abraham remain standing together. Finally, alone with God, Abraham "came near and said." And so, the conversational prayer opens.

All of the narrative information setting the stage for Abraham "coming near" the Lord constitutes an effective context of the following conversational prayer. As conversation analysts remind us, the context of a conversation is all important to understand even the clearest and seemingly most straight forward of utterances. Ochs describes context as "social and psychological world in which the language user operates at any given time."[21] When making observations about the significance of context in a conversation, two conditions apply:[22]

1. Is the context invoked by the analyst relevant to the participants themselves? This may include status between the participants, topic of conversation, and prior interactions of the participants.
2. Does the context have consequence? Is it demonstrable that the fact the conversation is occurring in this setting and not that setting have consequence for the interaction of the parties?

The above two conditions make clear that context is more than setting. J. Lyons details the following aspects of context, influential in conversation:[23]

---

21. Ochs, "Introduction," 1.
22. Sidnell, *Conversation Analysis*, 240.
23. Lyons, *Semantics*, 574.

1. Knowledge of the role and status of the participants
2. Knowledge of special and temporal location
3. Knowledge of formality level
4. Knowledge of medium (varieties between written and spoken conversation)
5. Knowledge of topic
6. Knowledge of province

The conversation between Abraham and God, following dinner with Sarah, is contextualized for the reader by the narrator and so meets Sidnell's first criterion above. The prayer will take place "on the way," in a moment of transition, removed from the social expectations of dwelling or sanctuary. The context of the conversation is further advanced by the narrator's exposé of the Divine inner thoughts as God contemplates whether or not to speak with Abraham concerning his intent for Sodom. Although the fate of the residents of Sodom and Gomorrah hang in the balance, the exchange between God and Abraham will be as much about character (just and righteous) as Divine punishment. And finally, the context removes any doubt that the following conversation is a one-on-one between God and Abraham. The conversation is private, not for public view, addressing a topic and in a manner shared uniquely by God and Abraham. There are no concerns about being overheard or misunderstood by a third party. The conversation participants are free to shape their statements fully to the design of the recipient. God and Abraham can be frank and air their full apprehensions about each other's moral character.

Standing

The standing between the conversational partners of this conversational prayer is set up quite differently than that of Gen 15:1. In Genesis 15, the LORD came to Abram in a vision, and so assuming all initiative and agency in beginning the conversation. Here, Abraham "came near" and initiates the conversation, asking a question and so assuming the right to the knowledge he seeks. The relationship between Abraham and the LORD has evolved from where it was in chapter 15. What is striking about the conversation of Genesis 17 is its lack of formality. Abraham barters with God, driving down the price, as if he were buying a sheep or plot of land.[24] And oddly, this seems to address

---

24. See Kimelman, "Prophecy as Arguing with God," 17–18.

Sidnell's second criterion for context. The conversation is consequential, and it is precisely the contextual lack of formality and supporting social props that allows the consequence of the conversation to clearly revolve around the key topic—the moral character of God and Abraham.

In conversation, it isn't just the *what* of the conversation, but the *how*, *when*, and *where* that add meaning to the exchange. The context of this prayer points the reader to the main issue at the heart of the ensuing debate. The partners of the conversation are "on the way." In a sense, this conversation occurs neither here nor there. They have left Abraham's tent and so are no longer encumbered by the expected rights and privileges of either guest or host.[25] But, neither is the conversation "in a vision," as have been previous conversations between Abraham and God (15:1). Nor is the conversation in a cultic site or near an altar (12:7). That is, the conversation is absent any of the religious accoutrements accentuating the sacred and thereby preventing challenges to the Divine character. And Abraham has not assumed any posture that might communicate reverence or even respect (17:3). No, the participants in this conversation have only their character to give them standing before each other. And "standing" is an issue in v. 22. The text of v. 22 originally had the Lord "standing" before Abraham. This was considered unseemly for Deity and so changed by the Masoretic scribes (and others, see LXX)[26] to make Abraham the one "standing" before the Lord. So, it would seem, the original set up for the following conversation pictured the Lord standing, present for questioning by Abraham.

Abraham's initial speech is cast in response to an implied invitation from the Lord when announcing his intention to visit Sodom. Although destruction of Sodom is not part of the Divine deliberation or an articulated outcome of the intended visit, Abraham presumes the inhabitants of Sodom are in imminent danger and pleads for their safety by appealing to the character of the Lord. Abraham challenges the plan of (as of yet only implied) indiscriminate Divine destruction by suggesting it would not be just and, as such, an inappropriate action for the Judge of all the earth. Abraham's appeal on behalf of the residents of Sodom and protest of Divine injustice are unmistakably connected to the narrative set up in which Abraham receives Divine commendation for charging "his household and children to keep the way of the Lord by doing righteousness and justice." Although on the surface, the conversation is about the people of Sodom, the context of the conversation indicates that something quite different is going on—this conversation is

---

25. This is seemingly emphasized in the closing when Abraham returns to his place (18:33).

26. The well-known *tiqqune sof^erim* explained by Speiser, *Genesis*, 134; and Brueggemann, *Great Prayers of the Old Testament*, 3-4.

about Divine character.[27] This context is necessary to understand if the full outrage of the following series of turns is to be appreciated.[28]

The LORD's pause, giving Abraham time to "approach near," is a consequence of his conclusion that Abraham is righteous and just. Now that same character quality, and whether it is possessed by the LORD, is up for examination. The context for the conversation has stripped away all supporting props and actors. Alone and far from religious or social constraints, through the conversation to follow, the LORD and Abraham will conclude something about each other's moral standing.

Rounds

The conversation begins with a statement by Abraham in which three questions are posed. These questions will guide the following conversational exchange.

1. Will you indeed sweep away the righteous with the wicked?
2. Suppose there are fifty righteous within the city; will you then sweep away the place and not forgive it for the fifty righteous who are in it? Far be it from you to do such a thing, to slay the righteous with the wicked, so that the righteous fare as the wicked! Far be that from you!
3. Shall not the Judge of all the earth do what is just?

Will the LORD indiscriminately destroy the wicked and the righteous? Can destruction be averted if fifty righteous can be found? Will not the Judge of all the earth do what is just? Although three questions are posed, the LORD only responds to the second. This selective response is worth considering. The implied accusation of Divine indiscriminate punishment and not doing what is right follow from violating Abraham's suggested measure of punishing fifty righteous. In agreeing to spare punishment on behalf of fifty non-deserving innocents, the LORD acquiesces to Abraham's conditions by which it will be known that the Judge of all the earth does what is just. And so, while focus is on the observable conditions (fifty righteous),

---

27. See the discussion by Macdonald, "Listening to Abraham," 30–31.
28. That the focus is on Divine character and not the people of Sodom is evident from the lack of consideration given to determining who, in Sodom, is righteous. Who should be included among the initial fifty? What makes any of these more righteous than anyone else? Can a person be "mostly righteous" and still qualify for the exempted group? And who chooses? Does Abraham determine who is righteous? Does the LORD? And if so, how is the choice made?

the last question is the real point (Shall not the Judge of all the earth do what is just?) as the bartering session to follow will show.

The conversation is constructed in a series of five rounds, each initiated by Abraham and answered directly by the LORD. Each round includes a request for a reduction in the number of righteous required to spare Sodom (the first-round reduction of five, otherwise reduced by ten righteous). In each case, the LORD offers a direct and brief preferred response to the reduction request.

Abraham discloses much more that is not addressed in the LORD's response. In rounds one, three, four, and five, Abraham announces his self-appointed permission to speak. In the first round, this self-appointed standing is followed by a self-deprecating description (dust and ashes) thereby mitigating the apparent arrogance of Abraham's presumed familiarity with the Divine. In rounds three and five, Abraham includes a plea, asking the LORD to not be angry, presumably with Abraham's repeated bartering. Both of these, (the repeated announcement to speak and plea for Divine restraint) amount to a reinforcement of standing between the conversation partners. None of this is explicitly answered in the LORD's response, but we can conclude that the Divine agreement to Abraham's terms includes an implicit acceptance of Abraham's standing in the conversation. Abraham's challenge of the LORD's moral character is met with acceptance and a series of preferred responses minus any repair or correction.

The *How* of the Conversation

It isn't simply the outcome of the conversation, but the series of rounds constructing the conversation, that is important. In terms of the hoped-for consequential action, Abraham could have initially presented his minimum requirement (ten righteous) to the LORD. To achieve this result, the bartering was unnecessary. But that would have eliminated the series of rounds and changed the *how* of the conversation. The repeated preferred response to Abraham's bartering allows for more than simply a reduction in the number of righteous required, staving off the Divine punishment. The repeated preferred response allows reaffirmation of moral standing between the conversation participants. The LORD's anger is restrained and Abraham's presumed familiarity with the Divine is accepted, confirming that Abraham does what is righteous and just. Further, the Divine moral character is reaffirmed. The Divine preferred responses are paired to all three of Abraham's initial queries, repeatedly affirming that the LORD does not indiscriminately punish the righteous with the wicked and that the Judge of all the earth will do what is just.

Closing

In contrast to the detailed contextual preparation for the opening in 18:16–22, this conversation has only a brief narrative closing: "he had finished speaking to Abraham; and Abraham returned to his place." The closing is brief but significant, with two distinct components:

1. He (the LORD) had finished speaking to Abraham
2. Abraham returned to his place

The statement indicating that the LORD had finished speaking is paralleled in Abraham's previous conversations with the LORD only in 17:22. And, just like that conversation, the topic of this conversation is now exhausted. The moral character of both, the LORD and Abraham, has been established and the standing of both, the LORD and Abraham, has been confirmed.

The second element of the closing is also significant, especially when compared to that in 17:22. There, "God went up." Here, Abraham, "returned to his place." The liminal setting in which the conversation took place vanishes. Having affirmed that the Judge of all the earth will do what is just, normalcy is restored. The Divine is free to continue his journey and Abraham free to return to his accustomed place. Having stilled both space and time, by pausing the narrative in order to consider the morality of God, the narrator allows resumption and the story now continues.

Genesis 20:3–8: You Are About to Die!

³ But God came to Abimelech in a dream by night,

A: and said to him, "You are about to die because of the woman whom you have taken; for she is a married woman."

⁴ Now Abimelech had not approached her;

B: so he said, "Lord, will you destroy an innocent people? ⁵ Did he not himself say to me, 'She is my sister'? And she herself said, 'He is my brother.' I did this in the integrity of my heart and the innocence of my hands."

A¹: ⁶ Then God said to him in the dream, "Yes, I know that you did this in the integrity of your heart; furthermore it was

I who kept you from sinning against me. Therefore I did not let you touch her. ⁷ Now then, return the man's wife; for he is a prophet, and he will pray for you and you shall live. But if you do not restore her, know that you shall surely die, you and all that are yours."

B¹: (Consequential Action) ⁸ *So Abimelech rose early in the morning, and called all his servants and told them all these things; and the men were very much afraid.*

Context

This conversational prayer comes to us within two contexts. The first is the context established by the narrator for the reader, the second is the context in which the conversational partners operate.

Within its Genesis setting, the narrator establishes a context directing the reader's approach to this conversational prayer. In previous conversations with God, Abraham's moral standing has been established. Abraham is recipient of an everlasting covenant with God (Gen 17:13), father of a great and mighty nation (Gen 18:18), a channel by which all the nations of the earth will be blessed (Gen 12:3), and progenitor of those who will "keep the way of the Lord by doing righteousness and justice" (Gen 18:18–19). The fact of God's promise has also been reaffirmed in the context leading to this conversation between God and Abimelech. Ishmael will not be the promised heir, instead a child of Abraham and Sarah will be the recipient of God's everlasting covenant (Gen 17:19). But now, Abraham's dishonesty has placed Abimelech in immediate danger, requiring extraordinary intervention by God. Further, Abraham's dishonesty has placed the integrity of God's promise at risk. The promise of a son born to Sarah, Abraham's wife, is now in danger, as Abimelech has unwittingly fallen victim to Abraham's lies.

The second context, established by the conversational participants, is more immediate and governs the initial interaction between God and Abimelech. The context is simple: God came to Abimelech in a dream by night (20:3). It is significant that the context is repeated in v. 6. The importance placed on this context by the narrator should give us pause. For the narrator, a dream is more than an opportunity for the brain to sort out the day's experiences, or a way of expression for the unconscious self. A dream can be a venue for communication from the outside. It can be a mysterious realm in which Divine secrets and predictions of the future are unveiled. Most of all, its uncontrolled by the dreamer (the dreamer cannot even choose to turn away or to stop her ears and not listen) and so is susceptible to an intervention that demands the attention of the dreamer. That God chooses to communicate with Abimelech in this fashion is itself an expression of power.[29] Abimelech has no choice. He did not invite the dream, or the conversation transmitted in the dream. The narrator has placed importance on this context, an importance that will become more apparent in the conversation itself.

Opening

Like many of the conversational prayers of the Abraham Cycle, this conversation, between God and Abimelech, has no opening. It simply begins: "You are about to die." There is no need for a Divine introduction. God comes unannounced and unexpected. Yet, the appearance in a dream gives to God immediate moral standing, eliminating the need to establish the credibility of the Divine threat, or the truthfulness of the revelation about Sarah. Abimelech offers no protest regarding God's right to confront, nor does Abimelech question God's ability to make good on this threat. And this immediate recognition raises several important questions. Why should Abimelech be answerable to this unknown God? Abimelech doesn't protest the validity of the moral standard threatened against him.[30] Nor does he protest God's right to impose that standard and mete out punishment. He simply argues that the standard is being wrongfully applied. The only clue to understanding Abimelech's reaction is that God comes in a dream. The narrator emphasizes the dream context of the conversation indicating that the *how* of this conversation is necessary for us to understand the *what* of the conversation. And the *what* of this conversation is important.

Rounds

The path taken by this conversation, a dispreferred response followed by two preferred responses, is important in understanding the *what-is-being-accomplished* of the conversation.

---

29. It is no doubt significant that God never uses a dream venue when speaking with Abraham, instead he simply appears (12:7; 17:1; 18:1), or comes in a vision (15:1), or speaks (12:1; 13:14; 21:12; 22:1).

30. The expression of power in this conversation is vital. Many have addressed the manner power relationships are expressed in conversation, noting that real power needs minimal verbal articulation, while those attempting to achieve power tend to be more verbally assertive. Stevanovic and Peräkylä, "Deontic Authority in Interaction," 191.

A
    } Dispreferred
B
    } Preferred
A¹
    } Preferred
B¹

Abimelech's initial dispreferred response, (B, v. 4) raises the same question posed by Abraham (18:23): "will you slay an innocent people?" Once again, the moral integrity of the Divine is open for question. The remainder of the response (v. 5) offers support for Abimelech's claim of innocence while at the same time bringing to the fore the deception from both Abraham and Sarah. Abimelech's dispreferred response reopens two topics also found in previous conversations:

1. The suspect nature of God's morality

2. The integrity of God's promise of descendants for Abraham

This dispreferred response from Abimelech allows expansion, articulated in the second round of this conversation.

The conflict established in the first dispreferred response allows for resolution (A¹) that confirms God's moral integrity and Abimelech's innocence. There are four parts to the Divine preferred response, relating directly to Abimelech's protest:

1. Affirmation of Abimelech's innocence

2. Revelation of God's unseen intervention

3. Command to restore Sarah to Abraham

4. Threatened punishment for noncompliance

The Divine response to Abimelech's protest of innocence seems designed to clearly affirm God's morality. In fact, the initial threat, "You are about to die" loses its legitimacy as God acknowledges Abimelech's innocence and reveals that he has intervened in an unseen fashion to keep Abimelech from violating Sarah. At most, the threat of death, by which the conversation began, functioned as an attention getter and a springboard to allow a repeated affirmation that God does not slay innocent people.

In addition, and quite unexpectedly, the second speech by God allows for the introduction of a description of Abraham as prophet, whose prayers are effective in changing Divine action in a manner reminiscent of the bartering episode of Genesis 18. But this insertion of Abraham, as prophet, also seems forced.[31] In the Divine response (v. 7), God acknowledges that no sin had yet been committed, and so presumably no offense deserving of death. If, however, now knowing Sarah's true identity and relationship to Abraham, Abimelech does not restore Sarah to her husband, God is quite clear—Abimelech will die. And so, the conditional action, averting or confirming the death sentence, is Abimelech's. Yet, the prayers of the prophet Abraham are also presented as effective in preserving Abimelech's life.[32]

Closing

This conversation has no closing. Instead, there is a narrative consequential closing with an implied preferred response to God's speech that becomes enacted the following day and involving both a preferred response by Abimelech and Abraham. In the narrative to follow, both Abimelech and Abraham perform consequential actions. Abimelech does restore Sarah (vv. 8–16) and Abraham does pray (vv. 17–18), but the actions do not have the results anticipated earlier in the conversation. Abimelech's actions result in Abraham's enrichment, not in preserving Abimelech's life, and Abraham's prayer results in the "healing" of Abimelech, his wife, and female slaves, allowing children to be born to Abimelech (vv. 17–18) reversing the Divinely enacted childlessness visited on Abimelech's household because of Sarah—a condition not even alluded to in the conversation. And so, if the conversation is not tied to the consequential action to follow, and not tied to the previous Divine action, preventing Abimelech from violating Sarah, what is the function of the conversation in this episode? It must be simply this: to reaffirm that God does not slay the innocent (20:4), the central protest and driver of the conversation between God and Abimelech. In the Abraham Cycle, recurring doubt concerning God's morality is articulated by both insider (Abraham) and outsider (Abimelech) and is of such importance that it deserves repeated conversational address.

---

31. Although consistent with his vision experience in Gen 15:1, rather than the dream appearance made available to Abimelech.

32. While Abraham's status as prophet seems unnecessary in this conversational prayer, that status will be an important feature of a later conversational prayer in Genesis 26.

Genesis 21:16–19: What Troubles You, Hagar?

¹⁶ *Then she went and sat down opposite him a good way off, about the distance of a bowshot; for she said, "Do not let me look on the death of the child." And as she sat opposite him, she lifted up her voice and wept.* ¹⁷ *And God heard the voice of the boy; and the angel of God called to Hagar from heaven,*

A: *and said to her, "What troubles you, Hagar? Do not be afraid; for God has heard the voice of the boy where he is.* ¹⁸ *Come, lift up the boy and hold him fast with your hand, for I will make a great nation of him."*

Aa: (Consequential Action) ¹⁹ *Then God opened her eyes and she saw a well of water. She went, and filled the skin with water, and gave the boy a drink.*

Context

It's hard to imagine a more disparate context operative for conversational partners. Hagar speaks from need and helplessness, dying of thirst in a barren desert. The angel of God, meanwhile, addresses Hagar from heaven, a position of power and privilege. This disjointed context emphasizes the *how* of this conversation. Previously, the Divine conversationalist "came down" (implied in the returning "going up" of 17:22) after speaking with Abraham, or in near proximity allowing Abraham to "draw near" in 18:23, or even in "finding" Hagar in their previous conversation of 16:7, but here remains steadfast in heaven, only "calling down" to the beleaguered woman (21:17). Hagar comes to the conversation from a position of dependency, near death, and overwhelmed with despair. The angel of God addresses Hagar without need and confirmed in power. The *how* of this conversation is accomplished through the establishment of extremely uneven positions of status and power. These positions of power are evidenced in the context established for the conversation and in the structure of the conversational round.[33]

Status and Power

This conversational prayer consists of only one round and its structure is quite unusual. It is unusual in that one of the conversation partners speaks (Hagar) but is never heard by the other partner in conversation, while a third

---

33. Heritage, "Conversation Analysis as Social Theory," 303–4.

party (Ishmael), not participant to the conversation, offers an inarticulate cry and is heard but never addressed by the conversational partner (angel of God). Hagar, expresses her anxiety, speaking presumably to herself: "Let me not look upon the death of the child." Meanwhile, her child also cries out, apparently inarticulately, but no less in despair and need. God hears the inarticulate need of the child but responds to the unheard cry of the mother. The result of this structure is to deny Hagar voice in the conversation.[34]

Opening

There is no opening or introduction offered by the Divine conversationalist. Perhaps, no Divine introduction is required. Perhaps, the setting in which Hagar found herself was enough. God and Hagar have spoken once before, maybe fourteen or fifteen years earlier, also in the desert and in direr circumstances (Gen 16:7-14). In that conversation, the birth of Ishmael to Hagar had been promised by God, but now the life of that child is in doubt—at least in doubt as far as Hagar knows.

Round

God responds to Hagar in a most inappropriate manner. First, is the initial question of the Divine response: "What troubles you, Hagar?" The desperation of the mother and child is answered with calm, almost casual interest. Wasn't the nature of the problem clear? There is no water and mother and child are both in grave danger! Following the initial Divine response, indicating that the cry of the child has been heard (again, not the cry of Hagar), Hagar is directed to lift the boy up and take him by the hand. The boy does indeed have a future—the promise is repeated—from Ishmael God will make a great nation. Finally, as affirmation of the future destined for Ishmael, God opens Hagar's eyes to a well of water (21:19). The water had been there all the time. It is not supernaturally called from a rock or made drinkable from a foul and stagnant pool. The water had been there, it was simply hidden to Hagar. Why were Hagar's eyes closed to the well of water? If the water was there and always available, why did Hagar need to go through such despair? Why didn't God open her eyes before this desperate

---

34. Nevertheless, Hagar converses with Divine personages more than any other woman in the Hebrew Bible (Gen 16:7-12; 21:17-19). Manoah's wife receives an address from the angel of the LORD but reports to her husband that the message came from a man of God (Judg 13:3-7). Eve is allowed only one statement of protest to God (Gen 3:13) as is Sarai (Gen 18:15).

moment? Because this conversational prayer was never about the water. Just as Hagar's desperate need led to an interaction with the angel of God in which dependency was evident, so, too, the future of Ishmael is equally dependent solely upon the act of God.

Here, it is quite clear that access to knowledge (the presence of the well) is also an expression of status.[35] Denied both voice and knowledge, Hagar is devoid of any agency in the conversation.[36] She has no autonomy or self-determination, only dependency. But it isn't only in the conversational prayer that Hagar is cast in this position of dependency. The whole tragic episode is set in motion by Abraham, who acting at God's command, listens to Sarah's complaints about Hagar and Ishmael, and banishes Hagar and the child into the desert, provisioned only with bread and a skin of water (21:11–14). Abraham (the just and righteous), and God (who does not slay the innocent), send the young mother and child into the desert, condemning them to almost certain death, simply to satisfy Sarah's jealousy. Throughout the whole series of events, Hagar is acted upon. Her only self-determined act is to sit in the desert, lift her voice in despair, and wait for death.[37] The cumulative effect of Hagar's dependency is to portray the consequential action of the conversational prayer as solely God's.

Consequential Action

Following the last turn of the conversational prayer, ending with the Divine promise, "I will make a great nation of him," God opens Hagar's eyes to the lifesaving well of water, and she gives her son a drink. Hagar and her son are saved, allowing the next and summary statement of consequential action: "God was with the boy" (21:20). On the verge of death in the desert, without voice or agency, and totally dependent, the conversational prayer makes clear that the future for Hagar and Ishmael, as detailed in 21:21, is

---

35. See the discussion by Clift, *Conversation Analysis*, 229.

36. Unlike her earlier conversation with God in 16:7–14. There, she is beside a well of water when the angel of the LORD found her. She has a plan of action—she has run away from her mistress, Sarai, presumably to return to Egypt. She has a voice, able to even name God (El-roi). And she has volition, able to either, conform to the angel of the LORD's directive (return to Sarai), or continue her way, fleeing from Sarai and from God's design for her unborn child. On the history of these stories, see Yoo, "Hagar the Egyptian," 215–35.

37. Aron Pinker understands the Genesis 21 episode as showing Hagar to be vindictive and cruel, seeking to kill her son and thereby exercising vengeance on Abraham. He concludes, "For Ishmael's agony of perishing from thirst in the desert and Hagar's sad prospects was of her own making." Pinker, "Expulsion of Hagar and Ishmael," 21.

an act of God and an act of God only. There are two sons of Abraham, Ishmael and Isaac, the destiny of both firmly in the hand of God (Gen 21:20; 22:12).[38] Yet, this consequential action leaves the conversation unsettled. Hagar, the immediate conversational partner quickly recedes into the background as God focuses the conversation on the boy.[39] God responds to the voice of the boy (v. 18), the promise of a future is for the boy, and even the life giving water is primarily for the boy (v. 19). The *who-we-are-to-one-another* assigned to Hagar in the conversational prayer is unfulfilled. The whole conversation and accompanying interaction come close to the exact opposite of a prayer—it's an anti-prayer denying to Hagar the status typically assigned to conversational participants that, nevertheless, gains its strength by violating normal conversational conventions.[40]

---

38. It is interesting that the other sons of Abraham, six born to Keturah and an unknown number to his concubines, have no interaction with God at all (Gen 25:1–6).

39. At times disparaged by later commentators. See Freedman and Simon, *Midrash Rabbah*, 474.

40. See the discussion by Claassens, "Just Emotions," 1–6.

4

Jacob Cycle

CONVERSATIONAL PRAYERS WITH GOD are structured very differently in the Jacob Cycle (Gen 25b–36)[1] than the conversational prayers presented in the Abraham Cycle (Gen 12–25a) or the conversations with God in the Creation Story. Most noticeably, in the Jacob Cycle there are no conversational rounds, as only one conversational participant speaks. Consequently, it is best to consider these excerpts not as conversations, but as employing "conversational activity" similar to the talk that may take place in a courtroom, classroom, or other settings that may appear conversational but clearly employ an overlaying structure.[2]

The absence of conversational rounds, a most basic conversational structure, from the prayers in the Jacob Cycle impacts the speech and consequential activity offered by both conversational participants. Obviously, there is no opportunity for a verbal response, either preferred or dispreferred, and so we must look to the consequential action to infer the disposition of the silent conversational participant. Less obvious, but no less significant, the conversational participant that does speak is also impacted by the way these conversational prayers are formed. The speaker's words demonstrate little if any recipient design, suggesting that the spoken address could just as well appear in a different context or in a different conversation with a different conversational participant. Further, the lack of exchange does not allow the speaker to repair or confirm understanding on the part of the other participant. The first speaker displays no orientation to how his actions or words are being received.[3] Recipiency is what extends a re-

---

1. The Isaac material of Genesis 26 is here included, but see the discussion by Blum, "Jacob Tradition," 181–82. See also Fishbane, "Composition and Structure in the Jacob Cycle," 15–38.

2. Levinson, *Pragmatics*, 318.

3. Heath, "Talk and Recipiency," 247.

lationship in conversation. Consequently, absent conversational exchange, the conversational prayers in the Jacob Cycle are snapshots, demonstrating little movement in the status relationship of the conversational partners. Particularly with Isaac, the absence of concern about status between the conversational participants will play a significant role.[4]

In addition to the differences, distinguishing the Jacob Cycle from other conversational prayers in the Abraham Cycle and the Creation Story, there are differences within the Jacob Cycle, distinguishing conversational prayers involving Isaac (two conversations, both in Genesis 26) and those prayers involving Jacob (three conversations). Two of the differences are most noticeable. First, Isaac never speaks to God,[5] while Jacob does address the Deity, but receives no reply.[6] Secondly, while the topic of the Divine speech to both Isaac and Jacob is a repetition of similar addresses made to Abraham, practically all of the content of the Divine speech to Isaac can be reconstructed from Divine speech made to Abraham.

Isaac

Genesis 26:1–5: Isaac Went to Gerar

[1] *Now there was a famine in the land, besides the former famine that had occurred in the days of Abraham. And Isaac went to Gerar, to King Abimelech of the Philistines.*

A: [2] The LORD appeared to Isaac and said, "Do not go down to Egypt; settle in the land that I shall show you. [3] Reside in this land as an alien, and I will be with you, and will bless you; for to you and to your descendants I will give all these lands, and I will fulfill the oath that I swore to your father Abraham. [4] I will make your offspring as numerous as the stars of heaven, and will give to your offspring all these lands; and all the nations of the earth shall gain blessing for themselves through your offspring, [5] because Abraham obeyed my voice and kept my charge, my commandments, my statutes, and my laws."

B: [6] *So Isaac settled in Gerar.*

---

4. See Steinmetz, *From Father to Son*, 88.

5. Boase characterizes Isaac as "a largely passive figure." Boase, "Life in the Shadows," 313.

6. Even in the wrestling episode of Gen 32:22–32, there is no dialogue with the Divine after his true identity is discovered.

Context

The context of this conversational activity is reminiscent of the episode presented in Genesis 20, also involving Abimelech of Gerar, but conflated with the episode in Egypt (Gen 12:10–20). In fact, the narrator seems to take special care that the two accounts not be confused, mentioning a famine that led to Isaac's journey to Gerar beside the famine in the days of Abraham, not part of the Abraham Abimelech story of Genesis 20, but part of the set-up to the story involving Pharaoh in Gen 12:10–20. This differentiation, from the story involving Abraham, seems significant in establishing the integrity of the Isaac episode, all the more so given the similarity between the Divine speech of Gen 22:17–18 and the Divine speech of Gen 26:2–5. In other words, the conversational activity with Isaac of Gen 26:2–5 is just as close in form and content to an earlier conversation between Abraham and God, as is the narrative involving Abraham and Abimelech now paralleled by the narrative featuring Isaac and Abimelech and repeating features of the earlier Abraham Pharaoh story.[7] All of this means that recipient design[8] is lacking in this Divine address to Isaac. Within the conversation, Isaac is functionally present as a "second Abraham"—the inheritor of Abraham's standing with the LORD.[9] The overlap between the angel's address to Abraham in Genesis 22 and the LORD's address to Isaac in Genesis 26 is unmistakable:

Gen 22:16–18

[16] "By myself I have sworn, says the Lord: Because you have done this, and have not withheld your son, your only son, [17] **I will indeed bless you, and I will make your offspring as numerous as the stars of heaven** and as the sand that is on the seashore. And your offspring shall possess the gate of their enemies, [18] and *by your offspring shall all the nations of the earth gain blessing for themselves,* <u>because you have obeyed my voice</u>."

Gen 26:2–5:

[2] The LORD appeared to Isaac and said, "Do not go down to Egypt; settle in the land that I shall show you. [3] Reside in this land as an alien, and I will be with you, and **will bless you;** for to you and to your descendants I will give all these lands, and I will fulfill the oath that I swore to your father Abraham. [4] **I will**

---

7. See Boase, "Life in the Shadows," 322–24.
8. Sidnell, *Conversation Analysis*, 5.
9. See Boase, "Life in the Shadows," 313–14.

make your offspring as numerous as the stars of heaven, and will give to your offspring all these lands; *and all the nations of the earth shall gain blessing for themselves through your offspring,* ⁵ because Abraham obeyed my voice and kept my charge, my commandments, my statutes, and my laws."

While the same topic (the covenant blessing first given to Abraham in Genesis 12) will occupy the other Divine conversational activity in the Jacob Cycle, the speech in Genesis 26 overlaps in content with Divine speech in the Abraham Cycle more than any other.[10] Additionally, just as the integrity of God's promise, fulfilled through the descendants of Abraham, is the focus of the trouble with Pharaoh in Genesis 12 and the Abimelech affair in Genesis 20, so now the same focus is apparent in Genesis 26, Isaac's version of the Abimelech affair.

Opening

The opening provided to this conversational activity is abrupt. The LORD appears to Isaac. As far as we, the readers, know this is the first direct interaction between the LORD and Isaac, besides the intervention of the angel of the LORD to prevent Abraham's sacrifice of Isaac in Genesis 22, which if audible in the literary world of the narrative, Isaac may have overheard, or if visual, he may have witnessed as a third party observer. This being the case, one wonders why no introduction was required here. There is no establishment of status and no introduction of a shared topic of conversation. The abruptness of the appearing is not unusual. What is unusual is that it happens without mentioning the mode of appearance; either in a vision (Gen 15:1), by a spring of water (Gen 16:7), by the oaks of Mamre (Gen 18:1), in a dream (Gen 20:3), the same night (Gen 26:24), while standing above (Gen 28:13), or after a journey from Paddan-aram (Gen 35:9). Neither is this episode prefaced with an introduction by which the Deity makes himself known like that given to Abraham (Gen 17:1) or to Jacob (Gen 28:13). This initial interaction between the LORD and Isaac is most similar to the first Divine speech to Abraham in Gen 12:1–3, also presented without introduction or mode of appearance.

---

10. The promise of Divine presence is also given to Jacob in Gen 28:15.

Status

The abrupt opening in Gen 12:1 establishes the Divine status to command, requiring not cooperation but obedience on Abraham's part. That same effect is established with Isaac in Gen 26:2. Unlike Abraham, however, where the initial conversational activity with God was followed by subsequent occasions for conversational give and take, no such opportunity is given to Isaac. The initial *who-we-are-to-one-another* between God and Isaac does not change or develop. The fulfillment of God's promise to Abraham through Isaac and his descendants will be brought to fruition because of the oath taken by God, not because of the status achieved by Isaac.[11]

Consequential Activity

The preferred response by Isaac, in the form of consequential action, allows the reintroduction of Abimelech, who will once more serve as an unwitting foil for the fulfillment of the Divine promise made to Abraham. This time, however, Abimelech, himself, will discover Isaac's ruse and take corrective action, apart from any prompting or conversational intervention by the Lord (as occurred in Genesis 20). Is this change in the role played by Abimelech simply part of the narrator's desire to establish the integrity of the episode with Isaac, or does the more active role played by Abimelech serve the goals of this conversation? In the Genesis 20 appearance of the Lord to Abimelech, the Lord discloses that Abraham is a prophet and that Abraham will pray for Abimelech and so avert the Divine punishment. The disclosure as prophet and Abraham's prophetic prayer have no consequential part to play in Genesis 20. The prayer does not produce the Divine intent. When compared to the episode with Isaac, however, the difference is striking. Abimelech's initiative in Genesis 26, without Divine intervention, prevents any disclosure about Isaac to Abimelech and so eliminates any possible Divine affirmation of Isaac's status. Although recipient of the same Divine promise, it is clear Isaac does not have the same standing with God as did his father, Abraham. Abraham's status before God will dominate the next and last conversation between God and Isaac.

Genesis 26:24–25: I Am the God of Your Father Abraham

A: [24] And that very night the Lord appeared to him and said, "I am the God of your father Abraham; do not be afraid, for I am

---

11. See Boase, "Life in the Shadows," 320.

with you and will bless you and make your offspring numerous for my servant Abraham's sake."

B: (Consequential Action) ²⁵ *So he built an altar there, called on the name of the Lord, and pitched his tent there. And there Isaac's servants dug a well.*

Opening

In this appearance[12] to Isaac, the LORD (YHWH) introduces himself as the "God of Abraham." Yet, somehow, Isaac knows that this Deity, the God of Abraham, is also the LORD (YHWH) for it is this name that is used to describe Isaac's response to the encounter (26:25).[13] This awkward introduction will prove useful in helping to connect and perhaps enfold this conversational activity with Isaac into the shadow of God's relationship with Abraham.

Context

The Divine conversational activity is contextualized, "that very night." That is, it occurred the night following Isaac's move to Rehoboth where another well was dug, finally ending a succession of disputed wells in two previous locations (26:17–22). More, it follows Isaac's proclamation (to no one in particular): "Now the LORD has made room for us, and we shall be fruitful in the land" (26:22). Other than this lead in by Isaac (which is just as easily connected to 26:4), the Divine conversational activity of 26:24 assumes no context, no setting, in fact, no particularity at all.

Direct Speech

The Divine speech contains four statements of relational status and consequent activity:

- Do not be afraid
- I am with you
- I will bless you
- I will make your offspring numerous

---

12. Deity also chooses "appearing" as the mode of being present to Abraham (12:7; 17:1; 18:1) and earlier to Isaac (26:2).
13. Also addressed by Isaac in prayer (25:21) and addressing Isaac (26:2).

None of these statements are unique.[14] The Divine speech of 26:24 repeats elements of the Divine announcement in 26:4-5 (particularly in the mention of Abraham) and although addressed to Isaac, references Abraham twice in a manner that is almost wistful in the Divine recall of Isaac's father. Abraham is identified as "your [Isaac's] father" and "my [the LORD's] servant." This is the only time the LORD identifies Abraham as his servant.[15] The title is used sparingly (only here in Genesis) and connotes a place of honor.[16] Here, Abraham's standing with God serves as the context by which conversations with Isaac will be conducted.[17]

Despite the important role the connections to Abraham play in the opening of this conversation, differences between Abraham and Isaac are just as important. The exchanges between conversational partners, so characteristic of the conversations between God and Abraham, are conspicuously absent with Isaac. The *who-we-are-to-one-another* between the conversational participants so dynamically present in the conversational rounds, the moral commands given by God, and the animation so impressively expressed by the bartering between God and Abraham, are not present at all in the conversational activity with Isaac. In fact, if recipient design guides this conversational activity, it could be argued that "Isaac" as such is not present. The recipient of the conversational activity is the son of Abraham, who just happens to be Isaac. It is tempting to conclude that the true recipient of the Divine speech in 26:24 is not Isaac, but a third-party observer, the reader, who is in need of the Divine reaffirmation of the LORD's covenantal intent.

---

14. Parallels to earlier conversations with Abraham can also be noted: the admonition to not be afraid (15:1), Divine blessing (12:2), numerous offspring (13:16; 15:5; 22:17) as well as the promise of Divine presence repeated with Jacob (28:15; 31:3).

15. Twice in Moses prayers, Abraham, Isaac, and Jacob (or Israel) are also identified as servants of God (Exod 32:13; Deut 9:27). Interestingly, Jacob self-identifies as "your [God's] servant" (Gen 32:10), a status not confirmed by God in this conversation. Jacob addresses God as "God of Abraham" and "God of Isaac" and not his God.

16. Moses is also identified as "my [God's] servant" elevating him above the prophets because he is: (1) entrusted with all my [God's] house, (2) beholds the form of the LORD, and with him (3) I [God] speak face to face (Num 12:7-8). Both, Abraham and Moses speak with God and are accorded servant status.

17. Boase argues that the Abraham material is dependent upon the Jacob tradition. Boase, "Life in the Shadows," 330-33.

Closing

Although the Divinely initiated speech calls for no response, and commands no reaction, the preferred response by Isaac, in the form of consequential action, is, just as the Divine speech, fourfold:

- Isaac builds an altar there
- Calls upon the name of the LORD
- Pitched his tent there
- A well is dug by Isaac's servants

Pitching the tent implies an intent to reside at the location, at least for a time (perhaps in response to the earlier Divine conversational activity of 26:2), and building the altar and digging the well imply an intent to return to the site should Isaac ever travel elsewhere. Otherwise, the activity is reminiscent of the activity performed by Abraham, and the Divine speech certainly reminds the reader of the Divine address to Abraham in Genesis 12 conflated with a return to the site in Genesis 13.[18] In these episodes, Abraham:

- Builds an altar (12:8; 13:4)
- First calls on the name of LORD (13:4)
- Pitched his tent (12:8)

Even in his response to the Divine conversational activity, Isaac remains in the shadow of his father, Abraham.

While, from the outside, the relationship between Isaac and God looks much the same as the relationship between Abraham and God, something is missing. Despite the parallels in consequential activity, and even the parallels in the promises made by God to Abraham, Isaac, and later Jacob, the *who-we-are-to-one-another* between God and Abraham is not at all like the *who-we-are-to-one-another* between God and Isaac (or later Jacob). The friendship between God and Abraham, kept warm by frequent conversation, has grown cold with Isaac. There is no dialogue, no give and take, no closeness in the relationship.

---

18. Arguably, the digging of the well by Isaac's servants is simply to conform the consequential activity to the prior succession of wells dug forming the context for the conversational prayer.

Jacob

Genesis 28:13–22: The LORD Is in This Place

A: ¹³ And the LORD stood beside him and said, "I am the Lord, the God of Abraham your father and the God of Isaac; the land on which you lie I will give to you and to your offspring; ¹⁴ and your offspring shall be like the dust of the earth, and you shall spread abroad to the west and to the east and to the north and to the south; and all the families of the earth shall be blessed in you and in your offspring. ¹⁵ Know that I am with you and will keep you wherever you go, and will bring you back to this land; for I will not leave you until I have done what I have promised you."

B: (Consequential Action) ¹⁶ *Then Jacob woke from his sleep* and said, "Surely the LORD is in this place—and I did not know it!"

Bª: (Consequential Action) ¹⁷ *And he was afraid*, and said, "How awesome is this place! This is none other than the house of God, and this is the gate of heaven."

Bᵇ: (Consequential Action) ¹⁸ *So Jacob rose early in the morning, and he took the stone that he had put under his head and set it up for a pillar and poured oil on the top of it.* ¹⁹ *He called that place Bethel; but the name of the city was Luz at the first.*

Bᶜ: (Consequential Action) ²⁰ *Then Jacob made a vow*, saying, "If God will be with me, and will keep me in this way that I go, and will give me bread to eat and clothing to wear, ²¹ so that I come again to my father's house in peace, then the LORD shall be my God, ²² and this stone, which I have set up for a pillar, shall be God's house; and of all that you give me I will surely give one-tenth to you."

Context

This first communication between God and Jacob is abrupt and unexpected. Jacob, on his journey to Haran, arrived at Bethel, a site at least proximate to the same site visited by Abraham (12:8; 13:4) but apparently unknown to Jacob. The narrative context for the conversation indicates that Jacob "came to a certain place" (28:11) giving no hint that Jacob was aware he was in a place previously visited by Abraham or aware of the altar constructed by his grandfather in the vicinity (12:8). Even as the narrator makes plain that Jacob is unaware of the history and significance of the place at which he has arrived, the narrator also wants the connection to be clear to the reader, even using the place name given by Jacob, Bethel (28:19), when describing the journey of Abraham years earlier (12:8; 13:3).

Having traveled all day and now, because the sun was setting and daylight fading, Jacob stopped for the night intending to sleep with his head resting on a pillow of stone. While asleep, Jacob dreams a dream. The dream venue of the ensuing conversation is reminiscent of the encounter between Abimelech and the Lord (20:3), but there is a difference. In Abimelech's encounter, the Lord is said to have "come in a dream by night" (20:3), giving no doubt that the Lord was present to Abimelech through the dream, and able to command Abimelech in a fashion that required immediate action. With Jacob it's different. In Genesis 28, Jacob is dreaming about a ladder (roadway?) reaching to heaven, on which angels are ascending and descending.[19] During the dream the Lord stood beside the sleeping Jacob—or is at least effectively proximate to Jacob.[20] Is the ladder actually present? Is the Lord actually present, able to pronounce a command as with Abimelech? Is Jacob's dream about the ladder of the same nature as any dream Jacob may have had about a recent event, or a family conflict, or his recent travels from Beer-sheba? Or is this dream different, immediately recognizable as a Divine intrusion in the same way Abimelech understood the Lord's intrusion in Genesis 19? There is nothing in the dream itself, or the Divine speech of vv. 13–15, to help answer these questions. There are no Divine commands that require a response from Jacob. There is no exchange between the conversational participants (as did occur with Abimelech) to indicate that Jacob and the Lord are present to each other. The answer is not immediate in the dream but must wait Jacob's response after waking from his sleep, in vv. 16–17.[21] In the consequential action, following the Divine speech in the dream, actions are taken to make the Deity's presence sure.

Opening

This conversational activity is unusual in that it does include an introduction by which the Deity identifies himself as the Lord. This is the first

---

19. See Wolde, "Stairway to Heaven?," 735.

20. As rendered in RSV and others. The preposition, עליו may in fact mean next to or above the ramp or roadway (ladder) reinforcing the status that accompanies the Lord's heavenly abode. Regardless, the phrase in v. 15 introduces the matter of the Lord's location, a topic that will be of prime concern for Jacob in the following conversational activity.

21. The composite nature of this passage is discussed by Westermann, *Genesis 12–36*, 454–57; see also Krüger, "Where Is God?," 247.

introduction between the LORD and Jacob and so the identification is expected but does not follow the pattern established by the initial interaction between Abraham or Isaac, in which no introduction is offered. As with Isaac before him, the LORD's introduction also contextualizes this Jacob conversation within the previous interactions shared with Abraham (and now Isaac). To Jacob it is made clear, the LORD is the God of Abraham your father and the God of Isaac (v. 13).

Divine Direct Speech

Following the introduction, the Divine direct speech is constructed in two parts. First, is a promise of land and offspring very similar to that promised earlier by the LORD to Abraham (12:1–3; 13:14–17; 15:5; 22:17–18) and Isaac (26:3–5). The second part of the direct speech (28:15) is emphatic in nature, introduced by a particle (הנה) often used to call attention to the following action or condition.[22] Here, attention is drawn to the fact that the LORD himself will be present, actively involved in fulfilling his promise of land and offspring.[23] A promise not made to Abraham or made so emphatically to Isaac (Gen 26:24). The sense of v. 15 is: Look—I, myself am always with you.

The surety of the promise made in vv. 13–14 is the continued and immediate presence of the LORD with Jacob. It is the strength of the *who-we-are-to-one-another* between the LORD and Jacob that forms the foundation for the consequential action following the conversational prayer. Interestingly, it is the surety of the LORD's presence, made clear in v. 15, that is directly challenged through Jacob's consequential action performed the next day.

Consequential Action

At first glance, this episode appears to be a Divine speech followed by a preferred response (in a series of consequential actions) performed by the human actor, Jacob. The consequential action is fourfold:

> B: (Consequential Action) [16] *Then Jacob woke from his sleep* and said, "Surely the LORD is in this place—and I did not know it!"

---

22. Waltke and O'Conner, *Introduction to Biblical Hebrew Syntax*, 627. See also Muraoka, *Emphatic Words and Structures in Biblical Hebrew*, 138.

23. Hence the use of the long form of the first-person pronoun (אנכי).

B^a: (Consequential Action) ¹⁷ *And he was afraid*, and said, "How awesome is this place! This is none other than the house of God, and this is the gate of heaven."

B^b: (Consequential Action) ¹⁸ *So Jacob rose early in the morning, and he took the stone that he had put under his head and set it up for a pillar and poured oil on the top of it.* ¹⁹ *He called that place Bethel; but the name of the city was Luz at the first.*

B^c: (Consequential Action) ²⁰ *Then Jacob made a vow*, saying, "If God will be with me, and will keep me in this way that I go, and will give me bread to eat and clothing to wear, ²¹ so that I come again to my father's house in peace, then the LORD shall be my God, ²² and this stone, which I have set up for a pillar, shall be God's house; and of all that you give me I will surely give one-tenth to you."

The third and fourth consequential actions (28:18–22) contain two elements that require consideration. First, Jacob took the stone on which he rested his head during the previous night's dream, erected it as a pillar, claiming that it "shall be God's house." Sacred pillars (מצבת) are not uncommon in ancient Israel and were erected to commemorate a special event (Josh 4), represent a Deity (Deut 12), or, as here described, house a Deity. The sacred pillar, housing the Deity, is certainly reflected in the name Jacob gives to the site, Bethel (house of God),[24] and fits better the conversational activity of Genesis 28 than its parallel rendition of Genesis 35.

The second element of this consequential activity that gives us pause and which adds to the significance of the sacred pillar, is the use of second person address in v. 22. The similarity of Jacob's vow with the liturgical formula found in Deut 26:5–10 (especially v. 10) has been noted,[25] but here, as consequential activity extending a conversation between Jacob and Deity, the vow has a more immediate meaning that includes the establishment of a sacred shrine, effectively ensuring the presence of Deity who now can be addressed in second person. The vow made by Jacob begins in v. 20 by addressing the Deity in third person, forming a response to the Deity's speech of vv. 13–15, especially the promise of Divine accompaniment in v. 15. Jacob then addresses God as immediately present in v. 22, formally, at least, continuing the conversation begun by the Deity in vv.

---

24. Note the change between vv. 17 and 19. In Gen 28:17, Jacob refers to the House of the Gods/God (בית אלהים) while in v. 19 the place is called House of El/God (בית אל). Interestingly, while also commenting on the structures and site at Bethel, a plural verbal form is used in Gen 35:7 (נגלו) describing the revelation of the Gods (האלהים) to Jacob.

25. Westermann, *Genesis 12–26*, 460.

13–15. In fact, v. 15 followed by vv. 20–22 form a recognizable round when isolated from the intervening consequential responses of vv. 16–19. Once the Lord's (YHWH's) presence has been secured, in the form of the pillar housing God (28:22a), the Lord can be addressed as immediately present, in the second person (28:22b).

Jacob's actions, intent on securing the presence of God, are not in conformity to the Divine promise of v. 15, but function as an effort to independently guarantee the Divine presence, casting doubt on the trustworthiness of the promise from v. 15. God's presence is valued by Jacob, but the Divine promise ensuring that presence is not enough, requiring the pillar to magically guarantee God's presence.

Notable, too, are the conditions, confirming the continued presence of God, presented in v. 15, and a separate set of conditions presented for establishing Jacob's subsequent and exclusive worship in v. 20.[26] In v. 15, the Divine presence is evidenced in ownership of the land and numerous progeny. Jacob's conditions, by which Divine presence will be concluded, are protection and prosperity (v. 20). In Jacob's subsequent travels, God is involved to secure children (29:31, 33; 30:22), prosperity (30:27), and provide protection (the subject of Jacob's prayer in 32:9–12), but Divine presence with Jacob is illusive,[27] connected to the "land of your [Jacob's] ancestors" (31:3) and the pillar at Bethel (31:13).[28]

So, what are we to make of the consequential action closing this conversational prayer? Oddly, this act of worship and devotion is in reality a dispreferred response to the promise made by the Lord in the conversational prayer. The unfettered *who-we-are-to-one-another*, promised by the Divine "Look—I myself will be with you" is countered by a very controlled *who-we-are-to-one-another* in the construction of the House of God (Bethel)[29] by means of which Jacob will address the Lord directly and attempt to ensure his continued presence. Jacob's act of religious devotion was effectively an attempt to control God and so ironically demean the very Divine promise prompting the devotion. And this very unequal sense of presence to one another will be maintained in the episodes to follow. God will be present in an unfettered manner, interacting at will with Leah, Rachal, Laban, and in most unexpected ways with Jacob, providing what he promised quite apart from any response offered by Jacob. Meanwhile, Jacob will continue his

26. A promised act of worship that goes unfulfilled even though protection and prosperity are provided.

27. Even the Divine Name is withheld in the famous wrestling episode of 32:22–32.

28. The MT of Gen 31:13 is defective, probably incorporating phrases from 28:20–21.

29. See Krüger, "Where is God?," 247–49.

efforts to control the Divine, literally seeking to wrestle from God promised benefits, while all the time reneging on his promised acts of devotion. This conversational prayer and its consequential actions will shape Jacob's relationship to God the rest of his life.[30]

Genesis 32:9–12:[31] Deliver Me, Please

A: ⁹ And Jacob said, "O God of my father Abraham and God of my father Isaac, O LORD who said to me, 'Return to your country and to your kindred, and I will do you good,' ¹⁰ I am not worthy of the least of all the steadfast love and all the faithfulness that you have shown to your servant, for with only my staff I crossed this Jordan; and now I have become two companies. ¹¹ Deliver me, please, from the hand of my brother, from the hand of Esau, for I am afraid of him; he may come and kill us all, the mothers with the children. ¹² Yet you have said, 'I will surely do you good, and make your offspring as the sand of the sea, which cannot be counted because of their number.'"

B: Silence

Context

This prayer for help is situational, applying only to Jacob at this particular point in his life. Reminding God of his earlier command to return to "your country and your kindred" (31:3), but now in immediate threat from his brother Esau, Jacob further reminds God of an earlier promise (28:13–15), although the actual wording quoted in Jacob's prayer is closer to a Divine promise delivered to Abraham (22:17).

Jacob's Turn

Jacob's prayer is abrupt, interrupting what might be considered a narrative flow connecting Gen 32:8 and Gen 32:13. Even the brief introduction to Jacob's prayer, "And Jacob said," is sudden, not accompanied by a posture

---

30. See even the Divine promise including presence made by God in 31:3 and referenced later by Jacob in Gen 32:9 but with the substitution of prosperity for presence. This awkward and at times troublesome relationship shared by God and Jacob is referenced also in Gen 32:28. This relationship has been noted, perhaps best described by Gunkel, *Genesis*, 300–302 but without noting the conversational dynamics in which this relationship is partially cast.

31. MT: Gen 32:10–13.

of prayer or an indication that the following words are intended as prayer. While others have made the same observation and concluded the prayer an intrusion,[32] the sudden, abrupt nature of the prayer gives to the conversational activity a sense of urgency; a desperation equal to that of Hagar in Genesis 21. The urgency expressed in Jacob's address makes the Deity's response all the more striking.

The Jacob turn is constructed in three parts:[33]

1. An opening establishing the *who-we-are-to-one-another* of the conversational partners (vv. 9–10).
2. A plea (v. 11).
3. A reminder of God's past promises (v. 12).

The opening of the Jacob turn establishes the *who-we-are-to-one-another* that Jacob hopes will guide the consequential action of the conversation. Jacob first reminds God of God's previous relationship and commitments to his grandfather and father followed by reference to the Divine command (Gen 31:3) to return to his country and kindred (the very people he now fears). Jacob's recitation of that command contains a subtle but very important change. Jacob claims that God commanded him to:

> Return to your country and to your kindred, and *I will do you good*

While the Divine command, as given in Gen 31:3 is:

> Return to the land of your ancestors and to your kindred, and *I will be with you*

Jacob habitually exchanges Divine presence for prosperity, and here he finds the substitution particularly attractive. The *who-we-are-to-one-another* of the conversation is completed by Jacob's self-description of unworthiness,[34] yet recipient of Divinely given enrichment—a position he hopes to retain. He further self-identifies as "your [God's] servant." This designation is not confirmed by God and, in fact, is attributed by God in Genesis only to Abraham. Jacob seems intent on appropriating some of Abraham's good standing with God to himself by claiming to be God's servant. Without question, it is Jacob's description of standing between the

---

32. Rad, *Genesis*, 318.

33. A pattern that will become familiar in the Moses prayers (see Exodus 32 and parallels).

34. Self-deprecation can be a strategy for securing a preferred response form a conversational partner. See Sidnell, *Conversation Analysis*, 83.

conversational partners that forms the basis for the plea articulated in the next part of his direct address.

The second part of the Jacob address forms a plea for Divine protection especially for the innocent and defenseless—"the mothers with the children" (v. 11). Presented in this manner, how could God refuse! This back loading of unexpected information or detail is designed to prevent a dispreferred response[35] and so secure Divine beneficence.

The third part of the Jacob turn references previous Divine promises of prosperity (this time stated emphatically[36]—"surely do you good") and progeny. The promise of progeny is similar to that made by God in Gen 28:14. And, if this is the promise referenced by Jacob now in Gen 32:12, he has once again substituted prosperity (nowhere to be found in the Divine direct speech of 28:13–15) for Divine presence (28:15). Jacob's citation (with changes) of previous promises is an attempt to convince his conversational partner that, to not act as requested, would be inconsistent with God's character and a violation of the *who-we-are-to-one-another* not only with Jacob but Abraham and Isaac, as well. This carefully crafted turn is designed at every point to elicit a preferred response from God. Urgent in its delivery and content, the turn is met with a disturbing response.

Divine Response

Jacob's direct address is met with Divine silence. Within conversational exchanges, silence can be a powerful turn.[37] Silence may communicate acquiescence or agreement with the previous statement, especially when no verbal reply is expected. Or, as in this case, silence can be a powerful dispreferred response leaving the conversational partner in an unknown standing and without information relative to the consequential activity of the conversation. Here, Jacob constructed his direct speech to reaffirm his standing with the LORD and based upon that standing formed a request for protection. The Divine silence leaves all that in question. Certainly, the comfort and reassurance for which Jacob was seeking will not be offered.

At times, a dispreferred verbal response can be joined with a preferred consequential action, with the preferred action dominating the verbal response.[38] We are tempted to conclude that this is the case here,

35. Pomerantz and Heritage, "Preference," 210–20.

36. By use of the personal pronoun and verbal formation היטב איטיב beginning the statement.

37. Clift, *Conversation Analysis*, 130–34.

38. Schegloff, *Sequence Organization in Interaction*, 77.

as despite the Divine silence, the anticipated reunion with Esau goes as Jacob had hoped. But this is in fact not the case, as there is no preferred consequential action. The anticipated reunion with Esau, feared by Jacob and for which Jacob pled for Divine protection, will go well, but, significantly, without Divine involvement. There is no consequential action to this conversation, at least there is none evident in the family reunion with Esau. The next time Jacob and God speak, they will be in conflict with each other. Here, Jacob's status will be affirmed by God as Jacob receives from God a new name accompanied by an indelible mark on his body, a mark that he will carry with him the rest of his life (32:26–32).

Genesis 35:9–15: Israel Shall Be Your Name

⁹ God appeared to Jacob again when he came from Paddan-aram, and he blessed him.

A: ¹⁰ God said to him, "Your name is Jacob; no longer shall you be called Jacob, but Israel shall be your name."

So he was called Israel.

A¹: ¹¹ God said to him, "I am God Almighty: be fruitful and multiply; a nation and a company of nations shall come from you, and kings shall spring from you. ¹² The land that I gave to Abraham and Isaac I will give to you, and I will give the land to your offspring after you."

¹³ Then God went up from him at the place where he had spoken with him. ¹⁴ Jacob set up a pillar in the place where he had spoken with him, a pillar of stone; and he poured out a drink offering on it, and poured oil on it. ¹⁵ So Jacob called the place where God had spoken with him Bethel.

Setting

The conversational activity and the consequential actions in this episode are remarkable for the duplication in other episodes found in the Abraham and Jacob Cycles of Genesis.[39] Genesis 35 shares characteristics of both Gen 17:1–8 and 28:18–22. The conversational activity has two parts:

---

39. See the discussion by Blum, "Jacob Tradition," 191–92. According to Blum's reckoning, following Nöldeke, "Die s.g. Grundschrift des Pentateuchs," only this conversational prayer comes from the "P" source. Blum, "Jacob Tradition," 191. This observation has implications concerning the purpose of Gen 35:9–15 and its

1. Jacob's name change to Israel
2. Repetition of the Abrahamic covenant (presented as a compilation of elements also appearing in a previous Divine statement to Abraham and perhaps from Isaac's parting blessing to Jacob)
   - I am God Almighty (17:1; 28:3)
   - be fruitful and multiply (17:6; 28:3)
   - a nation and a company of nations shall come from you (17:6; 28:3)
   - and kings shall spring from you (17:6; also 17:16)
   - The land which I gave to Abraham and Isaac I will give to you, and I will give the land to your descendants after you (17:8; 28:4)

Both parts of the conversational activity result in name changes—name changes that also occur elsewhere, under different circumstances.

1. Name change from Jacob to Israel (Gen 32:28; alluded to in 33:20)
2. Naming of Bethel (Gen 28:18; a site name previously occurring in 12:8; 13:3; 35:1; 35:5)

The consequential activity closing the episode also repeats action in earlier accounts:

- And Jacob set up a pillar in the place where he had spoken with him, a pillar of stone (parallel to 28:18)
- and he poured out a drink offering on it
- and poured oil on it (parallel to 28:18)
- So Jacob called the name of the place where God had spoken with him, Bethel (parallel to 28:19)

The only consequential action unique to this episode is the drink offering that Jacob poured on the pillar of stone. In fact, this is the only time a drink offering is mentioned in Genesis and its appearance in this context is unusual. Drink offerings are described most thoroughly in Exodus 29, Leviticus 23, and Numbers 15 and 28, and generally are performed in the vicinity of an altar.[40] The pillar (מצבה), usually a dressed stone (and so involving more labor and effort than simply setting a stone up on edge),

---

relationship to the conversational activity of Gen 28:13–17. See also Krüger, "Where Is God?," 254.

40. Jeremiah 44 describes drink offerings poured out to the queen of heaven, without explicitly mentioning an associated altar.

erected by Jacob may commemorate an event or be intended to represent the Deity. Certainly, the stone was intended to secure the presence of the Deity in Gen 28:22.[41] Here, and now accompanied by a drink offering, the pillar has a different function.[42] The drink offering performed in 35:14 may be designed to bring to mind the altars erected by Abraham at or near the same site (12:7; 13:4).

Genesis 35 and Genesis 17: Name Changes and Standing between Conversationalists

There are several significant points of similarity between the conversational activity in Genesis 35 with that of Genesis 17. First, Genesis 17 is the only other time in the Abraham Cycle or Jacob Cycle where the Divine identifies as *God Almighty*. Second, it is worth observing that Genesis 17 involves name changes: from Abram to Abraham (17:5) and from Sarai to Sarah (17:15) and Genesis 35 includes a name change; from Jacob to Israel (35:10) and renaming of Bethel (35:15). There is a third similarity between Genesis 35 and Genesis 17. In Gen 35:13 and again in v. 15, the narrator states that God spoke *with* Jacob. The preposition used (את) is unusual when describing the Divine human conversations in Genesis, appearing elsewhere only in Gen 17:3, 22. Typically, the preposition communicates a companionship, or an association that lasts over time. The preposition is used to describe a journey, or walking together (7:7, 13; 8:18), a sense of shared experience (6:18), or even the formation of the covenant between God and Abraham (17:4).[43] The appearance of this preposition in Genesis 17, describing a lengthy address by God to Abraham, is consistent with the notion of duration seen in other uses of the preposition in Genesis. In Genesis 35, however, the conversational activity is brief and the three appearances of the preposition (35:13, 14, 15) seem designed to emphasize the "togetherness" or "closeness"[44] of God Almighty and Jacob and not primarily the conversational activity. This sense of unity is consistent with the narrative

---

41. He also erected an altar in Gen 33:20 naming it "El, the God of Israel." Naming the altar in this manner may also represent an effort to localize Deity thereby effecting control over that Deity.

42. The fact that the pillar has a function different than that assigned to it in Genesis 28 is important and helps describe the changed standing between God and Jacob/Israel.

43. "את expresses closer association than עם." BDB 87A. Also GKC 103B, 458.

44. Waltke and O'Conner suggest the preposition may communicate a sense of spatial closeness. Waltke and O'Conner, *Introduction to Biblical Hebrew Syntax*, 195.

function of the conversational activity, a function that is complemented by the opening and closing to this conversational activity.

Opening/Closing

This conversation has both an opening ("God appeared to Jacob again, when he came from Paddan-aram, and blessed him" 35:9) and a closing ("Then God went up from him in the place where he had spoken with him" 35:13). The same opening and closing frame the conversation between Abraham and God in Genesis 17,[45] but are not used elsewhere with the conversational activity involving Jacob / Israel. The specificity of the opening and closing are unexpected and given the replicative nature of the conversational activity itself, there seems little doubt that the narrator wants a clear connection between the conversations of Genesis 17 and Genesis 35. So, why the strong connection between these two conversational prayers?

In the narrative run up to the conversational activity in Genesis 35:9–15, Jacob progressively becomes differentiated from the peoples surrounding him. For Jacob and those with him; foreign gods are disavowed (35:2, 4), appearance (clothes, jewelry) is changing (35:2, 4), and the surrounding peoples are distancing themselves because of a "terror from God" (35:5). At the same time, Jacob and his household are progressively becoming exclusively related to God Almighty (expressed in Jacob's name change to Israel 35:10), and will become sole possessor of the land now occupied by numerous people groups (35:11, 12). In other words, the narrative activity shapes the developing identity of "insider" and "outsider" that will now be reinforced through the conversational prayer in Genesis 35:9–15.[46] The insider designation is reinforced by the name change granted to Jacob and the preposition repeatedly used to describe the Divine human communication. This same discrimination between insiders (the child of Sarah) and outsiders (Ishmael and his descendants) dominates the conversational exchange of Genesis 17. Abraham's standing with God and the promise made to him by God are now appropriated to enrich and deepen the sometimes-questionable standing afforded to Jacob / Israel and the certainty of the promise now repeated to him by God at Bethel.

The last time Jacob was at Bethel (Gen 28) he sought to exercise control and agency over his relational standing with God through the erection of the pillar housing God. This time, the relationship between God and

---

45. God also "appears" to begin his conversation with Abraham (17:1) and "goes up" after conversing with Abraham (17:23).

46. See Lee, "גוים in Genesis 35:11," 482.

Israel is quite different. There is no bargaining, no promise of future religious devotion, no attempt to control coming from Jacob. This time, Israel's religious devotion is not performed as an attempt to control Deity but is simply a commemoration of Deity's free act of grace.

5

Moses

Just as there are observable structural differences between the conversational prayers in the Abraham Cycle and the Jacob Cycle, so, too, the conversational prayers with Moses have their own structural characteristics. Most noticeably, the conversational prayers involving Moses are devoid of any introduction whereby the Divine is made present in the conversation. When conversing with Abraham, Deity may *appear*, or *come down*, or in some other way become present. With Moses, there is none of that. With Moses, God is simply present as are all other conversational partners with whom Moses may engage. If movement is required in order to engage in conversation, it is Moses who *turns* to the Lord and so becomes effectively present. This structural peculiarity of the conversational prayers between Moses and God implies a *who-we-are-to-one-another* not shared by other conversationalists in the Hebrew Bible. This implied immediacy of the conversational prayers between God and Moses was not lost on the writer of Exodus. When describing the special relationship developed between God and Moses, it was their conversation that seemed most noteworthy:

> Thus the Lord used to speak to Moses face to face, as one speaks to a friend. (Exod 33:11)

Exodus 3:4—4:17

A: [4] *When the Lord saw that he had turned aside to see,* God called to him out of the bush, "Moses, Moses!"

B: And he said, "Here I am."

A^1: [5] Then he said, "Come no closer! Remove the sandals from your feet, for the place on which you are standing is holy ground." ⁶ He said further, "I am the God of your father, the God of Abraham, the God of Isaac, and the God of Jacob."

B¹: *And Moses hid his face, for he was afraid to look at God.*

A²: ⁷ Then the Lord said, "I have observed the misery of my people who are in Egypt; I have heard their cry on account of their taskmasters. Indeed, I know their sufferings, ⁸ and I have come down to deliver them from the Egyptians, and to bring them up out of that land to a good and broad land, a land flowing with milk and honey, to the country of the Canaanites, the Hittites, the Amorites, the Perizzites, the Hivites, and the Jebusites. ⁹ The cry of the Israelites has now come to me; I have also seen how the Egyptians oppress them. ¹⁰ So come, I will send you to Pharaoh to bring my people, the Israelites, out of Egypt."

B²: ¹¹ But Moses said to God, "Who am I that I should go to Pharaoh, and bring the Israelites out of Egypt?"

A³: ¹² He said, "I will be with you; and this shall be the sign for you that it is I who sent you: when you have brought the people out of Egypt, you shall worship God on this mountain."

B³: ¹³ But Moses said to God, "If I come to the Israelites and say to them, 'The God of your ancestors has sent me to you,' and they ask me, 'What is his name?' what shall I say to them?"

A⁴:¹⁴ God said to Moses, "I am who I am." He said further, "Thus you shall say to the Israelites, 'I am has sent me to you.'" ¹⁵ God also said to Moses, "Thus you shall say to the Israelites, 'The Lord, the God of your ancestors, the God of Abraham, the God of Isaac, and the God of Jacob, has sent me to you':

This is my name forever,
and this my title for all generations.

¹⁶ Go and assemble the elders of Israel, and say to them, 'The Lord, the God of your ancestors, the God of Abraham, of Isaac, and of Jacob, has appeared to me, saying: I have given heed to you and to what has been done to you in Egypt. ¹⁷ I declare that I will bring you up out of the misery of Egypt, to the land of the Canaanites, the Hittites, the Amorites, the Perizzites, the Hivites, and the Jebusites, a land flowing with milk and honey.' ¹⁸ They will listen to your voice; and you and the elders of Israel shall go to the king of Egypt and say to him, 'The Lord, the God of the Hebrews, has met with us; let us now go a three days' journey into the wilderness, so that we may sacrifice to the Lord our

God.' ¹⁹ I know, however, that the king of Egypt will not let you go unless compelled by a mighty hand. ²⁰ So I will stretch out my hand and strike Egypt with all my wonders that I will perform in it; after that he will let you go. ²¹ I will bring this people into such favor with the Egyptians that, when you go, you will not go empty-handed; ²² each woman shall ask her neighbor and any woman living in the neighbor's house for jewelry of silver and of gold, and clothing, and you shall put them on your sons and on your daughters; and so you shall plunder the Egyptians."

B⁴: Then Moses answered, "But suppose they do not believe me or listen to me, but say, 'The LORD did not appear to you.'"

A⁵: ² The LORD said to him, "What is that in your hand?"

B⁵: He said, "A staff."

A⁶: ³ And he said, "Throw it on the ground."

B⁶: (Narrative Response) *So he threw the staff on the ground, and it became a snake; and Moses drew back from it.*

A⁷: ⁴ Then the LORD said to Moses, "Reach out your hand, and seize it by the tail"

B⁷: (Narrative Response)—*so he reached out his hand and grasped it, and it became a staff in his hand*—

A⁸: ⁵ "so that they may believe that the Lord, the God of their ancestors, the God of Abraham, the God of Isaac, and the God of Jacob, has appeared to you."

A⁹: ⁶ Again, the LORD said to him, "Put your hand inside your cloak."

B⁹: (Narrative Response) *He put his hand into his cloak; and when he took it out, his hand was leprous, as white as snow.*

A¹⁰: ⁷ Then God said, "Put your hand back into your cloak"

B¹⁰: (Narrative Response)—*so he put his hand back into his cloak, and when he took it out, it was restored like the rest of his body*—

A¹¹: ⁸ "If they will not believe you or heed the first sign, they may believe the second sign. ⁹ If they will not believe even these two signs or heed you, you shall take some water from the Nile and pour it on the dry ground; and the water that you shall take from the Nile will become blood on the dry ground."

B¹¹: ¹⁰ But Moses said to the Lord, "O my Lord, I have never been eloquent, neither in the past nor even now that you have spoken to your servant; but I am slow of speech and slow of tongue."

A¹²: ¹¹ Then the LORD said to him, "Who gives speech to mortals? Who makes them mute or deaf, seeing or blind? Is it not I, the Lord? ¹² Now go, and I will be with your mouth and teach you what you are to speak."

B¹²: ¹³ But he said, "O my Lord, please send someone else."

A¹³: ¹⁴ *Then the anger of the Lord was kindled against Moses* and he said, "What of your brother Aaron the Levite? I know that he can speak fluently; even now he is coming out to meet you, and when he sees you his heart will be glad. ¹⁵ You shall speak to him and put the words in his mouth; and I will be with your mouth and with his mouth, and will teach you what you shall do. ¹⁶ He indeed shall speak for you to the people; he shall serve as a mouth for you, and you shall serve as God for him. ¹⁷ Take in your hand this staff, with which you shall perform the signs."

Context

The context established for this conversation is remarkable in several ways. Certainly, the miraculous appearance of Deity, present in a burning bush that is not consumed, presents an impressive display of power for the exiled shepherd. In addition, the narrator seems to take pains to impress upon the reader the immediacy of the Divine presence in this encounter. Moses came to the *mountain of God*, where the *angel of the Lord* appeared to Moses in the flame. When the *Lord* saw Moses approaching, *God* addressed the curious shepherd. With this fourfold reference to Deity, the reader can have no doubt that what is about to follow is a Divine human encounter.

Structure

The conversation in Exodus 3–4 is easily the most extended and complex conversation between God and Moses.[1] Embedded in the conversation are

---

1. Most understand this encounter between the LORD and Moses as a composite rendition. Two very different approaches are illustrated by the work of: Polak, "Storytelling and Redaction," 454–58; and Van Seters, *The Life of Moses*, 35–36. See also Jeon, *Call of Moses*; Römer, "Exodus 3–4," 65–79.

characteristics applicable to prayer. An examination of the structure of the conversation yields interesting results.

Preference Responses

The conversation flows by means of the strategic placement of dispreferred responses (3:11, 13; 4:1, 10, 13). Each dispreferred response allows the introduction of a new topic (including the signs of rounds six through eleven) even though, on at least one occasion, the topic is intrusive to the conversation (3:12). The dispreferred response of 4:10 (B[11]) is repeated in 6:30.

The function of preference responses in conversation can be intricate. In preference construction, there can be a distinction between format and action.[2] At times, the preference structure of the consequential action can functionally dominate the verbal response,[3] and that is the tendency we see in the Exodus 3–4 conversation. The consequential action by Moses remains cast in preferred responses even though the verbal replies offered by Moses tend to dispreferred responses.

Pre-expansion

The conversation is prefaced by a pre-expansion (3:4–6), providing an opening for the conversation and establishing a context in which the conversational partners negotiate status through response and repair.[4] In the pre-expansion, the LORD is presented as initiator through the miraculous appearance in the burning bush and the Divine direct address, using Moses' name. The short and direct preferred response, "Here am I," functions as a recognition of the LORD's status, commanding attention, and Moses' vulnerability to the LORD. While the LORD is aware of Moses' name, Moses is denied reciprocal knowledge of the Deity's name until the question ending the third round of the conversation (3:13) is answered. This unequal access to knowledge furthers the unequal standing between the conversational participants.[5]

While pre-expansions, in the form of invitations and summons (as in 3:4), or announcements (as in 3:5–6), are often designed to lessen

---

2. Clift, *Conversation Analysis*, 149. See also the chart in chapter 2: "Conversation Analysis."
3. Schegloff, *Sequence Organization in Interaction*, 77.
4. Sidnell, *Conversation Analysis*, 95.
5. Heritage, "Epistemics in Conversation," 376–78.

the likelihood of a dispreferred response,[6] the following conversation progresses by means of dispreferred responses. The same Moses, who is "afraid to look at God" in 3:5, has no hesitation to argue with God in the ensuing conversation.

The pre-expansion also includes an unusual element of recipient design. In 3:6, God identifies himself as "the God of your father, the God of Abraham, the God of Isaac, and the God of Jacob." The description is nearly repeated in 3:15, with one major difference. In addressing Moses in 3:6, God claims to be "God of your father" (singular)[7] while the description in 3:15 reads "God of your fathers" (plural). The sense in 3:6 is "I am God of your father, *and also* God of Abraham," while the sense of 3:15 (also 3:16; 4:5) is "I am God of your fathers, *that is* God of Abraham."[8] The effect is to intensify the directness by which God addresses Moses. The following conversation is for Moses alone. In the story, it is possible that Moses had only vague knowledge of his father's identity, let alone the Deity worshipped by his father. Any question of mistaken address is removed by this one simple proclamation, "I am God of your father." Moses, as of yet, knows nothing of the Deity addressing him, while that Deity knows everything about Moses. In response, Moses hides his face out of fear.[9]

Rounds One through Four

The first and second rounds of the conversation include statements that have near parallels in the fifth round (3:6–8; parallel to 3:15–17) of the conversation. Additional parallels occur outside the conversation (3:7; parallel to 2:24 and similar to the nation list in Gen 15:19–21).[10]

The third round (3:7–11) of the conversation includes interruptions in the first adjacency pair (3:7–10) indicating a break in speech or perhaps a conflation of speeches (3:9 "And now"; 3:10 "Come").[11] Although these

---

6. Sidnell, *Conversation Analysis*, 95–97.

7. Also in LXX. Plural in SP.

8. The singular is occasionally used in address to the patriarchs when obviously they could not be referenced as a group (e.g., Gen 26:24; 28:13; 31:29). The singular is also used occasionally of David when addressing a descendant of David (2 Kgs 20:5; 1 Chr 28:9; 2 Chr 21:12).

9. Middlemas, "Exodus 3 and the Call of Moses," 137.

10. O'Connell, "List of Seven Peoples in Canaan," 222.

11. Both verses begin with "And now" (וְעַתָּה). Turn constructional units (TCU) are "coherent self-contained" utterances "recognizable in context as 'possibly complete.'" Clayman, "Turn-Constructional Units," 151.

interruptions could function as openings or redactional seams,[12] each of which could easily follow immediately after the "Then the LORD said" of 3:7, within the conversational turn, these breaks or pauses represent moments of self-repair as the speaker, anticipating a dispreferred response, modifies, adjusts, or adds to the speech in an effort to elicit a preferred response from the conversational partner.[13] Self-initiated repair can have a variety of functions within conversation[14] including shaping or altering the trajectory of the progress of the turn.[15] Here, we see that self-repair at 3:9 allows reinforcement to the initial statement of intended action in 3:7 (v. 9 adds no new information, but reinforces the declaration of v. 7). The self-repair at 3:10 alters the progress of the turn by unexpectedly including Moses in the Divine plan.

In response, the Moses turn of the third round ends with a question (v. 11), functioning as a dispreferred response to A^2 (vv. 7–10). The self-deprecation (Who am I?) beginning the Moses response is an attempt to mitigate the dispreferred response.[16] That question (and so the dispreferred response articulated by the question) is ignored in the next round (vv. 12–13) with v. 12 (the Divine response—A^3) seemingly out of place and intrusive in the conversation. Moses' question of 3:11 is never answered and the introduction of the mountain as sign in 3:12 is off topic and dysfunctionally anachronistic as the doubt addressed by the "sign" would be long resolved by the time the people of Israel were led to the mountain.

The exchange between the end of round four and the response in round five is structured to demonstrate a change in the standing between the conversationalists. The unanswered question, ending round three is quite different than the structure of the fourth round (concluding in v. 13). The fourth round also ends in a question (also a dispreferred response) but followed by a Divine response (v. 14–22) in which Moses' question is directly addressed. The Moses dispreferred response, in the form of a question, in v. 13 allows the revelation of the Name in the Divine response. Moses, who hid his face in fear, is now bold enough to object to the Divine plan and ask for the Deity's name. Further, the LORD is willing to negotiate standing with Moses, entertaining Moses' dispreferred responses and giving to Moses the Divine Name. It is important to note that the Divine revelation is given in

---

12. See Propp, *Exodus 1–18*, 193; Weimer, *Die Berufung des Mose*, 30–31.
13. Clift, *Conversation Analysis*, 234.
14. Schegloff, "Ten Operations," 42.
15. A characteristic often used by source critics to suggest editorial activity. See here Schegloff, "Ten Operations," 46–47.
16. Clift, *Conversation Analysis*, 153–54.

response to Moses' question. Implicit in the answer is the acknowledgement by the LORD that Moses has a right to this knowledge. The *who-we-are-to-one-another* between God and Moses has changed. Agency is now shared between the conversationalists. Moses has a right to the Name.[17]

Following the revelation of the Divine Name, God provides an expanded version of his earlier statement from round three (vv. 7–10), detailing the events about to take place with Moses as emissary. This extended turn is followed by yet another dispreferred response from Moses (4:1). As with the previous dispreferred responses, this one, also, allows the introduction of a new element in the conversation, this time the signs forming the topic of rounds six through eleven.[18]

Rounds Six through Eleven

Rounds six through eleven (vv. 4:1–7) differ in structure compared to rounds one through four (3:5—4:1) and rounds twelve through thirteen (4:8–17). Rounds six through eleven are short, include consequential activity as preferred response, and appear more spontaneous than the lengthier rounds beginning and ending the conversation.

Round nine, consisting of only the LORD's turn (4:5) has no introduction formula ("And God said"), departing from the pattern established in all of the other rounds in this conversation. While the action of 4:4b (B^7), in response to the speech of 4:4a (A^7) could be moved to follow 4:5 (A^8) and so restore the normal pattern of turn introductions, doing so would significantly alter the *how* of this conversational activity. The structure of the round, as it appears, gives the sense of simultaneity or that Moses has interrupted the Divine speech reaching out and grabbing the serpent before the LORD had finished speaking. This interruption reinforces the intensity of the preferred response represented by Moses' action.[19] Dispreferred responses are frequently accompanied by a short delay or pause.[20] In this case, there is no pause. Moses appears eager, perhaps over eager, to respond in a preferred fashion to the directive given by God. The eager preferred response by Moses also isolates the purpose segment of the Divine speech, reinforcing the sign's function to cause belief "that the LORD,

---

17. Different than that expressed by Gowan, *Theology in Exodus*, 84.

18. Later to be performed in the presence of the elders of Israel (4:29–31).

19. Especially given that Moses usually responds in a dispreferred manner throughout the conversation.

20. Levinson, *Pragmatics*, 320.

the God of their fathers, the God of Abraham, the God of Isaac, the God of Jacob, has appeared to you" (4:5).

Rounds Twelve through Thirteen

Rounds twelve and thirteen return to the pattern earlier in the conversation (rounds one through five) with dispreferred responses moving the conversation forward. Following the signs of rounds six through eleven, Moses returns to self-deprecation as a means of offering a dispreferred response (4:10). It's no doubt ironic that having progressed this far in conversation with the LORD, demonstrating that he is quite capable of expressing himself and thinking on his feet, that Moses now describes himself as slow of speech and tongue (4:10). At any rate, the LORD will have none of it, this time meeting the attempt at Moses' self-deprecation head-on and using it as an opportunity to affirm his effective presence with Moses.

Having failed to dissuade the LORD by noting his own deficiencies, Moses finally offers an unmitigated dispreferred response with no attempt to soften its affect, "send someone else!" (4:13). Seemingly, tired of arguing, the LORD accommodates Moses by enlisting Aaron, Moses' well-spoken brother, to act as his assistant. And with that final accommodation, the conversation is over.

Rhetorical Function

This brief examination of structure reveals the uneven construction and reporting of the conversation leading to the conclusion that the conversation is here a literary device, used to summarize and introduce the subsequent plot activity of chapters 5–13. The conversation introduces major themes of the following plot: release by direct intervention of YHWH motivated by covenant loyalty; miraculous signs; the centrality of "this mountain"; confrontation with Pharaoh; the role of Aaron and Moses ("he [Aaron] shall be a mouth for you [Moses] and you shall be to him as God." 4:16). In other words, the writer of Exodus 1–13 chose to begin his account of the grandest redemptive event in the whole Hebrew Bible with a conversation. The conversation does much more than introduce narrative themes. The *how* of the conversation describes a developing *who-we-are-to-one-another* between Moses and the LORD. The strategic use of dispreferred responses within the conversation allows a depth of standing and inter-subjectivity between Moses and the LORD enjoyed by few other biblical characters.

Exodus 5:22—6:13

A: *²² Then Moses turned again to the Lord and said, "O Lord, why have you mistreated this people? Why did you ever send me? ²³ Since I first came to Pharaoh to speak in your name, he has mistreated this people, and you have done nothing at all to deliver your people."*

B: Then the Lord said to Moses, "Now you shall see what I will do to Pharaoh: Indeed, by a mighty hand he will let them go; by a mighty hand he will drive them out of his land."

A¹: ² God also spoke to Moses and said to him: "I am the Lord. ³ I appeared to Abraham, Isaac, and Jacob as God Almighty, but by my name 'The Lord' I did not make myself known to them. ⁴ I also established my covenant with them, to give them the land of Canaan, the land in which they resided as aliens. ⁵ I have also heard the groaning of the Israelites whom the Egyptians are holding as slaves, and I have remembered my covenant. ⁶ Say therefore to the Israelites, 'I am the Lord, and I will free you from the burdens of the Egyptians and deliver you from slavery to them. I will redeem you with an outstretched arm and with mighty acts of judgment. ⁷ I will take you as my people, and I will be your God. You shall know that I am the Lord your God, who has freed you from the burdens of the Egyptians. ⁸ I will bring you into the land that I swore to give to Abraham, Isaac, and Jacob; I will give it to you for a possession. I am the Lord.'"

⁹ Moses told this to the Israelites; but they would not listen to Moses, because of their broken spirit and their cruel slavery.

A²: ¹⁰ Then the Lord spoke to Moses, ¹¹ "Go and tell Pharaoh king of Egypt to let the Israelites go out of his land."

B²: ¹² But Moses spoke to the Lord, "The Israelites have not listened to me; how then shall Pharaoh listen to me, poor speaker that I am?"

¹³ Thus the Lord spoke to Moses and Aaron, and gave them orders regarding the Israelites and Pharaoh king of Egypt, charging them to free the Israelites from the land of Egypt.

Context

This conversational exchange has all of the prerequisite characteristics defining it as conversational prayer: it is initiated by the human conversational partner, expresses a request, and contains a conversational exchange with Deity. The context for the conversational prayer is specific. In response to God's command, Moses has approached Pharaoh, demanding the release of the Israelite people. Instead of securing their release, Moses has only managed to make the plight of the Israelites worse. In turn, the Israelite supervisors have blamed Moses and Aaron, complaining that they are now a foul smell to the Pharaoh and are in mortal danger by hand of the Egyptians (5:21). Faced with such a miserable failure, Moses "turns again to the Lord" (5:22).

Structure

This conversational prayer is constructed in three conversational rounds followed by a narrated conclusion. The rounds vary in structure, recipient design, and contextual specificity. The first and third rounds contain conversational exchanges between the participants, exchanges that are interrupted by the long speech of round two. The narrated response ending the Lord's second turn (v. 9) connects the conversational conclusion back to the precipitating context of 5:21. Round three and the narrated conclusion are more closely connected structurally and thematically with the conversation beginning in 6:28.[21] It seems clear that the conversation of 5:22—6:13 is synthesized by the narrator, created to advance the narrative design of chapters 5–6.

Round One: 5:22—6:1

The opening round of the conversation is contextualized by the conflict of 5:20–21. The condemnation heaped upon Moses and Aaron by the Israelite supervisors causes Moses to "turn again" to the Lord. Immediately, Moses addresses the Lord concerning the rejection by the Israelite supervisors. Moses offers no explanation or back story. The structure of the conversation implies that the Lord was present during the confrontation between Moses and the supervisors so that there was no need to inform the Lord about

---

21. Both turns in this round are framed by the infinitive "saying" as is the direct speech of 6:29. Otherwise the infinitive is not used in the direct speech of rounds one or two within this conversation.

the conflict and Moses needed to only turn again to the LORD and begin speaking. The LORD's response is immediate and, strangely, without opening.[22] The Israelite supervisors speak to Moses and Aaron, Moses turns to speak to the LORD, and the LORD responds. The inter-human conversational sequence quite unremarkably turns into a human Divine conversation.[23] The absence of any opening, heralding the Divine presence will become common throughout Exodus. Divine human conversations are generally introduced by simply indicating: "he said."[24] This simple introduction effectively indicates a familiarity between the conversational participants,[25] a familiarity that finds expression in Moses' opening address to God.

Without introduction, greeting, or hesitation, Moses begins a conversation with Deity by confrontation. Moses' complaint to the LORD has three parts, all leveling accusations against the LORD:

- Why have you mistreated this people?
- Why did you ever send me?
- You have done nothing at all to deliver your people.

There is no question as to whom Moses holds responsible for the present dilemma. In response, the LORD does not directly address the accusations leveled by Moses. There is no explanation, apology, or denial. In fact, the LORD's response has no necessary connection to Moses' accusations, or the conflict with the Israelite supervisors. The Divine response shows no recipient design. Functionally, the accusations articulated by Moses are denied, simply by ignoring them. Not only are the questions denied, but perhaps more importantly, the right of Moses to ask the questions is denied.[26] The LORD's reply indicates that he does not recognize Moses' right to information, or status to command a reply. The Lord's response shows no repair, no interest in achieving a common understanding regarding the accusations brought by Moses. Instead, the LORD describes events that will

---

22. Such as: he appeared (Gen 17:1); he called down Gen (21:17); he spoke by the word of the LORD (Gen 15:1); in a flame of fire (Exod 3:2).

23. Seen already in Exod 4:19, 21, with Aaron in Exod 4:27, and in the confrontation of Exod 4:24 in which the LORD tried to kill Moses.

24. The function of the infinitive, "saying" will be addressed in the conversational prayer of Num 16:1–50.

25. A familiarity addressed in Deut 34:10. "Never since has there arisen a prophet in Israel like Moses, whom the LORD knew face to face."

26. See the function of interrogatives in the Adam and Eve conversation with God in Genesis 3.

soon unfold. All the accusations will be swept away as the LORD enacts a miraculous release for the Israelites.

Round Two: 6:2–9

The second round of this conversation contains a lengthy speech by God[27] that seems out of place in this conversation.[28] The beginning of the second round is, in large, a repeat from 2:23 and 3:6–9.[29] The second round ends with a narrated preferred response (v. 9) that is also context specific (referencing the broken spirit of the Israelites and their cruel bondage in 5:21), perhaps related to the Divine speech in vv. 6–8, but not at all to the Divine speech in vv. 3–5. The conversational differences between the second round and the other rounds of the conversation suggest that it is an intrusion and that the conversation may have originally ended at 6:1 with vv. 10–13 connected to the conversation beginning in 6:28. If an intrusion into the conversation, the question must be asked, why is the round of 6:2–9 included? This question will be addressed below.

Round Three: 6:10–12

The third round ends with a dispreferred response (v. 12) that repeats Moses' objection (first raised in 4:10 and alluded to in the accusations of 5:21), insisting that he is not qualified to function as a spokesperson before Pharaoh. The objection cites the rebuff from the Israelite supervisors (5:21) as evidence leading him to suspect that Pharaoh will not listen to him either. That he has already appeared before Pharaoh (5:1) resulting in negative consequences, as Moses acknowledges in 5:23, seems a better objection to God's command than the noncompliance of the Israelite supervisors. By citing the opposition from the Israelite supervisors, this round becomes loosely situated in the same context as round one.

---

27. Interestingly, Divine speech in rounds one, three, and four is prefaced by "the LORD spoke" while round two prefaces Divine speech with "God spoke." Deity is present in a different form in round two when compared to the other rounds of this conversational prayer.

28. See Polak, "Storytelling and Redaction," 454. Childs considers this a sequel to the call of chapter 3. Childs, *Book of Exodus*, 114.

29. Fretheim, *Exodus*, 88.

Narrated Consequence 6:13

The closing to the conversation has a narrated response that functions to end the conversation but seems out of place, thematically connected more closely with 4:10–17. In the narrated consequence, the charge given by God to Moses and Aaron in 6:13[30] shows no recipient design. The response reinforces the command given in vv. 10–11, ignoring the protest by Moses in v. 12, and could just as well follow v. 9 instead of its present location following v. 12. Moses' objection of v. 12 is resumed in the conversation of 6:28–7:7. In fact, the third round (6:10–12) and narrated consequence (6:13) of this conversation seem better situated with the conversation beginning in 6:28.

Why Round Two?

Of the whole conversation, vv. 2–8 show the least amount of recipient design and the unit seems only marginally connected to the rest of the conversation. The question must be asked, why are these verses here? How would the conversation be different without vv. 2–8? It seems clear that the passage is a whole unit, beginning and ending with the Divine self-identification, "I am YHWH." Thematically, vv. 2–8 could serve as an abstract for the whole book of Exodus. This passage has caught the attention of biblical scholarship in two regards. First, the parallel between 3:1–15 and 6:1–8 has been noted.[31] This parallel would make the repeated call in chapter 6 superfluous if not for the particular inclusion of 6:3.

In 6:2–3, God introduces himself by saying:

> I am the Lord. I appeared to Abraham, to Isaac, and to Jacob, as God Almighty, but by my name the Lord I did not make myself known to them.

Rightfully, focus has been placed on the presence of the name, Lord (YHWH), in v. 3 and its obvious importance in this passage (repeated in vv. 6, 7, 8), and in the third round and closing (vv. 10, 12, 13). The notation that this is a new revelation in v. 3, "by my name 'the Lord' I did not make myself known to them" has been explained source critically since, in fact, the Name does appear previously (Gen 15:2; 27:27; 28:13, etc.).[32] Here, in Exodus 6, the introduction, "I am the Lord," serves to introduce the Divine speaker[33] and

---

30. Aaron is present in 5:20 but not mentioned in the conversation of 5:22—6:12.
31. See, for instance, Childs, *Book of Exodus*, 112–13.
32. Propp, *Exodus 1–18*, 268.
33. Greenburg, *Understanding Exodus*, 130–31; followed also by Propp, *Exodus*

in the context of this conversation, establishes status and position allowing for the command that will follow in v. 6.

Also, appearing in v. 3 is the name, "God Almighty," immediately taking the reader back to Gen 17:1 where the name is also used by way of introducing God's covenant with Abraham. Again, in Gen 35:9–5 the name "God Almighty" is used when the covenant is repeated to Jacob. Finally, Isaac uses the name, God Almighty in Gen 28:3 when blessing Jacob and wishing for him the benefits of God's covenant with Abraham. That covenant will now occupy center stage in Exod 6:2–8 as motivation for the LORD's redeeming acts.

Round two of this conversation redirects the conversation, and more redirects the attention of the reader. The release of the Israelites from bondage in Egypt will be accomplished solely by the mighty hand of the LORD in fulfillment of his covenant to Abraham, Isaac, and Jacob. Round two of the conversation places the immediate situation (5:21), within an unfolding history of redemption reaching back to the patriarchs and forward to possession of the land of promise.

Exodus 17:4–7 // Numbers 20:6–9

The conversational prayer of Exodus 17:4–7 has a parallel rendition in Numbers 20:6–9. The two accounts structure the conversational prayer quite differently making the prayers distinct from one another in both rhetorical function and consequential effect.

Exodus 17:4–7

A: ⁴ So Moses cried out to the Lord, "What shall I do with this people? They are almost ready to stone me."

B: ⁵ The LORD said to Moses, "Go on ahead of the people, and take some of the elders of Israel with you; take in your hand the staff with which you struck the Nile, and go. ⁶ I will be standing there in front of you on the rock at Horeb. Strike the rock, and water will come out of it, so that the people may drink."

A¹: *Moses did so, in the sight of the elders of Israel.* ⁷ *He called the place Massah and Meribah, because the Israelites quarreled and tested the Lord, saying, "Is the Lord among us or not?"*

1–18, 270.

Numbers 20:6–9

⁶ *Then Moses and Aaron went away from the assembly to the entrance of the tent of meeting; they fell on their faces, and the glory of the Lord appeared to them.*

A: ⁷ The LORD spoke to Moses, saying: ⁸ Take the staff, and assemble the congregation, you and your brother Aaron, and command the rock before their eyes to yield its water. Thus you shall bring water out of the rock for them; thus you shall provide drink for the congregation and their livestock.

B: ⁹ *So Moses took the staff from before the Lord, as he had commanded him.*

Context

This short conversational prayer is contextualized in an episode of immediate need: "there was no water for the people to drink" (Exod 17:1).[34] Faced with this life threatening situation, the people of Israel "quarreled" with Moses, bringing their complaint before him. In response, Moses challenges their "quarrel" claiming that their action is tantamount to "testing" the LORD. Undeterred, the people press their issue once again, complaining to Moses that they are near death. At which, "Moses cried out to the LORD."

Structure

This conversational prayer is structured in one round, followed by a narrative describing consequential action. The round is introduced by: "Moses cried to the LORD."[35] As is common in Exodus, conversations involving Moses present a Divine immediacy as the conversation easily transitions between human participants and the Divine participant. This immediacy becomes evident when contrasted with the parallel account of this episode in Numbers 20.[36] There, Moses and Aaron move location, leaving conversa-

---

34. For indications of redactional activity in this episode, see MacDonald, "Anticipations of Horeb," 10–12.

35. Following the introduction, the infinitive "saying" is used to frame the following direct speech. The metapragmatic verb, *cried*, aids in establishing the immediacy and intensity of the following exchange. See C. Miller, *Representation of Speech*, 248, 439.

36. Harrison argues that Exodus 17 and Numbers 20 represent two different events. Harrison, *Numbers*, 267–68. Philip Budd acknowledges that Numbers is a "retelling" of Exodus, but with a different purpose in mind. Budd, *Numbers*, 219–20. See also

tion with the leaders of the people, and enter the tent of meeting where they fall on their faces as the glory of the LORD appears to them.[37]

Immediacy in the Exodus 17 conversational prayer (and so status) is expressed in several additional ways, also more clearly seen when compared to Numbers 20. First, the conversational round structuring the Exodus dialogue is missing in the Numbers account. The Exodus 17 dialogue is begun with a question and a complaint that are context specific:

> "What shall I do with this people? They are almost ready to stone me."

As seen earlier (Gen 3), questions can serve a variety of functions in conversation.[38] In Exodus 17, the opening question is at once, a plea for direction and a recognition of status as Moses explicitly recognizes his inability to solve the present dilemma and implicitly recognizes God's ability to reach a solution. This status is muted by the absence of the opening question in the Numbers prayer, and further by the Moses statement to the congregation, claiming his own agency in producing the needed water (Num 20:10).[39]

The response (Exod 17:5-6) is also specific, nontransferable to another conversational participant or context. The immediacy of the Exodus conversation is expressed in the presupposed knowledge on the part of God and assumed by Moses. The topic of conversation is already known and needs no opening. Moses has no need to explain to God that there is no water. The articulated complaint and question, by which Moses addresses Deity, presupposes that God is already aware of the situation and that Moses is simply asking for direction. In this specificity, the dialogue displays a recipient design quite distinct from the parallel account in Numbers.[40] The same presupposed knowledge is characteristic of the Numbers account, however, without the initiating question opening the Exodus version. In Numbers, there is no rehearsal of need, no context, no request. In Numbers, Moses and Aaron do not even speak. Strictly speaking, there is no prayer in Numbers.

Immediacy is also expressed by the manner in which God's presence is described. In Exodus, God is present as the LORD (YHWH) in the

---

Levine, *Numbers 1-20*, 484. Knierim and Coats suggest the Numbers 20 and Exodus 17 accounts derive from different literary strands. Knierim and Coats, *Numbers*, 228.

37. Interestingly, Moses and Aaron do not converse with God in Numbers 20. They do not express their need. They simply listen as God speaks and then act in accordance with God's directive as articulated in Exodus, not as given in Numbers.

38. See Appendix 1.

39. See Fretheim, *Exodus*, 190.

40. Or the prayers of the Jacob Cycle in Genesis.

conversation with Moses. He does not appear. He does not draw near or establish presence in any other fashion. Instead, YHWH is never absent in Exodus 17, always accessible to Moses. In Numbers, it's quite different. YHWH is replaced by the "glory of the Lord" (YHWH) whose appearance is announced as Moses and Aaron lay face to the ground at the door of the tent of meeting.

The structure of the Divine response in Exod 17:5 also emphasizes the notion of Divine immediacy. In the Divine response, the Lord promises to be present during the consequential action performed by Moses. YHWH tells Moses that "I will stand before you there on the rock at Horeb" (v. 6). YHWH standing before Moses, brings to mind the same with Abraham (Gen 18:22), indicating more than physical proximity but a sense of accountability or vulnerability.[41] In Numbers, God is present as "the glory of the Lord" and makes no promise of presence in the consequential action. And in fact, the misdeeds of Moses and Aaron in Num 20:9–11 prompt Divine speech (Num 20:12), emphasizing Divine holiness without making Deity present.

Consequential Action—Theme

The narrative describing the consequential action following the conversation has been cited as the reason for the inclusion of the conversation in the narrative.[42] The conversation functions as an etiology for the doubly named Massah (translated: *quarrel*) and Meribah (translated: *test*).[43] That the consequential action following the Exodus conversation also dominates and follows the Numbers conversation (violating the directives given to Moses by God in Numbers) may be an indication of the primacy of the Exodus conversational prayer. Yet, an examination of the conversational structure of Exodus 17 and Numbers 20 points to a fundamental thematic difference presented in Exodus and Numbers.

The structure of each of the two accounts is designed to assist the two separate themes developed in Exodus and Numbers. In Exodus, the repeated affirmation of the immediacy of YHWH, seen even in the structure of the

---

41. Apparently deemed unseemly and so deleted by *Targum Neofiti 1* and modified in LXX making the "before you" temporal. Similar to the *tiqqune sofᵉrim* of Gen 18:22. See Propp, *Exodus 1–18*, 602.

42. See discussion in Durham, *Exodus*, 229.

43. Massah appears alone as a place name in Deut 6:16; 9:22, and Meribah appears alone in Num 20:13; Deut 32:51; Pss 81:8; 106:32. Both Massah and Meribah appear in Deut 33:8; Ps 95:8. But see Childs, *Book of Exodus*, 306–7.

conversational exchange, points to the main point of the whole episode—answering the question: "Is the LORD among us or not?" (Exod 17:7).[44] In Numbers, it isn't the presence of YHWH that is a concern, but the holiness of YHWH that becomes clearly seen by the waters of Meribah (Num 20:13). In both, however, it is striking that a conversation is the medium chosen to express the *who-God-is-to-Moses* [Israel].

Exodus 32:7–14; 31–34 // Numbers 14:11–35 // Deuteronomy 9:11–14, 25–29

The conversational prayer in Exodus 32 is divided into two parts (32:7–14 and 32:31–34) by intervening narrative. The two parts are here considered one conversational prayer for the second part presumes the first and the second may be said to compliment if not conclude the first. The uneven contextualization of the conversational prayer and the parallels to this conversational activity in Numbers 14 and Deuteronomy 9 suggest that the conversational prayer in Exodus 32 represents a variation on a formally stylized conversational prayer between the LORD and Moses.

Exodus 32:7–14

A[1]: [7] The LORD said to Moses, "Go down at once! Your people, whom you brought up out of the land of Egypt, have acted perversely; [8] they have been quick to turn aside from the way that I commanded them; they have cast for themselves an image of a calf, and have worshiped it and sacrificed to it, and said, 'These are your gods, O Israel, who brought you up out of the land of Egypt!'"

[9] The LORD said to Moses, "I have seen this people, how stiff-necked they are. [10] Now let me alone, so that my wrath may burn hot against them and I may consume them; and of you I will make a great nation."

B[1]:[11] But Moses implored the LORD his God, and said, "O Lord, why does your wrath burn hot against your people, whom you brought out of the land of Egypt with great power and with a mighty hand? [12] Why should the Egyptians say, 'It was with evil intent that he brought them out to kill them in the mountains,

---

44. This is also the concern of Exodus 32–34 as described by Timmer, "Small Lexemes, Large Semantics," 92, 98–99.

and to consume them from the face of the earth'? Turn from your fierce wrath; change your mind and do not bring disaster on your people. ¹³ Remember Abraham, Isaac, and Israel, your servants, how you swore to them by your own self, saying to them, 'I will multiply your descendants like the stars of heaven, and all this land that I have promised I will give to your descendants, and they shall inherit it forever.'"

A²:¹⁴ *And the Lord changed his mind about the disaster that he planned to bring on his people*

Exodus 32:31–34

A: ³¹ So Moses returned to the LORD and said, "Alas, this people has sinned a great sin; they have made for themselves gods of gold. ³² But now, if you will only forgive their sin—but if not, blot me out of the book that you have written."

B: ³³ But the LORD said to Moses, "Whoever has sinned against me I will blot out of my book. ³⁴ But now go, lead the people to the place about which I have spoken to you; see, my angel shall go in front of you. Nevertheless, when the day comes for punishment, I will punish them for their sin."

Context

The Divine human conversation in Exodus 32 is unevenly connected to the narrative context in which it resides. Moses has been on the summit of Mount Sinai where he received the "two tablets of the covenant, tablets of stone, written with the finger of God" (Exod 31:18). Impatient and even doubting his return, the people of Israel press Aaron to fashion for them gods made of the gold taken from their former Egyptian overlords. Hearing the commotion raised during the revelry of the people, the LORD orders Moses to descend the mountain and return to the camp of the people.

The prayer embedded in this conversation begins in 32:11–14 and continues in vv. 31–34.[45] Although obviously separated by the narrative of vv. 15–30, the conversation is also thematically disjointed. In its present structure, vv. 11–13 are presented as a dispreferred response to the Divine speech of 32:7–10. Yet, as a dispreferred response, it is remarkable that the prayer of vv. 11–13 is not connected to the complaint of vv. 7–8. The initial

---

45. See the analysis provided by Polak, "Storytelling and Redaction," 458.

Divine statement is presented in two parts: vv. 7–8 and 9–10. The response (vv. 11–13) is connected to vv. 9–10 (evidenced by the repetition of: *wrath burning hot*: vv. 10 and 11; *consume*: vv. 10 and 12) but shows no connection to the precipitating events forming the topic of vv. 7–8. Alternately, the continuation of the conversation in vv. 31–34 does show thematic connection to vv. 7–8 but no continuity to vv. 9–14.[46] Consequently, the dialogue could be presented in the form of two separate compositional conversations:

Conversation One: Exodus 32:7–8, 31–34

A[1]: [7] The LORD said to Moses, "Go down at once! Your people, whom you brought up out of the land of Egypt, have acted perversely; [8] they have been quick to turn aside from the way that I commanded them; they have cast for themselves an image of a calf, and have worshiped it and sacrificed to it, and said, 'These are your gods, O Israel, who brought you up out of the land of Egypt!'"

A: [31] So Moses returned to the LORD and said, "Alas, this people has sinned a great sin; they have made for themselves gods of gold. [32] But now, if you will only forgive their sin—but if not, blot me out of the book that you have written."

B: [33] But the LORD said to Moses, "Whoever has sinned against me I will blot out of my book. [34] But now go, lead the people to the place about which I have spoken to you; see, my angel shall go in front of you. Nevertheless, when the day comes for punishment, I will punish them for their sin."

Conversation Two: Exodus 32:9–14

[9] The LORD said to Moses, "I have seen this people, how stiffnecked they are. [10] Now let me alone, so that my wrath may burn

---

46. Source critics consider vv. 7–14 a Deuteronomic addition and vv. 25–29 a separate tradition. See Childs, *Book of Exodus*, 558; Beer, *Exodus*, 152–55; Lehming, "Versuch zu Ex XXXII," 30–50; Noth, *History of Pentateuchal Traditions*, 243–46. Arguments for the unity of Exodus 32 have been put forth in a series of articles by Hendrix culminating in "A Literary Structural Overview of Exodus 25–40," 123–38. Expanded upon by Hayes, "Golden Calf Stories," 62–63. See also Moberly, *At the Mountain of God*. Hayes also argues that the Deuteronomy 9 is dependent upon the Exodus 32 material (48–49) as does Begg, "Destruction of the Calf," 208–20. For our purposes, dependence is not as important as difference. The structural differences between the conversational prayers highlight the unique aspects of each.

hot against them and I may consume them; and of you I will make a great nation."

B¹:¹¹ But Moses implored the LORD his God, and said, "O Lord, why does your wrath burn hot against your people, whom you brought out of the land of Egypt with great power and with a mighty hand? ¹² Why should the Egyptians say, 'It was with evil intent that he brought them out to kill them in the mountains, and to consume them from the face of the earth'? Turn from your fierce wrath; change your mind and do not bring disaster on your people. ¹³ Remember Abraham, Isaac, and Israel, your servants, how you swore to them by your own self, saying to them, 'I will multiply your descendants like the stars of heaven, and all this land that I have promised I will give to your descendants, and they shall inherit it forever.'"

A²: ¹⁴ *And the Lord changed his mind about the disaster that he planned to bring on his people.*

Standing

The first turn (32:7–8) begins the conversation with a shocking and highly charged Divine emotional exclamation:

> Go down at once! Your people, whom you brought up out of the land of Egypt, have acted perversely.

The LORD begins the conversation, distancing himself by denying association (your [Moses'] people) or agency (whom you [Moses] brought up from the land of Egypt) with the now idolatrous people of Israel. This denial strikes at the very heart of the status relationship between the LORD and Israel, a relationship elsewhere used to preface the Decalogue,[47] later commemorated in liturgy,[48] and woven throughout the national narrative.[49] That relationship also forms the basis for Moses' dispreferred response (32:11):

---

47. Both Exod 20:2 and Deut 5:6.
48. Ps 81:10.
49. See Exod 12:42, 51; 13:16; Lev 11:45; 19:36; 22:33; 23:43; 25:38, 42, 55; 26:45; Num 15:41; 20:16; 21:5; 23:22; 24:8; Deut 1:27; 4:37; 6:12, 21; 8:14; 9:12, 26; 13:5; 16:1; 20:1; 26:8; 29:25; Josh 24:6, 17, 32; Judg 2:12; 6:8, 13; 1 Sam 8:8; 10:18; 12:6, 8; 2 Sam 7:6; 1 Kgs 8:16, 21, 51, 53; 9:9; 12:28; 2 Kgs 17:7; 17:36; 2 Chr 6:5; 7:22.

O Lord, why does your wrath burn hot against your people, whom you brought out of the land of Egypt with great power and with a mighty hand?

This conversation is about the Lord's standing with Moses and the nation of Israel, what preserves that standing, and what might threaten that standing.

Structure

When separated into two constituent conversations, structural differences become evident in the dialog. In conversation one, Moses offers a dispreferred response (32:32), prefaced by a preferred response (32:31), seemingly to mitigate the contestable nature of the dispreferred response. In turn, the Lord offers a dispreferred response (32:33) softened, to a degree at least, by the follow-up (32:34), offering what may appear to be a compromise with Moses. Conversation two is quite different. Conversation two contains a dispreferred response from Moses (32:11–13), without any preferred preface, but fashioned with rhetorical questions designed to win the agreement of the Lord. Structurally, two quite different conversational designs are operative.

Topic

In this reconstruction, both conversations follow the same general plot. The misbehavior of the people threatens to ignite God's anger, upsetting the Lord's relationship with the nation and ending in the destruction of the nation. Moses intervenes and the threatened destruction is averted.

In detail, however, significant topical differences express themselves.

- Precipitating Context:

    - Conversation one: The people have corrupted themselves, making for themselves a molten calf (gods)

    Contrasted with

    - Conversation two: The people are stiff-necked (no immediate infraction cited though contextualized in the golden calf incident of Exodus 32)

- Threatened Punishment

- Conversation one: The sinners blotted from the LORD's book[50]

  Contrasted with

- Conversation two: The nation consumed replaced by a great nation from Moses

- Moses Intervention

  - Conversation one: Moses offers to accept punishment on behalf of the people (*blot me, I pray you, out of your book which you have written*)

  Contrasted with

  - Conversation two: Moses reminds the LORD of his covenant with Abraham, Isaac, and Israel, invalidated by the threatened punishment. Moses cites consequent Egyptian slander should the punishment be enacted.

- Divine Response

  - Conversation one: Punishment delayed

  Contrasted with

  - Conversation two: The LORD repents of the evil he thought to do to his people.

When structured, however, as one conversation, the combined dialogue is significantly different than either of the constituent conversations. In the combined conversation:

- The corrupt action of the people in making the golden calf (calves) is not an isolated event but characteristic of a stiff-necked people.
- The covenant with Abraham, Isaac, and Israel is maintained despite the grave misbehavior of the people.[51]
- Although immediate punishment is averted, Divine judgment is forthcoming, postponed until after possession of the "place of which I have spoken to you" and meted out upon "whoever has sinned against me."

This combined conversation provides the perfect backdrop, connecting this conversation to the oft mentioned Jeroboam incident of 1 Kgs

---

50. See also: Pss 69:28; 139:16; Isa 4:4; Ezek 13:9.

51. The reference to Abraham, Isaac and Israel is unusual appearing elsewhere at: 1 Kgs 18:36; 1 Chr 29:18; 2 Chr 30:6.

12:28. In fact, it may have been that this combined conversation was created to function as a polemic against Jeroboam.[52]

The conversational prayers of Exodus 32 have additional inter-biblical connections: Num 14:11–35 and Deut 9:26–29.

Parallel: Direct Moses Address in Numbers 14:11–35 and Deuteronomy 9:26–29

The conversation, here structured as Conversation two, has parallels in Num 14:11–20 and Deut 9:26–29. The Numbers account is contextualized at Kadesh-barnea, following the ill report of the spies reporting on the formidable inhabitants of Canaan. The Deut 9:26–29 account seems to apply to the golden calf incident as well as events occurring at Taberah, Massah, Kibroth-hattaavah and Kadesh-barnea.

Although set in a context quite different than Exodus 32, Numbers 14 contains a direct address from Moses that shares features with Conversation two from the Exodus 32 Moses address. In Numbers 14, spies have returned to the Israelite camp at Kadesh, reporting on the nature of the land before them and the strength of the nations living there.[53] All of the spies except Caleb (and presumably Joshua) warn the Israelites not to venture an attack. In response, the people weep and complain against Moses and Aaron.

Numbers 14:11–35

A: [11] And the LORD said to Moses, "How long will this people despise me? And how long will they refuse to believe in me, in spite of all the signs that I have done among them? [12] I will strike them with pestilence and disinherit them, and I will make of you a nation greater and mightier than they."

B: [13] But Moses said to the Lord, "Then the Egyptians will hear of it, for in your might you brought up this people from among them, [14] and they will tell the inhabitants of this land. They have heard that you, O Lord, are in the midst of this people; for you,

---

52. Childs comes to a similar conclusion concerning Exodus 32, but without consideration of a CA examination of the dialogue between Moses and God. Childs, *Book of Exodus*, 560. But see Hayes, "Golden Calf Stories," 88–90.

53. Levine writes, "We have in Num 14:11–25 the reuse of themes first conveyed in the context of the Sinai theophany, and reapplied, as it were, to the situation at Kadesh." Levine, *Numbers*, 380. Wellhausen calls Num 14:11–25 a "free composition" based upon a "small kernel" from Exod 32:12; 34:6–7; Ezek 20. Cited in Gray, *Numbers*, 155.

O Lord, are seen face to face, and your cloud stands over them and you go in front of them, in a pillar of cloud by day and in a pillar of fire by night. ¹⁵ Now if you kill this people all at one time, then the nations who have heard about you will say, ¹⁶ 'It is because the Lord was not able to bring this people into the land he swore to give them that he has slaughtered them in the wilderness.' ¹⁷ And now, therefore, let the power of the Lord be great in the way that you promised when you spoke, saying,

¹⁸ 'The Lord is slow to anger,
and abounding in steadfast love,
forgiving iniquity and transgression,
but by no means clearing the guilty,
visiting the iniquity of the parents
upon the children
to the third and the fourth generation.'

¹⁹ Forgive the iniquity of this people according to the greatness of your steadfast love, just as you have pardoned this people, from Egypt even until now."

A¹: ²⁰ Then the Lord said, "I do forgive, just as you have asked; ²¹ nevertheless—as I live, and as all the earth shall be filled with the glory of the Lord— ²² none of the people who have seen my glory and the signs that I did in Egypt and in the wilderness, and yet have tested me these ten times and have not obeyed my voice, ²³ shall see the land that I swore to give to their ancestors; none of those who despised me shall see it. ²⁴ But my servant Caleb, because he has a different spirit and has followed me wholeheartedly, I will bring into the land into which he went, and his descendants shall possess it. ²⁵ Now, since the Amalekites and the Canaanites live in the valleys, turn tomorrow and set out for the wilderness by the way to the Red Sea."

A²: ²⁶ And the Lord spoke to Moses and to Aaron, saying: ²⁷ How long shall this wicked congregation complain against me? I have heard the complaints of the Israelites, which they complain against me. ²⁸ Say to them, "As I live," says the Lord, "I will do to you the very things I heard you say: ²⁹ your dead bodies shall fall in this very wilderness; and of all your number, included in the census, from twenty years old and upward, who have complained against me, ³⁰ not one of you shall come into the land in which I swore to settle you, except Caleb son of Jephunneh and Joshua son of Nun. ³¹ But your little ones, who you said would become booty, I will bring in, and they shall know the land that you have despised. ³² But as for you, your dead bodies shall fall in this wilderness. ³³ And your children shall be shepherds in the wilderness for forty years, and shall suffer for your faithlessness, until the last of your dead bodies lies in the wilderness. ³⁴ According to the number of the days in which you spied out the land, forty days, for every day a year, you shall bear your iniquity, forty years, and you shall know my displeasure." ³⁵ I the Lord have spoken; surely I will do thus to all this wicked congregation gathered together against me: in this wilderness they shall come to a full end, and there they shall die.

The most obvious topical difference between Numbers 14 and Conversation two of Exodus 32 is the inclusion of Num 14:18.

> The Lord is slow to anger,
>
> and abounding in steadfast love,
>
> forgiving iniquity and transgression,
>
> but by no means clearing the guilty,
>
> visiting the iniquity of the parents
>
> upon the children
>
> to the third and the fourth generation.

Paralleled elsewhere in Exodus and Deuteronomy (Exod 20:5, 6; 34:6, 7; Deut 5:9, 10; 7:9, 10), this confessional statement begins with a declaration,

> The Lord is slow to anger,
> and abounding in steadfast love,

found even more frequently (Pss 86:15; 103:8; 145:8; Neh 9:17; Joel 2:13; Jonah 4:2), and so appears to be a formalized insertion into the dialogue of Numbers 14. The Conversation two of Exodus 32 and the Numbers 14 conversation, minus the confessional insertion of Num 14:18, seem to be structured in a basic conversational pattern suitable for modification and use in a context supplied by a prose narrator.

Numbers 14 contains a conversational prayer between Moses and the Lord that shares significant topical characteristics with the reconstructed Conversation two from Exodus 32.

- Precipitating Context:

    - Exodus 32 Conversation two: The people are stiff-necked (no immediate infraction cited though contextualized in the golden calf incident of Exodus 32).

    - Numbers 14: The people fear the Canaanites, threaten insurrection against Moses and return to Egypt. Interpreted as despising the Lord (Num 14:11).

- Threatened Punishment

    - Exodus 32 Conversation two: The nation consumed replaced by a great nation from Moses.

    - Numbers 14: The nation struck by pestilence, disinherited by the Lord, and replaced by a greater and mightier nation from Moses.

- Moses Intervention

    - Exodus 32 Conversation two: Moses reminds of covenant with Abraham, Isaac, and Israel invalidated by threatened punishment. Cites consequent Egyptian slander should the punishment be enacted.

    - Numbers 14: Moses pleads for forgiveness. Cites Egyptian slander, spread to all the inhabitants of this land, should punishment be enacted.

- Divine Response

    - Exodus 32 Conversation two: Lord repents of the evil he thought to do to his people.

    - Numbers 14: Divine forgiveness granted, none of the people who have tested the Lord will see the land promised to their ancestors (implying covenant with Abraham, Isaac, and Israel).

Parallels also occur between Exodus 32 and Deuteronomy 9 that are not shared by Numbers 14. The Deuteronomy 9 account also separates the conversational dialogue by intervening narrative but in a manner unlike the presentation in Exodus 32. Direct speech from the Lord is found in Deut 9:12–14, while Moses direct speech is in Deut 9:26–29. Verbal similarities between the accounts are marked below.

Deuteronomy 9:12–15

¹² Then the LORD said to me, "Get up, *go down* quickly from here, *for your people whom you have brought from Egypt have acted corruptly. They have been quick to turn from the way that I commanded them; they have cast an image for themselves.*"

¹³ Furthermore the LORD said to me, "**I have seen that this people** is indeed a stubborn people. ¹⁴ **Let me alone** that I may destroy them and blot out their name from under heaven; and I will make of you a nation mightier and more numerous than they."

¹⁵ So I turned and went down from the mountain, while the mountain was ablaze; the two tablets of the covenant were in my two hands.

Exodus 32:7–10, 15

⁷ And the LORD said to Moses, "*Go down; for your people, whom you brought up out of the land of Egypt, have corrupted themselves;* ⁸ *they have turned aside quickly out of the way which I commanded them; they have made for themselves* a molten calf, and have worshiped it and sacrificed to it, and said, 'These are your gods, O Israel, who brought you up out of the land of Egypt!'"

⁹ And the LORD said to Moses, "**I have seen this people**, and behold, it is a stiff-necked people; ¹⁰ now therefore **let me alone**, that my wrath may burn hot against them and I may consume them; but of you I will make a great nation."

¹⁵ Then Moses turned and went down from the mountain, carrying the two tablets of the covenant in his hands, tablets that were written on both sides, written on the front and the back.

Although there are instances of verbal agreement in the reporting of the direct speech, there is also variation in the reported speech between Exodus 32 and Deuteronomy 9. Further, the Deuteronomy version eliminates the conversation between Moses and the LORD found in Exod 32:11–14, placing that part of the conversation within the context of a report by the spies at Kadesh-barnea.

Deuteronomy 9:26–29

The following prayer is recited by Moses in Deut 9:26–29 as direct speech in response to the Lord's direct speech earlier in the chapter. In Deuteronomy 9 the direct speech is introduced as a prayer of Moses to the Lord, spoken "Throughout the forty days and forty nights that I lay prostrate before the Lord when the Lord intended to destroy you" (9:25). It is not altogether clear if the prayer is contextualized at the incident of the golden calf (9:9),[54] or at Taberah or Massah (9:22), or at Kadesh-barnea (9:23), or is cited in Deuteronomy 9 as a summary collation of all the Moses intercessions on behalf of the nation. The prayer cited is substantively the same topic and structure as the prayer in Exod 32:11–13, but also has parallels to Num 14:13–16.

Deuteronomy 9

²⁶ I prayed to the Lord and said, "Lord God, do not destroy the people who are your very own possession, whom you redeemed in your greatness, whom you brought out of Egypt with a mighty hand. ²⁷ *Remember your servants, Abraham, Isaac, and Jacob*; pay no attention to the stubbornness of this people, their wickedness and their sin, ²⁸ otherwise **the land from which you have brought us might say,** 'Because the Lord was not able to bring them into the land that he promised them, and because he hated them, he has brought them out to let them die in the wilderness.' ²⁹ For they are the people of your very own possession, whom you brought out by your great power and by your outstretched arm."

Numbers 14

¹³ But Moses said to the Lord, "**Then the Egyptians will hear of it,** for in your might you brought up this people from among them, ¹⁴ and they will tell the inhabitants of this land. They have heard that you, O Lord, are in the midst of this people; for you, O Lord, are seen face to face, and your cloud stands over them and you go in front of them, in a pillar of cloud by day and in a pillar of fire by night. ¹⁵ Now if you kill this people all at one time, then the nations who have heard about you will

---

54. Also suggested by the statement in Deut 10:1, but see the statement in 10:10 following the intervening Israelite journey from Beeroth-bene-jaakan to Moserah.

say, ¹⁶ <u>'It is because the Lord was not able to bring this people into the land he swore to give them</u> that he has slaughtered them in the wilderness.'

Exodus 32 (Conversation Two)

¹¹ But Moses implored the LORD his God, and said, "O Lord, why does your wrath burn hot against your people, whom you brought out of the land of Egypt with great power and with a mighty hand? ¹² **Why should the Egyptians say,** 'It was with evil intent that he brought them out to kill them in the mountains, and to consume them from the face of the earth'? Turn from your fierce wrath; change your mind and do not bring disaster on your people. ¹³ *Remember Abraham, Isaac, and Israel,* your servants, how you swore to them by your own self, saying to them, 'I will multiply your descendants like the stars of heaven, and <u>all this land that I have promised</u> I will give to your descendants, and they shall inherit it forever.'"

The parallels between the three prayers can be charted as follows:

Parallels within the Conversational Activity

	Exodus	Numbers[55]	Deuteronomy
Go down, corrupt people	32:7–8a		9:12
Stiff-necked, stubborn	32:9		9:13
Consume, make new nation	32:10	14:12	9:14
Your people, mighty hand	32:11		9:26
Egyptians	32:12	14:13	9:28a
Malign the LORD	32:12b	14:16	9:28b
Abraham Isaac Jacob (Israel)	32:13		9:27

There is enough verbal overlap[56] in the three renditions to conclude a common source. At the same time verbal variation exists, suggesting

---

55. The Numbers account has an additional parallel to Exodus 34 (Num 14:18 // Exod 34:6–7).

56. See especially: Num 14:16 // Deut 9:28; Exod 32:7–8a // Deut 9:12; Exod 32:11b // Deut 9:26b.

fluidity in reporting the conversational activity.[57] It may be significant that although the Numbers account has details not paralleled in either Exodus or Deuteronomy, when parallels do occur, they appear in both Exodus and Deuteronomy.[58] Except for the parallel between Exod 32:7–8a and Deut 9:12, all of the other parallels between Numbers and Deuteronomy are with the portion of Exodus we have identified as Conversation two. There are no parallels to the conversational activity found in Exod 32:31–34.

All three direct speeches contain the same themes and follow a similar structure. Moses seeks to convince the LORD not to destroy his people, arguing that the Egyptians will hear of the Israelites' fate and malign the LORD, claiming that he was not able to fulfill the promises he made to his nation, Israel. Separated from the surrounding dialogue found in Exodus and Numbers, the Deuteronomy 9 rendition may be said to summarize the Exodus and Numbers conversations, but as a summarization lacks the structural conversation dynamics present in either Exodus or Numbers. Deuteronomy seems to use the direct speech of the LORD and of Moses in a formalistic fashion and, through the insertion of Deut 9:22–24, applies the direct speech to the whole of the wilderness wandering experience, not limiting the speech to a specific event. The conversation has a skeletal form to which additional items may be added as needed.

1. LORD's Complaint:

    - Israel has sinned
    - The LORD will destroy the nation
    - A new nation will be formed from Moses

2. Moses Intercession:

    - Plea to withhold destruction
    - The Egyptians will malign the LORD
    - Destruction of Israel would violate the LORD's covenant

3. The LORD withholds punishment

---

57. For example: Exod 32:10 (of you I will make a great nation); Num 13:12 (I will make of you a nation greater and mightier than they); Deut 9:14 (a nation mightier and more numerous than they); Exod 32:13 (Abraham, Isaac, and Israel); Deut 9:27 (Abraham, Isaac, and Jacob).

58. Those parallels include both verbal agreement (Num 14:16 with Deut 9:28) and variation (Num 14:12 with both Exod 32:10b and Deut 9:14). Levine is of the opinion that "In literary terms, it seems reasonable to regard Numbers 13–14 as having been based to a considerable extent on Exodus 32 and 34." Levine, *Numbers*, 380.

This repetitive use of conversational direct speech, conversational structure, and application of conversation to various contexts in Exodus, Numbers, and Deuteronomy suggests that this conversational prayer (or its stock form) is included in these narratives for its ability to powerfully express standing between conversational partners. When key events unfolded to threaten standing between the Lord and Israel, that crisis was met with talk. Talk that detailed the nature of the threat, its repair, and was essential in forming a joint understanding preserving the *who-we-are-to-one-another* of the conversationalists. There are few, if any, clearer examples in the Hebrew Bible of conversational prayer as powerfully efficacious in changing real events. Through conversational prayer, Moses and the Lord enter partnership to form a joint understanding affecting a whole nation of people for generations to come.

Numbers 11:11–24: Now You Shall See Whether My Word Will Come True for You or Not

A: [11] So Moses said to the Lord, "Why have you treated your servant so badly? Why have I not found favor in your sight, that you lay the burden of all this people on me? [12] Did I conceive all this people? Did I give birth to them, that you should say to me, 'Carry them in your bosom, as a nurse carries a sucking child, to the land that you promised on oath to their ancestors'? [13] Where am I to get meat to give to all this people? For they come weeping to me and say, 'Give us meat to eat!' [14] I am not able to carry all this people alone, for they are too heavy for me. [15] If this is the way you are going to treat me, put me to death at once—if I have found favor in your sight—and do not let me see my misery."

B: [16] So the Lord said to Moses, "Gather for me seventy of the elders of Israel, whom you know to be the elders of the people and officers over them; bring them to the tent of meeting, and have them take their place there with you. [17] I will come down and talk with you there; and I will take some of the spirit that is on you and put it on them; and they shall bear the burden of the people along with you so that you will not bear it all by yourself. [18] And say to the people: Consecrate yourselves for tomorrow, and you shall eat meat; for you have wailed in the hearing of the Lord, saying, 'Who will give us meat to eat?[59] Surely it was better for us in Egypt.' Therefore the Lord will give you meat, and you shall eat. [19] You shall eat not only one day, or

---

59. Question format preserved as rendered in RSV and elsewhere.

two days, or five days, or ten days, or twenty days, [20] but for a whole month—until it comes out of your nostrils and becomes loathsome to you—because you have rejected the Lord who is among you, and have wailed before him, saying, 'Why did we ever leave Egypt?'"

A[1]: [21] But Moses said, "The people I am with number six hundred thousand on foot; and you say, 'I will give them meat, that they may eat for a whole month'! [22] Are there enough flocks and herds to slaughter for them? Are there enough fish in the sea to catch for them?"

B[1]: [23] The Lord said to Moses, "Is the Lord's power limited? Now you shall see whether my word will come true for you or not."

[24] *So Moses went out and told the people the words of the Lord; and he gathered seventy elders of the people, and placed them all around the tent.*

Context

As with all conversations, the Numbers 11 conversation between Moses and God must be understood in context. That context is framed, beginning in Num 11:1, as the people complain in the "hearing of the LORD." Reacting to the complaining, the LORD consumes some of those on the margins of the Israelite camp, the fiery death only averted after the people cry out to Moses, who in turn, appeals in prayer to the LORD (11:2). Yet again, some of the "rabble" dissatisfied with the manna provided to them, express longing for the food they had in plenty while in Egypt and cry out "If only we had meat to eat!" (11:4). Hearing the weeping of the people, scattered throughout the camp at the entrance to every tent, the LORD becomes very angry and Moses becomes displeased. Without further preamble, a displeased Moses addresses in conversation a very angry LORD.

There are several contextual components of special significance in setting the conversation between Moses and the LORD. First, the context gives the conversation a sense of immediacy about it. Moses need not go to the tabernacle, need not fall on his face, need not separate himself in any fashion prior to speaking with God. The LORD is present to Moses. Further, the LORD is present in an unusual fashion throughout the whole episode. The context establishes that the people "complained in the hearing of the LORD" reaffirmed in the conversation itself as the LORD instructs Moses to say to the people, "you have wailed in the hearing of the LORD."

The phrase "in the hearing of the LORD" is unusual, here replacing the more common "in the eyes of the LORD."[60] The phrase, "in the eyes of" generally indicates understanding or assessment on the part of the subject. The phrase, "in the hearing of," while here an appropriate pairing to the complaining (11:1), generally indicates the presence or immediacy of the subject.[61] The LORD's immediacy is reinforced by the punishment meted out in 11:1-2. The "fire of the LORD" frequently indicates the presence or immediacy of the LORD (16:35).[62] And "presence" seems to be at the heart of the central complaint articulated by the LORD in conversation with Moses: "because you have rejected the LORD who is among you" (11:20). The complaining of the people, interpreted as rejection by the LORD who is among them, results in angry and displeased dispositions on the part of the conversational partners beginning in Num 11:11.

Structure

Questions are integral to the structure of this conversation. Moses' initial turn is formed in a series of questions. Questions are included as part of the direct address that the LORD commands Moses to give to the people. Questions serve as a form of protest in Moses' second turn. And a question is presented in the LORD's final turn, a question that functions as the focus of the whole conversation.

Round One

Without introduction or pre-expansion, Moses uses a series of questions to begin the conversation with God.

- Why have you treated your servant so badly?
- Why have I not found favor in your sight, that you lay the burden of all this people on me?
- Did I conceive all this people?

---

60. Indeed, some manuscripts read "in the eyes of," as noted in *BHS*. See also Gray, *Numbers*, 100, and Budd, *Numbers*, 115.

61. And slightly different in nuance than the phrase "he heard" (Num 12:2; 14:27) which can signify knowledge of (also Exod 2:24; 6:5; 16:7, 8; Deut 1:34).

62. Milgrom, *Numbers*, 82 describes the complaint as "directly, brazenly to God." See also Exod 3:2; 19:18; Lev 10:2; 1 Kgs 18:38; 2 Kgs 1:10; Isa 33:14; Mal 3:2; Job 1:16.

- Did I give birth to them, that you should say to me, "Carry them in your bosom, as a nurse carries a sucking child, to the land that you promised on oath to their ancestors?"
- Where am I to get meat to give to all this people?

Each of the questions is designed to elicit a dispreferred response.[63] The dispreferred response has a multifaceted function in the conversation. All at once; Moses is exonerated of any wrongdoing, the Lord is found responsible for the predicament, and the impossibility of the present situation is emphasized. The series of questions, expecting a dispreferred response, effectively indicts the Lord, while avoiding direct accusation. The questions are designed to force the respondent, in this instance the Lord, to articulate the impossibility of the situation into which Moses has been placed. The turn ends with a call for action from the respondent, also expressing the desperation motivating the questions.

- I am not able to carry all this people alone, for they are too heavy for me.
- If this is the way you are going to treat me, put me to death at once—if I have found favor in your sight—and do not let me see my misery.

And the absurdity of the situation is not lost on Moses.[64] The prayer in Num 11:11–24 contains one of the most fundamental dilemmas of prayer. Moses asks, quite literally: "Why have you done this evil to your servant?" The God to whom Moses prays, and the One from whom relief is sought is also the One who has caused the crises. The question is put to God allowing no compromise. The crises didn't just happen. Nor did the maltreatment result from any fault attributed to the petitioner. The crisis was God's doing and now Moses must appeal to this same God for relief.

The Lord's reply to the complaint offered by Moses is formed in two parts. In vv. 16–17 the Lord instructs Moses to gather seventy elders from among the people, bring them to the tent of meeting, and there the Lord will come down and talk with Moses, while taking "some of the spirit which is upon you" [Moses], placing it upon the elders, and so designating leadership among the group.

---

63. Termed *reversed polarity questions*, (questions that convey a bias toward the opposite valence than the valence of the sentence) questions like these used by Moses are used to indirectly disaffiliate from the position or actions of the respondent. See Hayano, "Question Design in Conversation," 410.

64. The addition of the pronoun (אנכי) is here understood to express the desperateness of the situation in which Moses found himself.

The second part of the Lord's reply (11:18–20) addresses the complaint raised by the people and contains a lengthy direct address that Moses is to repeat to the people. The address is specific in detail, implying that Moses was to repeat it verbatim, which apparently, he did, telling the people the "words of the Lord" (11:24). The direct address also contains two questions, quoting the complaints of the people.

- Who will give us meat to eat?
- Why did we ever leave Egypt?

Round Two

The question format, structuring the conversation, is continued in Moses' second turn. In the Lord's direct address of round one (v. 18b–20), meat is promised in abundance, so much so that it will become "loathsome" to the Israelites. This unlikely promise gives rise to additional reverse polarity questions in Moses' second turn:

- Are there enough flocks and herds to slaughter for them?
- Are there enough fish in the sea to catch for them?

Once again, the questions are designed as a dispreferred response, functioning as a challenge to the direct address of the Lord in vv. 16–20. The challenge posed by these questions is met by a question in return.

Is the Lord's power limited?

And it is this question that is the point of the whole conversation. The series of reverse polarity questions designed to exonerate Moses through absurd and exaggerated propositions in the form of questions, lead the reader to evaluate the last reversed polarity question in the same manner. The Lord is guiltless, and it is preposterous that he will not fulfill his promises.

The Covenant with Abraham, Isaac and Jacob

One of the unusual aspects of the conversation, especially when compared to conversations in Genesis and Exodus, is that the covenant with Abraham, Isaac, and Jacob plays no part in the Lord's response and only a minimal part in the complaint given by Moses (11:12). The response is limited to the immediate need even though the questions offered by Moses could invite reaffirmation of the Lord's covenant relationship with the people.

Did I conceive all this people? Did I give birth to them, that you should say to me, "Carry them in your bosom, as a nurse carries a sucking child, to the land that you promised on oath to their ancestors?"

Why does the LORD's reply fail to address this aspect of Moses' complaint, especially sense it is routinely mentioned in other conversational prayers (Exod 3:7–8; 6:2–6; 32:13; Num 14:23, 30)? Why is there no Divine defense bringing to mind the LORD's power witnessed by the plagues in Egypt or the escape at the Red Sea? The absence of a defense in round one permits Moses to press his complaint and, through additional reverse polarity questions, describe the helpless situation facing him and the Israelites. Throughout the whole conversation, no defense is offered by God to Moses' scathing and relentless complaint. No Divine protest of innocence or dispute of the facts is coming. Rather, after listening to the extent of Moses' indictment, the Divine offers redemption. It will be made right.

As with the conversations in Exodus 32, paralleled in Numbers 14 and Deuteronomy 9, this conversation explores the effective standing the LORD maintains with Moses and Israel (*Is the power of the Lord limited?* and *Why have you treated your servant so badly?*). These two questions are frequently asked in conversational prayer and are at the deepest level of the *who-we-are-to-God* in prayer. Is God good? And Is God powerful? The experience of apparent limits to both presence and power form the need to pray. Yet, a positive affirmation of God's goodness and power is implicit in the impetus to pray. From the shadows comes a plea for help. Belief is held in suspension, waiting desperately to hear:

Now you shall see whether my word will come true for you or not (Num 11:23).

Numbers 12:13–14: No Please!

A: [13] And Moses cried to the LORD saying,[65] "No Please! Please heal her!"[66]

B: [14] But the LORD said to Moses, "If her father had but spit in her face, should she not be shamed seven days? Let her be shut up outside the camp seven days, and after that she may be brought in again."

---

65. In Heb: לאמר.
66. For translation, see Levine, *Numbers*, 333.

Context

This prayer is in the simple form of request and response, made even more pointed by the context in which it is presented. Miriam, along with her brother, Aaron, oppose the marriage of their brother, Moses, to a Cushite woman and mount a challenge to his authority and to his assumed role as sole spokesperson for God. The LORD hears the opposition and suddenly speaks to all three, commanding them to make their way to the tent of meeting.[67] There, the LORD "comes down" in a pillar of cloud and "stood" at the entrance of the tent. Calling Miriam and Aaron, the LORD describes his special relationship with Moses; entrusting to Moses "all his house," speaking to him "face to face," and allowing Moses to "behold the form of the LORD." Given this special relationship with Moses, the LORD asks Miriam and Aaron why they were not afraid to speak against Moses (i.e., challenge his authority). Becoming angry, the LORD departs, but as the cloud (signifying the LORD's presence) moves away, or dissipates, Miriam is struck with leprosy. Witnessing his sister's sudden affliction, Aaron turns to Moses and pleads for her (12:12), admitting that their complaint was foolish (12:11), and so implying his recognition of shared guilt.[68] In response, Moses cries to God.

Structure

The conversational prayer in Num 12:13–14 is context specific,[69] showing a degree of recipient design that is not always matched by other conversational prayers in the Hebrew Bible.

The Moses turn is quite brief,

> No, please! Please heal her!

This brevity is unusual in the instances of Moses' direct speech to God. The word translated "please" or "beseech" נא, elsewhere always follows a particle

---

67. Num 12:1 contains two textual difficulties that do impact the context to the conversational prayer. See Yoo, "He Married a Cushite Woman," 37–48.

68. Certainly, the fact that only Miriam is punished when both Aaron and Miriam share guilt is one of the story's details that has raised objections. Although the ethic informing this selective punishment may be unsettling, it is worth noting that the conversation embedded in the account holds true to the elements of the plot even when that plot is troublesome. See Blidstein, "Midrashim on Aharon and Miriam," 1–12. See also Knierim and Coats, *Numbers*, 180.

69. Although, some have suggested 12:14–16 is a later addition to the story. See *Levine*, Numbers, 333. See also Forsling, *Composite Artistry*, 114.

or verb[70] but here follows the אל,[71] pointed in MT as "God" but is better rendered as a negation: "NO!" or perhaps "STOP!"[72]

The sentence is translated:

> No, please! Please heal her![73]

The point is, Moses expresses his request in an intensity never paralleled in his communication with God, even when his own fate or the fate of the entire nation is hanging in the balance (Numbers 11, 14). Given the strong contextualization of this conversation, we must look to the context of the conversation for possible explanations for the unusual form in which the Moses request is made. We might suspect that it was filial love motivating Moses. But the fact that Miriam is Moses' sibling isn't mentioned in the story at all. Instead, we must conclude that the strength of Moses' plea is related to the earlier description of the close bond between the Lord and Moses, in which Moses is designated as one who speaks with God face to face. It is the fact that Moses speaks with God that gives to Moses freedom to object so strongly to Divine action. Moses is granted great freedom and great influence with God because of his familiarity with God. The bond of the relationship is not threatened by the strength of this direct confrontation. Even though God responds to the request in a dispreferred manner, Moses is not admonished for his opposition to Miriam's punishment. The Moses turn of the conversation is structured in a way to reinforce the main thrust of the episode: The unique close bond shared by the Lord and Moses.

The Lord's Response

The whole controversy revolves around access to and familiarity with the Lord. Throughout the episode, "presence" is an important element in developing the argument of the piece. Divine presence is described by the introduction given to each conversational exchange. In v. 3 the Lord addresses all three, Moses, Aaron, and Miriam without any sign of Divine presence (cloud, glory, flame). When confronting Miriam and Aaron at the tabernacle, the Lord is present in a pillar of cloud that disappears immediately after the Divine speech. Moses, however, is still able to speak directly to the Lord, pleading for his sister, Miriam, even after the cloud disappears. And the idea of "presence" makes Miriam's punishment of leprosy especially

---

70. Gray, *Numbers*, 128.
71. See the note by Milgrom, *Numbers*, 98.
72. Levine, *Numbers*, 333. An alternate view is presented by Milgrom, *Numbers*, 98.
73. See similarly Gen 18:3.

effective, requiring her seven-day banishment from the camp[74] and illustrating to all her detachment from God.

In response to Moses' request, the LORD justifies the punishment by comparing it to a parental rebuke,[75] implying that an offence against Deity deserves a more severe punishment. While healing may have been granted,[76] Miriam will still be expelled from the presence of the LORD and the people for a period of seven days.[77] The Divine assessment is that Miriam has been presumptuous in claiming an equal familiarity with God as that given to Moses, a presumption that will now remove her from the presence of the LORD—and the people, isolating her outside the camp. Following her forced removal, she will eventually be restored, undoubtedly humbled by the experience.

Why is Moses granted presence, even though he opposes God in pleading for Miriam, while Miriam is denied presence after opposing Moses? Even though articulated through an idiom (speak against him), it is interesting that the verb used to describe the affinity between God and Moses (speak) is also the verb used to describe Miriam and Aaron's offense (speak).[78] Habitual "speaking" is the means for developing an inter-subjectivity, a shared outlook. The shared outlook between Moses and God, developed through conversation, could include opposition in a manner never achieved by the more distant Miriam.

Numbers 16:1–50: The Korah Rebellion

Narrative Pre-expansion ¹ *Now Korah son of Izhar son of Kohath son of Levi, along with Dathan and Abiram sons of Eliab, and On son of Peleth—descendants of Reuben—took* ² *two hundred fifty Israelite men, leaders of the congregation, chosen from the assembly, well-known men,*[79] *and they confronted Moses.* ³ *They assembled against Moses and against Aaron, and said to them, "You have gone too far! All the congregation are holy, every one of them, and the Lord is among them. So why then do you exalt yourselves above the assembly of the Lord?"* ⁴ *When Moses heard*

---

74. Lev 13:4; 14:3.
75. Spitting is an act of shaming. See Deut 25:9; Isa 50:6.
76. Gray, *Numbers*, 128.
77. It is likely that a leprosy affliction here would have disqualified Aaron from the priesthood—a complication that our narrator probably did not want to navigate. See Lev 21:21–23.
78. דבר; Num 12:8.
79. Num 16:2 Heb. reads: *and they confronted Moses, and two hundred fifty men.*

it, he fell on his face. ⁵ Then he said to Korah and all his company [saying],⁸⁰ "In the morning the Lord will make known who is his, and who is holy, and who will be allowed to approach him; the one whom he will choose he will allow to approach him. ⁶ Do this: take censers, Korah and all your⁸¹ company, ⁷ and tomorrow put fire in them, and lay incense on them before the Lord; and the man whom the Lord chooses shall be the holy one. You Levites have gone too far!" ⁸ Then Moses said to Korah, "Hear now, you Levites! ⁹ Is it too little for you that the God of Israel has separated you from the congregation of Israel, to allow you to approach him in order to perform the duties of the Lord's tabernacle, and to stand before the congregation and serve them? ¹⁰ He has allowed you to approach him, and all your brother Levites with you; yet you seek the priesthood as well!¹¹ Therefore you and all your company have gathered together against the Lord. What is Aaron that you rail against him?"

¹² Moses sent for Dathan and Abiram sons of Eliab; but they said, "We will not come! ¹³ Is it too little that you have brought us up out of a land flowing with milk and honey to kill us in the wilderness, that you must also lord it over us? ¹⁴ It is clear you have not brought us into a land flowing with milk and honey, or given us an inheritance of fields and vineyards. Would you put out the eyes of these men? We will not come!"

A: ¹⁵ (Consequential Action): *Moses was very angry* and said to the LORD, "Pay no attention to their offering. I have not taken one donkey from them, and I have not harmed any one of them."

Narrative Expansion: ¹⁶ And Moses said to Korah, "As for you and all your company, be present tomorrow before the Lord, you and they and Aaron; ¹⁷ and let each one of you take his censer, and put incense on it, and each one of you present his censer before the Lord, two hundred fifty censers; you also, and Aaron, each his censer." ¹⁸ So each man took his censer, and they put fire in the censers and laid incense on them, and they stood at the entrance of the tent of meeting with Moses and Aaron. ¹⁹ Then Korah assembled the whole congregation against them at the entrance of the tent of meeting. And the glory of the Lord appeared to the whole congregation.

---

80. Heb. reads: לאמר.
81. Num 16:6 Heb. reads: *his*.

A¹: ²⁰ Then the Lord spoke to Moses and to Aaron, saying: ²¹ Separate yourselves from this congregation, so that I may consume them in a moment.

B¹: (Consequential Action): ²² *They fell on their faces,* and said, "O God, the God of the spirits of all flesh,⁸² shall one person sin and you become angry with the whole congregation?"

A²: ²³ And the Lord spoke to Moses, saying: ²⁴ Say to the congregation, [saying]:⁸³ Get away from the dwellings of Korah, Dathan, and Abiram.

B²: (Consequential Action): ²⁵ *So Moses got up and went to Dathan and Abiram; the elders of Israel followed him.* ²⁶ He said to the congregation [saying],⁸⁴ "Turn away from the tents of these wicked men, and touch nothing of theirs, or you will be swept away for all their sins."

Narrative Expansion: ²⁷ *So they got away from the dwellings of Korah, Dathan, and Abiram; and Dathan and Abiram came out and stood at the entrance of their tents, together with their wives, their children, and their little ones.* ²⁸ *And Moses said, "This is how you shall know that the Lord has sent me to do all these works; it has not been of my own accord:* ²⁹ *If these people die a natural death, or if a natural fate comes on them, then the Lord has not sent me.* ³⁰ *But if the Lord creates something new, and the ground opens its mouth and swallows them up, with all that belongs to them, and they go down alive into Sheol, then you shall know that these men have despised the Lord."*

³¹ *As soon as he finished speaking all these words, the ground under them was split apart.* ³² *The earth opened its mouth and swallowed them up, along with their households—everyone who belonged to Korah and all their goods.* ³³ *So they with all that belonged to them went down alive into Sheol; the earth closed over them, and they perished from the midst of the assembly.* ³⁴ *All Israel around them fled at their outcry, for they said, "The earth will swallow us too!"* ³⁵ *And fire came out from the Lord and consumed the two hundred fifty men offering the incense.*

A³: ³⁶ [17:1 in MT] Then the Lord spoke to Moses, saying: ³⁷ Tell Eleazar son of Aaron the priest to take the censers out of the

---

82. See also Num 27:16. The only other use of the phrase is also spoken by Moses as part of a request presented to the Lord.

83. לאמר.

84. לאמר.

blaze; then scatter the fire far and wide. ³⁸ For the censers of these sinners have become holy at the cost of their lives. Make them into hammered plates as a covering for the altar, for they presented them before the LORD and they became holy. Thus they shall be a sign to the Israelites.

B³ (Consequential Action): ³⁹ *So Eleazar the priest took the bronze censers that had been presented by those who were burned; and they were hammered out as a covering for the altar—* ⁴⁰ *a reminder to the Israelites that no outsider, who is not of the descendants of Aaron, shall approach to offer incense before the Lord, so as not to become like Korah and his company—just as the Lord had said to him through Moses.*

Narrative Expansion: ⁴¹ *On the next day, however, the whole congregation of the Israelites rebelled against Moses and against Aaron, saying, "You have killed the people of the Lord."* ⁴² *And when the congregation had assembled against them, Moses and Aaron turned toward the tent of meeting; the cloud had covered it and the glory of the Lord appeared.* ⁴³ *Then Moses and Aaron came to the front of the tent of meeting,*

A⁴: ⁴⁴ and the LORD spoke to Moses, saying, ⁴⁵ "Get away from this congregation, so that I may consume them in a moment."

B⁴ (Consequential Action): *And they fell on their faces.*

Narrative Post-expansion: ⁴⁶ *Moses said to Aaron, "Take your censer, put fire on it from the altar and lay incense on it, and carry it quickly to the congregation and make atonement for them. For wrath has gone out from the Lord; the plague has begun."* ⁴⁷ *So Aaron took it as Moses had ordered, and ran into the middle of the assembly, where the plague had already begun among the people. He put on the incense, and made atonement for the people.* ⁴⁸ *He stood between the dead and the living; and the plague was stopped.* ⁴⁹ *Those who died by the plague were fourteen thousand seven hundred, besides those who died in the affair of Korah.* ⁵⁰ *When the plague was stopped, Aaron returned to Moses at the entrance of the tent of meeting.*

Context

This conversational prayer (Num 16:15, 20–24) is interwoven with a Moses address to Korah and narrative action, providing a dynamic context for the developing conversation with the LORD, a developing context that cannot be separated from an analysis of the conversational prayer.[85] Many see in the episode an intertwining of two or three main lines of tradition, JE and P (P^G, P^S), each with a distinct central issue occupying the attention of the component.[86] JE (16:12–15, 25–34) addresses the question of Moses' leadership. P addresses the nature of and limits to priestly function and office, accompanied by the threat of Divine punishment.[87] The initial complaint precipitating the action of this episode is a complaint that has been heard before (12:2). Korah, Dathan, Abiram, On, and two hundred fifty respectable men from the congregation complain that Moses and Aaron have taken too much authority upon themselves, saying:

> You have gone too far! All the congregation are holy, every one of them, and the LORD is among them. So why then do you exalt yourselves above the assembly of the LORD?

The argument escalates as Moses suggests a test to see whom the LORD has chosen (16:6–7),[88] accuses Korah and the Levites of not valuing the special role of service assigned to them (16:8–10), claiming that they are in opposition to the LORD (16:11), and summoning Dathan and Abiram (16:12).[89] These two instigators refuse Moses' summons, claiming that his promise of a land "flowing with milk and honey" has been false and that he is a threat to the people (16:14).[90]

The refusal mounted by Dathan and Abiram infuriates Moses and he "said to the LORD." The Moses turn has three components:

- Pay no attention to their offering.
- I have not taken one donkey from them.
- I have not harmed any one of them.

---

85. Mary Douglas places chapters 16–17 at the center of a chiastic structure forming Numbers. Douglas, *In the Wilderness*, 102–3.

86. The complex and uneven development of this episode has been addressed source critically. See Gray, *Numbers*, 195–211; Levine, *Numbers*, 405. Jaeyoung Jeon posits three sources behind the current narrative. Jeon, "Zadokites in the Wilderness," 381–40. The discrepancies and unevenness of the episode do impact the structure of the conversations as now appearing.

87. Yoo considers the narrative a "defense of the exclusively priestly prerogatives and polemics against other competing groups" in Yehud. Jeon, "Zadokites in the Wilderness," 383.

88. Thus, Moses turns Korah's accusation, "you have gone too far," back on the accuser.

89. See also Ps 106:16–18. See Jeon, "Zadokites in the Wilderness," 393–95.

90. Interestingly, Egypt is here also described as "flowing with milk and honey."

Opening

As with other conversations between Moses and the LORD, there is no need for an opening to either establish the topic of the conversation or the status of the conversational participants. Moses begins abruptly with a command, assuming that the LORD is aware of recent events and that the LORD is predisposed to act as Moses commands. The command is legitimized through two statements of proclaimed innocence. The first statement is not related to the context, no one having accused Moses of theft.[91] The second protest of innocence: "I have not harmed any one of them" may relate to the retort given by Dathan and Abiram in v. 14, although it seems most likely they had in mind a metaphorical blinding to what was apparent to all—the wild goose chase led by Moses that had, so far, failed to achieve the prosperity expected by the people (16:13–14).

The basic structure of the episode is familiar.

- The nation, or parts of the nation, offend the LORD by challenging Moses' assigned leadership. (vv. 3, 41–42)
- Moses brings the complaint to the LORD. (vv. 15, 43)
- The whole congregation is threatened by punishment from the LORD. (vv. 20, 45)
- Moses and Aaron intervene, averting the destruction of the entire nation. (vv. 22, 46–50)

The conversation embedded in the narrative, especially the Divine human conversation, gives to the episode its unique character. Two details, helping to contextualize conversations within this episode, combine to establish the conflict that will drive the narrative. In 16:4, Moses falls to his face upon hearing the complaint from Korah and his company that Moses has exalted himself above the assembly of the LORD. Again, in 16:22 and 45, Moses and Aaron with him fall to their faces following the Divine pronouncement of impending punishment that will consume the congregation. This posture, framing Moses' initial and final conversational activity, places Moses (and Aaron like him) in the role of supplicant, seeking to heal a fracture between the congregation and the LORD, even though he is the focus of the controversy.

---

91. The denial used by Moses is probably meant to convey absolute innocence from any theft or perhaps innocence from any related abuse of power.

Moses Turn One

The command issued by Moses, ordering the Lord to deny status to the people by not respecting their offering, is not effectively sustained by the two supporting statements.[92] The two supporting statements address Moses's status relative to the people in which he argues the benevolence of his leadership since he has neither, stolen from, or harmed any of the people. Moses has felt an affront and, in the command given to the Lord, is seeking solidarity from the Lord in opposition to the people (i.e., the enemy of my enemy is my friend).

The Lord Direct Speech

The direct address of this opening round is designed to emphasize the strength of the bond between the Lord and Moses. Without validating his right to do so, Moses immediately commands the Lord, effectively forcing the Lord to choose sides. And choose he does. The complex series of narratives and direct addresses that follow make clear that the Lord does indeed stand in solidarity with Moses. The Lord responds to Moses' command with four direct speeches:

- Then the Lord spoke to Moses and to Aaron, saying: Separate yourselves from this congregation, so that I may consume[93] them in a moment. (16:21)

- And the Lord spoke to Moses, saying: Say to the congregation: Get away from the dwellings of Korah, Dathan, and Abiram. (16:24)

- Then the Lord spoke to Moses, saying: Tell Eleazar son of Aaron the priest to take the censers out of the blaze; then scatter the fire far and wide. For the censers of these sinners have become holy at the cost of their lives. Make them into hammered plates as a covering for the altar, for they presented them before the Lord and they became holy. Thus they shall be a sign to the Israelites. (16:36–38)

- And the Lord spoke to Moses, saying: Get away from this congregation, so that I may consume them in a moment. (16:45)

---

92. Gray, *Numbers*, 202, notes that "the connection between v. 15a and v. 15b is not very close, and the two clauses may be from different sources."

93. אכל used with YHWH as subject appears in the Pentateuch only in this narrative.

In three of these speeches (1, 2, and 4), separation is commanded. The third address, also a direct address from the LORD, is a message given to Moses that he, in turn, is to pass on to Eleazar. That message concerns censers, on which incense was placed, that were used by the two hundred fifty who, along with Korah, challenged the authority of Moses and consequently were consumed by the fire that "came out from the LORD" (16:35), even as Korah and his household were swallowed by the earth, going "down alive to Sheol" (16:33). The censers were to be repurposed, hammered out as a covering for the altar, and serve as a "reminder to the Israelites that no outsider, who is not of the descendants of Aaron, shall approach to offer incense before the LORD" (16:40).

As with the initial Moses turn, structured to emphasize status between Moses and the LORD, the four responses from the LORD topically reinforce the Moses status by segregating Moses (and secondly Aaron) from the congregation.

Saying...

An interesting feature of the conversational presentation in this episode is the use of the infinitive לאמר (not always translated, but when translated is usually rendered "saying," as in the NRSV).[94] On five occasions within this conversational dialogue, the infinitive is used to frame direct speech from the LORD (the LORD spoke to XXX, *saying* ... ; 16:20, 23, 24, 36, 44). Twice the infinitive frames direct address from Moses (16:5, 26). And once, the infinitive is used to frame speech from the Israelites (16:41). The infinitive is often used to signify direct speech, but as we can see in this episode, not all direct speech is so framed,[95] and the use of the infinitive may help structure the conversational activity and narrative integration.[96] In its present form, there are sixteen speech events in this episode (16:1–46 [17:11] in Heb). If we consider the dialogue between the LORD and

---

94. Cynthia Miller contends that לאמר tends to appear in the first part of an adjacency pair, followed by a finite form (דבר, אמר, etc.) in the second part of the adjacency pair. In this structure the infinitive frames the adjacency pair and can be used as a clue, connecting parts of the conversation. Miller is right when considering the direct speech events from the LORD. Her observation is not correct, however, when the direct speech presented by Korah, the congregation, Dathan, or Abrim is considered. Also, not included in Miller's consideration is the conversational function of narrative expansions (pre-expansion) or consequential action apart from which the direct speech is incomplete. C. Miller, *Representation of Speech*, 250.

95. C. Miller, *Representation of Speech*, 174.

96. C. Miller, *Representation of Speech*, 248.

conversational partners as the focus of the analysis, and narratives with additional conversation embedded as expansions or insertions into that conversation, the following structural outline results:

Pre-expansion	16:1–14 (v. 5 Moses saying)
A: Moses turn	16:15
Narrative Expansion	16:16–19
B: LORD turn	16:20–21 (saying)
A¹: Moses and Aaron turn	16:22
B¹: LORD turn	16:23–24 (saying v. 23, 24)
A²: Moses turn (Consequential Action)	16:25–26 (saying)
Narrative Expansion	16:27–35
A³: LORD turn	16:36–38 (saying)
B³: Implied Moses turn (Consequential Action) 16:39–40	
Narrative Expansion	16:41–43 (v. 41 saying)
A⁴: LORD turn	16:44–45a (saying)
B⁴: Moses turn (Consequential Action)	16:45b
Narrative Post Expansion	16:46–50

The strategic use of the infinitive also serves to bind together the conversational activity, narrative expansions, and consequential actions. The first direct speech by Moses (16:5–11) in this episode is framed by the infinitive, while the initial Moses turn of direct speech to the LORD (16:15) is not framed by the infinitive, perhaps signifying the necessary connection between the pre-expansion, the first Moses turn of the Divine human conversation, and the first narrative expansion (16:16–19). The same unifying function may be evident in 16:20 (binding the first round of conversation; 16:20–22), 16:36 (binding the direct speech of the LORD in 16:37–38 to the consequential action of 16:39–40), and 16:44 (binding the fourth round of conversation and the narrative post-expansion; 16:44–50). The conversation between the LORD and Moses in 17:1 (Heb 17:16), initiating the next episode in the narrative, also uses the infinitive to frame the direct speech.

Of special interest is the concentrated use of the infinitive (saying) in 16:23–24. In v. 24 the LORD gives to Moses a command separating the congregation from the tents of Korah, Dathan, and Abiram. That command is obeyed, but Moses expands the message by connecting consequent Divine action to his own status:

> This is how you shall know that the LORD has sent me to do all these works; it has not been of my own accord: If these people die a natural death, or if a natural fate comes on them, then the LORD has not sent me. (16:28, 29)

That Moses' interpretation of the fateful events is correct is underscored by the double use of the infinitive (לאמר) in vv. 23–24. There is no doubt as to the source of the message. Here, the infinitive provides additional evidence in support of the central contention of the whole episode:

> This is how you shall know that the LORD has sent me [Moses] to do all these works. (16:28)

Numbers 27:12–23: Joshua, Successor to Moses

> A: ¹² The LORD said to Moses, "Go up this mountain of the Abarim range, and see the land that I have given to the Israelites. ¹³ When you have seen it, you also shall be gathered to your people, as your brother Aaron was, ¹⁴ because you rebelled against my word in the wilderness of Zin when the congregation quarreled with me. You did not show my holiness before their eyes at the waters." (*These are the waters of Meribath-kadesh in the wilderness of Zin.*)
>
> B: ¹⁵ Moses spoke to the LORD, saying, ¹⁶ "Let the LORD, the God of the spirits of all flesh,[97] appoint someone over the congregation ¹⁷ who shall go out before them and come in before them, who shall lead them out and bring them in,[98] so that the congregation of the LORD may not be like sheep without a shepherd."
>
> A¹: ¹⁸ So the LORD said to Moses, "Take Joshua son of Nun, a man in whom is the spirit, and lay your hand upon him; ¹⁹ have him stand before Eleazar the priest and all the congregation, and commission him in their sight. ²⁰ You shall give him some of your authority, so that all the congregation of the Israelites may obey. ²¹ But he shall stand before Eleazar the priest, who shall inquire for him by the decision of the Urim before the LORD; at his word they shall go out, and at his word they shall come in, both he and all the Israelites with him, the whole congregation."

97. See Num 16:22.
98. "Go out and come in" an inclusive indicating totality.

MOSES 133

B¹ (Consequential Action): ²² *So Moses did as the Lord commanded him. He took Joshua and had him stand before Eleazar the priest and the whole congregation;* ²³ *he laid his hands on him and commissioned him—as the Lord had directed through Moses.*

Context

In structure, this conversation is simple and straightforward. In consequence, this conversation is remarkable for its presumed authority. A leadership transition is in the making.[99] Moses will be "gathered to his people as was his brother Aaron" (27:13) and a successor is needed.[100] This is a moment of uncertainty in the life of the fledgling and refugee nation. Not everyone has been satisfied with the way Moses has wielded authority (12:2; 14:2), and open revolt was put down in a very bloody fashion (16:1–35). So, the smooth succession of power is not at all assured. Yet, a smooth succession is exactly what is accomplished—all based upon the report of a private conversation between Moses and the LORD. Within the Numbers narrative, the power of the conversation is amplified by the plot twists, separating the announcement of succession from the actual death of Moses by eight additional chapters in Numbers and the whole of Deuteronomy, finally realized in Deut 32:48–52. In Numbers, the visible confirmation of the transfer of the political succession from Moses to Joshua rests solely on this conversational prayer.

In Deuteronomy, it's quite another matter. In Deuteronomy, the Divine command ordering Moses to ascend the mountain of Abarim, Mt. Nebo, is preceded by a similar command for Moses to ascend Pisgah in order to view the land given to Israel by God (Num 3:23–28) and by Moses' choice of Joshua as successor in Deut 31:1–8, followed later by God's choice of Joshua (Deut 31:14–23). In Deuteronomy, the choice of Joshua is publicly affirmed, in the sight of all Israel (Deut 31:7), and publicly commissioned, accompanied by the pillar of cloud at the entrance to the tent of meeting (Deut 31:15).

---

99. The account may in fact be designed to address political leadership questions in Yehud. See Kislev, "Investiture of Joshua," 440–43.

100. The parallel to Aaron's death in Num 20:22–29 is unmistakable. Vaulx suggests that the Num 27:12–23 is modeled after the account of the death of Aaron in Num 20. Vaulx, *Les Nombres*, 322–25.

The LORD Turn One: 27:12–14

The initial direct speech from the LORD begins with a command, assuming an unequal status in the Divine human relationship. Status is maintained as the command is followed by a pronouncement of death.[101] Rationale for the death sentence is given using the same phraseology as appears in Num 20:12 (not evident in Deut 32:51–52). In the consequential action to follow (27:22–23), it is not clear if the command given by God (to ascend this mountain) is obeyed. Certainly, Moses does not die, as is implied he would, following the view from the summit (27:13).[102] The command functions as the precipitating context for the request voiced by Moses in response to the LORD's direct speech. The action required by the LORD's command plays no part in the subsequent narrative, and so the function of the command in the conversation is not to direct action—but to introduce the threat of Moses' death, thereby allowing for the request from Moses for a successor.

Moses Turn One: 27:15–17

Moses replies to the LORD with a dispreferred response, acknowledging his threatened imminent death, while ignoring (seemingly) the command to climb the mountain. The dispreferred response is in the form of a request, asking "the LORD, the God of the spirits of all flesh" to appoint his successor, someone to lead the Israelite nation so that "they not become like sheep without a shepherd."

The way Moses addresses his conversational partner communicates the recognized status operative in the conversation. The title, "God of the spirits of all flesh" is used only here and in Num 16:22.[103] Both are voiced by Moses in prayer as introducing a dispreferred response to a threatened destruction of the Israelite nation (16:22), or his own imminent death (27:13). By using the title, Moses acknowledges the LORD's inherent right over matters of life and death, while still seeking to change Divine behavior. There is a difference, however, between the prayers in Numbers 16 and 27 that also has a bearing on the expression of status between the conversational partners. In Numbers 16, Moses addresses the LORD in the

---

101. The same dynamic is operative, even more starkly in the divine pronouncement to Abimelech: "Behold, you are a dead man" (Gen 20:3).

102. See also Num 31:2 which uses the same phraseology to describe the death of Moses in a different context.

103. The title does appear (with variations) in later literature: Jub 10:3; 2 Macc 3:24; 14:46. In Jubilees 10 and 2 Maccabees 14, the title is also used in the context of a prayer—a rather gruesome prayer in 2 Maccabees 14.

second person, while, here, in Numbers 27, Moses uses a more formal and distant third person. While Moses still seeks to change Divine behavior, a certain loss of intimacy has developed.[104]

The first round of the conversation establishes three conditions that are important for the following narrative:

- Moses remains alive—yet initiates the request for succession.
- Joshua is chosen successor.
- Divine command drives the succession.

In the first round, the integrity of Moses' leadership is maintained, while reaffirming the Divine authority to appoint leadership. Had the threat of death not been given, there would be no motivation for a successor and had the threat of death actually been fulfilled, there would be no transfer of authority, no laying on Moses' hands, and no public role for Moses in the transfer of authority.

Round Two

In the second round of conversation (consequential action from Moses), the LORD offers a preferred response to Moses' request, directing the manner of succession that will take place.[105] That preferred response is specific in its direction given to Moses. In response to Moses' request, a successor has been chosen, Joshua son of Nun. The commissioning will be public, affirming both the new authority given to Joshua[106] and the continued role that Moses will play. And the whole process will be validated by Eleazar, the priest. Further, Joshua will be guided by the "decision of the Urim before the LORD" when making decisions impacting the whole congregation. The specificity of the LORD's direct speech leaves no doubt as to his involvement in the succession of Israel's leadership. That involvement is reinforced in the manner that the Moses consequential action is expressed. The action is introduced with: "Moses did as the LORD commanded him," and is concluded with: "as the LORD had directed through Moses" (27:22–23).[107]

104. This distancing is characteristic of all subsequent communication between Moses and the LORD in Numbers.

105. A chiasm exists between the Moses turn of v. 17 and the LORD's response in vv. 21–22. Mittmann, *Deuteronomium*, 110.

106. "Your authority" (מהודך) used only here in the Pentateuch. Noth raises the possibility that the transfer may have included a visible manifestation of the authority. Noth, *Numbers*, 215. See also Kislev, "Investiture of Joshua," 430–31.

107. See Kislev, "Investiture of Joshua," 433.

Without this conversation, the whole succession episode would appear to be planned and executed solely at Moses' initiative. The inclusion of the private conversation between the Lord and Moses into the narrative corrects this perception by describing God's active role and making clear that the initiative, choice, and timing of Joshua's commissioning rests with the Lord. Once again, we find that at the very heart of this pivotal national moment, a conversation is key. Fate, chance, and even Divine providence are all transformed by the agency of talk.

Deuteronomy 3:23–28: Moses' Farewell

A: [23] At that time, too, I entreated the Lord, saying: [24] "O Lord God, you have only begun to show your servant your greatness and your might; what god in heaven or on earth can perform deeds and mighty acts like yours! [25] Let me cross over to see the good land beyond the Jordan, that good hill country and the Lebanon."

B: [26] But the Lord was angry with me on your account and would not heed me. The Lord said to me, "Enough from you! Never speak to me of this matter again! [27] Go up to the top of Pisgah and look around you to the west, to the north, to the south, and to the east. Look well, for you shall not cross over this Jordan. [28] But charge Joshua, and encourage and strengthen him, because it is he who shall cross over at the head of this people and who shall secure their possession of the land that you will see."

Context

This prayer comes to us as a representation (quoted direct speech in Deut 3) of a representation (Moses' recounting) of the conversational prayer. This twice removed rendition is structured remarkably in that it is still presented as direct quoted speech even though it appears in a speech delivered by Moses intent on summarizing events since the nation of Israel left Sinai (Horeb in Deut 1:6).[108] Further, the conversation includes phrases (Deut 3:27 parallel to Deut 34:4) and describes events (Num 27:12–23; Deut 32:48–52; 34:1–4)

---

108. Joshua Berman compares the Deuteronomy retelling to Hittite treaty traditions in which historical accounts were redrafted "in accord with the needs of the moment." Berman, "Histories Twice Told," 230.

found elsewhere,[109] making it even more likely to represent a composite summary and not direct speech. The difference between Deuteronomy 3 and its parallels in Numbers 27 and Deuteronomy 32 and 34 is the conversation. The topic of the conversation is not unique. Rather, the uniqueness of Deuteronomy 3 is largely the conversation itself, and the contribution it makes to the Deuteronomy 1–4 Moses address by the *who-we-are-to-one-another* and the *what-it-does* in the plan of Deuteronomy.

The *Who-We-Are-to-One-Another*

The *who-we-are-to-one-another* of this conversation is established by the verbs used to describe Moses' initial request, and the manner of the LORD's response. Moses *entreats* (אתחנן) the LORD YHWH (a name used by Moses only here) and the LORD was *angry* (יתעבר)[110] in response. Both of these verbal forms are unusual in Deuteronomy and establish the emotional intensity of the scene. Moses' entreaty is a desperate plea[111] and the LORD's anger teeters on the edge of control, going beyond the bounds,[112] even more intense than that directed against the idolatrous (Exod 32) or complaining (Num 16) Israelites or the presumptuous Miriam (Num 12). The emotion of the moment is palpable.

In his plea, Moses uses language of contrition and devotion (the LORD's servant) while emphasizing the incomparability of the LORD, borrowing phrases at home in public discourse (Pss 89:7–9 [ET 6–8]; 113:5–6). Moses states that the LORD has only *begun* (Deut 3:24) to show him his greatness and might. Clearly, Moses hopes that the LORD will continue what he has begun and phrases the request so that a dispreferred response from the LORD must result in changed (and, implied by Moses, uncharacteristic) behavior on the LORD's part.

---

109. A recent discussion of the tangled relationship between parallel texts can be found in Yoo, "Four Moses Death Accounts," 423–41; Eckart, "Deuteronomiumstudiem I," 86–236.

110. Notice the same root is used to describe the LORD's anger and the "crossing" Moses petitions (v. 25), and the LORD prohibits for Moses (v. 27) but allows for Joshua (v. 28).

111. Nelson, *Deuteronomy*, 55.

112. Driver, *Deuteronomy*, 60.

The What-It-Does

In the presentation of the conversation in Deuteronomy 3, this highly charged emotional context accomplishes several purposes. For the conversational participants, the emotion establishes the importance of the topic, and the strength of the social relationship between the conversationalists. The strong dispreferred response does not weaken the standing between Moses and the LORD. While Moses is plainly constructing a request to best achieve his purpose (entering the Promised Land) and so the outcome of the conversation has immediate and literally life extending ramifications, its reproduction here in the Moses speech of Deuteronomy 1–4, allows the wider audience (the listening audience present in Deuteronomy 1–4 and the reading audience of Deuteronomy) to observe the emotion and experience the conversation as a performance. The *who-we-are-to-one-another* of the conversation allows Moses to risk the LORD's out of control anger, without fear of losing his standing with the LORD. Moses is confident in his social standing with the LORD so that no request is off limits. This emotional exchange is made available to audiences. The *who-we-are-to-one-another* between Moses and the LORD is witnessed by the audiences, in order for the audiences to adjust their *who-we-are-to-God*. The conversation is crafted to impact the emotional affiliation of the witnessing audience.[113] Empathy for Moses is intended to result in obedience to God by the observing audiences; a renewal of Israel's affinity to the LORD.

The emotional affective intent of the conversation becomes clearer when compared to the conversation of a parallel account in Num 27:12–23. In that conversation, Moses is also informed by the LORD that he will not enter the land given to the Israelites and that he should appoint Joshua as his successor to lead the people. Just like the conversation in Deuteronomy 3, the conversation in Numbers 27 is guided by the Moses request voiced in the initial turn:

> Deut 3:25   Let me cross over to see the good land beyond the Jordan, that good hill country and the Lebanon.
>
> Num 27:16–17   Let the LORD, the God of the spirits of all flesh, appoint someone over the congregation who shall go out before them and come in before them, who shall lead them out and bring them in, so that the congregation of the LORD may not be like sheep without a shepherd.

---

113. See the discussion in Ruusuvuori, "Emotion, Affect, and Conversation," 343–44.

While the appointment of Joshua (Num 27) or the charge given to Joshua (Deut 3) forms the concluding topic to the conversations, the place of Joshua in each conversation is quite different. In Numbers, Joshua's legitimacy is of prime importance and he is beneficiary of some of Moses' authority (Num 27:20), while in Deuteronomy 3, Joshua represents a necessary closure to Moses' leadership, a practicality insuring the finality of the *who-Moses-is-to-the-Lord* developed through the conversation.

In addition, the Numbers 27 and the Deuteronomy 32 parallels contain an important element not found in Deuteronomy 3. In Numbers 27, Moses is accused of rebelling against the Lord's word and did not "show my holiness before their eyes at the waters" (Num 27:14). Similarly, in Deuteronomy 32, Moses is said to have broken faith by failing to "maintain my holiness among the Israelites" (Deut 32:51). In Deuteronomy 3, the Lord is angry with Moses "on your (the Israelite's) account" and would not heed Moses. In Numbers 27 and Deuteronomy 32, Moses suffers because of his own failures. In Deuteronomy 3, Moses suffers on behalf of the nation.

The presentation of the Deuteronomy 3 conversation, in all its emotional intensity, is designed to encourage the empathetic identification of the audience. Moses is denied entrance to the Promised Land and suffers the Lord's anger because of his willingness to mediate on behalf of the nation now attentive to his address. The conversation is designed to create empathy with this tragic hero sprinkled with regret for causing the misfortune now suffered by Moses. These emotional attachments will be channeled into motivation for future action (Deut 4:1).[114] In this presentation, Moses seeks to impact the future relationship between the nation of Israel and the Lord. Reported conversational exchange was chosen as the venue for this motivational event because of the central role conversation plays in human relationships and in human Divine relationships.

---

114. MacDonald summarizes the contribution of the piece as articulating four main themes that will recur throughout Deuteronomy: Divine presence, human obedience, election, and the land. MacDonald, "Literary Criticism," 214–23.

6

Balaam, Joshua, and the Judges

THE CONVERSATIONAL PRAYERS INVOLVING Balaam, Joshua, and the Judges are remarkable for the inclusion of surprising and sometimes miraculous consequential activity. Talking donkeys, military defeat, burning rocks, and even the stilling of the sun in its march across the sky all accompany the conversational prayers in this section. Yet, most remarkably it isn't the miraculous that captures attention—it is the conversational prayer, itself, that remains the focus of attention. The truly amazing is a conversational prayer with God.

The tendency of the conversational prayers with Balaam, Joshua, and the Judges is to emphasize the *who-we-are-to-one-another*, the standing between the conversational participants, above the *what*, or the topic and outcome, of the prayer. A notable aspect of this emphasis on the *who-we-are-to-God* in conversational prayer is that these prayers include Israelite and non-Israelite alike. Abimelech (from Genesis), Balaam, Joshua, or Gideon; it seems to make no difference to God. The groupings by which we tend to identify and discriminate among ourselves are, in these prayers, of no importance to God. All are given access to Deity through conversational prayer and more, Deity is free to converse with anyone at any time, whether expected and welcomed or not.

Numbers 22:9–35: Balaam

A: [9] God came to Balaam and said, "Who are these men with you?"

B: [10] Balaam said to God, "King Balak son of Zippor of Moab, has sent me this message: [11] 'A people has come out of Egypt and has spread over the face of the earth; now come, curse them for me; perhaps I shall be able to fight against them and drive them out.'"

A¹: ¹² God said to Balaam, "You shall not go with them; you shall not curse the people, for they are blessed."

B¹: ¹³ *So Balaam rose in the morning, and said to the officials of Balak, "Go to your own land, for the Lord has refused to let me go with you."*

¹⁴ *So the officials of Moab rose and went to Balak, and said, "Balaam refuses to come with us."* ¹⁵ Once again Balak sent officials, more numerous and more distinguished than these. ¹⁶ They came to Balaam and said to him, "Thus says Balak son of Zippor: 'Do not let anything hinder you from coming to me; ¹⁷ for I will surely do you great honor, and whatever you say to me I will do; come, curse this people for me.'" ¹⁸ But Balaam replied to the servants of Balak, "Although Balak were to give me his house full of silver and gold, I could not go beyond the command of the Lord my God, to do less or more. ¹⁹ You remain here, as the others did, so that I may learn what more the Lord may say to me."

A²: ²⁰ That night God came to Balaam and said to him, "If the men have come to summon you, get up and go with them; but do only what I tell you to do."

B²: ²¹ *So Balaam got up in the morning, saddled his donkey, and went with the officials of Moab.*

²² *God's anger was kindled because he was going, and the angel of the Lord took his stand in the road as his adversary. Now he was riding on the donkey, and his two servants were with him.* ²³ *The donkey saw the angel of the Lord standing in the road, with a drawn sword in his hand; so the donkey turned off the road, and went into the field; and Balaam struck the donkey, to turn it back onto the road.* ²⁴ *Then the angel of the Lord stood in a narrow path between the vineyards, with a wall on either side.* ²⁵ *When the donkey saw the angel of the Lord, it scraped against the wall, and scraped Balaam's foot against the wall; so he struck it again.* ²⁶ *Then the angel of the Lord went ahead, and stood in a narrow place, where there was no way to turn either to the right or to the left.* ²⁷ *When the donkey saw the angel of the Lord, it lay down under Balaam; and Balaam's anger was kindled, and he struck the donkey with his staff.* ²⁸ *Then the Lord opened the mouth of the donkey, and it said to Balaam, "What have I done to you, that you have struck me these three times?"* ²⁹ *Balaam*

said to the donkey, "Because you have made a fool of me! I wish I had a sword in my hand! I would kill you right now!" ³⁰ *But the donkey said to Balaam, "Am I not your donkey, which you have ridden all your life to this day? Have I been in the habit of treating you this way?" And he said, "No."* ³¹ *Then the Lord opened the eyes of Balaam, and he saw the angel of the Lord standing in the road, with his drawn sword in his hand; and he bowed down, falling on his face.*

A³: ³² The angel of the Lord said to him, "Why have you struck your donkey these three times? I have come out as an adversary, because your way is perverse¹ before me. ³³ The donkey saw me, and turned away from me these three times. If it had not turned away from me, surely just now I would have killed you and let it live."

B³: ³⁴ Then Balaam said to the angel of the Lord, "I have sinned, for I did not know that you were standing in the road to oppose me. Now therefore, if it is displeasing to you, I will return home."

A⁴: ³⁵ The angel of the Lord said to Balaam, "Go with the men; but speak only what I tell you to speak."

B⁴: *So Balaam went on with the officials of Balak.*

Context

The most amazing thing about this conversation is that it seems so normal. Balaam has been approached by servants of Balak, king of Moab, in order to secure his assistance in cursing Israel because of his fear of the Israelite newcomers to his territory. Curious as to the identity of the emissaries, God comes to Balaam, in a nighttime visit, and asks him about his guests. Balaam accurately and fully explains their identity and what they want. God orders Balaam not to cooperate with Balak. In the morning, Balaam does as God commands, telling his visitors, "Go to your own land, for the Lord has refused to let me go with you." Undeterred, Balak sends a second group to Balaam, more distinguished than the first, asking once again for Balaam to come and assist him against Israel. Once again, God comes to Balaam in a dream, this time ordering Balaam to accompany the men but to do only as he commands.² Balaam complies with God's directive, saddling his donkey,

---

1. Heb. uncertain.

2. The inconsistencies in the story have been explained in a variety of manners. See Budd, *Numbers*, 256–63; Moberly, "Learning to Be a True Prophet," 14.

and setting out with the men sent by Balak. Whereupon, God must have had a change of heart for he becomes angry with Balaam and the angel of the LORD appears as an adversary[3] to Balaam. Balaam is blind to the presence of the angel of the LORD, while his donkey sees clearly and does what he can to avoid the imminent danger threatening his master. After three attempts to avoid the danger, and thinking that his donkey is simply being obstinate, Balaam strikes the donkey with his staff, at which the LORD opens the donkey's mouth and he protests his master's cruelty by asking, "What have I done to you, that you have struck me these three times?" Showing absolutely no surprise, Balaam begins a conversation with his donkey. Skillfully, the donkey employs reverse polarity questions[4] designed to elicit a dispreferred response from Balaam, removing any defense he may offer for his behavior, and forcing Balaam to admit his own error. At which point, the LORD opened Balaam's eyes, allowing him to see the angel of the LORD standing with sword drawn. Whether in response to the Divine presence or the drawn sword, Balaam falls to the ground. Balaam admits that he has sinned, for, he offers, "I did not know that you were standing in the road to oppose me" (22:34). He then offers to return home. The angel of the LORD seems to change his mind again, telling Balaam to continue on his journey, and directing Balaam to only speak "what I tell you to speak" (22:35).[5]

This strange encounter, including the prayer of 22:32–35, is unnecessary for the plot of the larger narrative. The directive given to Balaam by the angel of the LORD in 22:35 is essentially the same as given to Balaam by God in 22:20. The story could easily have progressed from 22:20 directly to v. 36. The intervening episode, with the threatening angel of the LORD and talking donkey, plays no further part in the story, is never mentioned again, and seems to interrupt the progression of the plot by diverting attention away from the plight of the invading Israelite nation. So, why is it

---

3. לשטן the same root from which "Satan" is derived. See also 1 Chr 21:1.

4. A polarity question is a question framed for a *yes-no* response, often formed from a corresponding assertion. The donkey asks, "Am I not your donkey?" a question form of the assertion, "I am your donkey." A reverse polarity question, in this case, forces Balaam to recognize his error and come to agreement with the donkey. For more on polarity questions, see Hayano, "Question Design in Conversation," 396–98; Clift, *Conversation Analysis*, 207–10.

5. Even though the conversational series begins with God as participant in the nighttime visit (notice a dream venue is not specified), and identified as the LORD by Balaam to the emissaries from Balak (22:8), the conversation changes to involve the angel of the LORD beginning with 22:32. Balaam doesn't seem to differentiate between God, the LORD, or the angel of the LORD.

here? What does the prayer of 22:32–35 and the surrounding inter-species conversation add to the passage?[6]

Perhaps it's in the beginning and ending that the purpose of the story is found. The story allows the repetition of God's command to Balaam to "do only what I tell you to do" (22:20) and from the angel of the LORD to speak "what I tell you to speak" (22:35).[7] Through mortal threat from the angel of the LORD and a unique deliverance accomplished by a donkey, the story places Balaam in a contingent position without agency, unable to act without direction from another. This lack of agency is key in the episode to follow as the theme of "speaking only what the LORD tells him" will be repeated over and over (23:5, 12, 16, 19, 26; 24:13).

Structure

If the purpose of the section 22:22–35, including the conversational prayer of 22:32–35, is to present Balaam without agency, it is remarkable that the conversation itself is structured exactly to accomplish the same purpose. The conversation in this section is constructed in two rounds of conversational activity between the angel of the LORD and Balaam.

Round One

The first round begins with a question: "Why have you struck your donkey these three times?" (22:32). Just as in the conversation with the donkey (2:28), Balaam is on the receiving end of a question, a question that requires him to answer an implied accusation and so establish status with his conversational partner. And, just like the conversation with the donkey (22:30), defense is impossible, and Balaam must assume a subordinate position of status relative to his conversational partner, this time, under threat of death (22:33). In response to the angel's question, Balaam replies: "I have sinned" (22:34) presumably in his ill treatment of the donkey, for it has not yet been established that journeying on to meet Balak is offensive. In sinning against his donkey, Balaam's status is effectively reduced even further in the conversation with the angel of the LORD. Balaam has already fallen to the ground on his face before the angel of the LORD (22:31). Now Balaam must admit that even the donkey has more integrity and standing before the angel, for

---

6. The same question posed by Frisch, "Story of Balaam's She-Ass," 103, 111. Frisch explains that the episode effects a potential change for Balaam's character not his circumstances (111).

7. See Moyer, "Who Is the Prophet, and Who the Ass?," 181–82.

he has sinned against the donkey and could not see what was plain to the beast on which he was riding (22:34), confirming his own statement to the donkey, "you have made a fool of me" (22:29).[8] Following his admission of guilt, and so recognition of reduced standing before the angel of the LORD, Balaam seeks some level of restoration, offering to return home, if continuing on with the men sent by Balak, is "displeasing to you" (22:34). Pleasing the angel of the LORD is the main concern, and whether to journey on or not is simply the means to achieve that restored status.

Round Two

The angel of the LORD replies to Balaam's offer to return home with a dispreferred response, commanding him to continue on but to speak "only what I tell you to speak" (22:35).[9] The dispreferred response, without explanation or mitigation, in the form of a command demanding Balaam's subordinate role is quite powerful in concluding this conversational prayer. Balaam will have a role to play in the unfolding drama to follow, but that role will be carefully scripted. Having established the fact of Balaam's subordinate standing and lack of independent agency, he is free to continue on the journey, and the narrator is free to continue on with the plot of the story.

Who-We-Are-to-God

There are numerous facets of this conversational prayer that appear bewildering and contradictory. Certainly, there is enough here to explain Balaam's confusion and perplexity. Balaam emerges from the encounter a changed man. Humbled by both his donkey and the angel of the LORD, Balaam can have no idea that something much bigger is happening through this conversational prayer.[10] Subsequent to this encounter, Balaam will deliver a series of four oracles (Num 23–24) he receives from God (23:19; 24:4, 16), the Most High (24:16), the Almighty (24:4, 16), who is also the LORD

---

8. While beyond evidence in the text of Numbers, establishing agency and status for Balaam may have been of interest to the narrator as Balaam is a character of international recognition and therefore important to establish Balaam acting, in at least this instance, at the command of YHWH. See Hackett, *The Balaam Text from Deir 'Alla*. Also suggested by Heckl, "Balaam," 9.

9. Expressed emphatically through the inclusion of the pronominal object (אתו). Wendland, "Two Dumb Donkeys Declare the Word of the LORD," 177.

10. The connections to the larger literary unit are described by Wendland, "Two Dumb Donkeys Declare the Word of the LORD," 171. The humiliating results of the episode are summarized by Wendland, "Balaam becomes the ass of the LORD" (178).

their (Israel's) God (23:21). These oracles will describe the destiny of the nations within the orb of Balaam's horizon. Balaam's experience of submissive contingency, susceptible to the acts of God, will serve as a model for the nations. The *what* of the prayer, either continuing the journey or returning home, is overshadowed by the status relationship developed between the conversational partners. Balaam's standing with Deity assures that he will only speak as directed by God and in so doing function as the catalyst for national events beyond his imagining.[11]

Joshua 7:6–16: The Defeat at Ai

⁶ Then Joshua tore his clothes, and fell to the ground on his face before the ark of the Lord until the evening, he and the elders of Israel; and they put dust on their heads.

A: ⁷ Joshua said, "Ah, Lord God! Why have you brought this people across the Jordan at all, to hand us over to the Amorites so as to destroy us? Would that we had been content to settle beyond the Jordan! ⁸ O Lord, what can I say, now that Israel has turned their backs to their enemies! ⁹ The Canaanites and all the inhabitants of the land will hear of it, and surround us, and cut off our name from the earth. Then what will you do for your great name?"

B: ¹⁰ The Lord said to Joshua, "Stand up! Why have you fallen upon your face? ¹¹ Israel has sinned; they have transgressed my covenant that I imposed on them. They have taken some of the devoted things; they have stolen, they have acted deceitfully, and they have put them among their own belongings. ¹² Therefore the Israelites are unable to stand before their enemies; they turn their backs to their enemies, because they have become a thing devoted for destruction themselves. I will be with you no more, unless you destroy the devoted things from among you. ¹³ Proceed to sanctify the people, and say, 'Sanctify yourselves for tomorrow; for thus says the Lord, the God of Israel, "There are devoted things among you, O Israel; you will be unable to stand before your enemies until you take away the devoted things from among you." ¹⁴ In the morning therefore you shall come forward tribe by tribe. The tribe that the Lord takes shall come near by clans, the clan that the Lord takes shall come near by households, and the household that the Lord takes shall come

---

11. An alternate tradition is preserved in Josh 24:10. There, God does not listen to Balaam and Balaam's presumptive curse is tuned into a blessing.

near one by one. ¹⁵ And the one who is taken as having the devoted things shall be burned with fire, together with all that he has, for having transgressed the covenant of the LORD, and for having done an outrageous thing in Israel."

A¹: ¹⁶ *So Joshua rose early in the morning, and brought Israel near tribe by tribe, and the tribe of Judah was taken.*

Context

Under Joshua's leadership, Israel has suffered a military defeat. Israel's attack force has been routed by the men of Ai, who chased the fleeing Israelites away from their city and killed about thirty-six of the frightened Israelites. The resultant despondency that swept through the Israelite camp was all the greater because of the confidence felt leading into the engagement with Ai.[12]

Equally significant to the setup for the conversation between Joshua and the LORD, but unseen, was that the Israelites broke faith and the anger of the LORD burned against Israel.[13] Not privy to this hidden dynamic, Joshua and the elders of Israel are devastated, bewildered, and stricken with anguish. Expressing their sorrow by tearing their clothes, falling to the ground[14] before the ark of the LORD, and covering their heads with dust, Joshua and the elders[15] remain prostrate until evening when, finally, Joshua prays.

In a visible act of contrition and sorrow, Joshua and the elders fall to the ground before the ark of the LORD.[16] The ark plays no further role in the episode and its mention here is to help establish the status between the conversational participants. Joshua has assumed a position of subservience and grief. The LORD is represented by an instrument of holiness and power while Joshua and the elders appear humble and helpless. The conversation to follow is not between equals or, as was so often with Moses, unmediated and familiar.

---

12. Joshua Berman understands this "bloated sense of self-confidence" shared by the whole nation but articulated by the spies (Josh 7:3), the heart of the dilemma in the defeat at Ai. Berman, "Making of the Sin of Achan," 128.

13. A helpful discussion of corporate responsibility can be found in Kaminsky, *Corporate Responsibility in the Hebrew Bible*; Clements, "Achan's Sin," 120–22.

14. Once before, Joshua has fallen to the ground on his face (5:14). Then, it was out respect for the commander of the army of the LORD.

15. This the first time the "elders" appear in Joshua, undoubtedly present to signify a national lament.

16. This detail is missing in LXX.

Conversational Round

This conversational prayer is constructed in one round followed by consequential activity. Within the conversation both, the topic of conversation and the status of the participants, are dynamic, helping to shape the conversational activity. The status of participants changes drastically yet, remains unsettled at the conclusion of the conversation.

Joshua Turn

The Joshua direct address contains familiar themes. The military defeat before the men of Ai will, in Joshua's opinion, only escalate as word of the defeat spreads to the Canaanites and all the inhabitants of the land. The Israelites will be surrounded by hostile forces and Israel's name will be cut off from the earth. The consequences of this loss will be devastating for the honor of the LORD's "great name." Threat to Israel's existence, resulting in insult from the inhabitants of the land, will lead to the LORD's defamation. The same pattern for petition in prayer is found in Exodus 32 and Numbers 14.

Joshua's direct speech begins with an inarticulate guttural sigh (Ah!)[17] born of grief and despair (7:7). Quickly, Joshua's desperation gives way to abandonment, for in an emphatic fashion (Why have you . . . ?) Joshua holds the LORD responsible for the predicament now facing Israel.[18] Yet, given Joshua's confrontational disposition, no request is made of the LORD in the prayer.[19] Rather than negotiating Divine action, the conversational activity from Joshua is designed to allow the LORD's conversational response.[20]

LORD Turn

The LORD's response (vv. 10–15) to Joshua's direct speech does not share the immediacy or emotional strength of that expressed by Joshua. Instead, the LORD's conversational activity is more like a monologue. The LORD's direct speech is in the form of a dispreferred response to Joshua, but allows no

---

17. Used also in Judg 6:22; 11:35; 2 Kgs 3:10; 6:5, 15. In prayer see Jer 4:10; 32:17; Ezek 9:8.

18. See GKC §113x. LXX mitigates the LORD's responsibility by reading: "Why did your servant bring this people . . . ?" See Soggin, *Joshua*, 93.

19. A similar strong emotional outburst is followed by a specific request from Moses in Num 12:13.

20. Richard Nelson recognizes the conversation "composed specifically for this particular literary context." Nelson, *Joshua*, 104.

opportunity for repair or clarification, even though it alters the status of the conversational partners and changes the flow of conversation, inserting unexpected elements into the topic. Other than the command in 7:10, the Lord's direct address shows very little recipient design.[21]

While Joshua's conversational activity is motivated by military threat, The Lord's direct response to Joshua is dominated by the restoration of status—first for Joshua and then for the sinful nation. In the Lord's direct speech, Joshua's initial question is matched by a command and a question of his own. Joshua is ordered to "Stand up!" (7:10). Joshua's disposition of grief and despair, expressed by his prostration is unacceptable to the Lord, signified so by the question "Why have you fallen upon your face?" (7:10). Joshua and the nation have not been abandoned by the Lord. Instead, the nation, by their own actions, has "become a thing devoted for destruction themselves" (7:12), absent the Divine Presence unless the illicitly obtained "devoted things" be destroyed from among them (7:12). The Lord explains that, through the actions of those yet unknown, devoted booty is being concealed,[22] making the whole nation devoted for destruction, evidenced in the rout before the men of Ai.

The logic of the Lord's response raises questions. If the removal of the contagion is the goal, it seems that it could be accomplished much more directly. The fact of illicit booty in the midst of the nation is revealed by the Lord to Joshua in the conversational activity, but the identity of those responsible (presumably also known to the Lord) must be discovered through the casting of lots. Why didn't the Lord simply tell Joshua where to look? Or, why wait until after the failed engagement with the men of Ai? Why did the thirty-six innocent men need to die? The removal of the things devoted, could have occurred much earlier.[23]

If, however, the process of sanctification involving all, both the innocent and the guilty, is the real goal of the conversational activity, then the Lord's response makes perfect sense.[24] Verse 13 (not present in LXX) forms a parallel to v. 9 and summarizes the consequential activity by one command: sanctify

---

21. The lack of recipient design suggests the conversation is created by the narrator and fulfills a rhetorical function apart from the direct communication to Joshua.

22. Berman argues that "contagion" terminology is missing in Joshua 7. Berman, "Making of the Sin of Achan," 118–21.

23. The ethical problems introduced in this story are addressed by Berman, "Making of the Sin of Achan," 115. For Clements, "it is difficult to find within the story of Achan's sin any residual merit or moral lesson." Clements, "Achan's Sin," 125.

24. The notion of corporate responsibility may be reinforced through the MT use of singular and plural pronouns beginning in v. 13.

yourselves. The process of identifying the guilty individual will involve the sanctification—the cleansing—of the whole nation.

Like so many other conversational prayers in the Hebrew Bible, the *who-we-are-to-one-another* between the conversational participants drives and shapes the *what* of the conversation and the *how* of the conversation. Here, the exclusive relationship between the Lord and Israel is reinforced through the expected shared moral character quality. This moral intersubjectivity, for good or ill, is a direct condition for and consequence of conversation with God.

In this conversational prayer, both parties of the conversation felt estranged, separated from the other conversational participant because of a disruption in that moral intersubjectivity. Joshua and the elders were devastated by what they thought to be God's abandonment and God, too, felt the weight of Israel's transgression. The repair of this breach in an interpersonal relationship began with talk.

Joshua 10:12–14: The Lord Listened to Joshua

¹² *On the day when the Lord gave the Amorites over to the Israelites, Joshua spoke to the Lord; and he said in the sight of Israel,*

A: "Sun, stand still at Gibeon,
and Moon, in the valley of Aijalon."

B: ¹³ And the sun stood still, and the moon stopped,
until the nation took vengeance on their enemies.

Is this not written in the Book of Jashar? The sun stopped in midheaven, and did not hurry to set for about a whole day. ¹⁴ *There has been no day like it before or since, when the Lord heeded a human voice; for the Lord fought for Israel.*

Context

The conversational activity inserted into this narrative,[25] comes to us mediated. The presumptive conversational activity is presented in the form of a poem[26] (song), quoted from a source—the Book of Jashar.[27] Consequently, if an actual conversation resides behind the preserved song, that conversation

---

25. See Leonard-Fleckman, "Stones from Heaven and Celestial Tricks," 386–87.
26. See Boling and Wright, *Joshua*, 283.
27. Giles and Doan, *Twice Used Songs*, 25–27.

has been so restructured as to make its recovery impossible.[28] The portion of the Joshua address preserved in this conversational prayer, lifted from the Book of Jasher, is recontextualized to now apply to a singular setting, the day when the LORD gave the Amorites over to Israel.

Structure

The conversational activity comprising this short exchange is structured in the form of one round; direct speech by Joshua followed by consequential activity from the LORD in response to Joshua's address. It's the editorial comment in v. 14 (the LORD heeded a human voice) that allows us to consider this short address as conversational prayer. And this point was important to the editor of the piece. Joshua utilizes a previously known poem or song, taken from a recognizable source, now employed to address the LORD. It seems that, for the editor of Joshua 10,[29] the important thing to remember is not the words of the conversational activity, but that those words, now in the form of a song, were uttered in conversation (*Joshua spoke to the Lord*).

Consequential Activity

There are significant literary issues raised by the insertion of this song in the narrative of Joshua 10 and a variety of settings have been suggested for the original composition of the song,[30] none of which need occupy us here. Instead, it is fascinating to think that the editor, while commenting on this episode, doesn't consider the stilling of the sun or the moon as the remarkable feature—but that *"the Lord heeded a human voice."*[31] That the events were the consequential activity of a conversation between a human and the

---

28. Some consider the poem to be hundreds of years older than the narrative in which it now resides. Holladay, "Day(s) the *Moon* Stood Still," 166–78; Boling and Wright, *Joshua*, 282.

29. See the compositional note by Trebolle, "Division Markers as Empirical Evidence," 190. Ed Noort suggests this episode may the climax of the book as a whole. Noort, "Joshua and Copernicus," 387–89.

30. See Dozeman, *Joshua 1–12*, 440–45; Kratz, *Composition of the Narrative Books*, 201.

31. *Heard* or *listened to* (שמע). Despite the claim of uniqueness in 10:14, Deity also heeds humans in Gen 30:17, 22; Num 21:3; Deut 10:10; Judg 13:9; 2 Kg 13:4; 2 Chr 30:30.

LORD[32] is more notable than the events themselves, even if those events are as singular as the stilling of the sun in its march across the sky![33]

And that conversation was conducted in the sight of Israel (10:12). The conversation is remembered as a public event, inviting others to witness and affirm the power of conversational prayer. The public nature of the event, while certainly enhancing the reputation of Joshua, becomes aspirational as others seek a similar engagement with God.

Judges 6:12–24: Gideon

Judges 6:12–7:11 is composed in a series of four conversations between Deity and Gideon, separated by narrative describing events related to the conversations.[34] These conversations between Gideon and Deity are remarkable for several reasons and appear at a pivotal point in the book of Judges, unfolding a prescriptive description of the LORD's relationship to Israel.[35] Although all four conversations are related topically, they are separated within the prose narrative and only the first is considered conversational prayer, including direct conversational activity, a topic initiated by the human participant and a petition met with a Divine response.

Conversation One

[11] *Now the angel of the Lord came and sat under the oak at Ophrah, which belonged to Joash the Abiezrite, as his son Gideon was beating out wheat in the wine press, to hide it from the Midianites.*

A: [12] The angel of the LORD appeared to him and said to him, "The LORD is with you, you mighty warrior."

B: [13] Gideon answered him, "But sir, if the LORD is with us, why then has all this happened to us? And where are all his wonderful deeds that our ancestors recounted to us, saying, 'Did not

---

32. Observed also by Leonard-Fleckman, "Stones from Heaven and Celestial Tricks," 400–401.

33. The event is sometimes postulated as a solar eclipse which, plausibly, may have taken place on October 30, 1207 BCE. See Vainstub, "Miracle of the Sun and Moon," 25–26.

34. Conversation two in one round 6:25–25. Conversation three in two rounds 6:36–40. Conversation four in five rounds 7:2–11.

35. For the role of Judges 6 in the rhetorical design of the book, see Martin, "Narrative Function of the Nameless Prophet," 137; Milstein, "Delusions of Grandeur," 214–25.

the LORD bring us up from Egypt?' But now the LORD has cast us off, and given us into the hand of Midian."

A¹: ¹⁴ Then the LORD turned to him and said, "Go in this might of yours and deliver Israel from the hand of Midian; I hereby commission you."

B¹: ¹⁵ He responded, "But sir, how can I deliver Israel? My clan is the weakest in Manasseh, and I am the least in my family."

A²: ¹⁶ The LORD said to him, "But I will be with you,³⁶ and you shall strike down the Midianites, every one of them."

B²: ¹⁷ Then he said to him, "If now I have found favor with you, then show me a sign that it is you who speak with me. ¹⁸ Do not depart from here until I come to you, and bring out my present, and set it before you."

A³: And he said, "I will stay until you return."

B³: *¹⁹ So Gideon went into his house and prepared a kid, and unleavened cakes from an ephah of flour; the meat he put in a basket, and the broth he put in a pot, and brought them to him under the oak and presented them.*

A⁴: ²⁰ The angel of God said to him, "Take the meat and the unleavened cakes, and put them on this rock, and pour out the broth."

B⁴: *And he did so.*

²¹ *Then the angel of the Lord reached out the tip of the staff that was in his hand, and touched the meat and the unleavened cakes; and fire sprang up from the rock and consumed the meat and the unleavened cakes; and the angel of the Lord vanished from his sight.*

A⁵: ²² Then Gideon perceived that it was the angel of the LORD; and Gideon said, "Help me, Lord God! For I have seen the angel of the LORD face to face."

B⁵: ²³ But the LORD said to him, "Peace be to you; do not fear, you shall not die."

---

36. Boling translates: "Because Ehyeh is with you," translating the verbal form as a variant of the personal name of God. Boling, *Judges*, 132. See also Freedman, "Name of the God of Moses," 151–56.

A⁶: ²⁴ *Then Gideon built an altar there to the Lord, and called it, The Lord is peace. To this day it still stands at Ophrah, which belongs to the Abiezrites.*

Storytelling

Gideon's conversational prayer is contextualized within the seven-year Midianite oppression suffered by the Israelites, having done "evil in the sight of the LORD" (6:1). Crying out for relief to the LORD, the God of Israel responds to the nation by sending a prophet with a message recounting the miraculous release from slavery in Egypt, defeat of all that opposed them in Canaan, and possession of the Canaanite land (6:8–10). This recital of Divine beneficence and Presence among the people of Israel becomes the core of Gideon's complaint as he asks:

> But sir, if the LORD is with us, why then has all this happened to us? And where are all his wonderful deeds that our ancestors recounted to us, saying, "Did not the LORD bring us up from Egypt?" (6:13)

The exodus story, embodying Gideon's understanding of the LORD's character and his relationship with the people of Israel, is at odds with Gideon's experience. The stories about "all his wonderful deeds that our ancestors recounted to us" formed a national narrative, now in question because of the disconcerting events of the past seven years. In the conversation, Gideon uses the story as shorthand to summarize his understanding of the LORD, God of Israel. Either the stories are not true, or God has abandoned his own people. The story of the past brings into sharp focus Gideon's disappointment in the present.

Status

One of the most prominent features of this segmented conversational prayer is the developing status between the conversational partners. Although the reader is aware of the identity of the conversationalists, Gideon becomes aware that he is addressing God only in round six of the segmented conversation.

Status is implicit in the opening of the conversation. The angel of the LORD appears to Gideon and establishes Gideon's status by declaring:

The LORD is with you (singular)

You mighty man of valor

The compliment paid to Gideon seems to go right past him and Gideon seems to miss the point. The affirmation of status (the LORD is with you—*Gideon*) is met with a dispreferred response, challenging the truthfulness of the LORD's presence with us (*Israel*). The status assigned to Gideon is not immediately received, allowing the progression of the conversation in rounds two through six. Gideon uses the angel of the LORD's opening statement to introduce the dilemma that will drive the plot of the following narrative. Gideon does not accept his assigned status and does not know the identity (status) of his conversational partner. The next several turns of the conversation sift out this identity problem.

Interestingly, the variable way in which the Deity is known is consistent throughout the conversational rounds. The changing references to Deity help mark off rounds in this conversation.[37]

- 6:12-24—angel of the LORD (angel of God in v. 21)[38] and LORD (LORD God in v. 22)
- 6:25-27—LORD
- 6:36-40—God
- 7:2-11—LORD

The first part of the conversation between Gideon and Deity is a three-way conversation: Gideon, the angel of the LORD, and the LORD. Boling concludes that at 6:14, the LORD "catches up" with his messenger (angel of the LORD) and a three way conversation follows.[39] In v. 21 the angel of the LORD vanishes from Gideon's sight, yet Gideon can immediately address his conversational partner—now as LORD God without any reappearing and the LORD can respond to Gideon's direct address. Literally, 6:21 has the angel of the LORD "walking away from his [Gideon's] eyes." More than simply unseen, but still present (as is the LORD), the angel of

---

37. Source critics have identified some of the same sections as independent episodes now woven into one narrative. Soggin, *Judges*, 104. See also Rofé, "Lo studio testo biblico," 140. While this may be true, the present structure of the narrative, and most importantly, the identifications assigned to the conversationalists, adds to the structure and impact of the conversational prayer.

38. LXX retains "angel of the LORD."

39. Boling, *Judges*, 131. Soggin, maintains the references used here are interchangeable, and only one Divine personage is present. Soggin, *Judges*, 114.

the LORD is now unseen and no longer present, no longer a continuing participant in the conversation.

Round One

Without introduction, and without any reaction from Gideon (surprise, astonishment, fear, etc.), the angel of the LORD appears[40] to Gideon and pronounces: "The LORD is with you." This initial statement of status functions to drive the conversation as Gideon responds in a dispreferred manner with a question, challenging the fact of the LORD's presence. The conversation seems to be structured to emphasize the centrality of this one topic: the question of the LORD's presence. The conversation begins between Gideon and the angel of the LORD, who converse about the presence of a third party—the LORD, himself. The angel of the LORD begins the conversation by stating that: "He [the LORD] is with you [Gideon]." Gideon replies effectively saying: "No—He isn't. He has thrown us [Israel] aside as our circumstances indicate" (6:13).

Round Two

At which point, the LORD, himself, breaks into the conversation at round two (6:14-15). As at the beginning of the conversation in 6:12, Gideon, once again, shows no reaction to the sudden presence of a new conversational partner. The LORD doesn't immediately address Gideon's dispreferred response of v. 13, but instead, commands Gideon in activity designed to change the circumstances by which Gideon concluded the LORD's absence. That command is answered with a second dispreferred response, again in the form of a question and self-deprecation, designed to lessen the confrontation embedded in the dispreferred response (6:15).

Round Three

Now, met with a second dispreferred response, the LORD directly answers Gideon's protest of 6:13 (Divine absence) with a direct affirmation "I will be with you" (6:16)[41] first voiced by the angel of the LORD in 6:12. The

---

40. The same introduction is used prefacing conversations with Abraham, Jacob and in Numbers (generally not so in Exodus) with Moses. The verb ראה is commonly rendered "to see," but when applied to Deity is frequently translated "appear."

41. Boling understands this as a variant on the personal name of God: אהיה.

LORD's statement is brief but powerful. Only two words, and perhaps bringing to mind a similar promise to Moses in Exod 3:12. The LORD's promise of his presence with Gideon is emphatic.[42] Oddly, this evokes yet a third dispreferred response, this time in Gideon's need for confirmation that he is actually speaking with the LORD. And further, in his request, asking the LORD not to go away!

Round Four

Gideon devises a plan whereby the status between the two conversational partners will be made clear (6:17). In 6:18, the LORD assures Gideon that he will stay present, while Gideon goes off to prepare an offering. The offering functions as consequential activity jointly understood as an expression of personal status between the conversationalists as negotiated through the conversation.

Round Five

At this point, the angel of God (v. 20, and the angel of the LORD in v. 21–22) reenters the conversation, instructing Gideon how to present the offering or gift. The fluidity of the Divine conversational partners is remarkable. At this point, Gideon is still unconvinced of the true nature of the status which has been negotiated in the preceding conversation. When Gideon finished doing as he was instructed, the angel of the LORD extends the staff he has been holding in his hand. He touches the food with the tip of the staff, at which fire springs up, consuming the offering, and He, the angel of the LORD, "walks away from Gideon's sight."[43] Ironically, when Gideon finally comes to full understanding as to the identity of his conversational partner—that partner leaves. Divine presence is confirmed even while Divine absence is observed. This paradox is central to the whole episode.

Boling, *Judges*, 132.

42. Emphatic כ suffix on עם strengthening the fact of the Deity's presence with Gideon. Gideon does seem to authentically search for Divine assurance throughout the episode. Scherer, "Gideon," 270.

43. Translated "vanished from his sight" in NRSV.

Round Six

Gideon is finally convinced that he has been in the presence of the angel of the LORD and is overcome by sudden fear, afraid that he will now die, having seen the angel of the LORD "face to face" (6:22). Gideon addresses the LORD God by means of an urgent plea: Help me! (v. 22). He is finally convinced that Deity is present—answering his initial objection of v. 13, but the consequence of that Presence is not what Gideon had expected. He now fears for his life and approaches the LORD God out of desperate need. Gideon's acknowledged dependency upon the LORD God is a quality of the shared interpersonal status between Gideon and the LORD that had not been part of Gideon's conversation until now.

Even as the angel of the LORD departs, the LORD God is still immediately present, and Gideon is able to speak to him directly. Oddly, the presence of the LORD, himself, doesn't seem to be a cause for fear or even astonishment as was generated by the angel of the LORD. At v. 23 the LORD reenters the conversation, calming Gideon's fears, reassuring him that he will not die, and offering to him peace. That peace Gideon commemorates in a monumental altar named appropriately: The LORD is Peace. Divine presence evokes Gideon's fear but results in Gideon's peace. The altar remains ("to this day it still stands," v. 24), a lasting consequence of Gideon's conversational prayer. The Divine Presence, evoking fear, but resulting in peace is made concrete and tangible, "to this day."

The Who-We-Are-to-God

The central topic of the conversation is the presence of the LORD. In every round, the presence of the LORD is either explicitly stated or implied (v. 6:14 in round two). Presence is unusually signified for the conversational participants. The angel of the LORD appears (6:12) and vanishes (6:21). The LORD, himself, however, neither comes nor goes. He is present to Gideon in conversation without interruption, extending into the continuation of the conversation in 6:25–7:11. The question of the LORD's presence is still a concern in the later conversations of this episode. The symbolic representation of any other god or goddess must be removed (6:25–33) and the strength of the Israelite army must be severely limited so as to cast no doubt on the LORD's effective presence to win the victory over the Midianites (7:1–8).

Ah, Lord God![44]

Gideon's question, persistent throughout this conversational prayer is a question often heard in prayer: "Where is God?" "If he is present, why hasn't he acted in the same miraculous fashion that we've heard about from the past?" (6:13). Circumstances indicate that God isn't present—at least in any effective fashion. So, the petitioner is driven to pray. Yet, the act of prayer assumes God is present. And that's the dilemma with prayer, especially conversational prayer. Conversational prayer is an act of immediacy with God at the very moment when that immediacy is cast into doubt. So, why is this problem of God's presence addressed in conversation? Why isn't the problem solved by ritual or commemorative object[45] (even the altar built by Gideon commemorates peace, not presence) guaranteed to make the Deity present?

The problem of God's presence is addressed through conversation. Conversation is one of the most fundamental of human activities. When the ability to converse, to communicate, is lost, something is very wrong. But conversation is also beyond the individual's control. Even the most skilled conversationalist must be open to the authentic and unforeseen contribution of the other conversational participants. In conversation, we are speaker and spoken to—actor and acted upon. In conversation we engage and are engaged by a person, not an idea, or a wish, or a dream. In conversational prayer, our projection into the world around us meets its limits as it is bounded by the reality of the Thou. In conversation, all participants are susceptible to change as relationships of status and preference, access to knowledge, and disposition toward consequential activity are dynamic, impressing unforeseen demands on the conversational participants.

The fact that God is encountered in conversational prayer is remarkable—almost unbelievable. God willingly and authentically makes himself susceptible, just like the human conversationalist, to the same dynamic forces of conversation. Could it be that just like with inter-human conversation—something is terribly wrong when we lose the ability to converse—so, too, something is terribly wrong when God stops communicating? This is the fundamental dilemma of prayer.

---

44. Josh 7:7; Jer 4:10; 14:13 32:17; Ezek 9:8.

45. Abraham also builds an altar (Gen 12:7) to commemorate an encounter with God. Jacob erects a pillar (Gen 28:22) to house God, but it plays no further role, eventually replaced by an altar (Gen 35:1) and a second pillar (Gen 35:14). These objects commemorate past encounters with God but have no power to produce a present encounter.

Judges 10:10–16: He Could No Longer Bear

A: ¹⁰ So the Israelites cried to the Lord, saying, "We have sinned against you, because we have abandoned our God and have worshiped the Baals."

B: ¹¹ And the Lord said to the Israelites, "Did I not deliver you[46] from the Egyptians and from the Amorites, from the Ammonites and from the Philistines? ¹² The Sidonians also, and the Amalekites, and the Maonites, oppressed you; and you cried to me, and I delivered you out of their hand. ¹³ Yet you have abandoned me and worshiped other gods; therefore I will deliver you no more. ¹⁴ Go and cry to the gods whom you have chosen; let them deliver you in the time of your distress."

A¹: ¹⁵ And the Israelites said to the Lord, "We have sinned; do to us whatever seems good to you; but deliver us this day!" ¹⁶ *So they put away the foreign gods from among them and worshiped the Lord;*

B¹: *and he could no longer bear to see Israel suffer.*

Context

This conversational activity is context specific. There is no doubt that this conversation is tailored to fit the narrative in which it is now embedded. The repetition of the word "abandoned" as well as mention of Ammonites, Amorites, and Philistines, both, in the narrative and the conversation, and the prominence given to the worship of other gods all tie this conversational activity to the narrative context.

This short conversational prayer, in Judges 10, presents Israel acting collectively to engage in conversation with the Lord. Having sinned against the Lord by worshipping the Baals and Astartes, the gods of the surrounding nations, they abandoned the Lord (10:6). As a result, the anger of the Lord was enflamed and he sold the Israelites into the hands of their enemies who crushed, oppressed, and distressed the Israelites for eighteen years (10:7–9). The cause and effect nature of the actions under consideration is clear, as is the active participation by both conversational partners: the Lord and the nation Israel. The narrative activity forms consequential actions stemming from a status relationship.

---

46. "Did I not deliver you" is missing in MT.

Structure

Composed in two rounds, the conversation displays a great deal of recipient design even though one participant in the conversation is an idealized construct, presenting the whole nation speaking with one voice and acting in concert.[47] The *how* of this exchange (collective Israel) is an intentional construction to accomplish rhetorical goals. Those goals include establishing a status intersubjectivity in which the Lord expresses a remarkable degree of empathy with his conversational partner.

Round One

The Israelites are confronted with unbearable foreign oppression, leading them to "cry" to the Lord. The conversational prayer is initiated by the Israelites, who, with one voice, address the Lord in direct speech. Yet, the oppression, the precipitating context for the prayer, finds no mention. Instead, their turn is an admission of misbehavior, (v. 10: "we have sinned against you, because we have abandoned our God and have worshipped the Baals") but includes no request directed to the Lord (not voiced until the end of the conversation, v. 15). The essence of the Israelite misconduct is that they have offended the Lord (sinned *against you*).

The break in interpersonal relationship forms the core of the Lord's dispreferred response. In response to Israel's cry, the Lord cites his previous deliverance of Israel when similar conditions of military threats faced the nation. Yet, the Lord contends, "you abandoned me and worshipped other gods." Therefore, the Lord will no longer deliver, telling the Israelites to "go cry to the gods you have chosen" and see if they will deliver you. The sense of personal abandonment is unmistakable. A deep relationship with the Lord has been broken by Israel's behavior and that change in status must be addressed before any consequential action is considered. The immediate and direct speech of the round enhances the interpersonal empathy and feeling of abandonment in a manner not possible through a prosaic description. The conversational round directs attention away from the idolatrous behavior or the military threat, focusing on the personal estrangement and feelings of abandonment felt by the Israelites, and more, felt by the Lord.

---

47. Emphasized by repeated mention: vv. 10, 11, 15.

Round Two

Round two is composed of a collective direct speech response by the Israelites, consequential activity from the Israelites, and consequential activity from the Lord. In response to the Lord's dispreferred response of round one, the Israelites offer a preferred response; repeating their confession ("we have sinned"), submitting to the prospect of punishment from the Lord, ("do to us whatever seems good to you"), and asking for immediate deliverance ("but deliver us today") (10:15). The request could have been included in the initial Israelite turn (v. 10) but is delayed until the status relationship is fully described by both conversational partners (the topic of round one, vv. 10–14). The national request is followed by consequential action whereby they remove the offending behavior (putting away the foreign gods) and resume a pattern of preferred relationship status (worshipped the Lord). The status altering consequential behavior from the Israelites is met with status altering behavior from the Lord—he could no longer bear to see Israel suffer (10:16).

Interpersonal Status

It is clear that this conversational activity recorded in Judges 10:10–16 is a literary construct.[48] The interaction between the Lord and the nation of Israel is portrayed in the form of a conversation in which all the people of the nation can converse as one participant, and the Lord is immediately present as a conversational partner to the whole nation. The observation that this is a literary construct begs the question—why? Why should the narrator interrupt the narrative activity with the insertion of this conversational prayer? What does the conversational prayer add to the plot? Precisely this—in the conversation a change of status between the conversationalists occurs that is more fundamental than the consequent military conflict in 10:17–11:33. This piece is more about the *who-we-are-to-one-another* of the conversation than it is about the *what* of the conversation.

---

48. First Samuel 12:10–17 apparently quotes part of this conversation, especially 1 Sam 12:10 quoting Judg 10:10, demonstrating verbal agreement with Judges 10 and indicating that either 1 Samuel knows of a Judges 10 tradition or both were dependent upon a common source. The Divine response, however, quoted by Samuel in 1 Samuel is updated, inserting Jephthah and either Samuel or Samson into the list of deliverance events occurring after Judges 10. Both use the verb עזבנו, translated by NRSV as "abandoned" in Judg 10:10 and "forsaken" in 1 Sam 12:10. Both also use the verb הצילנו, translated by NRSV as "deliver" in Judg 10:15 and "rescue" in 1 Sam 12:10.

And it is significant that this conversation effects a change in status for both Israel and the LORD. Israel puts away the implements devoted to rival gods and so seeks restoration with the LORD. But, the LORD changes just as much as Israel. The LORD "could no longer bear to see Israel suffer" (10:16).[49] The conversation allows the personal and intimate expression of Divine empathy, remorse, and perhaps guilt[50] not possible without the conversation. In developing an empathetic intersubjectivity, both conversational partners move. Both are deeply impacted by the words of the other. The LORD's expression of abandonment and empathy give hint to the value placed by God on interpersonal relationships formed and maintained by conversation.

Judges 13:8–23: Manoah and His Wife

A: ⁸ Then Manoah entreated the LORD, and said, "O LORD, I pray, let the man of God whom you sent come to us again and teach us what we are to do concerning the boy who will be born."

B: ⁹ *God listened to Manoah, and the angel of God came again to the woman as she sat in the field; but her husband Manoah was not with her.*

¹⁰ *So the woman ran quickly* and told her husband, "The man who came to me the other day has appeared to me." ¹¹ *Manoah got up and followed his wife, and came to the man*

A: and said to him, "Are you the man who spoke to this woman?"

B: And he said, "I am."

A¹: ¹² Then Manoah said, "Now when your words come true, what is to be the boy's rule of life; what is he to do?"

B¹: ¹³ The angel of the LORD said to Manoah, "Let the woman give heed to all that I said to her. ¹⁴ She may not eat of anything that comes from the vine. She is not to drink wine or strong drink, or eat any unclean thing. She is to observe everything that I commanded her."

---

49. תקצר נפשו, literally "his soul was cut." The verb is used elsewhere to indicate that the limits of endurance have been reached. In Judg 16:16, Samson is "tired to death" from Delilah's nagging. In Num 21:4 the Israelites experience "utter discouragement" (BDB 894a) as a result of their lack of provisions.

50. See Niditch, *Judges*, 121.

A²: ¹⁵ Manoah said to the angel of the LORD, "Allow us to detain you, and prepare a kid for you."

B²: ¹⁶ The angel of the LORD said to Manoah, "If you detain me, I will not eat your food; but if you want to prepare a burnt offering, then offer it to the LORD." (*For Manoah did not know that he was the angel of the Lord.*)

A³: ¹⁷ Then Manoah said to the angel of the LORD, "What is your name, so that we may honor you when your words come true?"

B³: ¹⁸ But the angel of the LORD said to him, "Why do you ask my name? It is too wonderful."

A⁴ (Post-expansion Consequential Acton): *¹⁹ So Manoah took the kid with the grain offering, and offered it on the rock to the Lord, to him who works wonders.*

B⁴ (Post-expansion Consequential Action): *²⁰ When the flame went up toward heaven from the altar, the angel of the Lord ascended in the flame of the altar while Manoah and his wife looked on; and they fell on their faces to the ground.*

²¹ *The angel of the Lord did not appear again to Manoah and his wife. Then Manoah realized that it was the angel of the Lord.* ²² *And Manoah said to his wife, "We shall surely die, for we have seen God."* ²³ *But his wife said to him, "If the Lord had meant to kill us, he would not have accepted a burnt offering and a grain offering at our hands, or shown us all these things, or now announced to us such things as these."*

Context

While the conversation of Judges 13:8–20 is contextualized to this particular narrative plot, it is worth noting that the episode includes an offering presentation (13:15–16, 19–20) that has similarities to Judges 6:20–21 and Genesis 18:4–8.[51] The conversation also brings to mind the interaction between Jacob and God in Genesis 32:24–31 in which the human conversationalist also asks the Deity's name.

---

51. Niditch thinks this a "traditional pattern" that presumably could be applied in various settings. Niditch, *Judges*, 146. If this is so, the inclusion of the offering episode suggests the active contribution of the narrator forming the shape of the conversational exchange.

Pre-expansion

The pre-expansion to this conversational prayer (structured in four rounds: 13:10–18) establishes the parameters of the conversation by identifying the participants. Manoah,[52] the LORD, the man of God, God, angel of God (angel of the LORD), and the woman are all potential conversationalists whose identities (sometimes hidden) are a significant backdrop for the following conversation. The man of God, angel of God, and angel of the LORD are identified for the reader as the same individual, although that fact remains unknown to Manoah or his wife and is part of the interpersonal status dynamic embedded in the conversational prayer.

The pre-expansion includes a direct address in which Manoah asks the LORD to send again the "man of God" in order to teach them how to treat the boy soon to be born to Manoah and his barren wife. As will be reinforced by the conversation to follow, the request is unnecessary, for the instruction has already been given to Manoah's wife and no further information will be forth coming. Additional information is not what this conversation is about. The LORD does "listen to Manoah" responding in a preferred fashion, and the angel of God (thought by Manoah to be the "man of God") comes again, but not to Manoah. The angel of God comes to "the woman as she sat in the field" (13:9). Even though the "man of God" (angel of God) is sent in response to Manoah's request, Manoah must relocate, guided by "the woman," before the conversation can begin. The liminal status of the conversationalists, occupying much of the conversation is matched by the spatial liminality characterizing the site of the conversation.[53]

In the pre-expansion, Deity is assigned multiple identities each expressing a different status relationship with Manoah. The multiple identities and unexpected response by the Deity in the pre-expansion, function to keep the status between the conversationalists in flux.

---

52. "Manoah" can be translated "rest" and his name may be significant in this conversation, concerned so much with identity and status. As the conversation concludes, Manoah finally realizes the identity of his conversational partner and despairs for his life (similar to Gideon's encounter of Judg 6). Rest is restored to Manoah only after the wise and comforting encouragement from his wife. Manoah's name is highlighted throughout the episode by the contrast to his unnamed wife. Adele Reinhartz offers a different explanation for her anonymity, thinking that it emphasizes her similarity to the angelic conversationalist. Reinhartz, "Samson's Mother," 29. See also the discussion presented by Mobley, *Samson and the Liminal Hero*, 85–86.

53. In this respect the conversational episode has parallels to the Gideon encounter of Judges 6 and the Elijah encounter in 1 Kings 19.

Round One: 13:11b

Identity is the topic of the first round. Manoah asks: "Are you the man?" Manoah's question is answered in the affirmative, simply and directly (one word in Hebrew: אָנִי; I am), without comment or amplification. The abruptness of the reply is an act of power establishing the status parameters of the ensuing conversation. Manoah is granted an answer but has no right to additional information obviously possessed by Manoah's conversational partner.

Round Two: 13:12–14

Round two also begins with a question. Manoah asks "the man" (whom we, as readers, know to be the "angel of the LORD") for information regarding the lifestyle of the promised son. The "man" answers, only repeating instructions previously given to "the woman" (13:4–5). New information doesn't seem to be the issue for Manoah. Rather, the answer by the "man," affirming the previous announcement, reassures Manoah that in fact, the man's words will come true (13:12). Manoah prefaces his question for additional information with the affirmation, "now when your [the "man's"] words come true." More than a statement of fact, Manoah's preface is a statement of trust, acquiescing to the status standing between the two conversationalists established by the "man" in v. 11. Manoah's question and the "man's" response are not about an exchange of information but an affirmation of status—a shared standing before each other.

Round Three: 13:15–16

Satisfied that he and the "man" share standing before one another, Manoah is prompted to offer his conversational partner a meal, cementing the relationship between the two.[54] Manoah's turn is in the form of a request: "Allow us to detain you." The turn by the angel of the LORD, is in the form of a preferred response, but with conditions. He will allow Manoah and his wife to detain him, but he will not eat the food prepared. Throughout the turn it is clear, agency remains with the "man" (angel of the LORD). Instead of joining Manoah and his wife in a meal, the "man" directs that an offering to the LORD be prepared.

---

54. Here and in Judg 13:19—similar to the Gideon story in Judg 6:19–21.

Round Four: 13:17–18

In round four of the conversation, Manoah also asks a question. Manoah asks his conversational partner to identify himself: "What is your name?" The question (similar to those in Gen 32:27; Exod 3:13) presses the relationship between the conversationalists. Oddly constructed, the question asked by Manoah is literally: *Who* is your name? (not *what*).[55] Throughout the conversation, and here explicitly through the request for the name, status between Manoah and the "man" is being negotiated. All the while, agency is retained by the "man" in the conversation. Manoah seeks to strengthen the bond with his conversational partner even further but does so hesitantly adding a statement of trust and so reducing the likelihood of a dispreferred response from his conversational partner. The question is appended to an affirmation of standing ("that we may honor you when your words come true") but is met with an unexpected response.

The response offered by "the man" to Manoah's question is vague and ambiguous at best. "The man" answers Manoah's question with a question of his own: "Why do you ask my name?" followed by a declaration: "It is Wonderful." A difficult phrase that must at least indicate it is beyond Manoah's expectations or understanding (we, as readers, are in on the secret identity, but Manoah is still in the dark). The declaration "Wonderful" finds no response. Manoah asks no further question, neither does he answer the question posed by the "man." In fact, the activity of v. 19 could easily have followed the angel of the LORD turn in v. 16. It isn't until the post conversation activity that the name "Wonderful" will be reinforced (v. 19). Although appearing in a phrase very difficult to translate, the same word (פלא) will be used to describe either, an amazing thing that happened during the sacrifice (JPS), or the character of the LORD (NRSV) worshipped by means of the sacrifice.

Post-expansion: 13:19–23

Status also dominates the post-expansion to the conversation in 13:19–23. As the flame consumed the offering, prepared by Manoah, "the man," now revealed to Manoah and his wife as the "angel of the LORD," ascends in the flame while Manoah and his wife watch in astonishment. Realizing that they have been conversing with Deity (variously identified as: the angel of the LORD, or God, or the LORD), they fall on their faces and Manoah despairs

---

55. See Boling, *Judges*, 222.

that he and his wife will die for "we have seen God."[56] In other words, the status established during the conversation is now believed to be at risk as the full import of the moment becomes known. Manoah's wife ventures to disagree with her husband arguing that, had God intended to kill them, he would not have accepted their offerings, or shown and announced to them these things (13:23). That is, he would not have conversed with them. More than the miraculous events that Manoah and his wife were recently privileged to witness; it was the conversational prayer that proved most compelling in verifying their standing with God.

Judges 15:18–20: Samson

[18] *By then he was very thirsty, and he called on the Lord,*

A: saying, "You have granted this great victory by the hand of your servant. Am I now to die of thirst, and fall into the hands of the uncircumcised?"

B: [19] *So God split open the hollow place that is at Lehi, and water came from it. When he drank, his spirit returned, and he revived. Therefore it was named En-hakkore which is at Lehi to this day.* [20] *And he judged Israel in the days of the Philistines twenty years.*

Despite Samson's remarkable and storied career in which the spirit of the LORD stirred in him (Judg 13:25) or rushed upon him (Judg 14:6, 19; 15:14), Samson only speaks to the LORD twice, here in 15:18 and again just prior to his death in 16:28, 30. Of these two, only 15:18–19 contains enough conversational activity to be included as a conversational prayer.[57]

Context

This conversational prayer follows the story of Samson's miraculous victory over a thousand Philistine warriors, slaughtering them armed only with a donkey's jawbone, but more, empowered by the spirit of the LORD that has rushed upon him (15:14). As is true with much of Samson's career, this story, too, is filled with contradictions. Samson, the mighty warrior, violates his Nazirite vow by using as his weapon of choice part of a carcass, an object

---

56. This is not the only time that "seeing God" is considered a dangerous prospect: Gen 16:13–14; Exod 19:21; 24:9–11; 33:20.

57. The place of the episode in the broader Samson story is discussed by Broida, "Closure in Samson."

he is strictly forbidden to touch (Num 6:6). Yet, despite his willful offense[58] Samson prevails and credits his victory to the LORD (15:18) whom Samson now holds responsible to quench his desperate thirst.

Structure

This conversational prayer is constructed in only one round, composed of Samson's direct speech followed by consequential activity in the form of a preferred response from God. Samson's speech appears in two parts, a declarative statement followed by a question:

> You have granted this great victory by the hand
> of your servant.
>
> Am I now to die of thirst, and fall into the hands
> of the uncircumcised?

The opening statement establishes agency and status between the conversational partners. The LORD is credited with agency resulting in the slaughter of the Philistines, accomplished only by the hand of Samson, the LORD's servant. The actor is the LORD and the servant is Samson. Both, agency and status are used in the following question in order to secure a desired outcome. Samson desires the same exercise of Divine agency to now provide water and so save the servant from death and capture by the uncircumcised (that is, those not "servants" as is Samson). The question posed by Samson is phrased to elicit a negative reply but a preferred response.[59] It is designed to put the recipient on the defensive, presented to prevent the absurd situation implied by the question.

In response, God (not the LORD upon whom Samson called) split open a depression in the bedrock and water gushed out.[60] Even though the consequential action provides what Samson requested, God's silence in the matter is noteworthy. In fact, and although the LORD's spirit repeatedly rushes upon Samson, God never speaks to Samson. This is all the more noticeable given the quite lengthy conversation between the Deity and Samson's parents when announcing his birth. God's silence prevents

---

58. Samson obviously is quite familiar with the contents of his vow as is made clear in his conversation with Delilah in Judg 16:17. See also Chepey, "Samson the 'Holy One,'" 97–99.

59. See Hayano, "Question Design in Conversation," 405–7. Reversed polarity questions are also posed by Moses in Num 11:11–24.

60. Similar to another episode also filled with contradictions, this time involving Moses (Num 20).

the development of a shared understanding, an inter-subjectivity, between God and Samson. Samson never develops a *who-we-are-to-one-another* with God in conversation. The conversational activity of this episode makes clear that, like the donkey's jawbone, Samson remains a questionable tool in the hand of God, but nothing more.[61]

---

61. Perhaps suggested also by Assis, "Structure and Meaning of the Samson Narratives," 11. Edward Greenstein suggests that Samson is Israel and that Samson's exploits and character are actually the storyteller's description of Israel. Greenstein, "Riddle of Samson," 252–53. Gregory Mobley characterizes Samson as a wild man about whom the biblical attitude is ambivalent. Mobley, *Samson and the Liminal Hero*, 114.

7

Parallel Prayers

Samuel–Kings, Chronicles, Isaiah

SAMUEL–KINGS, CHRONICLES,[1] AND ISAIAH present several prayers uttered by David, Solomon, or Hezekiah, cast in the form of conversation, and appearing in parallel texts. While it is certain that these prayers are stylized renditions, not actual reproductions of words uttered,[2] it is worth noting that they are cast in the form of conversational activity. Why? The writers of these three works seek to convey something about the relationship between David, Solomon, Hezekiah, and God that necessitated this conversational form of communication. The writers of all three works use conversational prayer as a means by which to express the bond between the conversational partners. Yet, the conversational prayers contained in these literary works are not structured like the conversational prayers elsewhere in the Hebrew Bible. They bear the mark of rhetorical design,[3] presented to advance the persuasive intent of the literary composition in which they now reside.[4]

David: 2 Samuel 7:18–29 // 1 Chronicles 17:16–27

2 Samuel 7:18–29

¹⁸ *Then King David went in and sat before the Lord, and said,*

---

1. Throughout this chapter, "Chronicler" will refer to the author or composer of the particular episode in Chronicles under discussion. No assumption is made concerning a single composition including Chronicles, Ezra, and Nehemiah.

2. Anderson, *2 Samuel*, 128.

3. Illustrated in the presentation made by Gary Knoppers in his discussion of 1 Kings 8. Knoppers, "Prayer and Propaganda," 236–38.

4. Martin Noth included prayers as marks of unifying design within the Deuteronomic literature. Noth, *Deuteronomic History*, 4–11.

A: "Who am I, O Lord God, and what is my house, that you have brought me thus far? [19] And yet this was a small thing in your eyes, O Lord God; you have spoken also of your servant's house for a great while to come. May this be instruction for the people,[5] O Lord God! [20] And what more can David say to you? For you know your servant, O Lord God! [21] Because of your promise, and according to your own heart, you have wrought all this greatness, so that your servant may know it. [22] Therefore you are great, O Lord God; for there is no one like you, and there is no God besides you, according to all that we have heard with our ears. [23] Who is like your people, like Israel? Is there another nation on earth whose God went to redeem it as a people, and to make a name for himself, doing great and awesome things for them, by driving out before his people nations and their gods?[6] [24] And you established your people Israel for yourself to be your people forever; and you, O Lord, became their God. [25] And now, O Lord God, as for the word that you have spoken concerning your servant and concerning his house, confirm it forever; do as you have promised. [26] Thus your name will be magnified forever in the saying, 'The Lord of hosts is God over Israel'; and the house of your servant David will be established before you. [27] For you, O Lord of hosts, the God of Israel, have made this revelation to your servant, saying, 'I will build you a house'; therefore your servant has found courage to pray this prayer to you. [28] And now, O Lord God, you are God, and your words are true, and you have promised this good thing to your servant; [29] now therefore may it please you to bless the house of your servant, so that it may continue forever before you; for you, O Lord God, have spoken, and with your blessing shall the house of your servant be blessed forever."

1 Chronicles 17:16–27

[16] *Then King David went in and sat before the Lord,*

A: and said, "Who am I, O Lord God, and what is my house, that you have brought me thus far? [17] And even this was a small thing in your sight, O God; you have also spoken of your servant's

---

5. MT uncertain. McCarter suggests "the generation to come" for the problematic "May this be instruction for the people" used in the NRSV. McCarter, *2 Samuel*, 233. See also Driver, *Notes on the Hebrew Text*, 276–77.

6. MT uncertain. Notice that 1 Chronicles uses second person "your people" (1 Chr 17:21) for the third person "his people" in 2 Sam 7:23.

house for a great while to come. You regard me as someone of high rank,[7] O LORD God! [18] And what more can David say to you for honoring your servant? You know your servant. [19] For your servant's sake, O LORD, and according to your own heart, you have done all these great deeds, making known all these great things. [20] There is no one like you, O LORD, and there is no God besides you, according to all that we have heard with our ears. [21] Who is like your people Israel, one nation on the earth whom God went to redeem to be his people, making for yourself a name for great and terrible things, in driving out nations before your people whom you redeemed from Egypt? [22] And you made your people Israel to be your people forever; and you, O LORD, became their God.

[23] "And now, O LORD, as for the word that you have spoken concerning your servant and concerning his house, let it be established forever, and do as you have promised. [24] Thus your name will be established and magnified forever in the saying, 'The LORD of hosts, the God of Israel, is Israel's God'; and the house of your servant David will be established in your presence. [25] For you, my God, have revealed to your servant that you will build a house for him; therefore your servant has found it possible to pray before you. [26] And now, O LORD, you are God, and you have promised this good thing to your servant; [27] therefore may it please you to bless the house of your servant, that it may continue forever before you. For you, O LORD, have blessed and are blessed forever."

Context

The context of this prayer is remarkable and the same in both accounts. First, King David "went in"—but *in* where? Neither account specifies the location. Instead, the focus of the statement is on the act of relocating, indicating that David approaches, or comes near, God in order for this conversation to take place. The second aspect of the context is more surprising. David sat down (2 Sam 7:18; 1 Chr 17:16) before the LORD.[8] Conversational prayers involving Moses or one of the patriarchs might have the human participant falling, face to the ground, or standing in respect before Deity.[9] For

---

7. MT uncertain. JPS renders, "you regard me as a man of distinction."

8. Anderson suggests that David assumed a kneeling position, a position of prayer, but admits it is not attested elsewhere in the Hebrew Bible. Anderson, *2 Samuel*, 126.

9. Gen 17:22 makes it clear that Abraham stands before YHWH.

the 2 Samuel and 1 Chronicles narrators, positioning David to "sit before the LORD" must have special significance. David has assumed a position of power and confidence as his conversational prayer with God begins. The following conversational prayer will describe the Davidic dynasty, a political reality central to the narratives constructed by both the Deuteronomic Historian and the Chronicler. David's posture, in conversation with the LORD, illustrates the high status given to David in the LORD's estimation. David's act of sitting illustrates his high standing before God.

This assumption of status before God was apparently not without risk, or at least it might have had the appearance of pretense, for David admits the courage required to speak so before God (2 Sam 7:27).[10] The Chronicles account emphasizes the honor given to David, inserting into the prayer the acknowledgment that the LORD God regards David as someone of "high rank" and "honored" (1 Chr 17:17–18). The Chronicler claims that God is doing these great deeds and making known great things for both "your servant's sake" and "according to your own heart" effectively elevating David to lofty status (1 Chr 17:19) while at the same time removing the reference to the "courage" it took on David's part to address God (1 Chr 17:25).

If evaluated only by content of the conversation, the prayer offered by David is unnecessary, for the topic is closed. The Davidic dynasty has already been established and need not be negotiated further.[11] But, the topic of conversation is only one element in the overall function of conversation. Through means of a conversational prayer, status is expressed, and David's reputation is being formed. While David's direct address is spoken to the LORD God, the recipient of the direct speech is now the reading audience. The direct speech of the conversational prayer is inserted in the respective Samuel and Chronicles narratives to accomplish the greater narrative design—a design thought by both, the Samuel and Chronicles compilers, to have lasting significance.[12] That significance, meaningful to an audience larger than the conversational participants, is also illustrated by Solomon's prayer, also rendered in parallel versions in 2 Samuel 7:25 and 1 Kings 8:26.

Structure

Although cast in the form of conversational activity, this direct speech by David displays few of the characteristics expected in conversational

---

10. Interestingly, the Chronicles account chooses to make no mention of this "courage" (את לבו; 1 Chr 17:25).

11. See Anderson, *2 Samuel*, 128.

12. See the repetitive use of "forever" (עולם and עד עולם).

exchange. The direct speech of David's prayer tends to the formal, shows little recipient design, allows for no repair, and asks for no response. Further, David's direct address elicits; no response from the LORD, no closing to the conversation, and no consequential action. The conversational activity of David's direct address is separated from the following narrative action in both 2 Samuel and 1 Chronicles by the notation, "Sometime afterward" (2 Sam 8:1; 1 Chr 18:1), effectively removing the conversational activity from any consequent action.

The opening question of the direct speech, "Who am I, O Lord God, and what is my house, that you have brought me thus far?" appearing verbatim in both renditions, introduces the topic of the direct speech and the status of the conversational partners. Although on the face of it, an expression of humility,[13] the question allows the description of an elevated status, appearing in the remainder of the direct speech. The David speech will describe the elevated status enjoyed by David but will describe that status as a result of the LORD's direct actions on behalf of first, the nation of Israel, and second on behalf of David, himself.

Variations between 2 Samuel and 1 Chronicles

Although the direct speeches in 2 Samuel 7 and 1 Chronicles 17 have essentially the same contexts, follow the same pattern, and share a great amount of actual text (1 Chronicles probably based on 2 Samuel),[14] variations do exist. Both versions quote "the saying" (2 Sam 7:26, 1 Chr 17:24) but render the saying with variation.[15] Inconsistencies in 2 Sam 7:23 are smoothed out

---

13. Anderson, *2 Samuel*, 126. Japhet, *1 and 2 Chronicles*, 339. Here, David's self-abasement simply provides the opportunity for aggrandizement.

14. See the survey by De Vries, *1 and 2 Chronicles*, 153. Trebolle argues that these two versions of David's prayer are based upon a common source. Trebolle, "Samuel/Kings and Chronicles," 96–108. While it is here concluded that the Chronicles rendition is based upon the Samuel version, in our comparison of the two parallel accounts, dependency is not as important as simply noting the differences and how these differences function in the respective versions. See Kalimi, *Reshaping of Ancient Israelite History*, 404; additional arguments cited by Merrill, "Chronicler," 398–99; Japhet, *Ideology of the Book of Chronicles*, 8; Knoppers, *1 Chronicles 1–9*, 66–68; Hurvitz, "Recent Debate on Late Biblical Data," 191–210. For a minority view on the priority of Chronicles, see Gray, *1 and 2 Kings*, 9. Graeme Auld contends a shared common source for the Deuteronomic History and Chronicles. See Auld, *I and II Samuel*. Raymond Person argues that the Deuteronomic History and the Chronicles are "contemporary literary works" both faithful to a broader tradition. Person, "Problem of 'Literary Unity,'" 226. Also, Person, *Deuteronomic School and the Book of Chronicles*, 163; Person, "Text Criticism as a Lens," 207.

15. Brueggemann, *David's Truth*, 80.

in 1 Chr 17:21 by use of the second person pronoun. In addition to these, perhaps, minor variations, there are differences that are more significant, rendering the two versions quite different in conversational function.[16]

There are five variations in the 1 Chronicles 17 version of this conversational prayer that effectively change the status between the conversational partners when compared to the rendition of the prayer given in 2 Samuel 7.

1. 1 Chr 17:17 "regarding me as someone of high rank" for the problematic phrase in 2 Samuel 7:19 "may this be instruction."
2. 1 Chr 17:18 insertion of "honoring your servant."
3. 1 Chr 17:24 inserts: "*your* [the LORD of hosts and God of Israel] *name will be established* and magnified" (2 Sam 7:26: reads: your name will be magnified) connecting to the "establishment" of the house of your servant David (1 Chr 17:24).
4. Lord God—In 2 Samuel 7: LORD God אדני יהוה) (literally: LORD YHWH) appearing in vv. 18, 19a, 19b, 20, 22 (some read יהוה אלהים), 25 (not in all manuscripts), 28, 29.[17] This form is used nowhere else in Samuel.[18] The appearance of this unique form in this conversational activity, not maintained in the 1 Chronicles version of the prayer, must give us pause.[19] What does the name, "Lord YHWH," mean for the status negotiated in the 2 Samuel prayer? The overwhelming preponderance of usage for this title appears in Ezekiel (217 occurrences). In Ezekiel, the title frequents messenger speeches. It may be that the title is here used as a sign of submissiveness on David's part.[20] If so, the removal of this name for God from the David speech in Chronicles is consistent with other 1 Chronicles 17 variations. The second variation in naming between 2 Samuel and 1 Chronicles is in the 2 Sam 7:27

---

16. Kalimi notes also the stylistic variation employed by the Chronicler. See, for example, the comparison between 2 Sam 7:27 and 1 Chr 17:25 Kalimi, *Reshaping of Ancient Israelite History*, 249.

17. MT *qere* and LXX[LMN] read LORD God throughout as in the 1 Chronicles 17 rendition. See McCarter, *2 Samuel*, 234. 2 Sam 6:17 reads את ארון יהוה (ark of the LORD), while the corresponding 1 Chr 17:2 reads ארון ברית יהוה (ark of the covenant of the LORD) only to substitute אלהים (Elohim) in the next verse.

18. Anderson, *2 Samuel*, 126.

19. Japhet considers the Chronicles variation motivated by "theological considerations." Japhet, *1 and 2 Chronicles*, 338. CA allows us to understand these variations as a depiction of status achieved in conversation, a status that is remembered for purposes different in 2 Samuel 7 and 1 Chronicles 17. When "LORD God" in 1 Chronicles 17 יהוה אלהים is used (1 Chr 17:16; 1 Chr 17:17).

20. See Greenburg, *Ezekiel 1–20*, 65.

reference: "LORD of Hosts, the God of Israel." 1 Chronicles 17:25 simply reads: "my God" appropriating a personal relationship and status to the before mentioned LORD of Hosts, the God of Israel, and Israel's God (1 Chr 17:24). The title "LORD of Hosts" may refer to a position of honor among the heavenly hosts.[21]

5. 2 Samuel ends with a statement of blessing on the house of David (2 Sam 7:28), while 1 Chronicles ends with a statement of blessing on the LORD (1 Chr 17:27).[22] The Chronicles conclusion, with David blessing the LORD, solidifies status between the conversational participants (consistent with the inclusions found in 1 Chr 17:17, 18). The pronouncement of blessing assumes the status and ability to bless and so the variation in ending creates a status relationship between the LORD and David that is very different in the two renditions.

The standing between the conversational partners in the two conversational prayers make the two prayers very different, even though they share many of the same words and are reported to have occurred at the same event. These variations have the effect of elevating the status of David and his house, effectively changing the relationship between the conversational partners in the Chronicles account when compared to the conversational prayer in 2 Samuel 7. This change of status for David and his house is consistent with the overall rhetorical design of both Samuel and Chronicles. That this change is made by the Chronicler through a conversational prayer, illustrates the importance of prayer in the estimation of the Chronicler. He understood well the vital nature of conversation in a Divine human relationship—a relationship the Chronicler hoped would be replicated among his readers.

David: 2 Samuel 24:10–17 // 1 Chronicles 21:8–17

Unlike other prayers so far investigated, this conversational prayer is partly mediated.[23] The first round allows David to address the LORD directly, but the LORD speaks through a mediator, Gad, the prophet, David's seer, using the stylistic introduction "thus says the LORD" (2 Sam 24:12; 1 Chr 21:9,

---

21. Mettinger, "YHWH SABAOTH," 126.

22. Japhet, *1 and 2 Chronicles*, 341. Elsewhere, Japhet suggests that Adonay had come to be identified with YHWH and so unnecessary or improper of the Chronicler to include both. Japhet, *Ideology of the Book of Chronicles*, 23.

23. As will be the prayers of Hezekiah in 2 Kgs 19:15–34; Isa 37:14–35; and 2 Kgs 20:1–7; Isa 38:3–8.

11). The 2 Samuel 24 rendition also uses the stylistic phrase, "the word of the Lord" (2 Sam 24:11). The mediation of Gad and the appearance of these stylistic introductions, preceding direct address from God, introduce an element of formality into the conversational prayers that will change the function of the conversational activity in the narratives. The dynamism of the status between the conversational participants will diminish as formal elements and mediation are added to the conversations.

2 Samuel 24:10–17

[10] But afterward, David was stricken to the heart because he had numbered the people.

A: David said to the Lord, "I have sinned greatly in what I have done. But now, O Lord, I pray you, take away the guilt of your servant; for I have done very foolishly."

[11] When David rose in the morning, the word of the Lord came to the prophet Gad, David's seer, saying,

B: [12] "Go and say to David: Thus says the Lord: Three things I offer you; choose one of them, and I will do it to you."

[13] So Gad came to David and told him; he asked him, "Shall three[24] years of famine come to you on your land? Or will you flee three months before your foes while they pursue you? Or shall there be three days' pestilence in your land? Now consider, and decide what answer I shall return to the one who sent me." [14] Then David said to Gad, "I am in great distress; let us fall into the hand of the Lord, for his mercy is great; but let me not fall into human hands."[25] [15] So the Lord sent a pestilence on Israel from that morning until the appointed time; and seventy thousand[26] of the people died, from Dan to Beer-sheba. [16] But when the angel stretched out his hand toward Jerusalem to destroy it, the Lord relented concerning the evil, and said to the angel who was bringing destruction among the people, "It is enough; now stay your hand." The angel of the Lord was then by the threshing floor of Araunah the Jebusite.

A¹: [17] *When David saw the angel who was destroying the people, he said to the Lord,* "I alone have sinned, and I alone have done

---

24. MT reads seven. LXX and 1 Chronicles 21 read three.

25. LXX includes the statement: "So David chose the pestilence, and it was the time of the wheat harvest."

26. MT reads 77,000. LXX and 1 Chronicles 21 reads 70,000.

wickedly; but these sheep, what have they done? Let your hand, I pray, be against me and against my father's house."

1 Chronicles 21:8–17

A: ⁸ David said to God, "I have sinned greatly in that I have done this thing. But now, I pray you, take away the guilt of your servant; for I have done very foolishly."

B: ⁹ The LORD spoke to Gad, David's seer, saying, ¹⁰ "Go and say to David, 'Thus says the LORD: Three things I offer you; choose one of them, so that I may do it to you.'"

¹¹ So Gad came to David and said to him, "Thus says the Lord, 'Take your choice: ¹² either three years of famine; or three months of devastation by your foes, while the sword of your enemies overtakes you; or three days of the sword of the Lord, pestilence on the land, and the angel of the Lord destroying throughout all the territory of Israel.' Now decide what answer I shall return to the one who sent me." ¹³ Then David said to Gad, "I am in great distress; let me fall into the hand of the Lord, for his mercy is very great; but let me not fall into human hands."

¹⁴ So the Lord sent a pestilence on Israel; and seventy thousand persons fell in Israel. ¹⁵ And God sent an angel to Jerusalem to destroy it; but when he was about to destroy it, the Lord took note and relented concerning the calamity[27]; he said to the destroying angel, "Enough! Stay your hand." The angel of the Lord was then standing by the threshing floor of Ornan the Jebusite. ¹⁶ David looked up and saw the angel of the Lord standing between earth and heaven, and in his hand a drawn sword stretched out over Jerusalem. Then David and the elders, clothed in sackcloth, fell on their faces.

A¹: ¹⁷ And David said to God, "Was it not I who gave the command to count the people? It is I who have sinned and done very wickedly. But these sheep, what have they done? Let your hand, I pray, O LORD my God, be against me and against my father's house; but do not let your people be plagued!"

---

27. Rendered by NRSV in 2 Sam 24:16 as "evil." Heb. uses הרעה in both 2 Sam 24:16 and 1 Chr 21:15.

Context

These two parallel passages are famous for the way in which the episode is introduced. In 2 Samuel 24, it is clear that the context is established through the agency of the LORD (2 Sam 24:1), one of the conversational participants, because the "anger of the LORD was kindled against Israel" (2 Sam 24:1), while in 1 Chronicles 21, it is the Satan,[28] not participant in the following conversation, who "stands up against Israel, and incited David to count the people" (1 Chr 21:1). This change in context certainly positions the following conversational prayers quite differently in 2 Samuel and 1 Chronicles. It is significant that this difference in context is known only to the reader. David seems unaware of the hidden agency prompting his actions and his direct speech to God is not impacted at all by the behind the scenes activity.

Structure

The conversational prayer is rendered in two rounds, followed by a series of consequential actions that are specifically described as flowing from the prayer (2 Sam 24:25; 1 Chr 21:26). While David speaks unmediated to the LORD (God in 1 Chronicles) and able to address his conversational partner in the second person, the LORD addresses David only through the mediation of Gad, the prophet (and presented as the *word of the Lord* in 2 Sam 24:11). At Divine direction, Gad must *go* and speak to David (2 Sam 24:12; 1 Chr 21:9). The LORD is immediately present to Gad, but not to David.[29] David may speak directly to the LORD, but the LORD chooses not to be in the presence of David.

Parallel Renditions

The conversational prayer by David in 2 Samuel and 1 Chronicles contains a number of discrepancies and textual problems that have long occupied

---

28. For a survey of interpretive suggestions, see Stokes, "Devil Made David Do It," 92–93. Stokes concludes that, as in the Balaam story of Numbers 22, the *Satan* is an angelic figure (106). See also the comments concerning the *Satan* by Ristau, "Breaking Down Unity," 207, 209. Also, Stokes, "Satan, YHWH's Executioner," 251–70.

29. Perhaps also indicated by the use of the infinitive, framing the LORD's direct speech to Gad in both 2 Sam 24:11 and 1 Chr 21:9.

commentator's attention.[30] There are several significant variations between the two renditions of David's conversational prayer.[31]

The same introduction is used prefacing conversations with Abraham, Jacob and in Numbers (generally not so in Exodus) with Moses. The verb, ראה, is commonly translated "to see," but when applied to Deity is frequently translated "appear."

2 Samuel 24	1 Chronicles 21
1. Incident is incited by LORD because he is angry at Israel (24:1). The precipitating action is that David numbered (ספר) the people.	1. Incident is incited by Satan (21:1). The precipitating action is that David numbered (מנה)[32] Israel.
2. The Divine punishment is three days of pestilence throughout the land.	2. The Divine punishment is described as three: • sword of the LORD • pestilence on the land • angel of the LORD destroying throughout the land (the insertion of the angel moderates the direct opposition by the LORD in 2 Samuel)
3. David's plea to Gad includes the nation delivered in first-person plural.	3. David's plea to Gad is consistently in first-person singular.
4. David's confession in 24:17 uses אנכי ("I") repetitively.	4. David's confession in 21:17 uses אני ("I") repetitively.[33]

30. Compositional schemes are surveyed by Rofé, "Writing, Interpolating and Editing," 318–20. Rofé contends that a harmonizing hand is at work in 1 Chronicles 21 separate from the Chronicler (323). See also Edenburg, "2 Sam 21–24," 189–222. For various views regarding the composition of Chronicles, see Knoppers, "Images of David in Early Judaism," 449–50.

31. It cannot be assumed that the Chronicles account is dependent upon a *Vorlage* identical to the MT of Samuel. No conclusion is here made about the nature of a shared textual tradition. For a survey of the DSS Samuel materials, see Feldman, *Dead Sea Scrolls Rewriting Samuel and Kings*, 5–8.

32. Typically, this root is used to indicate a numbering reserved to YHWH alone. See Ristau, "Breaking Down Unity," 209.

33. There is no functional difference between the long and short forms of the personal pronoun. See Waltke and O'Connor, *An Introduction to Biblical Hebrew Syntax*, 292. אנכי is rare in Chronicles and not to be expected in 1 Chr 21:17. Rather, its appearance in 1 Chronicles 21, in agreement with 2 Samuel 24 would be more noteworthy. The use of the first-person singular pronoun in both 2 Samuel 24 and 1 Chronicles 21 emphasizes the distinction between David and the nation: "*I* did it, not them." For possible implications dating the texts, see Rezetko, "Dating Biblical Hebrew," 215; Hurvitz,

2 Samuel 24	1 Chronicles 21
5. David's confession is directed to the Lord (24:17).	5. David's confession addresses "Lord my God" (21:17) and is witnessed by the elders (21:16).
6. The appearance of the angel of the Lord is on the threshing floor belonging to Araunah.	6. The appearance of the angel of the Lord is by the threshing floor belonging to Ornan (21:15) and again standing between heaven and earth with drawn sword over Jerusalem (21:17).[34]

In addition to the above, the 2 Samuel 24 and 1 Chronicles 21 versions contain a major variation in the manner that the Deity's address is expressed. In 2 Samuel 24:13, the Lord's address, mediated by Gad, is in the form of three questions:

- Shall three years of famine come to you on your land?
- Or will you flee three months before your foes while they pursue you?
- Or shall there be three days' pestilence in your land?

The questions are similar in structure, each requiring a simple yes or no response, and each implying a punishment of equal severity.[35] The question format is itself a form of power in this conversational prayer. The question demands an answer, without repair or explanation, placing the recipient of the question in a contingent position relative to the conversational partner. Even though David does not answer the questions directly, his direct reply (now mediated by Gad), is designed to reinforce his standing with his conversational partner (24:14).

In 1 Chronicles 21:12, the choices are in the form of propositions, each longer than the one before, and implying an increasing severity to the punishments. David is presented with a choice:

- Either three years of famine;
- Or three months of devastation by your foes, while the sword of your enemies overtakes you;

"Recent Debate on Late Biblical Data," 195–96.

34. Is the hovering angel a secondary addition? See Dion, "Angel with the Drawn Sword," 114–17.

35. Japhet, *1 and 2 Chronicles*, 382.

- Or three days of the sword of the Lord, pestilence on the land, and the angel of the Lord destroying throughout all the territory of Israel.

The expansion presented in 1 Chronicles allows for even greater distinction between punishment wrought through natural disaster, punishment accomplished through human hands, and punishment meted out directly by God. Formed as propositions, each allows for more than a yes or no reply as in 2 Samuel. Even though articulated by the exact same words in 2 Samuel and 1 Chronicles, David's decision to "fall into the hand of the Lord, for his mercy is great" as reply to the expanded propositions in 1 Chronicles 21, emphasizes David's trust in the Lord, that is, his standing before the Lord, to an even greater extent than described in 2 Samuel 24.[36]

Conversational Status

When compared to the 2 Samuel rendition, the Chronicles account allows the Chronicler to heighten the status granted to David before God. The Chronicler avoids an adversarial role assumed by the Lord toward David by introducing the *Satan* as the agent of incitement. In 1 Chronicles 21, David's plea to the Lord, voiced consistently in first person singular, stems from a personal standing before the Lord. And the address to the "Lord my God" once again emphasizes the personal standing David maintains before the Lord. This elevation in David's status is consistent with the manner the Chronicler tends to use the personal name "David" more than his title, "king" as in 1 Chr 21:21 contrasted to 2 Sam 24:20.[37] This, too, is important in describing the status between David and the Lord as the *who-we-are-to-one-another* between the conversational partners changes the *what-it-does* of the conversational activity between the 2 Samuel 24 and 1 Chronicles 21 renditions.

Likewise, the second conversationalist, the Lord, is present differently in 1 Chronicles than in 2 Samuel. The various names used for Deity throughout the episode describe that conversational presence. In Chronicles, יהוה (Lord) is the most common name for Deity. Consequently, David's use of "God," prefacing David's direct speech in 1 Chr 21:8, 17 is unusual and a departure from his earlier prayer in 1 Chronicles 17. Sinful David, the guilty servant, who has acted foolishly, petitions "God" (1 Chr 21:8) contrasted to the twice referenced "Lord," petitioned in 2 Sam

---

36. See Kalimi, *The Reshaping of Ancient Israelite History*, 342. Also, Muraoka, *Emphatic Words and Structures*, 55.

37. David is named twenty-five times in the 1 Chr 21:1–22 episode.

24:10. Similarly, it is "God" and "Lord my God" that David addresses directly, witnessed by the elders, interceding for the nation in 1 Chr 21:17, contrasted to the consistent reference to the "Lord" throughout 2 Sam 24:10–17. How do these name changes impact the conversational prayer? The use of "God" in David's initial petition (21:9) and mediation (21:17), both of which included David's admission of guilt, very subtly but very clearly distance the conversationalists from one another. This distance is matched by a subtle difference in David's confession:[38]

- I alone am guilty; *I alone have done wrong*. (2 Sam 24:17)
- I alone am guilty and *have caused severe harm*. (1 Chr 21:17)

This distance, emphasized by the Chronicler, is effectively overcome through David's humble repentance, petition, and intercession. The conversation does more than bring the punishment to an end. The conversation restores and enhances the status between the conversationalists. That renewed relationship, witnessed by the elders is now appropriated by the repentance, petition, and intercession of the post-exilic community in Jerusalem, for whom the Chronicles version was intended.[39]

Solomon: 1 Kings 3:5–14 // 2 Chronicles 1:7–12

1 Kings 3:5–14

[5] *At Gibeon the Lord appeared to Solomon in a dream by night*;

A: and God said, "Ask what I should give you."

B: [6] And Solomon said, "You have shown great and steadfast love to your servant my father David, because he walked before you in faithfulness, in righteousness, and in uprightness of heart toward you; and you have kept for him this great and steadfast love, and have given him a son to sit on his throne today. [7] And now, O Lord my God, you have made your servant king in place of my father David, although I am only a little child; I do not know how to go out or come in. [8] And your servant is in the midst of the people whom you have chosen, a great people, so numerous they cannot be numbered or counted. [9] Give your servant therefore an understanding mind to govern your people,

---

38. Both JPS and NRSV describes the enhanced description in 1 Chr 21:17 by rendering David's confession as having acted *very* wickedly.

39. See the relational emphases noticed by Ristau, "Breaking Down Unity," 209, 221.

able to discern between good and evil; for who can govern this your great people?"

A¹ (Consequential Action):¹⁰ *It pleased the Lord that Solomon had asked this.*

A¹ᵃ: ¹¹ God said to him, "Because you have asked this, and have not asked for yourself long life or riches, or for the life of your enemies, but have asked for yourself understanding to discern what is right, ¹² I now do according to your word. Indeed I give you a wise and discerning mind; no one like you has been before you and no one like you shall arise after you. ¹³ I give you also what you have not asked, both riches and honor all your life; no other king shall compare with you. ¹⁴ If you will walk in my ways, keeping my statutes and my commandments, as your father David walked, then I will lengthen your life.

2 Chronicles 1:7–12

⁷ *That night God appeared to Solomon,*

A: and said to him, "Ask what I should give you."

B: ⁸ Solomon said to God, "You have shown great and steadfast love to my father David, and have made me succeed him as king. ⁹ O Lᴏʀᴅ God, let your promise to my father David now be fulfilled, for you have made me king over a people as numerous as the dust of the earth. ¹⁰ Give me now wisdom and knowledge to go out and come in before this people, for who can rule this great people of yours?"

A¹: ¹¹ God answered Solomon, "Because this was in your heart, and you have not asked for possessions, wealth, honor, or the life of those who hate you, and have not even asked for long life, but have asked for wisdom and knowledge for yourself that you may rule my people over whom I have made you king, ¹² wisdom and knowledge are granted to you. I will also give you riches, possessions, and honor, such as none of the kings had who were before you, and none after you shall have the like."

Variations between the Two Accounts

There are several significant differences between these two accounts of the conversational prayer between God and Solomon.

Context and Editorial Insertions

1. 1 Kings indicates that the conversation occurred in a "dream by night" (1 Kgs 3:5, 15). The 2 Chronicles version makes no mention of a dream implying that the conversation was "a direct and immediate revelation to Solomon."[40] The Chronicler's alteration of the earlier Kings account, perhaps sensitive to the same reservation about the credibility of revelatory dreams as expressed in Jer 23:25-32,[41] shields Solomon from the questionable reputation of dream revelation. But more, the dream venue, establishes a power dynamic favoring the Divine apparition that is absent in the 2 Chronicles rendition.

2. The 1 Kings version contains an editorial insertion ("It pleased the Lord that Solomon had asked this" 1 Kgs 3:10), functioning as consequential action, that is not included in the 2 Chronicles version.

3. In 1 Kgs 3:5, the Lord (יהוה) appears to Solomon, while in 2 Chr 1:7, it is God (אלהים) who speaks with Solomon.[42]

Solomon Turn

1. Kings repeatedly identifies first David (1 Kgs 3:6), and then Solomon as God's servant (1 Kgs 3:7, 8, 9). The 2 Chronicles account does not use the servant designation.

2. In 1 Kgs 3:6, character qualities (faithfulness, righteousness, uprightness in heart) are used to describe David and listed as the conditions resulting in Divine blessing. This list of character qualities, or the conditional presence of these qualities, does not appear in the 2 Chronicles account.

3. Solomon's self-description of 1 Kgs 3:7 (go out or come in) is woven into the request for an understanding mind (1 Kgs 3:9) or wisdom and knowledge (2 Chr 1:10). The 1 Kings version presents Solomon as *only a little child* (3:7), a description not found in 2 Chronicles.

---

40. Kalimi, *Reshaping of Ancient Israelite History*, 54.
41. Coggins, *First and Second Books of Chronicles*, 148.
42. This usage is consistent with the Chronicler's preference when referencing Deity.

God's Turn

1. To the list of blessings not requested by Solomon, 2 Chronicles adds *possessions* and *honor* (1:11), blessings that will nevertheless be granted by God (1:12). *Honor*, appearing also in the 1 Kings list, while *possessions* does not (3:13).

2. The God direct speech in 1 Kgs 3:14 ends with a condition (*If you will walk in my ways, keeping my statutes and my commandments, as your father David walked*), followed by a promise (*then I will lengthen your life*) that does not appear in 2 Chronicles,[43] even though both accounts mention Solomon's refrain from requesting a long life (1 Kgs 3:11; 2 Chr 1:11) as commendable.

The variations between the two accounts effectively cast Solomon in a slightly different status relationship with God in 1 Kings 3 than that presented in 2 Chronicles 1. In Kings, Solomon's self-description is the LORD's servant, as was his father David, and only a little child. These descriptions are strategic. Identifying as the LORD's servant, presumes Divine action that is consistent with the LORD's patronage. And, in conversation, self-deprecation, especially when over-stated (only a little child) motivates the respondent to action negating the self-deprecation, in this case enhanced affiliation between God and Solomon.[44] These descriptives present a preferred status relationship of dependence and obedience that make the hoped for Divine consequential action only consistent with the current status relationship between the conversationalists.

When placed in its literary context, the positive portrayal of Solomon in 1 Kings 3:5–14 takes on a more nuanced hue.[45] The 1 Kings account presents Solomon as full of potential, supported by the LORD, should he only "walk in my ways, keeping my statues and my commandments" (1 Kgs 3:14). The narrative that follows describes just how far Solomon fell from this ideal. Beginning well, 1 Kings 4–10 describe the glories of Solomon's reign, enjoying the blessing of God. The story ends badly, however, as Solomon fails to maintain his fidelity to the God of Israel (1 Kings 11). The summary of Solomon's fall, culminating in the editorial statement of 1 Kgs 11:9–10, uses language similar and reminiscent of the 1 Kings 3

---

43. Perhaps reflecting Solomon's death at a relatively early age. Japhet, *1 and 2 Chronicles*, 532; Zalevski, "Revelation of God to Solomon," 258.
44. See Clift, *Conversation Analysis*, 151.
45. Sweeney, *1 and 2 Kings*, 530.

conversation with the LORD designed to make plain the unfulfilled potential that was Solomon's.[46]

In 2 Chronicles, the mood of this conversation between Deity and Solomon is different than 1 Kings.[47] Chronicles places the conversation under the thematic umbrella introduced in 2 Chr 1:1: "the LORD his God was with him and made him exceedingly great." Rather than showing unfulfilled potential (as in 1 Kings), the Chronicler uses the conversation to support the positive, almost ideal, portrait of Solomon in 2 Chronicles 1–9.

Structure

Several structural components of this conversation deserve attention. Both accounts follow essentially the same conversational structure (minus the consequential action formed by the editorial insertion of 1 Kgs 3:10). Neither account includes a greeting or an ending. Unannounced and without introduction, the LORD or God simply begins speaking (although contextualized in a "dream by night" in 1 Kings), even though this is the first encounter between the Deity and Solomon in both the Kings and Chronicles accounts.

And without a closing, the conversation simply stops.[48] Although not unusual in the conversational prayers of the Hebrew Bible, the absence of a closing suggests that exchange of information is not the primary function of the conversation. The conversation describes the status between the conversational participants. That status, although trending differently in both Kings and Chronicles, is dynamic and so the *who-we-are-to-one-another* of the conversation is open ended, continuing in the following narrative.

Although the conversation has no closing, the episode containing the conversation has a firm ending. 1 Kings provides a closure to the conversation, indicating that "Solomon awoke" (1 Kgs 3:15) reiterating that the conversation had been in a dream. Both 1 Kings and 2 Chronicles relocate Solomon from Gibeon to Jerusalem following the conversation, bringing the reader to a new chapter in Solomon's career.

---

46. The editorial insertion is presented in the form of a third conversation between the LORD and Solomon (1 Kgs 11:11), a conversation not mentioned in the Chronicles account.

47. Kalimi, makes this point appealing to several alterations between the earlier Samuel–Kings and the Chronicler's version the David–Solomon story. Kalimi, *The Reshaping of Ancient Israelite History*, 52.

48. "Participants cannot appropriately terminate occasions of interaction simply by stopping talking and/or walking away." Robinson, "Overall Structural Organization," 77. But this is exactly what happens between God and Solomon.

Both versions are constructed in two rounds, the second round consisting only of the Deity speech. Why doesn't Solomon respond to the Deity's promise? There is no astonishment. No thank you. No promise of fidelity. Solomon certainly is confident enough to speak to Deity as evidenced in round one. So, why is he silent, offering no response to God's promise? Silence is an important feature of conversation and here the silence is controlled by the Deity. Following the Deity's promise, Solomon awakes (1 Kgs 3:15) or the event simply ends, presumably with God disappearing (reversing the "appearing" of 2 Chr 1:7). Solomon is prevented an opportunity at response. The last word is God's. The effect of the conversational structure is that the reader's attention remains on the Deity's promise without any distraction a response from Solomon may have offered.

Solomon: 1 Kings 8:22–54 // 2 Chronicles 6:14–7:1

1 Kings 8:22–54

A: ²² *Then Solomon stood before the altar of the Lord in the presence of all the assembly of Israel, and spread out his hands to heaven.* ²³ He said, "O LORD, God of Israel, there is no God like you in heaven above or on earth beneath, keeping covenant and steadfast love for your servants who walk before you with all their heart, ²⁴ the covenant that you kept for your servant my father David as you declared to him; you promised with your mouth and have this day fulfilled with your hand. ²⁵ Therefore, O LORD, God of Israel, keep for your servant my father David that which you promised him, saying, 'There shall never fail you a successor before me to sit on the throne of Israel, if only your children look to their way, to walk before me as you have walked before me.' ²⁶ Therefore, O God of Israel, let your word be confirmed, which you promised to your servant my father David.

²⁷ "But will God indeed dwell on the earth? Even heaven and the highest heaven cannot contain you, much less this house that I have built! ²⁸ Regard your servant's prayer and his plea, O LORD my God, heeding the cry and the prayer that your servant prays to you today; ²⁹ that your eyes may be open night and day toward this house, the place of which you said, 'My name shall be there,' that you may heed the prayer that your servant prays toward this place. ³⁰ Hear the plea of your servant and of your

people Israel when they pray toward this place; O hear in heaven your dwelling place; heed and forgive.⁴⁹

³¹ "If someone sins against a neighbor and is given an oath to swear, and comes and swears before your altar in this house, ³² then hear in heaven, and act, and judge your servants, condemning the guilty by bringing their conduct on their own head, and vindicating the righteous by rewarding them according to their righteousness.

³³ "When your people Israel, having sinned against you, are defeated before an enemy but turn again to you, confess your name, pray and plead with you in this house, ³⁴ then hear in heaven, forgive the sin of your people Israel, and bring them again to the land that you gave to their ancestors.

³⁵ "When heaven is shut up and there is no rain because they have sinned against you, and then they pray toward this place, confess your name, and turn from their sin, because you punish them, ³⁶ then hear in heaven, and forgive the sin of your servants, your people Israel, when you teach them the good way in which they should walk; and grant rain on your land, which you have given to your people as an inheritance.

³⁷ "If there is famine in the land, if there is plague, blight, mildew, locust, or caterpillar; if their enemy besieges them in any of their cities;⁵⁰ whatever plague, whatever sickness there is; ³⁸ whatever prayer, whatever plea there is from any individual or from all your people Israel, all knowing the afflictions of their own hearts so that they stretch out their hands toward this house; ³⁹ then hear in heaven your dwelling place, forgive, act,⁵¹ and render to all whose hearts you know—according to all their ways, for only you know what is in every human heart— ⁴⁰ so that they may fear you all the days that they live in the land that you gave to our ancestors.

⁴¹ "Likewise when a foreigner, who is not of your people Israel, comes from a distant land because of your name ⁴² —for they shall hear of your great name, your mighty hand, and your outstretched arm—when a foreigner comes and prays toward this house, ⁴³ then hear in heaven your dwelling place, and do

---

49. 1 Kgs 8:30 and 2 Chr 6:21 both read שמעת, though translated inconsistently in NRSV.

50. MT: "in the land of their gates."

51. עשית (act) is not in 2 Chr 6:30.

according to all that the foreigner calls to you, so that all the peoples of the earth may know your name and fear you, as do your people Israel, and so that they may know that your name has been invoked on this house that I have built.

[44] "If your people go out to battle against their enemy, by whatever way you shall send them, and they pray to the LORD toward the city that you have chosen and the house that I have built for your name, [45] then hear in heaven their prayer and their plea, and maintain their cause.

[46] "If they sin against you—for there is no one who does not sin—and you are angry with them and give them to an enemy, so that they are carried away captive to the land of the enemy, far off or near; [47] yet if they come to their senses in the land to which they have been taken captive, and repent, and plead with you in the land of their captors, saying, 'We have sinned, and have done wrong; we have acted wickedly'; [48] if they repent with all their heart and soul in the land of their enemies, who took them captive, and pray to you toward their land, which you gave to their ancestors, the city that you have chosen, and the house that I have built for your name; [49] then hear in heaven your dwelling place their prayer and their plea, maintain their cause [50] and forgive your people who have sinned against you, and all their transgressions that they have committed against you; and grant them compassion in the sight of their captors, so that they may have compassion on them [51] (for they are your people and heritage, which you brought out of Egypt, from the midst of the iron-smelter). [52] Let your eyes[52] be open to the plea of your servant, and to the plea of your people Israel, listening to them whenever they call to you. [53] For you have separated them from among all the peoples of the earth, to be your heritage, just as you promised through Moses, your servant, when you brought our ancestors out of Egypt, O LORD God."

[54] *Now when Solomon finished offering all this prayer and this plea to the Lord, he arose from facing the altar of the Lord, where he had knelt with hands outstretched toward heaven.*

---

52. The incongruent mention of "eyes" is smoothed in LXX by insertion of "eyes *and ears.*"

2 Chronicles 6:12—7:1

A: ¹² Then Solomon stood before the altar of the Lord in the presence of the whole assembly of Israel, and spread out his hands. ¹³ Solomon had made a bronze platform five cubits long, five cubits wide, and three cubits high, and had set it in the court; and he stood on it.⁵³ Then he knelt⁵⁴ on his knees in the presence of the whole assembly of Israel, and spread out his hands toward heaven. ¹⁴ He said, "O Lord, God of Israel, there is no God like you, in heaven or on earth, keeping covenant in steadfast love with your servants who walk before you with all their heart— ¹⁵ you who have kept for your servant, my father David, what you promised to him. Indeed, you promised with your mouth and this day have fulfilled with your hand. ¹⁶ Therefore, O Lord, God of Israel, keep for your servant, my father David, that which you promised him, saying, 'There shall never fail you a successor before me to sit on the throne of Israel, if only your children keep to their way, to walk in my law as you have walked before me.' ¹⁷ Therefore, O Lord, God of Israel, let your word be confirmed, which you promised to your servant David.

¹⁸ "But will God indeed reside with mortals⁵⁵ on earth? Even heaven and the highest heaven cannot contain you, how much less this house that I have built! ¹⁹ Regard your servant's prayer and his plea, O Lord my God, heeding the cry and the prayer that your servant prays to you. ²⁰ May your eyes be open day and night toward this house, the place where you promised to set your name, and may you heed the prayer that your servant prays toward this place. ²¹ And hear the plea of your servant and of your people Israel, when they pray toward this place; may you hear from heaven your dwelling place; hear and forgive.

²² "If someone sins against another and is required to take an oath and comes and swears before your altar in this house, ²³ may you hear from heaven, and act, and judge your servants, repaying the guilty by bringing their conduct on their own head,

---

53. In conversation, both place and position are important. In 2 Chr 6:12, as in 1 Kgs 8:22, Solomon engages in conversation "before the altar of the Lord" that is, in the inner court of the temple. This location is changed in v. 13, bringing the intimate conversation between Solomon and the Lord into a public arena.

54. In 1 Kings 8, Solomon remains standing, although in 8:54 he does "arise" following the prayer.

55. את־האדם added in 2 Chr 6:18. See the discussion by Japhet, *Ideology of the Book of Chronicles*, 82.

and vindicating those who are in the right by rewarding them in accordance with their righteousness.

[24] "When your people Israel, having sinned against you, are defeated before an enemy but turn again to you, confess your name, pray and plead with you in this house, [25] may you hear from heaven, and forgive the sin of your people Israel, and bring them again to the land that you gave to them and to their ancestors.

[26] "When heaven is shut up and there is no rain because they have sinned against you, and then they pray toward this place, confess your name, and turn from their sin, because you punish them, [27] may you hear in heaven, forgive the sin of your servants, your people Israel, when you teach them the good way in which they should walk; and send down rain upon your land, which you have given to your people as an inheritance.

[28] "If there is famine in the land, if there is plague, blight, mildew, locust, or caterpillar; if their enemies besiege them in any of the settlements of the lands; whatever suffering, whatever sickness there is; [29] whatever prayer, whatever plea from any individual or from all your people Israel, all knowing their own suffering and their own sorrows so that they stretch out their hands toward this house; [30] may you hear from heaven, your dwelling place, forgive, and render to all whose heart you know, according to all their ways, for only you know the human heart. [31] Thus may they fear you and walk in your ways all the days that they live in the land that you gave to our ancestors.

[32] "Likewise when foreigners, who are not of your people Israel, come from a distant land because of your great name, and your mighty hand, and your outstretched arm, when they come and pray toward this house, [33] may you hear from heaven your dwelling place, and do whatever the foreigners ask of you, in order that all the peoples of the earth may know your name and fear you, as do your people Israel, and that they may know that your name has been invoked on this house that I have built.

[34] "If your people go out to battle against their enemies, by whatever way you shall send them, and they pray to you toward this city that you have chosen and the house that I have built for your name, [35] then hear from heaven their prayer and their plea, and maintain their cause.

[36] "If they sin against you—for there is no one who does not sin—and you are angry with them and give them to an enemy, so that they are carried away captive to a land far or near; [37] then if they come to their senses in the land to which they have been taken captive, and repent, and plead with you in the land of their captivity, saying, 'We have sinned, and have done wrong; we have acted wickedly'; [38] if they repent with all their heart and soul in the land of their captivity, to which they were taken captive, and pray toward their land, which you gave to their ancestors, the city that you have chosen, and the house that I have built for your name, [39] then hear from heaven your dwelling place their prayer and their pleas, maintain their cause and forgive your people who have sinned against you. [40] Now, O my God, let your eyes be open and your ears attentive to prayer from this place.

[41] "Now rise up, O LORD God, and go to your resting place,

> you and the ark of your might.

Let your priests, O LORD God, be clothed with salvation,

> and let your faithful rejoice in your goodness.

[42] O LORD God, do not reject your anointed one.

Remember your steadfast love for your servant David."

B: [7:1] *When Solomon had ended his prayer, fire came down from heaven and consumed the burnt offering and the sacrifices; and the glory of the Lord filled the temple*

Context

Although very similar in content, and placed in the same setting, the context established by the writer of Kings[56] and the Chronicler positions these two renditions of Solomon's prayer very differently. Both begin by placing Solomon, standing on the altar. In Chronicles, however, just prior to addressing the LORD, Solomon kneels before the LORD in the presence of the whole assembly. 1 Kings 8 does have Solomon "arise" from "where he had knelt" (1 Kgs 8:54) after the prayer, but this, after the fact, notation presents a movement in the status relationship between Solomon and the LORD that is quite differently described in 1 Chronicles. Solomon also assumes a supplicant posture by "spreading out his hands toward heaven." Mentioned once in 1 Kgs 8:22, but twice in 2 Chr 6:12, 13, Solomon is

---

56. For a survey of constructional schemes applied to 1 Kings 8 see Knoppers, "Prayer and Propaganda," 230–31; De Vries, *1 and 2 Chronicles*, 255.

clearly establishing the status relationship contextualizing the words to follow and patterning similar behavior for "any individual or all your people Israel" (1 Kgs 8:38; 2 Chr 6:29).

And following the prayer, the consequential activity is quite different as well. In Kings, Solomon simply arises and turns to face the assembly, pronouncing a blessing upon them. In Chronicles, a miraculous response from God in the form of a consuming fire and glory of the LORD that filled the temple (2 Chr 7:1), is witnessed by all, providing a very public preferred response from God to the direct speech from Solomon. 1 Kings presents the temple as a place of prayer, accessible by all and essential to all.

Solomon Round

With few variations, the prayers by Solomon in 1 Kings 8 and 2 Chronicles 6 are essentially the same—until the ending. At 1 Kgs 8:50b, the 2 Chr 6:40 version leaves the 1 Kings text,[57] replacing 1 Kgs 8:50b–53 with a formalized conclusion very similar to, if not taken from, Ps 132:8–10.[58] The thematic differences between the 1 Kings 8 ending and that found in 2 Chronicles 6 are significant, each conforming to the overall rhetorical purpose of each writer.[59]

The first part of Solomon's direct address (1 Kgs 8:23–26; 2 Chr 6:14–17) establishes the status of the conversational participants. The incomparable greatness of the LORD, God of Israel, is recognized in such a fashion that enhances the promise made to David, the LORD's servant, and Solomon's father. A failure to honor the promise made to David (now the foundation for Solomon's address) would be paramount to denying the stature assigned by Solomon to the LORD, God of Israel. That promise is subject to a slight but important change in the 2 Chronicles 6 rendition. In 1 Kings 8, Solomon reminds God that the promise was conditioned:

> If only your descendants will look to their way and walk before me as you have walked. (1 Kgs 8:25)

While in 2 Chronicles the condition reads:

> If only your children will look to their way and walk in the path of my teachings [my torah] as you have walked. (2 Chr 6:16)

---

57. The point of departure, 1 Kgs 8:50, does appear elsewhere at 2 Chr 30:9.

58. Japhet, *1 and 2 Chronicles*, 601–05.

59. Knoppers argues that the 1 Kings account is designed to emphasize the temple as the "Divine-human nexus." Knoppers, "Prayer and Propoganda," 254.

The change of this one word (1 Kings: לְפָנַי; 2 Chronicles: בְּתוֹרָתִי) makes the 2 Chronicles version compatible with the post-exilic ideals of religious virtue.[60] This change will condition most of the petitions to follow in that the anticipated infractions, for which forgiveness is sought, become less relational (*walk before me*) as in 1 Kings, and more legislative (*in my teachings*) as in 2 Chronicles.

Based upon the acknowledged status articulated in the beginning of the direct address, Solomon next presents a formalized petition, asking the LORD to "regard" (1 Kgs 8:28; 2 Chr 6:19) and "hear" (1 Kgs 8:30; 2 Chr 6:21). The status negotiated between Solomon and the LORD expressed "today" (1 Kgs 8:28)[61] is extended into the future through the seven petitions that follow. The seven petitions forming the core of Solomon's prayer are pleas for answers to prayer.[62] All the petitions request that God hear *in* heaven (1 Kings 8 and 2 Chr 6:27) or *from* heaven (2 Chr 6).

1. 1 Kgs 8:31–32   //   2 Chr 6:22–23
2. 1 Kgs 8:33–34   //   2 Chr 6:24–25
3. 1 Kgs 8:35–36   //   2 Chr 6:26–27
4. 1 Kgs 8:37–40   //   2 Chr 6:28–31
5. 1 Kgs 8:41–43   //   2 Chr 6:32–33
6. 1 Kgs 8:44–45   //   2 Chr 6:34–35
7. 1 Kgs 8:46–50   //   2 Chr 6:36–39

Petitions 2–3, and 7 contemplate direr circumstances resulting from sin (in petition 1 the sin is directed toward a neighbor) and plead for relief from the circumstances, accompanied by Divine forgiveness. The fourth petition also envisions direr circumstances, presumably resulting from sinful behavior, for relief and forgiveness is here, also, requested. The fifth petition imagines the foreigner who, having heard of the LORD's great reputation appears at the temple in prayer. Solomon requests that person, too, be attended by the LORD.

The end of the prayer differs considerably between Kings and Chronicles. The formalized conclusion of 2 Chr 6:40–42 appropriates the status and authority of a presumably widely known liturgical piece, lending that authority now to the person of Solomon. The addition of this liturgical piece to the

---

60. See Gottlieb, "Mashal Le-Melekh," 109–10.

61. Missing in the 2 Chronicles 6 version.

62. Generalized in the opening (1 Kgs 8:28 // 2 Chr 6:19) and closing (1 Kgs 8:52) petitions and the central petition from the list of seven (1 Kgs 8:38 // 2 Chr 6:30).

end of the prayer in Chronicles amplifies what the Chronicler understood to be the main function of the prayer—articulating the high status given to Solomon, and, by extension, the high status given to the temple.

Status in 1 Kings 8 and 2 Chronicles 6

Although very similar in form (until the ending), the differences that do exist in the two renditions of Solomon's prayer are significant in describing the status relationship between the conversational participants. In 1 Kings, the nation ("your people Israel") is forged in the iron-smelter of Egypt, formed at the exodus, under the leadership of Moses, and should they be repentant of future sins against God, subject to a similar re-gathering from the land of their captors. 2 Chronicles is altogether different. In 2 Chronicles there is no mention of Egypt, the exodus, or Moses.[63] Instead, in 2 Chronicles we read of a Divine resting place, in the company of the ark, priests, and "your anointed one" (Solomon, himself) all clothed in remembrance of the Divine's steadfast love for "your servant David." The ending of the prayer in 2 Chronicles elevates the status of Solomon, placing him in the rarified company of the ark, David, and the resting place of God. Important also is the thrice repeated address "Lord God" (יהוה אלהים) found only in the 2 Chronicles ending.[64] The appellation is unusual in Chronicles,[65] but also used in Solomon's prayer of 2 Chr 1:9 (not appearing in the 1 Kings 3 parallel) and David's prayer of 1 Chr 17:16, 17 (also in the 2 Samuel 7 parallel).[66] The appearance of Lord (the personal name of Israel's God) together with the general term for Deity (God) unspecified by further attribution (God of the ancestors, God of Israel, God of Abraham, Isaac, and Jacob) allows Solomon familiarity with Deity unrestricted by land, ethnicity, or political boundaries. The Lord God effectively acts in the midst of his people, Israel, and the foreign captor, whether near or far, so that all the peoples of the earth may know his name and fear him (2 Chr 6:32). Unrestrained Divine prerogative and Divine immediacy is illustrated in the consequential activity to follow.

---

63. Consistent with the Chronicler's neglect of the exodus.

64. Elsewhere, in 1 Kings 8 and 2 Chronicles 6, the title, "Lord, God of Israel" is used. Likewise, the title "Lord God" is not found in Ps 132:8–10.

65. More common is "Lord, God of Israel" or "Lord, his (our, your) God," or "Lord, God of the ancestors," etc.

66. Elsewhere in Chronicles the title is only found in 1 Chr 22:1, 19, 28:20; 29:1; 2 Chr 32:16.

Significant is the turn added in 2 Chr 7:1, a Divine response to Solomon's turn, completing the round of conversation.[67] This remarkable and miraculous response is absent in 1 Kings, but consistent with the rhetorical function of Solomon's earlier prayer (2 Chr 1:7–10 parallel to 1 Kgs 3:6–9). The miraculous and demonstrable evidence of Divine presence in 2 Chronicles 7 elevates Solomon's status in a manner not desired in 1 Kings.

Hezekiah: 2 Kings 19:15–34 // Isaiah 37:14–35

2 Kings 19:15–34

A: [15] *And Hezekiah prayed before the Lord*, and said: "O Lord the God of Israel, who are enthroned above the cherubim, you are God, you alone, of all the kingdoms of the earth; you have made heaven and earth. [16] Incline your ear, O Lord, and hear; open your eyes, O Lord, and see; hear the words of Sennacherib, which he has sent to mock the living God. [17] Truly, O Lord, the kings of Assyria have laid waste the nations and their lands, [18] and have hurled their gods into the fire, though they were no gods but the work of human hands—wood and stone—and so they were destroyed. [19] So now, O Lord our God, save us, I pray you, from his hand, so that all the kingdoms of the earth may know that you, O Lord, are God alone."

B: [20] Then Isaiah son of Amoz sent to Hezekiah, saying, "Thus says the Lord, the God of Israel: I have heard your prayer to me about King Sennacherib of Assyria. [21] This is the word that the Lord has spoken concerning him:

She despises you, she scorns you—
    virgin daughter Zion;
she tosses her head—behind your back,
    daughter Jerusalem.

[22] "Whom have you mocked and reviled?
    Against whom have you raised your voice
    and haughtily lifted your eyes?
Against the Holy One of Israel!

[23] By your messengers you have mocked the Lord,
    and you have said, 'With my many chariots
I have gone up the heights of the mountains,
    to the far recesses of Lebanon;

---

67. This response allows this episode to be included in conversational analysis.

I felled its tallest cedars,
  its choicest cypresses;
I entered its farthest retreat,
  its densest forest.

²⁴ I dug wells
  and drank foreign waters,
I dried up with the sole of my foot
  all the streams of Egypt.'

²⁵ "Have you not heard
  that I determined it long ago?
I planned from days of old
  what now I bring to pass,
that you should make fortified cities
  crash into heaps of ruins,

²⁶ while their inhabitants, shorn of strength,
  are dismayed and confounded;
they have become like plants of the field
  and like tender grass,
like grass on the housetops,
  blighted before it is grown.

²⁷ "But I know your rising and your sitting,
  your going out and coming in,
  and your raging against me.

²⁸ Because you have raged against me
  and your arrogance has come to my ears,
I will put my hook in your nose
  and my bit in your mouth;
I will turn you back on the way
  by which you came.

²⁹ "And this shall be the sign for you: This year you shall eat what grows of itself, and in the second year what springs from that; then in the third year sow, reap, plant vineyards, and eat their fruit. ³⁰ The surviving remnant of the house of Judah shall again take root downward, and bear fruit upward; ³¹ for from Jerusalem a remnant shall go out, and from Mount Zion a band of survivors. The zeal of the LORD of hosts will do this.

B¹: ³² "Therefore thus says the LORD concerning the king of Assyria: He shall not come into this city, shoot an arrow there, come before it with a shield, or cast up a siege ramp against it. ³³ By the way that he came, by the same he shall return; he shall not come into this city, says the LORD. ³⁴ For I will defend this city to save it, for my own sake and for the sake of my servant David."

Isaiah 37:14–35

A: ¹⁴ *Hezekiah received the letter from the messengers and read it. Then he went up to the temple of the Lord and spread it out before the Lord.* ¹⁵ *And Hezekiah prayed to the Lord,* saying: ¹⁶ "O LORD of hosts, God of Israel, who are enthroned above the cherubim, you are God, you alone, of all the kingdoms of the earth; you have made heaven and earth. ¹⁷ Incline your ear, O LORD, and hear; open your eyes, O LORD, and see; hear all the words of Sennacherib, which he has sent to mock the living God. ¹⁸ Truly, O LORD, the kings of Assyria have laid waste all the nations and their lands, ¹⁹ and have hurled their gods into the fire, though they were no gods, but the work of human hands—wood and stone—and so they were destroyed. ²⁰ So now, O LORD our God, save us from his hand, so that all the kingdoms of the earth may know that you alone are the LORD."

B: ²¹ Then Isaiah son of Amoz sent to Hezekiah, saying: "Thus says the LORD, the God of Israel: Because you have prayed to me concerning King Sennacherib of Assyria, ²² this is the word that the LORD has spoken concerning him:

She despises you, she scorns you—
    virgin daughter Zion;
she tosses her head—behind your back,
    daughter Jerusalem.

²³ "Whom have you mocked and reviled?
    Against whom have you raised your voice
and haughtily lifted your eyes?
    Against the Holy One of Israel!

²⁴ By your servants you have mocked the Lord,
    and you have said, 'With my many chariots
I have gone up the heights of the mountains,
    to the far recesses of Lebanon;
I felled its tallest cedars,
    its choicest cypresses;
I came to its remotest height,
    its densest forest.

²⁵ I dug wells
    and drank waters,
I dried up with the sole of my foot
    all the streams of Egypt.'

²⁶ "Have you not heard
    that I determined it long ago?
I planned from days of old
    what now I bring to pass,
that you should make fortified cities
    crash into heaps of ruins,

²⁷ while their inhabitants, shorn of strength,
    are dismayed and confounded;
they have become like plants of the field
    and like tender grass,
like grass on the housetops,
    blighted before it is grown.

²⁸ "I know your rising up and your sitting down,
    your going out and coming in,
    and your raging against me.

²⁹ Because you have raged against me
    and your arrogance has come to my ears,
I will put my hook in your nose
    and my bit in your mouth;
I will turn you back on the way
    by which you came.

³⁰ "And this shall be the sign for you: This year eat what grows of itself, and in the second year what springs from that; then in the third year sow, reap, plant vineyards, and eat their fruit. ³¹ The surviving remnant of the house of Judah shall again take root downward, and bear fruit upward; ³² for from Jerusalem a remnant shall go out, and from Mount Zion a band of survivors. The zeal of the LORD of hosts will do this.

B¹: ³³ "Therefore thus says the LORD concerning the king of Assyria: He shall not come into this city, shoot an arrow there, come before it with a shield, or cast up a siege ramp against it. ³⁴ By the way that he came, by the same he shall return; he shall not come into this city, says the LORD. ³⁵ For I will defend this city to save it, for my own sake and for the sake of my servant David."

Context:

Faced with the threat of Assyrian conquest at the hand of Sennacherib, both 2 Kings 19 and Isaiah 37 present Hezekiah praying before the LORD. Hezekiah's prayer sets the stage for a lengthy Divine judgment speech against Sennacherib. This judgment speech, presented as a Divine turn within a conversational prayer, assumes a personal dynamic that would otherwise be absent had the prayer not been included.

Variations:

Although essentially the same in both 2 Kings and Isaiah, there are minor differences in the two renditions.[68]

2 Kings 19	Isaiah 37
• LORD, the God of Israel (v. 15)	• LORD of hosts, God of Israel (v. 15)[69]
• "Please" particle נא (v. 19)	• No particle present (v. 19)
• LORD are God alone (v. 19)	• You alone are the LORD (v. 20)
• Messengers (v. 23)	• Servants (v. 24)[70]
• Retreat (v. 23)	• Remotest height (v. 24)
• Foreign waters (v. 24)	• Waters (v. 25)

Structure:

Like a prayer of David (2 Sam 24:10–17; 1 Chr 21:8–17) and a later prayer offered by Hezekiah (2 Kgs 20:1–7; Isa 38:3–8), this prayer is partly mediated by a third party—the prophet Isaiah, son of Amoz. In this conversational prayer, the prophet's mediation provides an appropriate venue for the inclusion of the lengthy judgment poem against Sennacherib. But, the prophet's mediation of the LORD's reply to Hezekiah also highlights the lack of recipient design in the LORD's reply to Hezekiah. Aside from the

---

68. It is here concluded that Isaiah is dependent upon the Kings account. See Blenkinsopp, *Isaiah 1–39*, 469; Peursen and Talstra, "Computer-Assisted Analysis of Parallel Texts in the Bible," 50. For a minority view see Smelik, "Distortion of Old Testament Prophecy," 71–74.

69. The title "LORD of Hosts" (and near variants) is a favored title for God in Isaiah and is not a surprising modification in Isaiah's rendition of the prayer.

70. Perhaps extending the contrast between Sennacharib and his servants to the LORD of Hosts and his presumed servants.

sign described in 2 Kgs 19:29 and Isa 37:30, there is nothing that connects the LORD's turn (B) to Hezekiah's request. Recipient design is minimal in B, with the concerns expressed by Hezekiah only addressed in B¹. The response B, in both 2 Kings and Isaiah, is unnecessary for the conversation, which more naturally flows from A directly to B¹. This observation naturally leads to the question: Why embed the judgment poem against Sennacherib into a conversational prayer?

This conversational prayer, in both renditions,[71] now serves as the context for a lengthy judgment poem against King Sennacherib.[72] The judgment against Sennacherib is couched in a Divine preferred response to Hezekiah. Presenting the judgment in this fashion, the Divine action accomplishes two purposes: Sennacherib's misdeeds are punished, and the standing of Hezekiah is preserved. The judgment is not a dispassionate act of moral retribution or legal penalty. Instead, God's judgment against Sennacherib is part of the *who-we-are-to-one-another* between Hezekiah and God. The function of the shared standing between the conversationalists described in this conversational prayer can be seen clearly when compared to 2 Chr 32:20 where the prayer is only mentioned and the defeat of the Assyrian army is described minus the shared standing developed in conversation.

An interesting feature in the response of B¹, however, is the way in which the central request of A, "save us" in 2 Kgs 19:19 (amplified by the inclusion of the particle נא, "please") and Isa 37:20 is modified to "save this city" (2 Kgs 19:34; Isa 37:35).[73] The consequential action to the conversational prayer is repeated verbatim in both accounts (2 Kgs 19:35–37; Isa 37:36–38) and even though the action accomplishes what Hezekiah had hoped, saving Hezekiah and his compatriots does not seem to be the Deity's first concern.[74] Instead, the Divine consequential action, the salvation of Jerusalem, is a fitting response to the boast and threat from Rabshakeh, citing numerous other cities that have fallen before the Assyrian might (2 Kgs 19:12–13; Isa 37:12–13).

---

71. Interestingly, this prayer is only mentioned, but not recited, in 2 Chr 32:20.

72. Montgomery calls it an "unbidden oracle." Montgomery, *Book of Kings*, 494.

73. Jenkins argues that Sargon's threat occasioned the judgment poem. Jenkins, "Hezekiah's Fourteenth Year," 293. Some see the whole account composed during the sixth century Babylonian crises. See Baruchi-Unna, "Story of Hezekiah's Prayer," 282.

74. Contrast this with the repetition of request and response seen in the Elisha conversational prayer of 2 Kgs 6:17–21.

Storytelling in Conversation

Jerusalem was spared Assyrian devastation at the hand of Sennacharib in or around 704 BCE. The Assyrian account of the conflict is quite different than that presented in 2 Kings or Isaiah. In Sennacharib's rendition of the event:

> As for Hezekiah, the Jew, who did not submit to my yoke, 46 of his strong, walled cities as well as the small cities in their neighborhood which were without number,—by levelling with battering-rams (?) and by bringing up siege-engines (?), by attacking and storming on foot, by mines, tunnels and breaches (?), I besieged and took (those cities). 200,150 people, great and small, male and female, horses, mules, asses, camels, cattle and sheep without number, I brought away from them and counted as spoil. Himself, like a caged bird I shut up in Jerusalem his royal city.[75]

Remembered quite differently by the Judeans as recorded in the texts of the Hebrew Bible, Jerusalem is not a cage in which Hezekiah was confined but the object of a unique and remarkable act of Divine protection. The inclusion of the conversational prayer articulating both, Divine favor for Jerusalem and Divine contempt for Sennacharib, moves the story from one of military prowess and might (decidedly favoring the Assyrians) to a story of Divine empathy and activism. Here, it isn't military machines or the spoil of war that concerns the story, but a Divine human relationship forged in the give and take of conversation. How stories are told tells a great deal about the storyteller.

Hezekiah: 2 Kings 20:1–7 // Isaiah 38:3–8

2 Kings 20:1–7

¹ *In those days Hezekiah became sick and was at the point of death.*

A: The prophet Isaiah son of Amoz came to him, and said to him, "Thus says the Lord: Set your house in order, for you shall die; you shall not recover."

B: ² *Then Hezekiah turned his face to the wall and prayed to the Lord* [saying]: ³ "Remember now, O Lord, I implore you, how I have walked before you in faithfulness with a whole heart, and have done what is good in your sight."

---

75. Luckenbill, *Annals of Sennacharib*, 32–33.

Hezekiah wept bitterly.

A¹: ⁴ *Before Isaiah had gone out of the middle court, the word of the Lord came to him* [saying]: ⁵ "Turn back, and say to Hezekiah prince of my people, Thus says the Lord, the God of your ancestor David: I have heard your prayer, I have seen your tears; indeed, I will heal you; on the third day you shall go up to the house of the Lord. ⁶ I will add fifteen years to your life. I will deliver you and this city out of the hand of the king of Assyria; I will defend this city for my own sake and for my servant David's sake."

⁷ Then Isaiah said, "Bring a lump of figs. Let them take it and apply it to the boil, so that he may recover."

Isaiah 38:1–8

¹ *In those days Hezekiah became sick and was at the point of death.*

A: The prophet Isaiah son of Amoz came to him, and said to him, "Thus says the Lord: Set your house in order, for you shall die; you shall not recover."

B: ² *Then Hezekiah turned his face to the wall, and prayed to the Lord* ³ [He said]: "Remember now, O Lord, I implore you, how I have walked before you in faithfulness with a whole heart, and have done what is good in your sight."

And Hezekiah wept bitterly.

A¹: ⁴ *Then the word of the Lord came to Isaiah* [saying]: ⁵ "Go and say to Hezekiah, Thus says the Lord, the God of your ancestor David: I have heard your prayer, I have seen your tears; I will add fifteen years to your life. ⁶ I will deliver you and this city out of the hand of the king of Assyria, and defend this city. ⁷ "This is the sign to you from the Lord, that the Lord will do this thing that he has promised: ⁸ See, I will make the shadow cast by the declining sun on the dial of Ahaz turn back ten steps."

So the sun turned back on the dial the ten steps by which it had declined.

Structure

As with the prayers of David (2 Sam 24:10–17; 1 Chr 21:8–17) and Hezekiah's earlier prayer (2 Kgs 19:15–34; Isa 37:14–35) this conversational prayer, too, is mediated, in part, by a prophet. While Hezekiah can speak directly to the LORD, the Divine response comes through Isaiah the son of Amoz and as the word of the LORD (2 Kgs 20:4; Isa 38:4).

There are several structural details found in both versions of the conversational prayer that deserve our attention. Although mediated by the prophet, Isaiah, this conversational prayer establishes a firm and unequal status relationship between the conversational partners. The opening turn, spoken by the LORD, announces the imminent death of the conversational partner. Even though Hezekiah offers a dispreferred response to the opening turn, that response is structured to make clear that he is in a powerless position, unable to offer any counter to the Divine announcement. It is worth noting that Hezekiah's response is labeled a "prayer,"[76] both in the introduction to B and the Divine response of A¹. This label, "prayer," appears relatively infrequently, used in Kings only for prayers articulated by Elisha and Hezekiah. The prayer uttered by Hezekiah is given urgency through its opening "O LORD" (אנה) and "please" (the particle (נא), matched by the accompanying action of turning to the wall and weeping bitterly. The *how* of Hezekiah's response helps us understand the *what* of his response. Hezekiah asks the LORD to "remember."[77] Specifically, Hezekiah asks the LORD to "remember" his past standing; having been faithful and having done good in the LORD's sight. Hezekiah draws attention to his moral uprightness, in terms that emphasize his standing with the LORD, in an effort to dissuade the LORD from his threatened action. This dispreferred response is non-confrontational but nevertheless forms a dispreferred prayer for healing.[78]

Round Two

In contrast to the verbatim agreement found in the conversation's first round, there are three structural details that differ in the two versions of the conversational prayer contained in round two of the conversation. The first structural detail to note may, at first, appear insignificant.[79] The first round

---

76. See discussion of Elisha's prayer in 2 Kings 6:17–21.

77. D. T. Williams suggests that the prayer is not a prayer for healing. Williams, "Dial and the Boil," 32.

78. Sidnell, *Conversation Analysis*, 78–79.

79. We assume here the 2 Kings account is the source for the Isaiah account. See

of this conversation (A and B) is the same in both versions. The framing of B, however, is not the same in both versions. In 2 Kings 20:2, B is introduced by the infinitive, "saying" (לאמר)[80] while Isaiah 38:3 uses the finite form, "he said" (ויאמר). The infinitive, often used to frame an exact quote, only appears in A of 2 Kgs 20:2, even though A in both versions is identical. Conversely, Isaiah 38:4 introduces A[1] with the infinitive as does 2 Kgs 20:4 even though variations exist between the two versions of A[1]. So, what does the use of the infinitive in 2 Kgs 20:2 signify and why is it not repeated in Isa 38:3? If we are to assume that the infinitive is intended to frame a direct quote, then it appears the Isaiah 38 version is careful to present the LORD's statement accurately (even if it differs from the source in 2 Kgs 20), in a manner not desired or needed for Hezekiah's statements.

Second, in both accounts, a statement is inserted about the king of Assyria and the LORD's rescue of the city of Jerusalem from the king of Assyria's hand (2 Kgs 20:6b; Isa 38:6). The two renditions of the rescue are essentially the same except for the rationale provided in 2 Kings 20 (for my sake and for my servant David's sake) that does not appear in Isaiah. In Isaiah, the rationale for the rescue of the city is as a response to Hezekiah's prayer and tears. Isaiah grants to Hezekiah a greater standing with God than does 2 Kings. This observation is consistent with the inclusion of the "writing" (Isa 38:10–20) which might otherwise be an intrusive addition[81] but which also functions to detail the standing Hezekiah enjoys with God.

The third structural detail to note involves the ending of the conversation. In Isaiah 38, Isaiah continues A[1] with a statement concerning the reversal of the sun dial (Isa 38:7–8), a sign that a miraculous healing for Hezekiah is forthcoming.[82] In Isaiah 38, the sign is proffered by the LORD, without any initiating request from Hezekiah. In 2 Kings, the sun dial becomes the subject of a subsequent conversation between Isaiah and Hezekiah (2 Kgs 20:8–9) in which Hezekiah initiates the request for a sign to verify the healing will take place. In 2 Kings 20, Isaiah and Hezekiah discuss the nature of the sign and then having reached agreement, Isaiah "cried to the LORD," presenting the request for a sign to which the LORD complies.

Blenkinsopp, *Isaiah 1–39*, 484.

80. Cynthia Miller notes that often the infinitive is used in the first part of an adjacency pair. C. Miller, *Representation of Speech*, 250. Here, the infinitive appears in the second part of the adjacency pair, framing the verb פלל (2 Chr 30:18 the only other such usage of לאמר). See C. Miller, *Representation of Speech*, 439.

81. See Goswell, "Literary Logic and Meaning of Isaiah 38," 170–75.

82. Hezekiah is promised fifteen additional years of life, not permanent healing. See Wieringen, "Notes on Isaiah 38–39," 28.

I–Thou

Taken collectively, these differences in the two renditions of the conversational prayer result in an enhanced standing of Hezekiah in the Isaiah version when compared to the 2 Kings version. If we assume that the Isaiah version is a variation of the version from Kings,[83] and that the variations are intentional, why were they constructed? The answer must be this: the writer of Isaiah viewed the *who-we-are-to-God* in conversational prayer as the catalyst for the effective consequential action.[84] God responds to the *who* of this prayer every bit as much as to the *what* of the prayer.

---

83. Wagner argues that the prayer in Isaiah 38 represents the last stage of literary history for the Hezekiah story in Isaiah. Wagner, "From Salvation to Doom," 101.

84. See also Wagner, "From Salvation to Doom," 94–95.

8

Elijah/Elisha Cycle

THE PRAYERS IN THE Elijah / Elisha stories are quite different in structure than the prayers in Kings attributed to David, Solomon, or Hezekiah. Structurally, these conversational prayers resemble more the prayers of Joshua or Minoah and are quite unlike the prayers found in the later prophetic books. It should also be noted that of the conversational prayers found in Kings, only these, the conversational prayers of Elijah and Elisha, have no parallel in Chronicles.[1] While the conversational prayers involving Elijah or Elisha are often accompanied by miraculous events, these events play a supportive role in the conversational exchange, never diverting attention from the more astonishing conversation with Deity.

1 Kings 17:20–22: Elijah and the Widow's Son

A: [20] Then he cried out to the LORD, "LORD my God, have you brought tragedy even on this widow I am staying with, by causing her son to die?"

A[1]: [21] *Then he stretched himself out on the boy three times* and cried out to the LORD, "LORD my God, let this boy's life return to him!"

B: [22] *The Lord heard Elijah's cry, and the boy's life returned to him, and he lived.*

---

1. Elijah is present in Chronicles only through a very unpleasant letter sent to Jehoram (2 Chr 21:11–15), a letter not mentioned in Kings (2 Kgs 3). And Elisha is not present at all in Chronicles.

Structure

This conversational prayer has no opening and no closing. The conversation is framed by the repeated notation that Elijah "cried out"[2] to the LORD (v. 20, 21). There is a sense of urgency, perhaps even desperation, in the address. Without time to waste, Elijah gets directly to the heart of the tragedy. The conversational prayer consists of one round in the form of a question and command spoken by Elijah followed by consequential action from the LORD in response. While it is clear that the whole episode is designed to verify Elijah's status as a man of God and that "the word of the LORD in your mouth is truth" (1 Kgs 17:24), it is fascinating that the narrator chose a conversation between Elijah and the LORD as the pivotal moment by which to validate Elijah.[3]

Question

Elijah's conversation with the LORD begins with an accusation in the form of a question. The question articulates the initial presuppositions guiding the conversational exchange.[4] Elijah blames the LORD for this tragedy, culminating in the death of the widow's son. He doesn't seek a rationale. He doesn't consider a higher motive. Nor does Elijah consider the LORD's noninvolvement. Elijah accuses the LORD of murder.[5] An accusation to which there is no reply.

---

2. The verb קרא is used relatively infrequently in Kings, clustered in 1 Kgs 13:2–32; 18:27–28; and three times in 2 Kgs 11:14; 18:28; 20:11.

3. For literary connections to the larger unit see Oancea, "Die Witwe und Israel," 130–41. Also, Steck, *Überlieferung und Zeitgeschichte*.

4. Levinson, *Pragmatics*, 178.

5. Commentators have struggled with the boldness of Elijah's accusation. Josephus says the boy "appeared to be dead." Josephus, *Jewish Antiquities*, 3.13.3. Marvin Sweeny agrees that the boy is not actually dead. But this seems to be more than Elijah's statement will allow. Sweeney, *1 and 2 Kings*, 215. Simon De Vries goes even further. He acknowledges that v. 20 states the boy has died but suggests that v. 20 "must be a secondary addition." Without any textual evidence for this conclusion, De Vries claims the verse makes three mistakes—one of which is bad theology because it implies "Yahweh might actually kill little boys." De Vries, *1 Kings*, 222.

Command

Elijah's initial accusatory question is quickly followed by a ritual act of magic[6] and a second address to the LORD, this time in the form of a command. Even though Elijah's ritual act, stretching out upon the body of the lifeless boy, has attracted much attention from commentators,[7] it is utterly ignored by the LORD. Verse 22 is quite clear. Elijah's words captured the LORD's attention. Elijah perceives that it is the LORD, his God, who possesses the agency required to permit the return of the boy's soul and so he commands the LORD accordingly.[8]

Elijah commands the LORD to permit the return of the child's soul, and the LORD does just that. The impact of the Divine consequential action is profound. Without uttering a word, the LORD confirms all that Elijah has spoken. Elijah's initial accusatory presuppositions are not challenged. And the bond between the LORD and Elijah is strengthened.[9]

The Divine silence of this conversation is intriguing. The LORD is accused of murder and then obeys the command of his accuser to undo the harm of which he has just been accused. The LORD's actions, in the form of a preferred response, acquiesce to the indictment of his accuser. Yet, through the whole episode the bond between accuser and Accused is strengthened, and in a fashion to enhance the reputation of the accuser! In this conversation, silence speaks loudly.[10]

The Power of Conversation

The inclusion of a ritual act of magic, embedded in Elijah's conversational prayer, provides an opportunity to see the effectiveness of conversation in stark contrast to other means of eliciting Divine action. Magic, when performed properly, is perceived by the performer to impose a compulsory response upon Deity.[11] The ritual begins an unbreakable cause and

---

6. See Montgomery, *Books of Kings*, 296; Cogan, *1 Kings*, 429; Kalmanofsky, "Women of God," 65.

7. Andrew Davis argues that Elijah is not performing a ritual act of magic but attempting to diagnose the boy's condition. Davis, "Rereading 1 Kings 17:21," 466.

8. This account is structured quite differently than its parallel involving Elisha in 2 Kgs 4:32–37.

9. Samuel Balentine notes the importance of perceived status in prayer in the Elijah stories. Balentine, *Prayer in the Hebrew Bible*, 51.

10. The silence here is even more powerful contrasted to the Divine rebuttal in conversation with Elijah at Horeb (1 Kgs 19:9, 13).

11. The belief that the action or spoken formula begins a chain of inevitable cause

effect chain of actions designed to achieve the desired end sought by the performer. The Deity must act. Conversation, on the other hand, has no such claim of inevitability. Conversation is dynamic and unscripted. It rests upon status negotiation in order to achieve an outcome. In this instance, the LORD's utter dismissal of the ritual act ensures both his status as a free agent and the power of conversation to produce Divine action.

1 Kings 18:36–38: Elijah on Carmel

A: *³⁶ At the time of the offering of the oblation*, the prophet Elijah came near and said, "O LORD, God of Abraham, Isaac, and Israel, let it be known this day that you are God in Israel, that I am your servant, and that I have done all these things at your bidding. ³⁷ Answer me, O LORD, answer me, so that this people may know that you, O LORD, are God, and that you have turned their hearts back."

B: *³⁸ Then the fire of the Lord fell and consumed the burnt offering, the wood, the stones, and the dust, and even licked up the water that was in the trench.*

Structure

Structurally, this conversational prayer is very similar to Elijah's prayer in 1 Kings 17. Elijah addresses Deity predicated upon an immediate and non-repeatable need. The Elijah address is answered by consequential action from Deity. And, like the prayer in 1 Kings 17, although this time much more explicitly, the conversation is focused on confirming status between the conversational partners.[12] Elijah's request of the LORD, God of Abraham, Isaac, and Israel is designed to result in public knowledge, making clear to all that: (1) you are God in Israel, and (2) that I am your servant, and that I have done all these things at your bidding (v. 36). The consequential action, fire of the LORD, is described as an emphatic affirmation

---

and effect also separates the magic from pious ritual. Although the actions or speech may be exactly the same, if not accompanied by the belief of inevitable Divine response, the pious act may be better considered as acted out prayer, founded on the same status negotiation and reliance on sincerity and authenticity as normal conversation. Sometimes the line between pious religious act and magic is blurred especially when the absence of desired Divine action is blamed upon the petitioner, effectively adding guilt to need.

12. Balentine, *Prayer in the Hebrew Bible*, 51–54.

of Elijah's status claim between himself and Deity, in stark contrast to the dismal failure of the prophets of Baal.[13]

Elijah Turn

The Elijah turn of the conversation is specific and detailed concerning the hoped-for consequence of the action requested from the LORD but is dependent upon previous conversation with the prophets of Baal (v. 24) to specify the Divine action requested. The God of Abraham, Isaac and Israel is immediately present, attending to the conversation between Elijah and the prophets, while, at least in Elijah's estimation, Baal must be meditating, or have wandered off, be on a journey, or has fallen asleep and must be roused (v. 27). Throughout the whole exchange, first between Elijah and the prophets, and then between Elijah and the LORD, the conversation is structured to make plain the effective presence of the LORD.

God of Abraham, Isaac, and Israel

The title given to the LORD by Elijah, "God of Abraham, Isaac, and Israel," is unusual, appearing elsewhere only in: 1 Chr 29:18; 2 Chr 30:6 and as an implied title in Exod 32:13. Commentators recognize the title as a variation of the more usual "God of Abraham, Isaac, and Jacob"[14] but have failed to notice that the title (or its implied) only appears in prayer (Exod 32:13; 1 Kgs 18:36; 1 Chr 29:18), or in official correspondence (2 Chr 30:6)[15] that may well be reliant on the David prayer of 1 Chr 29:18 and the Solomon prayer of 2 Chr 6:36–40. The common element in all these references is the intent to establish status between Deity and the nation, Israel. The status between God and Israel is here signified by the outcome of the desired action, "and that you have turned their hearts back" (1 Kgs 18:37).

The relationship between Elijah's conversational prayer (vv. 36–37) and the accompanying ritual act (vv. 30–35) is similar to the ritual and speech act of 1 Kings 17. Differences appear, however, when a comparison is made between the prophets of Baal on one hand and Elijah on the other, in the emphasis given to ritual and speech in the drama worked out on Mt Carmel.

---

13. Christina Fetherolf suggests that the consumption of the altar along with the sacrifice may indicate YHWH's displeasure with Elijah rather than a preferred response to Elijah's request. Fetherolf, "Elijah's Mantle," 203.

14. De Vries states the change "deliberate," designed to complement the following phrase, "God in Israel" (v. 36). De Vries, *1 Kings*, 230. See also Cogan, *1 Kings*, 443.

15. See Kalimi, *The Reshaping of Israelite History*, 192.

Elijah's request: "Answer me, O Lord, answer me" (v. 37)[16] is like that uttered by the prophets of Baal (v. 26). Unlike the request made by the prophets of Baal, however, Elijah's formulation of the request, repeating the phrase "answer me" draws attention away from the ritual and implies that the passionate plea of a person is the catalyst motivating God to act, while the Baal prophets rely upon repeated acts of ritual, including ecstatic dancing and self-cutting (vv. 26–29), but to no avail. The relational standing between Baal and his prophets could produce no consequential action, while the Lord would rend the heavens with fire in response to the plea of Elijah.

1 Kings 19:4–18: Elijah at Horeb

Of the three conversational prayers between Elijah and Deity appearing in the Hebrew Bible, this is the most private, yet the most extensive and complicated. This conversation, just like the previous two between Elijah and Deity (1 Kings 17 and 18), develops the status relationship between conversation partners, but, unlike the previous two conversations, the prolonged encounter in 1 Kings 19 will diminish Elijah's prophetic standing before Deity, yet, without impacting the personal standing between the two.[17] The dynamism of Elijah's standing before Deity is developed through changing context, doublets, assertive questions, and the various identifiers used for the Divine conversationalist.

> [4] *But he himself went a day's journey into the wilderness, and came and sat down under a solitary broom tree.*
>
> A: He asked that he might die: "It is enough; now, O Lord, take away my life, for I am no better than my ancestors." [5]
>
> *Then he lay down under the broom tree and fell asleep.*
>
> B: *Suddenly an angel touched him* and said to him, "Get up and eat."
>
> [6] *He looked, and there at his head was a cake baked on hot stones, and a jar of water. He ate and drank, and lay down again.*

---

16. Some LXX delete the repetition.

17. Admittedly, Elijah's relationship to Deity is complex, reflected in the many descriptions given by commentators to Elijah, ranging from insubordinate, overzealous, conceited, humorous, and plagued by an overinflated ego. For a survey of opinions see Hadjiev, "Elijah's Alleged Megalomania," 434.

A¹: ⁷ *The angel of the Lord came a second time, touched him,* and said, "Get up and eat, otherwise the journey will be too much for you."

B¹:⁸ *He got up, and ate and drank; then he went in the strength of that food forty days and forty nights to Horeb the mount of God. ⁹ At that place he came to a cave, and spent the night there.*

A²: Then the word of the Lord came to him, saying, "What are you doing here, Elijah?"

B²: ¹⁰ He answered, "I have been very zealous for the Lord, the God of hosts; for the Israelites have forsaken your covenant, thrown down your altars, and killed your prophets with the sword. I alone am left, and they are seeking my life, to take it away."

A³: ¹¹ He said, "Go out and stand on the mountain before the Lord, for the Lord is about to pass by."

Now there was a great wind, so strong that it was splitting mountains and breaking rocks in pieces before the Lord, but the Lord was not in the wind; and after the wind an earthquake, but the Lord was not in the earthquake; ¹² *and after the earthquake a fire, but the Lord was not in the fire; and after the fire a sound of sheer silence.*

B³: ¹³ *When Elijah heard it, he wrapped his face in his mantle and went out and stood at the entrance of the cave.*

A⁴: Then there came a voice to him that said, "What are you doing here, Elijah?"

B⁴: ¹⁴ He answered, "I have been very zealous for the Lord, the God of hosts; for the Israelites have forsaken your covenant, thrown down your altars, and killed your prophets with the sword. I alone am left, and they are seeking my life, to take it away."

A⁵: ¹⁵ Then the Lord said to him, "Go, return on your way to the wilderness of Damascus; when you arrive, you shall anoint Hazael as king over Aram. ¹⁶ Also you shall anoint Jehu son of Nimshi as king over Israel; and you shall anoint Elisha son of Shaphat of Abel-meholah as prophet in your place. ¹⁷ Whoever escapes from the sword of Hazael, Jehu shall kill; and whoever escapes from the sword of Jehu, Elisha shall kill. ¹⁸ Yet I will leave seven thousand in Israel, all the knees that have not bowed to Baal, and every mouth that has not kissed him."

Context

The context of a conversation,[18] including the setting of the conversation, exerts an important influence on the *what* of the conversation itself.[19] In this conversation, the context is established, first by the threat from Jezebel (19:2), second by Elijah's flight with his servant to Beer-sheba, and third by Elijah's solitary continuation into the wilderness a day's journey where he sits on the ground and, in desperation for his life, addresses Deity.[20] Further, as the setting changes, it segments the conversation between Elijah and Deity (vv. 8, 11, 13).[21] The angel of the LORD addresses Elijah (v. 7), telling him a journey awaits him (but without revealing the destination). Elijah, sustained by the one meal, travels forty days and nights, arriving at Horeb, where he finds a cave and settles in for the night (vv. 8–9). While in the cave, Elijah is addressed by the word of the LORD, commanding him to go out to the entrance of the cave (v. 13). In compliance, Elijah moves to the entrance of the cave where he is addressed by Deity again. As the setting for the conversation changes, so, too, does the persona of the Divine conversationalist. When in the desert, Elijah is addressed by the angel of the LORD (vv. 5, 7). After the setting moves to Horeb, the mount of God, it is the word of the LORD that speaks to Elijah (v. 9). Finally, as Elijah moves to the entrance of the cave (v. 13), a voice (v. 13) and the LORD (v. 15) converse with Elijah.

The movement of the setting for the conversation has an important influence on the structure of the conversation. Elijah's persona remains constant, yet he must move from space to space. Conversely, Deity does not move location, but changes persona as the setting for the conversation changes. Elijah is drawn in further and further, becoming more and more contingent as Deity becomes more and more the effective agent, controlling

---

18. As others have noted, the whole episode is designed to bring to the reader's mind Ishmael's journey to the wilderness, Jonah's flight and complaint under the bush, and Moses' encounter with God on Sinai. See Robinson, "Elijah at Horeb," 534–35.

19. Sidnell, *Conversation Analysis*, 245–55.

20. See also Jonah 4:2–11.

21. Mica Roi considers the story a departure on a journey story, a literary form seen elsewhere in the Hebrew Bible. Roi, "1 Kings 19," 44. See also the discussion describing the composite nature of 1 Kings, Hadjiev, "Elijah's Alleged Megalomania," 440–42. For arguments supporting a unified structure to the passage, see Robinson, "Elijah at Horeb," 533.

the conversation and its outcome. The changing venue of the conversation signals the shift in standing between the conversationalists.

Structure

The conversation between Elijah and Deity of 1 Kings 19 is constructed in six rounds, interspersed with action and a changing venue. The first two rounds contain preferred responses, establishing a rapport between Deity and Elijah. That rapport provides a foundation for the dispreferred responses in rounds three through six, presented in the form of indirect accusations and disapproval addressed by the conversationalists.

Doublets

A series of doublets, appearing throughout the conversational exchange, adds to the structure of the episode:

- Two appearances of the angel of the LORD
- Two commands to "get up and eat"
- Two questions by Deity: "What are you doing here?" (once voiced by the word of the LORD and once by a voice)
- Two statements of complaint by Elijah (in answer to Deity's question)

Repetition throughout the conversational exchange will highlight the formation of a shared understanding, an intersubjectivity, between the conversationalists.

Divine Identity

Throughout the conversation, Deity is referenced in four ways: angel (messenger) of the LORD (v. 7); word of the LORD (v. 9); a voice (v. 13); the LORD (v. 15). The structure of the conversation, including the repetition between rounds, suggests that all four represent the same conversational partner, yet, that partner is present to Elijah in a changing manner. The use of these changing labels for the Divine, mark movement in the fluctuating standing between the conversational partners. The relationship between the two conversationalists is changing.

Assertive Questions

The question posed by Deity (What are you doing here? vv. 9, 13) amounts to a rebuff. In these assertive questions,[22] not formed to seek information (after all, the journey leading Elijah to the Mount was at Deity's direction; v. 7), Deity challenges Elijah's complaint and implied accusation (vv. 10, 14). The accusatory nature of the questions becomes even clearer when combined with the Deity response in round six (19:15–18). In round six, the Deity attributes power to Elijah, recognizing his agency in anointing kings and prophets, while the questions earlier posed to Elijah implicitly accuse Elijah of a failure to use his power.[23]

Silence as a Dispreferred Response

Round four has a remarkable turn. Following the powerful phenomena of wind, earthquake, and fire (functioning in the conversation as consequential action in response to the Elijah statement of 19:10), came a "sound of shear silence" to which Elijah responded, "when he heard it." Elijah heard the sound of shear silence.[24] Silence can be a powerful part of conversation, functioning in a variety of manners.[25] Here, the Divine silence is made even more prominent following the noisome phenomena of wind, earthquake, and fire. And it is the silence that seems to have attracted Elijah's attention, causing him to wrap his face in his mantle[26] and move to the entrance of the cave. Without saying a word, the Divine silence presents a powerful rejection of Elijah's accusation in 19:10.[27]

Elijah's Complaint

Elijah's complaint is given verbatim two times (vv. 10, 14), both in response to the Deity's question ("What are you doing here?"). The first time, Elijah's complaint is met with a dispreferred response as the word of the LORD,

---

22. Clift, *Conversation Analysis*, 206.

23. Rosenblum, "When is a Question an Accusation?," 153.

24. As rendered in NRSV. Lust suggests something quite different when he translates "a roaring and thunderous voice" instead of "shear silence" for the phrase קול דממה דקה. Lust's suggestion remains a minority view. Lust, "A Gentle Breeze or a Roaring Thunderous Sound?," 115.

25. Clift, *Conversation Analysis*, 130–34.

26. See Fetherolf, "Elijah's Mantle," 202.

27. Davidson, "Subsequent Versions," 103–4.

making no mention of Elijah's statement, simply commands Elijah to go out to the entrance of the cave. There, following the display of wind, earthquake, fire, and silence, a Divine voice asks Elijah once again "What are you doing here?" This repetition of the question would most generally be followed by a repair from the respondent, as the first answer to the question was evidently not the preferred response. In other words, the display in vv. 11–12 is designed to give Elijah an opportunity to rethink his answer to the question posed to him in v. 10.[28] Elijah's repeated response, makes clear that he has properly understood the question and the relational status of the person posing the question. Despite this clear understanding of the question, Elijah holds firm to his response. Something else is at work.

The problem, evidenced by the repeated question, is that the two conversationalists do not share a common understanding of the world around them. Elijah complains that he is alone in his zealousness for the LORD, surrounded by Israelites who have forsaken covenant and who are now seeking to kill him. Elijah's complaint brings with it the implicit accusation that it is Deity who is responsible for placing Elijah in such a precarious position. The Deity has quite a different assessment of the situation. This "problem of intersubjectivity,"[29] of two very different understandings, will be addressed by the Deity's final response to Elijah in 19:15–18. Rather than seeing Elijah a powerless victim, soon to be murdered, the Deity describes Elijah as an agent of power, the anointer of kings and prophets, surrounded by seven thousand loyalists. And behind the Divine's explicit statement is the implicit affirmation of Divine control. Elijah is not in as precarious position as he thought, and the Deity has not lost control of the situation, marginalized by the Israelite unfaithful. Instead, the Deity is active and firmly in control of events not only in Israel but in Syria as well.

Joint Understanding in Prayer

The central issue in Elijah's conversation with Deity at Horeb illustrates the problem of intersubjectivity, a common problem in conversational prayer. Liturgical prayer is generally formulated to bring the petitioner into alignment with God, to see things from God's point of view, by articulating religiously approved expressions of that Divine viewpoint. Conversational prayer, when voicing a request or objection, is an effort to move God, to move Deity into alignment with the petitioner's point of view. Conversational prayer is, at its core, presumptuous; presuming that the Deity should alter perceptions to

---

28. See Sidnell, *Conversation Analysis*, 117–18.
29. Schegloff, "Repair after Next Turn," 1295–300.

understand the world from the petitioner's point of view. Why should Deity attend to such a presumptuous request? The three Elijah conversational prayers detail movement by both conversational partners, each responding to the other in order to achieve a shared understanding of each other and the world around. The movement of the Divine is no less real and authentic than is the movement of the human petitioner. Conversational exchange is a risk for all participants; Divine and human alike.

2 Kings 6:17–20: Elisha

A: [17] Then Elisha prayed: "O LORD, please open his eyes that he may see."

B: *So the Lord opened the eyes of the servant, and he saw; the mountain was full of horses and chariots of fire all around Elisha.* [18] *When the Arameans came down against him,*

A[1]: Elisha prayed to the LORD, and said, "Strike this people, please, with blindness."

B: *So he struck them with blindness as Elisha had asked.* [19] *Elisha said to them, "This is not the way, and this is not the city; follow me, and I will bring you to the man whom you seek." And he led them to Samaria.* [20] *As soon as they entered Samaria,*

A[2]: Elisha said, "O LORD, open the eyes of these men so that they may see."

B[2]: *The Lord opened their eyes, and they saw that they were inside Samaria.*

Context

How something is said in conversation is just as important as *what* is said in conversation. With that in mind, it is worth noting that this conversational prayer between Elisha and the LORD is structured in a way to highlight a feature of the status relationship between the LORD and Elisha. The conversational prayer is unusual in that the first two rounds are actually described as an act of "prayer" (פלל).[30] In addition, the requests verbalized by Elisha

---

30. In 2 Kings only here and 4:33 (also voiced by Elisha) and 19:15, 20; 20:2 (prayers made by Hezekiah). Elsewhere, is used to describe the conversational prayer to a third party (Deut 9:25–29).

in 6:17, 18 (*open, strike*) have appended the particle, נָא,[31] intended to add urgency to the plea (translated, *please*) and consistent with the introductory description, "he prayed."[32] These observations immediately lead to a question. Why isn't Elisha's conversational prayer in the third round (v. 20) so described?[33] What is urgent about the first two rounds of conversation that does not impact the third round? The answer must be the changing context of the conversation. Rounds one and two of the conversation take place under the immediate threat of the surrounding Aramean army and so are desperate in their intent.[34] Round three finds that threat removed as the Aramean army has been deceived, now surrounded by Israelites in the city of Samaria, and at the mercy of Elisha.

Structure

In the first round, Elisha's turn identifies his conversational partner in the address (v. 17). In the second round, the Elisha turn is prefaced in a fashion that identifies the addressee (*Elisha prayed to the Lord*; v. 18). The editorial preface, framing the second Elisha turn, suggests that the second Elisha turn is a continuation of the first Elisha turn. The third round returns to the pattern seen in the first round as Elisha once again identifies the addressee in conversation (v. 20). This feature of the conversation can also be explained by the changing context. Rounds one and two are given in quick succession and there is no need for Elisha to repeat the identity of his conversational partner in round two. Round three, separated geographically and chronologically from rounds one and two requires a new address. Structurally then, this conversational prayer as it now appears is conflated, drawing into one conversation elements from two separate conversational prayers. Is there a consequence to this conflation? Yes, and that answer is also seen in the structure of the prayer.

There is a structural feature common to all three rounds that becomes more notable, given the differences existing between the first two rounds and the third round. The preferred responses (B, B¹, B²) are expressed

---

31. Used also in the Moses conversational prayer of Num 12:13 and the Hezekiah prayer of 2 Kgs 19:19 (but not in the parallel of Isa 37:20) and 20:3 (and its parallel in Isa 38:3).

32. See GKC, §105b. See also, Waltke and O'Connor, *An Introduction to Biblical Hebrew Syntax*, 578.

33. Apparently, others have asked this question and added the verb, "pray" (פלל). See footnote to 6:20 in *BHS*.

34. Similar to the use of the particle נָא (please) in Moses' plea for Miriam (Num 12:13).

repeating, almost verbatim, the requests (v. 18) from Elisha. This verbatim agreement strengthens the preferred response and gives a sense of structural continuity to the conversation. Although the preferred responses are in the form of consequential action, they are formed to repeat the request voiced by Elisha. "Repetitional responses" are designed to "confirm" rather than "affirm"[35] the initial proposition and emphasize the effective agency of the response. That is, the form of the preferred responses, in this conversation, shows the agreement between Elisha and Deity. There is no space between the two.[36] And, it is this empathetic agreement between Elisha and the LORD that becomes magnified by conflating two separate conversations into three rounds of one conversation.

The consequential action, a preferred response to Elisha's request, is as much a response to the *how* of the request as it is to the *what* of the request. The emotional intensity forming the initial Elisha turns sets the stage for the developing intersubjectivity between the LORD and Elisha, prompting the Divine action. Elisha's desperateness is part of the *who-we-are-to-one-another* in his conversational prayer. In this conversational prayer, emotion moves God to act.

---

35. Lee, "Response Design in Conversation," 425.

36. The close alliance between Elisha and the LORD places the king of Aram in a precarious position as he focuses on Elisha as his prominent enemy.

9

Conversational Prayers Only in Chronicles

THE CHRONICLER HAS A special interest in prayer and includes several conversational prayers not appearing in parallel passages of Samuel–Kings.[1] These prayers tend to emphasize the *who-we-are-to-one-another* of the conversationalists, depicting God as powerful and the human participant as dependent.[2] Several of the prayers (David in 1 Chr 29:10–19 and Jehoshaphat in 2 Chr 20:5–17) are free constructions of the Chronicler, borrowing from themes and phraseology found elsewhere in Chronicles and the Deuteronomic material. The Chronicler took this preexisting material and recast it into the form of conversational activity. The *how-its-said* and the *what-it-does* of a conversation is the dynamic appropriated by the Chronicler in these passages.

1 Chronicles 4:10: Jabez

A: [10] Jabez called on the God of Israel, saying, "Oh that you would bless me and enlarge my border, and that your hand might be with me, and that you would keep me from hurt and harm!"

B: *And God granted what he asked.*

Context

The point of this short interruption in the genealogies of 1 Chronicles is to illustrate the effective agency of God's power in the life of an individual (and

---

1. See Duke, *The Persuasive Appeal of the Chronicler*, 56.
2. See Throntveit, *When Kings Speak*, 62–65.

perhaps, by extension, the nation of Israel). That a conversational prayer is the chosen vehicle for illustrating this Divine intervention is remarkable.[3]

The conversation is set up in a noteworthy fashion. Verse 9 provides an etymology,[4] and a wordplay on the name Jabez that functions on two levels. First, Jabez's mother explains the name saying, "I bore him in pain,"[5] implying the name, Jabez, is derived from the same root as the word "pain" or "harm" (also in Jabez's own words; 4:10). But, this connection between "pain" and "Jabez" is not exact for it would require the transposition of the last two consonants in the name Jabez, forming "Jazeb," and this is where the second level of the word play comes into place. Jabez is given an unfortunate name that isn't even pronounced correctly![6]

Regardless, this name forms the central problem of the short narrative. The power of this name positions Jabez in a place of disadvantage. Nevertheless, the name does not restrict Jabez and he becomes more honored than his brothers (4:9).[7] How can this be! Given such an unfortunate start to life, Jabez does the only thing possible—he prays.[8] Seeing that we are provided so few details about Jabez, we must conclude that the information we are permitted is important. For the Chronicler, a connection is made between Jabez' act of prayer and the status afforded him.

Structure

The conversational prayer is constructed in one round: speech by Jabez, directed to the God of Israel, who responds with consequential action. Although framed by the statement, "Jabez called on the God of Israel," there is no relationship established between the two conversationalists. There is no introduction, no basis for the request, no rationale, no appeal to past interaction. Jabez addresses the God of Israel without claiming any prior relational status with his conversational partner. The *what* of Jabez' statement is just as impersonal. There is no recipient design in what Jabez

---

3. Especially if, as R. Christopher Heard suggests, this narrative belongs to a group also including 1 Chr 4:39–43 and 1 Chr 5:9–10; 18–22. Heard, "Echoes of Genesis in 1 Chronicles 4:9–10," 10–12.

4. Japhet, *1 and 2 Chronicles*, 109. Curtis and Madsen, *Book of Chronicles*, 107.

5. Certainly, bringing to mind Gen 3:16. Heard, "Echoes of Genesis in 1 Chronicles 4:9–10," 5; Kalimi, *Reshaping of Ancient Israelite History*, 252.

6. Was this transposition intended as humor or designed to elicit even more empathy? It's hard to say.

7. נכבד is translated "honored" with NRSV. See Heard, "Echoes of Genesis in 1 Chronicles 4:9–10," 3.

8. The Chronicler does seem to have a special interest in prayer.

has to say, and even though Jabez' statement is introduced by the infinitive (לאמר), probably indicating the following is intended to represent exact speech, the same request could be directed to any deity. Further, there is no thank you, no pledge of loyalty, no vow, no moral response offered, should the God of Israel respond positively.[9]

In like manner, the God of Israel responds in a very distant and impersonal fashion. The Divine gives no assessment, no rationale, no speech. The God of Israel never addresses Jabez. Simply, a preferred consequential action is performed with no indication of the Divine's disposition toward his conversational partner. Were the Deity's actions performed willingly, grudgingly, hesitantly, or eagerly? Structurally, this conversation is quite formal. Nothing in the conversation suggests anything other than a conversation between strangers. And, it is at this point that the constructed nature of the conversational activity is apparent. The request is made in a moment—the answer takes a lifetime.

The Power of Prayer

The prayer begins in an unusual fashion.[10] It begins with a particle most generally translated "if" (אם). Perhaps best here translated "If only"[11] the prayer is in the form of a wish: If only you would bless me! This initial request is then detailed by three subsequent phrases:[12]

- That you would enlarge my border
- That your hand would be with me

---

9. Myers, *1 Chronicles*, 28. Did Jabez "hedge his bets" by calling on other gods as well?

10. The text of the prayer is difficult, employing poetic structures confirming that the prayer is crafted and not a spontaneous expression.

11. GKC §151e.

12. Although the translation presented here is accepted by NRSV and, with variations, by additional translations (NAB, NIV, NASB, ESV, RSV), R. Christopher Heard presents persuasive argumentation for the following translation and chiastic structure:

(A) If Only you would really bless me

   (B) And extend my boundaries

(A¹) And if your hand will be with me

   (B¹) And make pastureland [available]

See Heard, "Echoes of Genesis in 1 Chronicles 4:9–10," 10. The differences in translation do not affect the core observations regarding the conversational activity considered here.

- That you would keep me from harm and hurt[13]

The first of the three requests (enlarge my borders) invites comparison to the manner in which Jabez' "brothers" acquired land elsewhere in the Chronicles genealogy. Although Jabez never appears in the Chronicles genealogies, the "brothers" may be broadly identified through comparison to other land acquisition narratives in 1 Chronicles 4-5. Those brothers, the Simeonites and Reubenites, gained land by fighting for it (Simeonites—4:39-43), or by asking God and then fighting for it (Reubenites—5:9-10; 18-22). Jabez, on the other hand, simply makes his request to God.[14]

The second and third requests continue Jabez' acknowledged reliance upon God. Whether the object of the request be protection from harm or additional pastureland (as with Heard's translation above), the conversational activity presented in 1 Chronicles 4 maintains the agency is God's alone. God granted what Jabez requested.

There are no commendable qualities assigned to Jabez that might result in the Divine's positive disposition toward his requests. It is striking that no rationale is offered for God's response. No additional considerations are brought to bear, no preexisting conditions, no influences outside this one simple conversational prayer. Jabez is more honored than his brothers, simply because he prayed. Rather than seeking some other means of achieving his desired end (blessing, land, peace), Jabez acknowledged his reliance upon the God of Israel in conversational prayer with the result that he was honored. Further, there is no prior relational status between Jabez and the God of Israel that might predispose God favorably toward Jabez' request. Jabez prayed. The catalyst for activating the efficacious power of God was simply prayer. But, not activated in a ritualistic cause and effect. No accompanying sacrifice or performed ritual was necessary to unlock God's good graces. The God of Israel grants the request simply because Jabez prayed. God answered the prayer of an otherwise unknown and unremarkable individual—simply because he prayed.

---

13. Not translated "that I may not cause pain" as in the NKJV and upon which Bruce Wilkerson's popular book was based. Wilkerson, *The Prayer of Jabez*. See Heard, "Echoes of Genesis in 1 Chronicles 4:9-10," 5-6.

14. Heard suggests this implies a nonviolent means of acquisition, an action by Jabez that results in the designation that Jabez was more honored than his brothers. "The Chronicler seems to want to imply that Jabez acquired additional land at no one's expense, in contradistinction to his 'brothers.'" Heard, "Echoes of Genesis in 1 Chronicles 4:9-10," 12.

1 Chronicles 29:10–19: David

A: [10] Then David blessed the LORD in the presence of all the assembly; David said: "Blessed are you, O LORD, the God of our ancestor Israel, forever and ever. [11] Yours, O LORD, are the greatness, the power, the glory, the victory, and the majesty; for all that is in the heavens and on the earth is yours; yours is the kingdom, O LORD, and you are exalted as head above all. [12] Riches and honor come from you, and you rule over all. In your hand are power and might; and it is in your hand to make great and to give strength to all. [13] And now, our God, we give thanks to you and praise your glorious name.

[14] "But who am I, and what is my people, that we should be able to make this freewill offering? For all things come from you, and of your own have we given you. [15] For we are aliens and transients before you, as were all our ancestors; our days on the earth are like a shadow, and there is no hope. [16] O LORD our God, all this abundance that we have provided for building you a house for your holy name comes from your hand and is all your own. [17] I know, my God, that you search the heart, and take pleasure in uprightness; in the uprightness of my heart I have freely offered all these things, and now I have seen your people, who are present here, offering freely and joyously to you. [18] O LORD, the God of Abraham, Isaac, and Israel, our ancestors, keep forever such purposes and thoughts in the hearts of your people, and direct their hearts toward you. [19] Grant to my son Solomon that with single mind he may keep your commandments, your decrees, and your statutes, performing all of them, and that he may build the temple[15] for which I have made provision."

Structure

As with other prayers quoted only by the Chronicler, this prayer by David seems to be a free composition of the Chronicler,[16] repeating themes and

15. Heb. fortress.

16. See especially Asa in 2 Chr 14:11–12 and Jehoshaphat in 2 Chr 20:5–17. Japhet notes the accumulation of nouns in the prayer, giving an abstract quality to the piece. Japhet, *1 and 2 Chronicles*, 509. Japhet's observation implies that the piece has a very low recipient design and so not characteristic of actual conversation. The introduction of the prayer using the finite form of אמר may also support that this is not intended to represent a quotation of David's direct speech. The same is true of the David prayer of 1 Chr 29:10, the Asa prayer in 2 Chr 14:11, and the Jehoshaphat direct speech of 2 Chr 20:6.

wording found elsewhere. This prayer shares certain structural features with David's prayer of 2 Sam 7:18–29 // 1 Chr 17:16–27. Both:

- are constructed in two parts
- transitioned by "and now" (עתה)
- begin with an opening self-deprecating question
- reserve the simple request to the end of the prayer

Conversation expresses the dynamism of an interpersonal relationship between the conversational partners, a dynamism that is absent in the first part of this prayer, but consistent with the setting established in v. 10. The first part of David's prayer (1 Chr 29:10–13) is abstract, dominated by a description of God's splendor and rule over all humanity. It is distant and formal. Throughout, David consistently uses a first-person plural, presenting himself as spokesperson for the whole group.[17] The only claim to unique status between the conversationalists is the descriptive, "the God of our ancestor Israel," found in the opening benediction. Otherwise, it is conceivable that the whole of the first part of the prayer could be uttered in a variety of circumstances by a variety of persons. There is nothing that necessitates it be mouthed by David.

The second part of the prayer is very different. In v. 14, David begins using the first person singular,[18] and will continue to speak in concrete terms that are specific to the immediate occasion, but in a fashion that no longer requires David to function as a spokesperson for the whole assembly. The opening question, "But who am I, and what is my people?" is similar to the opening question in David's earlier prayer, "Who am I" (2 Sam 7:18 // 1 Chr 17:16). The self-effacement, posed in the form of an opening question, is designed to secure a preferred response from the conversational partner.[19] That is, there is a hoped-for affinity between David and the LORD. Here, the question all at once acknowledges; Divine power, human weakness, and an implicit attitude of dependency and contrition from David. Even "the abundance we have provided for building you a house" (v. 16) and the moral achievement expressed in "the uprightness of my heart" (v. 17) are postured as simple acts of devotion for "all things come from you and of your own we have given you" (v. 14). The conversational prayer is constructed to emphasize the *who-we-are-to-one-another* of the conversational partners.

---

17. Similar to Asa's prayer of 2 Chr 14:11–12.

18. In a manner similar to the change of person used in the Jehoshaphat prayer of 2 Chr 20:5–17.

19. Sidnell, *Conversation Analysis*, 83.

The prayer culminates in the sole request made by David: "grant to my son Solomon . . ." (v. 19). Specifically, David requests that God would grant to Solomon fidelity to the commandments, decrees, and statutes of the LORD, and success in constructing the temple (fortress) for which David has made provision.[20] Throughout the prayer, the standing of David before Deity is expressed by referencing David's "uprightness of heart" a standing anticipated for Solomon also as he maintains single minded fidelity to the LORD, God of Abraham, Isaac, and Israel.

What-It-Does

Unlike Solomon's public prayer in 2 Chronicles 6 (2 Chr 7:1), but like the private prayers of 2 Samuel 7 and 1 Chronicles 17, David's prayer evokes no response from God. There is no clear indication that God was even attentive to David's direct address.[21] Instead, consequential action is elicited from the observing assembly (1 Chr 29:20–22). The conversationally styled address is effective in arousing the assembly, and for that reason has a pivotal role in the Chronicler's narrative. The whole episode (beginning in 1 Chronicles 28) is transitional, describing the royal succession from David to Solomon. That transition will be completed in 1 Chr 29:22b–25. The conversational prayer, if only in form, makes God present in the proceedings through the direct, immediate address of David's speech. Conversational prayer made Deity and a particular relationship to Deity present in the mind of those praying in a way not possible through more formal expressions. It is the *who-we-are-to-God* aspect of the conversational prayer that accounts for its inclusion here.

By the inclusion of this conversational prayer, the Chronicler appropriates the social power of conversation into the narrative. Conversational prayer makes God present in the mind of the petitioner. Even if no Divine response is forthcoming, conversational prayer makes attendant the *I* of the *I–Thou* conversational prayer. In this prayer, the *I* of the *I–It* is transformed into the *I* of the *I–Thou*. This change is clear in the progression of this prayer. David's formal and abstract manner in the opening of the prayer becomes personal and immediate in the second part of the prayer. For his reading audience, the Chronicler hopes the same.

---

20. Roddy Braun concludes that it is a prime objective of the Chronicler to portray Solomon as the "chosen temple builder." Braun, "Solomon," 590.

21. God's active response is reserved until 1 Chr 29:25 and follows the active response of the assembly, leaders, and mighty warriors.

2 Chronicles 14:11–12:[22] Asa

A: [11] Asa cried to the Lord his God, "O Lord, there is no difference for you between helping the mighty and the weak. Help us, O Lord our God, for we rely on you, and in your name we have come against this multitude. O Lord, you are our God; let no mortal prevail against you."

B: [12] *So the Lord defeated the Ethiopians*[23] *before Asa and before Judah, and the Ethiopians fled.*

Mention of this conflict between Asa and the Ethiopians, does not appear in the parallel Kings narrative. This, and the exaggerated numbers assigned to the opposing army (one million men and three hundred chariots, 2 Chr 14:9), together with the confusing place names mentioned in the battle and following rout, have led some commentators to consider the account a fabrication of the Chronicler.[24] Should this be true, it leads us to ask; if the Chronicler is free to compose the narrative as he wishes, why make the whole episode revolve around a conversational prayer?[25] If the episode is a free composition of the Chronicler, the prayer takes on even more importance, not less.

Structure

The structure shaping this conversational exchange appears elsewhere in Chronicles. Even though the prayer between Asa and Deity is structured the same as the prayer offered by Jabez (2 Chr 4), the prayers are worlds apart and a comparison between the two highlights peculiarities in the Asa prayer. Asa's prayer offers ample rationale for the desired consequential action. Asa appeals to Deity in a very personal manner, and even offers a motivation for the Deity to act ("let no mortal prevail against you"). While Jabez' prayer shows little recipient design, and addresses God in a formal fashion, Asa's prayer repeats the name of the Lord three times in this one sentence. Likewise, exclusive relationship to that Deity (his, our God) is

---

22. MT: 2 Chr 14:10–11.

23. Heb. *Cushites* inhabiting modern day Ethiopia.

24. Curtis and Madsen conclude, "The narrative is entirely artificial." Curtis and Madsen, *Books of Chronicles*, 383. Jacob Myers is more convinced of a historical core to the account of battle, although now exaggerated in order to "magnify the victory of Yahweh." Myers, *2 Chronicles*, 85.

25. Certainly, the account of prayer and battle supports the assessment offered in 2 Chr 14:2: "Asa did what was good and right in the sight of the Lord his God." See also the memory of the prayer in 2 Chr 16:7–10.

affirmed three times as well.[26] While Jabez' prayer could be offered to any number of deities, there can be little doubt as to the identity of the intended recipient of the Asa address.

Asa Turn

The first part of the prayer is difficult. Literally, the MT (v. 10) reads: "there is none with you to help between the weak and the mighty" (אין עמך לעזור בין רב לאין כח). Given the earlier admission regarding the overwhelming strength of his enemy (2 Chr 14:9), Asa's prayer should probably be understood as "there is none to help except you in a conflict between the strong (the Ethiopians) and the weak (Judah).[27] In concise fashion, the Asa statement establishes the *who-we-are-to-one-another* of the conversational partners and so establishes a rationale for the request to follow. Asa is fully and solely dependent upon his conversational partner.

The conclusion to Asa's prayer is fascinating. Asa offers as motivation for Divine action "let no mortal prevail against you." The intent of this statement is to depict the Ethiopians as adversaries of the LORD. Asa describes them simply as mortals. It is their status as mortals that makes it improper for the Ethiopians to impose their will and might over the LORD in an effort to prevent the LORD from accomplishing his purposes.[28] While, in this story, Asa is certainly no enemy of the LORD, he is, however, (just like the Ethiopians) a mortal and his prayer is also designed to effect a change in Divine action. Asa proposes to impose his will over the LORD in an effort to prevent the adversarial imposition by the Ethiopians. How is it that Asa can motivate the LORD to action by raising the threat of restrictions imposed upon God by other mortals? The answer is found in the very nature of conversational prayer. Asa's appeal for help rests in an interpersonal relationship with the LORD, a relationship that is maintained and given breath in prayer. The *who-we-are-to-God* is emphasized by Asa in the repetitions noted earlier and this standing between Asa and God is the key element motivating the consequential actions from God.

---

26. For the use of lists of three or repetitions of three see Atkinson, "Public Speaking and Audience Responses," 384–90.

27. See Japhet, *1 and 2 Chronicles*, 711.

28. The verb (עצר) is often translated "prevent" or "restrain." Sometimes used to indicate barrenness or a prevention of pregnancy (Gen 20:18).

Consequential Action

In response to Asa's prayer, the LORD defeated the Ethiopians (v. 12).[29] This consequential action is immediate and decisive. In vv. 13–15, the defeat is described in further detail, but all under the umbrella action; the LORD defeated the Ethiopians. The LORD is portrayed as the sole actor effecting the defeat, and the conversational prayer the sole catalyst prompting Divine intervention.

Asa's prayer is in the first-person plural. He presents himself as a spokesperson for the whole nation and the consequential action by the LORD, in response to Asa's prayer, is a response to the whole nation. Undoubtedly, the episode, including Asa's prayer of dependence, is intended, by the Chronicler, as illustrative of the relational commitment expressed by Azariah in 15:2: "The LORD is with you, while you are with him. If you seek him, he will be found by you, but if you abandon him, he will abandon you." In this statement, too, the *who-we-are-to-God* is the central catalytic concern.

2 Chronicles 20:5–19: Jehoshaphat

A: ⁵ Jehoshaphat stood in the assembly of Judah and Jerusalem, in the house of the LORD, before the new court, ⁶ and said, "O LORD, God of our ancestors, are you not God in heaven? Do you not rule over all the kingdoms of the nations? In your hand are power and might, so that no one is able to withstand you. ⁷ Did you not, O our God, drive out the inhabitants of this land before your people Israel, and give it forever to the descendants of your friend Abraham? ⁸ They have lived in it, and in it have built you a sanctuary for your name, saying, ⁹ 'If disaster comes upon us, the sword, judgment, or pestilence, or famine, we will stand before this house, and before you, for your name is in this house, and cry to you in our distress, and you will hear and save.' ¹⁰ See now, the people of Ammon, Moab, and Mount Seir, whom you would not let Israel invade when they came from the land of Egypt, and whom they avoided and did not destroy— ¹¹ they reward us by coming to drive us out of your possession that you have given us to inherit. ¹² O our God, will you not execute judgment upon them? For we are powerless against this great multitude that is coming against us. We do not know what to do, but our eyes are on you."

¹³ *Meanwhile all Judah stood before the Lord, with their little ones, their wives, and their children.* ¹⁴ *Then the spirit of the*

---

29. Indicated in the NRSV by "So" beginning the verse. In this instance, the connective ו does indicate consequence.

Lord came upon Jahaziel son of Zechariah, son of Benaiah, son of Jeiel, son of Mattaniah, a Levite of the sons of Asaph, in the middle of the assembly.

B: [15] He said, "Listen, all Judah and inhabitants of Jerusalem, and King Jehoshaphat: Thus says the LORD to you: 'Do not fear or be dismayed at this great multitude; for the battle is not yours but God's. [16] Tomorrow go down against them; they will come up by the ascent of Ziz; you will find them at the end of the valley, before the wilderness of Jeruel. [17] This battle is not for you to fight; take your position, stand still, and see the victory of the LORD on your behalf, O Judah and Jerusalem.' Do not fear or be dismayed; tomorrow go out against them, and the LORD will be with you."

A¹: [18] *Then Jehoshaphat bowed down with his face to the ground, and all Judah and the inhabitants of Jerusalem fell down before the Lord, worshiping the Lord.* [19] *And the Levites, of the Kohathites and the Korahites, stood up to praise the Lord, the God of Israel, with a very loud voice.*

Structure

Jehoshaphat's prayer of 2 Chr 20:5–17 is not conversational, per se, but does contain conversational activity that merits our attention. Although the LORD's reply to Jehoshaphat is mediated by a prophet and so does not meet the first criterion for conversational prayer established in the Introduction, Divine immediacy is indicated in the conversational activity. The way in which the initial Jehoshaphat statement is given direct address and evolves into the use of first person, and the description of the response of the people in attendance (standing before the LORD, v. 13), and the response of Jehoshaphat (bowing before the LORD, v. 18) all imply Divine immediacy in the episode, even if the Divine address is mediated by Jahaziel.

This entire episode, including the threat from an eastern coalition (2 Chr 20:1) and the prayer in 2 Chr 20:5–12 is missing from the 2 Kgs 22:41–50 account of Jehoshaphat's reign. Both 2 Chr 20:34 and 2 Kgs 22:45 make reference to a source document, *Book of the Annals of the Kings of Judah*, from which they presumably obtained information.[30] It seems apparent that the prayer of Jehoshaphat is a free and lengthy composition inserted by the Chronicler into what is otherwise a close reliance upon the Kings

---

30. See the discussion by Na'aman, "Prophetic Stories," 169–72; Na'aman, "Temple Library of Jerusalem," 142–45. 1 Kgs 22:41–50 is paralleled by 2 Chr 20:31–37. It is here concluded that the 2 Chronicles account is dependent upon the 2 Kings account. Kalimi, *Reshaping of Ancient Israelite History*, 116–18. Japhet, *1 and 2 Chronicles*, 785.

account. The inclusion of stylistic elements of a conversational exchange allows us to examine both, the *what* of the speech and the *how* of the speech. The Chronicler's composition of Jehoshaphat's prayer has parallels to other prayers, undoubtedly also composed by the Chronicler.[31]

1 Kings 8	2 Chronicles 6	2 Chronicles 7	2 Chronicles 20
Solomon	Solomon	Solomon	Jehoshaphat
[37] "**If there is famine in the land, if there is plague, blight, mildew, locust, or caterpillar**; if their enemy besieges them in any of their cities; whatever plague, whatever sickness there is; [38] whatever prayer, whatever plea there is from any individual or from all your people Israel, all knowing the afflictions of their own hearts *so that they stretch out their hands toward this house;* [39] then hear in heaven your dwelling place, forgive, act, and render to all whose hearts you know—according to all their ways, for only you know what is in every human heart— [40] so that they may fear you all the days that they live in the land that you gave to our ancestors.	[28] "**If there is famine in the land, if there is plague, blight, mildew, locust, or caterpillar**; if their enemies besiege them in any of the settlements of the lands; whatever suffering, whatever sickness there is; [29] whatever prayer, whatever plea from any individual or from all your people Israel, all knowing their own suffering and their own sorrows *so that they stretch out their hands toward this house;* [30] may you hear from heaven, your dwelling place, forgive, and render to all whose heart you know, according to all their ways, for only you know the human heart. [31] Thus may they fear you and walk in your ways all the days that they live in the land that you gave to our ancestors.	[13] When I shut up the heavens **so that there is no rain, or command the locust to devour the land, or send pestilence among my people**,	[9] "**If disaster comes upon us, the sword, judgment, or pestilence, or famine**, *we will stand before this house,* and before you, for your name is in this house, and cry to you in our distress, and you will hear and save."

---

31. Japhet writes that the prayer "bears the stamp of a Chronistic literary piece." Japhet, *1 and 2 Chronicles*, 788.

The prayer uttered by Jehoshaphat contains elements that are found elsewhere in prayers. In addition, there are thematic parallels between Jehoshaphat's prayer and the prayer of Asa in 2 Chronicles 14 and the prayer of David in 1 Chronicles 29.

2 Chronicles 14	2 Chronicles 20	1 Chronicles 29
Asa	Jehoshaphat	David
¹¹ Asa cried to the LORD his God, "O LORD, there is no difference for you between helping the mighty and the weak. Help us, O LORD our God, **for we rely on you, and in your name we have come against this multitude. O Lord, you are our God; let no mortal prevail against you."**	⁶ and said, "O LORD, God of our ancestors, are you not God in heaven? <u>Do you not rule over all the kingdoms of the nations? In your hand are power and might,</u> so that no one is able to withstand you. ¹² O our God, will you not execute judgment upon them? **For we are powerless against this great multitude that is coming against us.**	¹¹ Yours, O LORD, are the greatness, the power, the glory, the victory, and the majesty; <u>for all that is in the heavens and on the earth is yours; yours is the kingdom,</u> O LORD, and you are exalted as head above all. ¹² Riches and honor come from you, and you rule over all. <u>In your hand are power and might</u>; and it is in your hand to make great and to give strength to all.

In addition, Jehoshaphat's prayer contains elements that are familiar from other prayers recorded in Kings and Chronicles.[32]

- God alone rules over the nations of the world and he alone determines their fate. (v. 6)
- God gifted the land to Israel, the descendants of his friend, Abraham. (v. 7)[33]
- A temple has been built, making concrete God's presence in the land with his people. (v. 8)
- That temple serves as a focal point to pray for aid from God. (v. 9)
- Plea for help. (v. 12)

---

32. See the discussion in Japhet, *1 and 2 Chronicles*, 790–92. See also Hodossy-Takács, "On the Battlefield and Beyond," 167.

33. A theme consistent with the genealogies of 1 Chronicles 1–9. The exodus event is never used by the Chronicler as a dogma of faith. Instead, the Chronicler emphasizes an almost unbreakable bond between the people of Israel and the land, a bond that extended before the exodus and after the exile. The mention of the exodus in vv. 10–11, unusual for the Chronicler, sets the conditions for the conflict prompting Jehoshaphat's prayer and draws in God's involvement by depicting the land as "your [God's] possession that you have given us to inherit" (v. 11).

Jehoshaphat's prayer for aid certainly flows from the Solomonic dedication (1 Kgs 8; 2 Chr 6), but with a major difference. The Solomonic prayer indicates that the supplicant will "pray toward this house" while God will hear from heaven (1 Kgs 8:37–39). Jehoshaphat asserts that the "Name" inhabits "this house" (2 Chr 20:9).[34] For Jehoshaphat, God is immediately present in the temple.

The immediacy of the presence of God in the temple is complimented by a change occurring between v. 7 and v. 8 of Jehoshaphat's direct speech. The beginning of Jehoshaphat's prayer is cast in third person, referring to the ancestors and your people. That changes in v. 8 as Jehoshaphat begins speaking in first person terms, bringing the conversation into the immediate present.

The prayer ends with two requests followed by a causative clause:

- Execute judgment on them   for (כי)   we are powerless
- Teach us what to do   for (כי)   our eyes are on you

Even though elsewhere presented as a powerful monarch and military leader,[35] Jehoshaphat's prayer expresses reliance upon God who is immediately present to hear and answer. Both, the immediacy of Deity in the temple and the nature of the two requests emphasize the who-we-are-to-one-another between Jehoshaphat and God.

God's response to Jehoshaphat is mediated by a prophet, not presented as an exact quote, and refers to Deity in the third person.[36] Following Solomon's prayer of 1 Kings 8, there is a delayed but unmediated response from God (1 Kgs 9:3–9) and in the 2 Chronicles 6 version there is an immediate display of God's presence in the fire from heaven (2 Chr 7:1) and a delayed unmediated verbal response (2 Chr 7:12–22). In response to Asa (2 Chronicles 14), whose request is very similar to Jehoshaphat's, there is only consequential action. So, why the detailed verbal, but mediated, response by God in vv. 15–17? Certainly, there is a degree of military instruction contained in the response (v. 16), but most of the Divine response is relational in focus. Since the LORD will be with you (v. 17), the battle will be won, the nation need only stand still and see the victory of the LORD, and there is no need to fear or be dismayed. The observable outcome of the ensuing battle

---

34. Előd Hodossy-Takács has argued that the account is a "clear theological demonstration of the God-given success to the Temple-centered community." Előd Hodossy-Takács, "On the Battlefield and Beyond," 178.

35. Able to muster a million-man army! (2 Chr 17:14–19).

36. Even though it is prefaced by the common prophetic formula: Thus says the LORD.

CONVERSATIONAL PRAYERS ONLY IN CHRONICLES 237

is not the real issue of conversation. The who-we-are-to-God is the core of God's mediated verbal response.

2 Chronicles 30:19–20: Hezekiah

A: But Hezekiah prayed for them, saying, "The good LORD pardon all [19] who set their hearts to seek God, the LORD the God of their ancestors, even though not in accordance with the sanctuary's rules of cleanness."

B: [20] *The Lord heard Hezekiah, and healed the people.*

Context

Hezekiah's prayer is uttered in the midst of a dilemma. Pilgrims, intent on observing the Passover, are unable to maintain ritual purity and so risk violating Mosaic law (Lev 7:19–21). The situation has been previously anticipated and a provision for an alternate Passover observance is offered (Num 9:10–11), but the lengthy preparations required make it untenable in Hezekiah's case. So, what is to be done? Either, turn the pilgrims away, or permit their full participation even though in violation of ritual requirements, or allow the Levites to slaughter the animals to be used for sacrifice by the pilgrims. This third, middle ground solution seems to have been Hezekiah's alone and so his prayer on behalf of the multitude.

Structure

The prayer, itself, is straight forward. Circumstances have prevented the maintenance of ritual cleanness, but the intent, the desire, and the "heart" of those involved, was to seek God. Hezekiah concluded that the disposition of the heart should not be impeded by impossible ritual correctness, and so petitioned the good LORD for pardon on behalf of the multitude. Although similar to the liturgical refrain, "O give thanks to the LORD, for he is good; for his steadfast love endures forever" (1 Chr 16:34; 2 Chr 5:13; 7:3; et al) this is the only time the "good LORD" is addressed. By use of this title, Hezekiah emphasizes the ethical intersubjectivity between those who, even if ritually impure, have a "heart to seek God" and the "good LORD" now addressed by Hezekiah in prayer.

The equally straightforward response, shaped as consequential action, forms a preferred response to Hezekiah and indicates Divine agreement.

As no illness or sickness is mentioned by Hezekiah, the healing should be understood as preventative in nature, not imposing any penalty for ritual violation.[37] What permitted the suspension of cleanliness norms for this, a most special religious festival? The intent of the heart, expressed through conversation, found welcome compatibility with the good Lord who acted upon a shared ethical ethos.

He Prayed, Saying...

As noted earlier, the infinitive, "saying" (לאמר) can be used in the Hebrew Bible to signify direct speech, as seems to be the case in this prayer (v. 18). At times, additional verbs are used in concert with the infinitive to give added dimension and description to the spoken words themselves. These "metapragmatic" verbs inform us concerning the *how* of the speech in addition to the *what* of the speech.[38] Twice, and only twice, the verb "pray" is used as a metapragmatic verb followed by an infinitive to give a sense as to how the following speech was uttered (i.e., he prayed, saying . . .).[39] In both of these occasions, Hezekiah is the speaker (2 Kgs 20:2–3; 2 Chr 30:18–19). In 2 Kings, Hezekiah has just learned of his impending death and utters a prayer for healing, requesting that the Lord would "remember." In 2 Chr 30:18–19, the request is for pardon, but the Divine consequential action is healing.[40] In Hezekiah's prayers, healing is the consequential action in both instances and that healing is predicated upon a Divine assessment of moral character, the intent of the heart, including "perfect faith in God's power and complete trust in His help."[41] That shared moral character between petitioner and Deity is expressed in conversational prayer.

---

37. Japhet, *1 and 2 Chronicles*, 953.

38. Verbs such as: grumble, order, sing, ask, deceive, etc. Miller provides a comprehensive list. C. Miller, *Representation of Speech*, 437–40.

39. In Jonah 4:1, the verb "pray" is used as a metapragmatic verb, followed by a finite form (he said). Moral character is also a major component of the conversational exchange between God and Jonah.

40. Japhet, *Ideology of the Book of Chronicles*, 252.

41. Japhet, *Ideology of the Book of Chronicles*, 255. See also Rudolph, *Chronikbücher*, 303.

10

Prophets

CONVERSATIONAL PRAYER OCCURS RELATIVELY infrequently within the prophetic literature. Undoubtedly, there must be several reasons for this absence, ranging from, the rhetorical designs of the prophetic compilers, the religious sensitivities of the proposed reading audiences, and the way status relationships were envisioned between the prophetic office and Deity. Conversational activity with earlier prophetic figures, especially Moses and Elijah, included a sense of intimacy with God that is diminished with the classical prophetic figures.[1] By the classical prophetic period, prophetic conversational prayer with God has given way to prophetic vision and oracle. This makes those instances of conversational prayer that do occur even more significant. We will observe that when conversational activity between God and prophet does occur in the prophetic literature, it is in moments of intense emotion and dire circumstance for both the human and Divine conversationalist.

Jeremiah 14:11–14

> A: [11] The LORD said to me: Do not pray for the welfare of this people. [12] Although they fast, I do not hear their cry, and although they offer burnt offering and grain offering, I do not accept them; but by the sword, by famine, and by pestilence I consume them.
>
> B: [13] Then I said: "Ah, LORD GOD! Here are the prophets saying to them, 'You shall not see the sword, nor shall you have famine, but I will give you true peace in this place.'"

---

1. Notable exceptions are Jeremiah and Ezekiel.

A¹: ¹⁴ And the LORD said to me: The prophets are prophesying lies in my name; I did not send them, nor did I command them or speak to them. They are prophesying to you a lying vision, worthless divination, and the deceit of their own minds.

Context

This conversational prayer is presented within a series of oracles predicting Divine judgment for Israel's misdeeds. The constructed nature of this conversational prayer is suggested in several ways. First, the prayer utilizes themes, vocabulary, and phrases repeated elsewhere in the book of Jeremiah. The conversational prayer continues the themes of Divine displeasure, even including Divine instruction found elsewhere (14:14 // 7:16; 11:14), as well as a triad of destructive forces (sword, famine, and pestilence) also appearing elsewhere in the Jeremiah text.² In addition, it is notable that this section does not use the infinitive "saying" (לאמר), often used in Jeremiah to introduce a direct speech quotation, indicating that the author is not intent on presenting the direct speech of the conversational prayer. The composite nature of this whole section of Jeremiah is evidenced by the difficulty commentators have encountered in attempting to structure the piece, recognizing literary forms of both prose and poetry as well as a variety of thematic connections.³

Jeremiah 14:11–14 is a constructed conversation placed strategically to further the rhetorical design of the collection of material found in Jer 11:1–17:27. This observation begs the question: why a conversation? Why construct a conversation as a vehicle to communicate the message of 14:11–14? As we have seen elsewhere in our examination of conversational prayer—*how* something is said is often just as important as *what* is said.⁴ Unlike most other conversational prayers found in the Hebrew Bible, this prayer is narrated to the reader by one of the participants.⁵ Jeremiah reports to the reader what the LORD said in conversation. The conversation itself, quite apart from the details of what was said in the conversation, is part of the rhetorical design of the passage. The conversation places Jeremiah in opposition to the deceitful prophets who claim falsely to have obtained a command

---

2. See Jer 21:7, 9; 24:10; 27:8, 13; 29:17–18; 32:24, 36; 34:17; 38:2; 42:17, 22; 44:13.

3. See the discussion in Carroll, *Jeremiah*, 312; Holladay, *Jeremiah 1*, 423. See also Wessels, "Blame Game," 866–67.

4. Already considered in other Jeremiah conversations. Willis, "Dialogue between Prophet and Audience," 75.

5. Moses also reports on a conversational prayer in Deuteronomy 9, during a speech presented to a national audience.

to speak or a vision from the LORD. Yet, it is important that the LORD be represented accurately in this reported conversation. Consequently, Jeremiah reports the LORD's direct address in the first person, rather than the more expected third person. This form of reporting reduces Jeremiah's intermediary role and places the LORD in direct and immediate confrontation with the deceitful prophets (14:14) and wicked people (14:16). Even though reported by Jeremiah, these are the LORD's words, not the prophet's.

The first-person direct address also marks the boundaries of this reported conversational prayer. The conversational prayer is identified by the direct address in v. 11, separating it from the indirect address of v. 10 that seems to naturally continue the prophetic oracle introduction of v. 1 (The word of the LORD that came to Jeremiah). The direct address of v. 11 is followed by a response in v. 12, and a second direct address in v. 14. The beginning of v. 15 separates the conversation from what follows through the transition offered by "therefore" (לכן).

Structure

Direct Address A

The first thing to notice about the direct address in v. 11 is the familiarity Deity has with Jeremiah. The LORD anticipates the prophet's reaction to earlier judgments by commanding the prophet: "Do not pray for the welfare of the people" (14:11).[6] The command presupposes extended previous interaction allowing Deity to anticipate how his conversational partner will respond.[7] This is a conversation between acquaintances, if not friends. This prior interpersonal familiarity is important to nuance the dispreferred responses that will follow within the conversation. Jeremiah and the LORD are in disagreement, yet the disagreement doesn't undo the more fundamental bond between the two conversationalists. Even though the opening direct address to Jeremiah is a dispreferred command (a cease and desist order), there can be no doubt that this familiarity between the LORD and Jeremiah stands in stark contrast to the distance the LORD puts between himself and the deceitful prophets in v. 14.

Following the opening directive given to the prophet, the LORD declares that religious ritual will be ineffective in warding off the impending judgment. The die is cast, and nothing can dissuade the LORD from acting.

---

6. Mark Boda seeks to construct a liturgical place for the prayer mentioned in v. 11. Boda, "From Complaint to Contrition," 191.

7. See Stulman, *Jeremiah*, 140.

The immediacy of the LORD's involvement in the punishment is made clear: I do not hear (their cry), I do not accept (their offerings), and I consume.[8] The sword, famine, and pestilence are simply tools used by the Divine actor and should not cloud the unpleasant fact that this is the LORD's doing.

Response B

Just as the direct address of 14:11–12 presupposes familiarity between the conversationalists, so, too, does the response. Jeremiah offers a dispreferred response to the direct address of v. 11, doing, albeit quite indirectly, exactly what he was told not to do.[9] While complying with the directive by not praying for the welfare of the people, Jeremiah, nevertheless, offers information that might at least moderate the impending judgment. He protests that the people should not be held culpable, for they are being misled by the prophets who are offering the people a false sense of security instead of ominous warning. And more, that false security is proffered based upon a reported message from the LORD: "I (the LORD) will give you true peace in this place" (14:13). How can the people be held liable for simply responding to what was presented to them as the word of the LORD? Implicitly, Jeremiah blames the LORD for the condition of the people.[10]

The strength of the prophet's response is indicated by the opening exclamation: "Ah, LORD God!" (14:13). The particle "Ah" (אהה) elsewhere communicates protest (Jer 1:6; 32:17) and introduces a very similar statement, objecting to Divine deception that offers false security in the face of impending devastation (4:10).

The response of the prophet has a double function. Within the conversation, the prophet's dispreferred response attempts to dissuade the LORD by confronting him with his own words of safety mediated by "the prophets." Outside the conversation, Jeremiah's response provides the platform for the LORD to distance himself from the lying prophets who are now susceptible to more severe punishment (14:15–16).

---

8. See similar in Isa 1:15 and directly counter to the prayer of Solomon in 1 Kgs 8:22–53 and 2 Chr 6:14–7:1.
9. Thompson, *Book of Jeremiah*, 377. Stulman, *Jeremiah*, 141.
10. Stulman, *Jeremiah*, 142.

Direct Address A[1]

The LORD presents a dispreferred response to Jeremiah's reply (B). The LORD defends himself from Jeremiah's charge through a series of denials. The prophets, whom Jeremiah cited, are "lying prophets" (14:14)[11] spewing falsehoods in "my name."[12] The LORD denies involvement with these deceitful prophets stating that "I did not send them nor did I command them" (14:14), an expression also found elsewhere in Jeremiah (23:32).[13] And the "vision" (חזון), claimed by the prophets as the source of their message, is just as deceitful, nothing more than a product of their own imagination (14:14).[14]

Significantly absent from the LORD's response is any rebuke to Jeremiah for the prophet's attempt to seek leniency for the people, despite the LORD's instruction to the contrary. Even the prophet's attempt to indict the LORD, suggesting he needs to shoulder at least some of the blame for the current situation, doesn't elicit Divine rebuke. Jeremiah's words are rejected but the prophet is never turned away.

Consequential Action

The connection between the conversation of 14:11–14 and the oracle in 14:15–22 is strong.[15] The culpability of the prophets, used as an argument to dissuade the LORD from punishing the people in the conversation, is now given full expression as they become the object of Divine retribution in v. 15. But the guilt of the deceitful prophets does not mitigate the punishment to be visited upon "the people" (v. 16), for the LORD will "pour out their wickedness upon them" (v. 16). Despite Jeremiah's plea, the LORD will not offer a reprieve, for to do so would be to collude with the false prophets, with those who "misrepresent social and symbolic realities."[16] Only when the imminent suffering is felt fully, when all the supporting props are shattered, only then will "God's people discover God's hidden gift of hope and salvation."[17]

11. שקר הנבאים. The positioning of שקר the noun is certainly done to emphasize the deceitful nature of the prophets. See Overholt, *Threat to Falsehood*, 86–90.

12. "In my name" (בשמי) is an expression often used in Jeremiah to help characterize a true prophet: Jer 12:16, 23:25; 27:15; 29:9, 21, 23.

13. See also Jer 23:26.

14. See also Jer 23:16.

15. Verse 15 begins with "Therefore" (לקן), making it clear that the action described in 14:15–16 is a consequence of the Divine denunciation of v. 14.

16. Stulman, *Jeremiah*, 143.

17. Stulman, *Jeremiah*, 143.

Ezekiel 9:8–10

⁸ *While they were killing, and I was left alone, I fell prostrate on my face and cried out,*

A: "Ah LORD God! will you destroy all who remain of Israel as you pour out your wrath upon Jerusalem?" ⁹

B: He said to me, "The guilt of the house of Israel and Judah is exceedingly great; the land is full of bloodshed and the city full of perversity; for they say, 'The LORD has forsaken the land, and the LORD does not see.' ¹⁰ As for me, my eye will not spare, nor will I have pity, but I will bring down their deeds upon their heads."

Context

Despair. Utter despair is the only way to describe the context for this brief but intense exchange. The conversational prayer takes place within the context of a vision in which the hand of the LORD God fell upon Ezekiel on the fifth day of the sixth month of the sixth year, while Ezekiel was sitting in his house with the elders of Judah in his company (8:1). In the vision, Ezekiel is transported by a spirit, sent from God, to various vantage points in and around the temple where he is able to witness the ever-greater abominations being committed by the house of Judah. With each observation Ezekiel is addressed by God as "mortal" (8:5, 8, 12, 15, 17)[18] and directed to observe misdeeds, followed by the Divine warning that even greater abominations are to follow (8:6, 13, 15). Finally, unable to tolerate any more, God asks,

> Is it not bad enough that the house of Judah commits the abominations done here? Must they fill the land with violence, and provoke my anger still further? (8:17)

Having had enough, God tells the prophet,

> Therefore I will act in wrath; my eye will not spare, nor will I have pity; and though they cry in my hearing with a loud voice, I will not listen to them. (8:18)

Determined to act, God sends for the "executioners of the city" (9:1). Recognizing that there are those who "sigh and groan" over all the abominations being committed in the city and not participating in or advocating the misdeeds, a man in linen is sent to mark the innocents. Once the man in

---

18. Translated by other versions as "Son of Man."

linen has completed his task, the executioners are now freed to do their work, cutting down old men, young men and young women, little children, and women, all those not marked as innocent by the man in linen.

While the massacre proceeds, Ezekiel is left alone and in despair he falls to the ground and cries out: "Ah, Lord God."

Structure

Conversational activity establishes standing between the conversational participants. The standing operative within the conversational prayer of 9:8–10 is a continuation of the status established within the conversations of chapter 8. Throughout the book, God addresses Ezekiel by the title Son of Man (בן־אדם),[19] a practice continued in the visions of chapter 8 (vv. 5, 8, 12, 15, 17).[20] The significance of this attribution has been variously explained as: an emphasis on Ezekiel's mortal nature contrasting the divine beings Ezekiel frequently encounters especially in chapters 8–11,[21] or a designation from the Creator emphasizing Ezekiel's "creatureness," or a recognition of Ezekiel's "manhood, with whom God will have fellowship and with whom He will speak."[22] Perhaps the label's meaning is best explained by Walther Zimmerli, "In this summons the prophet was not being addressed in the uniqueness of his personal being, as would be expressed by his proper name, nor according to his office, but as an individual within the created order, the servant, who is summoned by his master in an act of unprecedented condescension by his Divine Lord."[23] This description of the "son of man," (the servant, summoned by his master) is significant for the nonuse of the title in the conversational prayer.

The surprise is that the label "son of man" is not used in the conversational prayer. In the previous direct address from God to Ezekiel, and throughout most of chapter 8, God uses the label, son of man, to address Ezekiel (8:5, 8, 12, 15, 17).[24] So why doesn't God address Ezekiel as son of man in this prayer, especially since Ezekiel's request of v. 8 represents a

---

19. "Mortal" in NRSV. See the discussion in Joüon and Muraoka, *Grammar of Biblical Hebrew*, 129j.

20. Over eighty occurrences throughout the book.

21. Greenburg, *Ezekiel 1–20*, 62; see also Hossfeld, "Tempelvision," 151–65.

22. Cooke, *Book of Ezekiel*, 31.

23. Zimmerli, *Ezekiel*, 1:131.

24. The label is not used in 8:6, 9, but these can be seen as continuation of the address begun in vv. 5 and 8.

challenge to the Divine activity and so stepping out of his expected role as creature and servant summoned by his master?

In answering this question, we must first note the broader connections between the conversational prayer and the accompanying vision. The conversation includes phrases used elsewhere in the vision of chapter 8 and seems to serve as a summary or a distillation of the vision:[25]

Conversation	Vision
The land is full of bloodshed (9:9)	they fill the land with violence (8:17)
They say the LORD has forsaken the land, and the LORD does not see (9:9)	they say, The LORD does not see, the LORD has forsaken the land (8:12)
My eye will not spare, nor will I have pity (9:10)	my eye will not spare nor will I have pity (8:18)

In addition, Ezekiel's protest in the conversational prayer finds a parallel later in the book:

Ah, LORD God! Will you destroy all who remain of Israel (9:8)	Ah, LORD God! Will you make a full end of the remnant of Israel? (11:13)

If so much of the conversation's content can be found elsewhere, what is added by the inclusion of the material, but now in the form of this brief conversational prayer? The added value of the conversation is the *how* of the content's presentation.

Conversation depends upon status negotiation and this standing between the conversational partners is the unique contribution made by the conversational prayer, a contribution that explains the absence of the son of man title. Within the conversation, the emotion of the moment has blurred the lines of status relationship. There is an immediacy and urgency in the conversation felt by both Ezekiel and God. Ezekiel begins his request with the particle "Ah!," perhaps best understood as an inarticulate groan of despair and sorrow. The shrieks and screams of those being slaughtered have reached Ezekiel's ears and while the executioners

---

25. Two devices have been observed as especially effective in gathering a positive response: list of three and contrast. When constructed well, the devices provide additional ease for respondents to anticipate a conclusion and proper place in the speech or dialogue to respond. These devises are effectively used here to help secure the prophet's empathetic identification with God. See Hutchby and Wooffitt, *Conversation Analysis*, 184–89.

continue their work, Ezekiel, alone in the house of the LORD, falls to the ground and cries out, "Ah! LORD God!"[26]

The intensity of Ezekiel's emotion is met with an equal emotional fervor from God. The problem of the guilt of the house of Israel and Judah has pushed all other considerations aside.[27] It does not matter that Ezekiel's request has taken him from his Divinely assigned status "son of man." It does not matter that the "servant summoned by his master" is now challenging the Master's actions. All that matters is the tragedy unfolding before these two conversational partners.

Ezekiel's empathy for the slaughtered is palpable. He is overcome, unable to stand or to see beyond the horror of the present bloodbath. But, at least in the mind of God, that empathy is misplaced. God's reply is not only a description of the tragedy at hand, but an effort to seek Ezekiel's affiliation,[28] an effort to have Ezekiel see things from God's point of view. And this seems to be the whole point of the conversational prayer, to secure Ezekiel's affiliation, but even more to secure the affiliation of the reader.[29] Intersubjectivity, a joint understanding of the world shared by the conversational participants, is the goal of presenting the conversation between Ezekiel and God. And here, that joint understanding of the world is both emotive and cognitive. God's pain is so great that he seeks the support of his friends—support offered in conversation.

Conversational prayer is reciprocal, a give and take, moving both participants. From Ezekiel 9 we learn that a sober reflection on conversational prayer must consider that God, too, experiences pain and grief for which he seeks emotional empathy and support from friends. An amazing change can take place in conversational prayer. The *I* in an *I-It* relationship can move from son of man (servant) to friend in an *I-Thou* relationship.

Amos 7:1–9

> [1] *This is what the Lord God showed me: he was forming locusts at the time the latter growth began to sprout (it was the latter growth after the king's mowings).* [2] *When they had finished eating the grass of the land,*

---

26. See similarly Josh 7:7; Judg 6:22; Jer 4:10; 14:13; 32:17.
27. See the discussion by Ruusuvuori, "Emotion, Affect, and Conversation," 347–48.
28. See Lindstöm and Sorjonen, "Affiliation in Conversation," 360–61.
29. Clayman, "Sequence and Solidarity," 250–53.

A: I said, "O Lᴏʀᴅ God, forgive, I beg you!
How can Jacob stand?
He is so small!"

B: ³ *The Lord relented concerning this*;
"It shall not be," said the Lᴏʀᴅ.

⁴ *This is what the Lord God showed me: the Lord God was calling for a shower of fire, and it devoured the great deep and was eating up the land.*

A¹: ⁵ Then I said, "O Lᴏʀᴅ God, cease, I beg you!
How can Jacob stand?
He is so small!"

B¹: ⁶ *The Lord relented concerning this*;
"This also shall not be," said the Lᴏʀᴅ God.

⁷ *This is what he showed me: the Lᴏʀᴅ was standing beside a wall built with a plumb line, with a plumb line in his hand.*

A²: ⁸ And the Lᴏʀᴅ said to me, "Amos, what do you see?"

B³: And I said, "A plumb line."

A³: Then the Lᴏʀᴅ said, "See, I am setting a plumb line
in the midst of my people Israel;
I will never again pass them by;
⁹ the high places of Isaac shall be made desolate,
and the sanctuaries of Israel shall be laid waste,
and I will rise against the house of Jeroboam with
the sword."

Structure

The series of visions in Amos 7 has long attracted the attention of commentators and they have suggested a variety of structures for the passage, including various connections to the following narrative.[30] Certainly, the conversational prayer incorporated into the vision report fits the larger rhetorical design of the book. To this point, however, none of the commentators have considered the conversational structure embedded in the vision report and how that structure fits into the rhetorical design of the

---

30. Wolf, *Joel and Amos*, 294–95; Paul, *Amos*, 223; Mays, *Amos*, 123–27; Jeremias, *Book of Amos*, 130; Campos, "Structure and Meaning in the Third Vision of Amos," 28; Gordis, "Composition and Structure of Amos," 217–29; Bulkeley, "Amos 7,1—8,3," 521–28.

book. Several observations are in order concerning the structure of this conversational exchange.

First, it should be noted that the infinitive, לאמר (saying), is never used in this conversational prayer to frame or introduce direct speech. The infinitive does appear elsewhere in the book to signify direct speech (2:12; 3:1; 7:10; 8:5), including the report of Amaziah's speech in the narrative immediately following the series of visions. This implies that the author acknowledges the constructed nature of the conversation and that the structure, the *how*, of the conversation is very important and intentionally composed by the author.

An obvious structural characteristic to note about this series of visions is the manner in which the conversationalists flip roles as initiator and respondent. The conversation is structured in three rounds, involving both Amos and the Lord, followed by a direct address from the Lord.

- Round one: vv. 2–3
- Round two: vv. 5–6
- Round three: v. 8

In rounds one and two, Amos is the initiator of conversation and the Lord is the respondent. In the third round, the Lord initiates the request, placing the prophet in the role of the responder. This transposition has several effects on the conversation.

In the first two rounds, Amos voices a dispreferred response to the preceding vision of destruction about to be visited on Israel. The prophet's prayer of protest and plea to avert the destruction allows the prophet to function as mediator and empathetic spokesperson for the nation. It also allows the Lord to be persuaded by the prophet's plea and so relent from the proposed destructive action.[31] Through the first two rounds, Amos is elevated in status, as he proves effective in persuading his conversational partner to respond to him in a preferred fashion.[32] This elevation in status might be construed as an equal reduction in status for the Lord, making him susceptible to the prophet's directives. That equivocation is removed in the third round.

The third round is different. This round is initiated by the Lord, who asks of his conversational partner: "What do you see?" (v. 8). The question is not a request for knowledge, but presupposes knowledge, possessed by the

---

31. Bulkeley, "Amos 7,1—8,3," 522.

32. Joining other intercessors: Abraham (Gen 20:7), Moses (Exod 32:11–14), Samuel (1 Sam 7:5–8), and Jeremiah (Jer 7:16; 11:14). See P. D. Miller, *They Cried to the Lord*, 274.

Lord, knowledge that will now be shared with Amos.[33] This use of a question places the Lord in a power position within the conversation, as he is now assumed to possess knowledge, not shared by the prophet, and is poised to explain the significance of the knowledge. The prophet is in a dependent role, relying upon the Lord for both knowledge and the meaning of that knowledge. In this fashion, the outcome of the exchange and any consequential activity to follow is still a result of the Lord's agency. Even though earlier he has been dissuaded by Amos, the Lord is still firmly in charge.

The presentation of Amos as effective intercessor and the Lord as the effective agent of the impending judgment is extremely important in the depiction of the prophet's conflict with Amaziah in 7:10–17. Amos must deny Amaziah's accusations and affirm that his prophetic mission is not compromised by either money or national affiliation. Amos argues his effective representation of the Divine message. The conversation between Amos and the Lord in the series of visions settles the status relation between the conversationalists and firmly establishes the roles each will play in the larger prophetic drama in the book of Amos.

Jonah 4:1–11

¹ *But this was very displeasing to Jonah, and he became angry.*

A: ² He prayed to the Lord and said, "O Lord! Is not this what I said while I was still in my own country? That is why I fled to Tarshish at the beginning; for I knew that you are a gracious God and merciful, slow to anger, and abounding in steadfast love, and ready to relent from punishing. ³ And now, O Lord, please take my life from me, for it is better for me to die than to live."

B: ⁴ And the Lord said, "Is it right for you to be angry?"

⁵ *Then Jonah went out of the city and sat down east of the city, and made a booth for himself there. He sat under it in the shade, waiting to see what would become of the city.* ⁶ *The Lord God appointed a bush, and made it come up over Jonah, to give shade over his head, to save him from his discomfort; so Jonah was very happy about the bush.* ⁷ *But when dawn came up the next day, God appointed a worm that attacked the bush, so that it withered.* ⁸ *When the sun rose, God prepared a sultry east wind, and the sun*

---

33. See Heritage, "Epistemics in Conversation," 379–84; see also Hayano, "Question Design in Conversation," 400–406.

beat down on the head of Jonah so that he was faint and asked that he might die.

A¹: He said, "It is better for me to die than to live."

B¹: ⁹ But God said to Jonah, "Is it right for you to be angry about the bush?"

A³: And he said, "Yes, angry enough to die."

B³: ¹⁰ Then the LORD said, "You are concerned about the bush, for which you did not labor and which you did not grow; it came into being in a night and perished in a night. ¹¹ And should I not be concerned about Nineveh, that great city, in which there are more than a hundred and twenty thousand persons who do not know their right hand from their left, and also many animals?"

Context

The introduction to the conversational prayer (4:1) establishes the antagonism that will be expressed in the opening exchange of the conversation.[34] Jonah has reluctantly obeyed God's command to go to Nineveh and preach a warning of imminent punishment from God. In response, the people of Nineveh, believe God, proclaim a fast (3:5), and turn from their evil ways (3:8, 10). As a result, God changed his mind and did not bring the calamity he threatened upon the people of Nineveh (3:10). God's change of mind caused Jonah to become displeased and angry. Jonah's anger is explained in his direct address to God (4:2–3). Jonah clearly recognizes that the LORD is a "gracious God and merciful, slow to anger, and abounding in steadfast love,[35] and ready to relent from punishing" (4:2). Jonah's objection is that these Divine qualities are applied equally to the residents of Nineveh and not reserved solely for Israel.

Structure

This conversation is structured in a fascinating manner. The questions in vv. 4 and 9 are framed for a yes-no response. Evidence suggests that questions, formed in this fashion, are designed to secure confirmations, to win the

---

34. See the repetitive use of first person, effectively emphasizing the confrontation between the conversationalists in the conversation. See Sasson, *Jonah*, 277.

35. A creedal statement found, with variation, elsewhere: Exod 34:6–7; Num 14:18; Neh 9:17; Pss 86:15; 103:8; 111:4; Joel 2:13. See Vanoni, *Buch Jonah*, 144.

agreement of the responder.[36] Securing Jonah's affiliation with the LORD is the whole point of this conversational prayer. The conversation begins with the conversationalists antagonistic toward one another.[37] The LORD's merciful disposition toward Nineveh has angered Jonah so much so that he pleads with the LORD to take his life, for life is no longer worth living (v. 3).[38] In response, the LORD asks simply, "Is it right for you to be angry?" knowing full well that, if given the opportunity to respond, Jonah's response would be, Yes! It is significant that Jonah does not respond, for his presumed answer, although affirmative, would still represent a dispreferred response and so continue the disagreement between Jonah and the LORD.

Following the episode of the withering bush and the resultant hardship inflicted upon Jonah by the relentless sun and wind, Jonah once again announces that it is better for him to die (v. 8). Once again, the LORD asks Jonah, is it right for you to be angry? (about the bush). This time Jonah is allowed to respond, and he does so in the affirmative, but this time, the affirmative answer forces him into agreement with the LORD, resolving the opening disagreement between Jonah and the LORD concerning the fate of Nineveh. If Jonah is right to express concern for the bush, how much more so is it right for the LORD to be concerned for the inhabitants of Nineveh? Jonah's affirmative answer to the previous two questions allows him no room to now disagree with the LORD. In the conversation:

- The precipitating complaint has not changed: It is better for me to die
- The Divine question has not changed: Is it right for you to be angry?
- The response to the question has not changed: Yes!

Structurally, the conversation remains constant. Yet, the constancy of the conversation forces a change in the affiliation between conversationalists (and more the reader) as Jonah is forced into accepting the LORD's point of view.

Closing

As with most of the conversational prayers in the Hebrew Bible, there is no closing to the conversation, it simply ends. Jonah offers no rebuttal to God's

---

36. Pomerantz and Heritage, "Preference," 214.
37. Person, *In Conversation with Jonah*, 44.
38. See also Elijah in 1 Kgs 19:4–18.

legitimate concern over the residents of Nineveh. Jonah's reluctant acceptance of God's point of view has already been accomplished through the questions posed by the Lord, and now Jonah's silence is telling. There is nothing more to say. Jonah (and the reader) may not be happy with the application of God's unbounded grace, but there is no objection yet to be formed.

The rhetorical importance of this conversational prayer, within the book of Jonah, cannot be overstated. The abrupt ending of the conversation also ends the book. The last word is God's. The last word is grace. For, as Jonah has already recognized, "deliverance belongs to the Lord!" (2:10).

11

General Observations

THE CONVERSATIONAL PRAYERS IN the Hebrew Bible give ample evidence for one foundational truth: The human relationship with God is built on talk. The quality and strength of the bond between God and human is measured by the quality of talk that transpires between the two. Abraham and Moses, identified as friends of God in the Hebrew Bible, are both identified as such because of their talk with God.[1] The conversational prayers of the Hebrew Bible, including those in which Abraham and Moses participated, demonstrate the rich and varied, yet, essential role of talk in the *who-we-are-to-one-another* between God and his conversational partners. These conversational prayers give voice to fundamental dilemmas, deep human questions, and relational dynamics that resonate even today in a prayerful encounter with God. Conversational prayer is founded on a relationship with God in which the petitioner is fully present to God, susceptible to a Divine human partnership that is uncontrollable and often unexpected by the human conversationalist. As presented in the conversational prayers in the Hebrew Bible, it's clear that conversing with God requires intention, humility, and courage. The conversational prayers are instructive for: *what-is-said*, *how-its-said*, and *what-it-does*.

What-Is-Said

Conversational prayer is rarely identified as prayer in the Hebrew Bible even though it is quite evident that the activity of prayer is present.[2] While it is probably correct not to make over much of this observation, it does suggest that conversational prayer goes beyond simple petitions or praise,

---

1. Abraham: 2 Chr 20:7; Isa 41:8. Moses: Exod 33:11; Num 12:8; Deut 34:10.
2. Exceptions are found in 2 Kgs 4:33; 6:17; 19:15, 20; 20:2; 2 Chr 30:18.

themes, and topics common in liturgical prayer. Conversational prayers are broad and venture beyond the realm of the religious. There is a dynamic present in conversational prayer that is not characteristic of liturgical or otherwise formalized prayer. Freed of formal constraints, conversational prayers are presented without pre-requisite formula, location, or personal status. Anyone, anywhere, anytime may address God in prayer when motivated by need and expressed with honesty and authenticity. Conversational prayer does not recognize national or religious boundaries. Even if unnoticed by others or absent comfort for the petitioner, the cry of the distressed reaches God. But it is equally true that the conversational prayers demonstrate, at times uncomfortably so, that God may address any of us, anywhere, at any time. Having approached God in conversation, it is often the case that the petitioner discovers she or he has been summoned and is simply responding to the invitation of the Divine.

Conversational prayers are not equally distributed throughout the Hebrew Bible. Contextualized in prose writing, the prayers are used to accomplish the larger purposes of the different writers choosing to include these prayers. Among these writers, the Chronicler has a special interest in prayer and uses conversational prayer to pointedly communicate ideology. "Chronicles is a comprehensive expression of the perpetual need to renew and revitalize the religion of Israel."[3] In renewing and revitalizing, the Chronicler makes extensive use of sources, changing those sources when needed, to make them applicable to his present time, place, and ideological outlook. The Chronicler uses the conversational prayers to make that bridge between the past and the present in a very pointed, personal, and immediate manner. Special affinity for conversational prayer is expressed by the Chronicler in Hezekiah's prayer of 2 Chronicles 30:18–19. For the Chronicler, as illustrated by Hezekiah, condition of heart is more important than ritual correctness. The same is true of the prayers by Jabez and Asa. These prayers (of Jabez, 1 Chr 4:10; and of Asa, 2 Chr 14:11) share the same structure yet are very different in conversational function. Jabez' prayer is formal and distant, while Asa's prayer is immediate, intimate, and urgent. Despite these relational differences, both prayers express sole reliance on Deity and both prayers move the Divine to act.

In the conversational prayers, we find themes that are perennial in prayer. In the Abraham Cycle, the conversational prayers are concerned with the trustworthiness of God. The prayers ask if God can be trusted to keep his promises, particularly as first introduced in Gen 12:1–3. Repeatedly, circumstances suggest that God is not trustworthy, and the matter is

---

3. Japhet, *Ideology of the Book of Chronicles*, 516.

raised, more than once, with God in conversational prayer. Even when the Divine promise is threatened by the petitioner's own duplicity, God proves faithful (Gen 12:10–20). Similarly, the prayer in Num 11:11–24 contains one of the most fundamental dilemmas of prayer. Moses asks, quite literally: "Why have you done this evil to your servant?" The God to whom Moses prays, and the One from whom relief is sought, is also the One who has caused the crises. The question is put to God allowing no compromise. The crises didn't just happen. Nor did the maltreatment result from any fault attributed to the petitioner. The crisis described in Numbers 11 was God's doing and now Moses must appeal to this same God for relief.

Surely, all who pray will at some time find themselves in the deep shadows of this same dilemma, questioning the character of the Divine, and able only to utter a cry of "Please!" (Num 12:13) or an inarticulate groan from a breaking heart (Ezek 9:8). Perhaps comfort can be found knowing that God has been in these conversations before, does not shy away from these most intimate of moments, and shares the deep heartache in conversation as would any good friend. Divine empathy, an intersubjectivity between God and the breaking human heart, provides comfort and solace when religious correctness fails.

How-It's-Said

Conversational prayer allows a status of friendship with God. Conversation is more than information exchange or the impetus for consequential action. Conversation allows a dynamic status between the conversational participants. As carrier of a dynamic relationship (an *I–Thou*), conversational prayer is fluid and can be familiar, but never formulaic. The very nature of conversational prayer will never allow certainty or completeness such as that permitted in formulaic prayer. And although the contextual catalyst, the problem or dilemma prompting the prayer, may be resolved, conversational prayer is never finished.

The biblical narrators all portray speech between God and human patterned after the speech between humans. The conversational prayers indicate that the way we speak to one another was the basis for the way in which God was addressed in prayer. This is consistent with the predominant Hebrew Bible conception of God as person. In conversation we meet God as person, not as idea or dogma. As person, the God whom we meet in prayer is always more, never fully captured by our previous understanding or interactions.

The basic pattern for these types of prayer is normal human conversational interaction. Within these conversational prayers, there is no literary formula or set pattern of speech outside of the normal human cultural conventions that govern address, be it petition, gratitude, etc. There are no uniquely religious speech introductions or formulae which are in and of themselves efficacious. There are no incantations or magical words in the conversational prayers. There is a profound simplicity and functionality to these conversational prayers.[4] In this immediate contact with the God who searches the human heart, a premium is placed on sincerity and authenticity.

Conversational prayer is presumptuous, challenging God to assume the petitioner's point of view and to act in a manner desired by the petitioner or answer an objection framed by the petitioner. Liturgical prayer is different. Liturgical prayer is validated by religious affirmation and effectively seeks to move the petitioner to see things from God's point of view (religious correctness), even when a petition or objection is voiced. While never denying the necessity or value of liturgical prayer, conversational prayer is otherwise. Conversational prayer seeks to move God to see things from the petitioner's point of view. Conversational prayer seeks to develop Divine human intersubjectivity through human agency. Why should God be so moved? In conversational prayer, the *I–Thou* relationship is reciprocal and authentic, affirming the personhood of both conversational partners. Conversational prayers are frequently inserted into biblical narrative because of the ability of the prayer to give expression to the personhood of the participants, both human and Divine. And that personhood demands that each is susceptible to the other.

Like inter-human speech, the effectiveness of the conversational prayers is not primarily conditioned by wording, but by the intersubjectivity achieved between the conversationalists. Among the interpersonal factors contributing to this intersubjectivity, the *who-we-are-to-one-another* in prayer plays a crucial role. The requirement of sincerity in prayer derives from the social nature of prayer as a transaction between persons. In communication, one affects another not so much by the form of the words but by the spirit that animates the words. Since conversational prayer puts no stock on a prescribed wording, the basis of its acceptance by God, that is, of God's being touched by it, must be the sincerity of the professions made by the individual in prayer. The essence of conversational prayer is the conformity of speech and thought. When placed before a third party, a hearing or reading audience, the conversational prayers of the Hebrew Bible force assessments

---

4. Powerfully illustrated by the Elijah prayer of 1 Kings 17.

to be made concerning the sincerity of all participants in and observers of the conversational prayers—both human and Divine.

The relational aspect of conversational prayer is important even when muted or prevented. In the Jacob Cycle, only one person speaks in conversational prayer. Consequently, the relationship between the person praying and God is static, not developed or enriched. The lack of give and take, the back and forth of conversation, prevents relational development. The same is true of the Samson prayer in Judg 15:18–19. The dynamism of the relationship between God and Moses is nowhere to be found with Jacob or Samson. In conversational prayer, character matters and when there is dissimilarity in the characters of those involved, conversation stops, and monologue begins.

In Exodus, introductions to the conversational prayers are rare. Moses speaks with God, absent the need for God to appear, come down, or give heed, and, generally, without the need for Moses to relocate to the tabernacle, bow to the ground, or in any other fashion acknowledge the presence of God. Without these introductory phrases, the impression is formed of a Divine immediacy or presence available to Moses that allows human to human conversational exchange to shift to Divine human conversational exchange without skipping a beat. This Divine immediacy is remarkable. If the conversational prayers by Moses are a model, it may be that we all pray much more than we are aware, and, in fact, speak in the presence of God more than we intend. It isn't a question *if* our utterances are heard by God, but *how intentional* we are about our conversation with God.

What allowed Moses to immediately address God when those around him were either unaware of God's presence or unable to direct speech to God? Certainly, it wasn't that Moses was always in agreement with either God's actions or demonstrated disposition. Some of the strongest protests in prayer come from Moses.[5] Nor did God always approve of Moses. It was because of a tragic misstep Moses was prevented from accompanying Israel to the Promised Land. Moses' freedom in prayer grew from an intentionality that made him mindful of Deity's presence even when that presence was hidden to other observers. That intentionality, when practiced, becomes habitual, characteristic of a long-term relationship, not just a moment in time.

This matter of intentionality is woven into the rhetorical design of the conversational prayers. Often, conversational prayers are used as a rhetorical device to bring the reader into conversation with God. For example, in Jonah 4 the conversational prayer involving Jonah is designed to win

---

5. The protests in Exodus 5, 32; Numbers 11, 12 are among the strongest ever verbalized to God.

the affiliation of the reader—bringing the reader to the point of recognition that the graciousness and mercy of God is not bounded by political, ethnic, or national identities.[6] While the exact nature of the affiliation between petitioner and God may change, this intersubjectivity, a shared point of view between conversational partners, is a constant consequence of conversational prayer. And it is important to remember that this intersubjectivity means a loss of control as the petitioner ventures into a shared outlook formed by partners in conversation and not dictated by a single actor in monologue. Consequently, conversational prayer always involves a risk. A risk of losing an outlook, plan, or expectation as the future is now molded jointly by both conversational partners.

What-It-Does

Conversational prayer is reciprocal, a give and take, moving both participants. Even though conversational prayers are effective in changing real events within the plot of the narratives in which they are now embedded, conversational prayers are as much about the relationship between the conversationalists as they are about a topic of discussion or a problem to be solved.[7] In Joshua-Judges, Divine identity is a repeated concern in the conversational prayers. A variety of names and identities are associated with the Divine conversationalist, often all within the same conversational prayer. The identification and character of the Deity *who-is-to-me* in prayer is a major concern of conversational prayer. That is, just like with other friends, it's in conversation that we get to know God and are known by God.

This relational dynamic of conversation is clearly present in the prayers of David and Solomon. In fact, it's the *who-we-are-to-one-another* of conversation that accounts for the form given to these prayers and, to a great extent, accounts for their inclusion in the Kings or Chronicles narratives. By and large, the prayers of David and Solomon are monologues (speeches) constructed in the form of conversation. Presented as conversation, the prayers add a level of attention that can be given to the *who-we-are-to-one-another* of the address and not just the *what* is said of the conversation. This conversational structure forces the reader to attend to the development of relationship status between the conversationalists.

This *I–Thou* relational status conveyed in conversational prayer keeps the awareness of God's presence a constant reality. Conversation keeps the conversational partner near to mind. Conversational prayer keeps God

6. The same may be said of the Ezekiel 9 prayer.
7. See, for example, the prayer in Judges 13.

near to mind. And part of the immediate *who-we-are-to-one-another* of conversational prayer is the intersubjectivity that tends to form shared character qualities. That is, God's character tends to rub off on the human conversational partner. For ancient Israel, this meant an expectation that a degree of holiness, a sense of shared time with God, could be experienced by everyone, not just priest, or prophet, or king (Num 11:29) and that the absence of this shared character noticeably impacts the quality of the Divine—human relationship (i.e., Jacob, Samson).

This *who-we-are-to-one-another* in conversational prayer seems to have been engrained in the prophetic understanding of God's disposition toward all humanity. For the prophets, the worshipper's character mattered far more than the form of worship. Isaiah is clear in his insistence that worship, like conversational prayer is inter-relational and devoid of any magical or necessary cause and effect value.[8] Worship, like conversational prayer, demands authenticity, which cannot be replaced by any properly performed sacrifice or liturgically correct prayer formula. And the *who-we-are-to-God* in prayer is presented as effecting change in real events! That is, authenticity in the *who-we-are-to-one-another* moves God to act no less than the human conversationalist is moved to act or change.

One of the amazing dynamics of the conversational relational status, seen especially in Ezekiel 9 and Jonah 4, is the empathy and emotional affiliation God seeks from those with whom he converses. From Ezekiel 9 we learn that a sober reflection on conversational prayer must consider that God, too, experiences pain and grief for which he seeks emotional empathy and support from friends. Accustomed to think that prayer provides emotional support for the human participant, comfort and strength in the face of tragedy, it is startling to think that God may seek the same thing. Moses is a friend of God (Exod 33:11) entrusted with his (God's) whole house (Num 12:7). What does it mean to be trusted by God, available for God to emotionally lean on (Ezek 9)? An amazing change can take place in conversational prayer. The *I* in an *I–It* relationship can move from son of man (servant—Ezekiel) to friend (Moses) in an *I–Thou* relationship. An *I–It* relationship is unilateral, a one way stream, existing for the sole benefit of the *I*. Conversational prayer strives for an *I–Thou* relationship that is reciprocal, placing both at the disposal of the other, susceptible to be acted upon, held to account, and available to the other. An *I–Thou* relationship with God should not be taken lightly or entered thoughtlessly. The demands are great. Can there be a greater privilege or greater responsibility than to, like Moses, be caretaker of Divine trust?

---

8. See famously Isa 1:12–17; see also Elijah in 1 Kings 17.

This drive for authenticity can be demanding on the human participant. The conversational prayers in the prophetic literature, though admittedly rare, make a profound addition to our understanding of prayer. In the process of developing an intersubjectivity, a joint understanding between the prophet and God, the prophet is encouraged to develop an emotional affinity with God. In Ezekiel, the crises giving context to the prayer of chapter 9 places God in need of the emotional support provided by friends and the prophet is encouraged to respond with that support.[9] Conversational prayer (like conversation with anyone) demands that at times we forgo our own point of view in order to empathetically enter the world view of our conversational partner (both cognitively and emotionally). Conversational prayer assumes a willingness to be changed and risks that an unknown outcome may forever leave its imprint.

That risk, that loss of control, is a problem considered in the conversational prayer of 1 Kings 19. A lack of shared understanding between God and Elijah is at the heart of the conversational prayer. In the conversational prayer between Elijah and God, the world looks one way through human eyes, but evidently quite differently from God's point of view. One of the fundamental problems in prayer, and certainly at the heart of the prayer in 1 Kings 19, is coming to a mutual understanding with God. While often, conversational prayer begins with an attempt to get God to see things as we see them (to get God to act upon our requests), recurrently we leave the prayer encounter compelled to see things from God's point of view. Frequently, coming to this shared intersubjectivity, this shared view of the condition prompting prayer, is not easy, and, if the conversational prayers in the Hebrew Bible are intended at least in part as exemplary, all too often we are not willing learners. As Elijah experienced, conversational prayer can be a struggle and we, too, may hide our faces from the Divine silence.

In Judges 6, Gideon poses a question often heard in prayer: "Where is God?" "If he is present, why hasn't he acted in the same miraculous fashion that we've heard about from the past?" (6:13). In Gideon's assessment, circumstances indicate that God isn't present—at least in any effective fashion. So, the petitioner is driven to pray. Yet, the act of prayer assumes God is present. And that's the dilemma with prayer, especially conversational prayer. Conversational prayer is an act of immediacy at the very moment when that immediacy is cast into doubt. So, why is this problem of God's presence addressed in conversation? Why isn't the problem solved by ritual or commemorative object[10] (even the altar built by Gideon commemorates

---

9. See also Jonah 4.
10. Abraham also builds an altar (Gen 12:7) to commemorate an encounter with

peace, not presence) guaranteed to make the deity present? Conversation forces the petitioner to give attention to the interpersonal relationship of the characters involved in a way not possible in ritual. Conversational prayer forces the petitioner to acknowledge the presence of God, uncontrolled, unfettered, and unrestrained by expectation. Conversational prayer forces us to leave an *I–It* in order to experience an *I–Thou*.

God. Jacob erects a pillar (Gen 28:22) to house God, but it plays no further role, eventually replaced by an altar (Gen 35:1) and a second pillar (Gen 35:14). These objects commemorate past encounters with God but have no power to produce a present encounter.

Postscript: The Last Word

Yesterday, I was riding on the tractor, doing spring yard work, when I noticed a little boy with a fishing pole walking along the creek that winds its way through our property. I stopped to show the little guy and his Grandma my favorite fishing hole. I went back to work, observing a little later that my wife had struck up a conversation with Grandma. It turns out the boy and his twelve-year-old sister had just lost their Mom to a heart attack. The children discovered their Mom and phoned Grandma, concerned because "Mommy won't wake up." Yesterday, Grandma had taken the boy out for the afternoon, looking for a place to fish and had stumbled upon our little creek. She was trying to give her grandson a break from the tremendous heartache that had now become his familiar companion. She was trying to let him be a little boy.

I can't get this little boy out of my mind. Everything in me wants to shout out in pain and grief. Do I simply groan in prayer with Ezekiel or Elijah? Do I protest with Moses and say "No! Please God. No!" Is there comfort to be found with Jonah knowing that God, too, feels this boy's pain more than I ever could? I'm sure I'll see this little boy again. He didn't catch any fish but fell in love with my wife's chickens and Grandma, too, seemed to need the peace and quiet of this little retreat.

Will the Judge of all the earth do what is right for this little boy? Any *I–Thou* relationship I might have with God, must help form my *I–Thou* relationship with this little boy just as certainly as my encounter with the boy is now part of the *I* that engages the Divine *Thou*.

I began this investigation expecting to be changed and I haven't been disappointed. But sometimes we need to be careful about what we wish. Frankly, I didn't understand the peril, the genuinely life changing consequences of conversing with God in prayer. I have discovered that along with the enticement and clear enjoyment of conversing with God, comes tremendous trepidation and risk. I'm being changed and I am not in control of either the process or goal. Conversational prayer requires courage—the willingness to be acted upon by the Divine conversationalist. For me, I think the journey is just beginning.

Appendix 1

Genesis 3:9–19: Adam and Eve

Interrogatives in Conversation

WHILE NOT A CONVERSATIONAL prayer, the conversation between Adam, Eve, and the LORD God in Genesis 3 deserves inclusion in this study because of a particular feature of this conversation that also appears in additional prayers.[1] The Genesis 3 conversation gives us opportunity to introduce the multifaceted function of questions in conversation.

In form, this conversation is remarkable. The adjacency pairs of the conversation are solely in the form of question and answer. The supply of information is only one function of questions offered in conversation.[2] Interrogatives can also function to; open a conversation (*How are ya?*), or they may contain implied directives (mother asking son: *Didn't I tell you to pick up those clothes?*), or threats (same mother to non-cooperative son: *Do you really want me to come up there?*), or designed to effect a preferred response, or attempted efforts to secure affirmation, or confirmation from the conversational partner (*Do you like this shirt I'm wearing?*), or as a dispreferred response communicating protest (*Who do you think you are to tell me that?*) or denial (*How should I know?*). In many instances, interrogatives function to assert a right to possess certain knowledge and so, as in Genesis 3, communicate status as the interrogator assumes authority in asking the question. The interrogator's right is recognized and reaffirmed in the compliant preferred response of the conversational partner.

---

1. Num 11, 22; 1 Kgs 19.
2. See Clift, *Conversation Analysis*, 152, 202–10.

Structure

⁹ But the Lord God called to the man, and said to him, "Where are you?"

B: ¹⁰ He said, "I heard the sound of you in the garden, and I was afraid, because I was naked; and I hid myself."

A¹: ¹¹ He said, "Who told you that you were naked? Have you eaten from the tree of which I commanded you not to eat?"

B¹: ¹² The man said, "The woman whom you gave to be with me, she gave me fruit from the tree, and I ate."

A²: ¹³ Then the Lord God said to the woman, "What is this that you have done?"

C: The woman said, "The serpent tricked me, and I ate."

A³: ¹⁴ The Lord God said to the serpent,

"Because you have done this,
cursed are you among all animals
and among all wild creatures;
upon your belly you shall go,
   and dust you shall eat
   all the days of your life.

¹⁵ I will put enmity between you and the woman,
   and between your offspring and hers;
he will strike your head,
   and you will strike his heel."

¹⁶ To the woman he said,

"I will greatly increase your pangs in childbearing;
   in pain you shall bring forth children,
yet your desire shall be for your husband,
   and he shall rule over you."

¹⁷ And to the man he said,

"Because you have listened to the voice of your wife,
   and have eaten of the tree
about which I commanded you,
   'You shall not eat of it,'
cursed is the ground because of you;
   in toil you shall eat of it all the days of your life;

¹⁸ thorns and thistles it shall bring forth for you;
   and you shall eat the plants of the field.

¹⁹ By the sweat of your face
   you shall eat bread
until you return to the ground,
   for out of it you were taken;
you are dust, and to dust you shall return."

Status Established and Challenged

The initial question of the conversation in Genesis 3 establishes status (the *who-we-are-to-one-another*) between the conversation partners. Authority is presumed by the LORD God and recognized by the conversational partners, requiring them to respond to the question in a preferred fashion. The question is not met with silence, which could imply disregard. Nor, is the question met with a dispreferred response (i.e., *Where are you? – None of your business*), effectively refusing or at least challenging the interrogator's status expressed in the initial question. The initiating question is met with a preferred response that implies the interrogator's right to ask the question.

First Round

   A: Where are you?"

   B: ¹⁰ He said, "I heard the sound of you in the garden, and I was afraid, because I was naked; and I hid myself."

The conversation is initiated by means of a question and that question is answered—eventually. The answer offered by Adam is in the form of a preferred response and provides more information than is immediately required by the initial question, implicitly recognizing the questioner's right to that knowledge. The additional information provided in the response also leads to the next question in the series. The answer short circuits the conversation by anticipating follow-up questions and pre-offering information in answer to those questions.[3] The long form of the conversation could have proceeded:

   A: Where are you?

   B: I hid myself.

   A¹: Why did you do that?

   B¹: I heard you in the garden and was afraid

---

3. A similar structure is evident in the exchange between the serpent and Eve in Gen 3:1–3.

A²: Why were you afraid?

B²: I was naked.

This longer conversational form forces the LORD God to reassert authority with each enquiry. Each enquiry provides the possibility of a dispreferred response and so holds the status of the interrogator in suspension. In this hypothetical long form of the conversation, the *who-we-are-to-one-another* of the conversation is less established. And indeed, in the conversation as we have it, a challenge to the LORD God's status becomes evident in the second round.

Second Round

In the second round of the conversation, two more questions are posed.

A¹: ¹¹ He said, "Who told you that you were naked? Have you eaten from the tree of which I commanded you not to eat?"

B¹: ¹² The man said, "The woman whom you gave to be with me, she gave me fruit from the tree, and I ate."

The answer to the first enquiry (*Who told you that you were naked?*) is given indirectly: "The woman gave me the fruit." The implication is that the woman, in providing the forbidden fruit, was the source of knowledge and the real culprit in breaking the command. But additional questions provide opportunity to challenge the status of the questioner—"whom you gave to be with me." The man's guilt is protested by placing responsibility on the woman and the LORD God. Adam responds to the LORD God's question and so complies, but the insertion of the phrase, "whom you gave to be with me," functions as a dispreferred response, challenging the status of the questioner. The *who-we-are-to-one-another* of the conversation is dynamic and changing and this changing status drives the conversation.

Third Round

A²: ¹³ Then the LORD God said to the woman, "What is this that you have done?"

C: The woman said, "The serpent tricked me, and I ate."

As the man before her, the woman answers the question posed to her by first presenting herself as the victim of another's action: *The serpent tricked me.* The other's action is prerequisite for the admission, *I ate.* The question addressed to the Woman assumes the Lord God's right to the knowledge He requests. While no direct challenge to the Lord God's status is given by the Woman (she does not claim the serpent is a gift from the Lord God in the manner the Man described the Woman), she none the less resists accountability by inserting information that, she hopes, will moderate her culpability.

It is significant that no question is posed to the serpent, and consequently the serpent is given no opportunity to respond. Nor does the serpent initiate participation in the conversation. In this conversation the serpent has no voice. If at least part of the function of the questions structuring this conversation is to articulate standing between the conversationalists, it seems probable that no question is asked of the serpent because no status between the serpent and the Lord God is envisioned or desired. The previous responses were designed for explanation that also displayed status standing between the Divine interrogator and human respondents. Each question is met with a preferred response that provides information leading to the next interrogatory.

Status Restored

Status is restored in the Lord God's final turn of the conversation. The *who-we-are-to-one-another* of the conversational participants is clearly described. In turn the serpent, woman, and man are given place and condition in relation to one another. The final response is highly stylized, deviating from the spontaneous conversational style of 3:9–13. It is also an interesting feature of this conversation that it forms a chiastic pairing.[4] In the series of questions initiating the first three rounds followed by the direct address to the serpent, the Lord God addresses: Adam, Eve, the Serpent. Followed by concluding speech addresses to: Eve, Adam. Resulting in the chiastic:

Adam
    Eve
        Serpent
    Eve
Adam

---

4. A literary device used frequently in Genesis. See, for example, God's pronouncement in Gen 9:6. Yudkowsky, "Chaos or Chiasm?," 110–14.

It may be that the initial sequence of address is designed to establish ranking or status and the way the serpent is offered no opportunity for response is an implicit denial of status.[5]

---

5. See Levinson, *Pragmatics*, 301. See also Raymond and Heritage, "The Epistemics of Social Relationships," 683.

Appendix 2

Non-Conversational Prosaic Prayers

The following are not included in the Conversational Prayer group. Either they appear in poetic contexts (common in Jeremiah) preventing conversational analysis, or they lack the requisite conversational activity, or the prayer is used as a formal greeting or similar speech act in which Deity is not the true addressee (i.e., Ruth).

1. Passages in which prosaic prayer is only mentioned.

    - Genesis 25:21; 30:6, 22
    - Exodus 2:23–24; 14:10; 14:15; 22:23
    - Leviticus 9:24; 16:21; 26:40
    - Numbers 11:2; 21:7
    - Deuteronomy 9:19
    - Judges 3:9
    - 1 Samuel 1:10, 12–15; 7:5; 7:8–9; 8:6; 8:18; 12:17–18; 12:19, 23; 15:11
    - 2 Samuel 6:18; 12:16; 21:1
    - 1 Kings 13:6; 18:42
    - 2 Kings 4:33
    - Isaiah 42:2–4; 56:7
    - Jeremiah 21:2
    - Ezekiel 22:30
    - Lamentations 3:8, 44
    - Daniel 2:18; 6:11

- Ezra 8:21–23
- Nehemiah 2:4
- 1 Chronicles 5:20; 21:26
- 2 Chronicles 13:14; 33:12–13

2. Passages in which the wording of prosaic prayers occurs.
    - Genesis 19:18–19; 24:11, 26–27
    - Judges 16:23–24; 16:28–30; 21:2–3
    - 1 Samuel 1:11; 7:6; 12:10
    - 2 Samuel 15:31
    - Jeremiah 3:22–25; 4:10; 7:16 (=11:14=14:11) 14:7–9; 14:19–22; 15:15–18; 16:19; 17:14–18; 18:19–23; 20:7–13
    - Jonah 1:14
    - Ruth 1:8–9; 2:4; 2:12; 4:11; 4:14
    - Daniel 2:19–23; 9:4–19
    - Ezra 9:6–15
    - Nehemiah 1:4–11; 4:4–5; 5:19 (6:14; 13:14, 22, 29, 31)

Bibliography

Alter, Robert. *The Art of Biblical Narrative*. New York: Basic, 1981.
Anderson, A. A. *2 Samuel*. WBC 11. Dallas: Word, 1989.
Arnold, Bill. "The Holiness Redaction of the Abrahamic Covenant (Genesis 17)." In *Partners with God: Theological and Critical Readings of the Bible in Honor of Marvin A. Sweeney*, edited by Shelley Birdsong and Serge Frolov, 51–61. Claremont Studies in Hebrew Bible & Septuagint 2. Claremont, CA: Claremont, 2017.
Assis, Elie. "The Structure and Meaning of the Samson Narratives (Jud. 13–16)." In *Samson: Hero of Fool? The Many Faces of Samson*, edited by Erik Eynikel and Tobias Nicklas, 1–12. Themes in Biblical Narrative 17. Leiden: Brill, 2014.
Atkinson, J. M. "Public Speaking and Audience Responses: Some Techniques for Inviting Applause." In *Structures of Social Action: Studies in Conversation Analysis*, edited by J. Maxwell Atkinson and John Heritage, 370–409. Studies in Emotion and Social Interaction. Cambridge: Cambridge University Press, 1984.
Auld, Graeme. *I and II Samuel: A Commentary*. OTL. Louisville: Westminster John Knox, 2011.
Balentine, Samuel. *Prayer in the Hebrew Bible: The Drama of Divine-Human Dialogue*. Overtures to Biblical Theology. Minneapolis: Fortress, 1993.
———. "Prayer in the Wilderness Traditions: In Pursuit of Divine Justice." *Hebrew Annual Review* 9 (1985) 53–74.
Baruchi-Unna, Amitai. "The Story of Hezekiah's Prayer (2 Kings 19) and Jeremiah's Polemic Concerning the Inviolability of Jerusalem." *JSOT* 39 (2015) 281–97.
Beer, Georg. *Exodus*. Handbuch zum Alten Testament 1/3. Tübingen: Mohr/Siebeck, 1939.
Begg, Christopher. "The Destruction of the Calf (Exod 32,20 / Deut 9,21)." In *Das Deuteronomium: Entstehung, Gestalt und Botschaft*, edited by Norbert Lofink, 208–51. Bibliotheca ephemeridum theologicarum lovaniensium 68. Leuven: Leuven University Press, 1985.
Berman, Joshua. "Histories Twice Told: Deuteronomy 1–3 and the Hittite Treaty Prologue Tradition." *JBL* 132 (2013) 229–50.
———. "The Making of the Sin of Achan (Joshua 7)." *Biblical Interpretation* 22 (2014) 115–31.
Blenkinsopp, Joseph. *Isaiah 1–39*. AYB 19. New York: Doubleday, 2000.

Blidstein, Gerald. "Midrashim on Aharon and Miriam." In *Shefa Tal: Studies in Jewish Thought and Hebrew Culture Presented to Brakha Sack*, edited by Zeev Gries et al., 1–12. Beer-Sheva: Ben-Gurion University Press, 2004.

Blum, Erhard. "The Jacob Tradition." In *The Book of Genesis: Composition, Reception, and Interpretation*, edited by Craig Evans et al., 181–211. VTSup 152. Leiden: Brill, 2012.

Boase, Elizabeth. "Life in the Shadows: The Role and Function of Isaac in Genesis—Synchronic and Diachronic Readings." *VT* 51 (2001) 312–35.

Boda, Mark. "From Complaint to Contrition: Peering through the Liturgical Window of Jer 14, 1–15, 4." *ZAW* 113 (2001) 186–97.

Boling, Robert. *Judges*. AB 7. Garden City, NY: Doubleday, 1981.

Boling, Robert, and G. Ernest Wright. *Joshua*. AB 6. Garden City, NY: Doubleday, 1982.

Braun, Roddy. "Solomon, the Chosen Temple Builder: The Significance of 1 Chronicles 22, 28, and 29 for the Theology of Chronicles." *JBL* 95 (1976) 581–90.

Broida, Marian. "Closure in Samson." *JHS* 10 (2010). https://jhsonline.org/index.php/jhs/article/view/11257.

Brown, Francis, S. R. Driver, and Charles A. Briggs. *Hebrew and English Lexicon of the Old Testament*. Oxford: Clarendon, 1907.

Brueggemann, Walter. *David's Truth in Israel's Imagination and Memory*. Philadelphia: Fortress, 1985.

———. *Great Prayers of the Old Testament*. Louisville: Westminster John Knox, 2008.

Buber, Martin. *I and Thou*. Translated by Ronald Gregor Smith. New York: Scribner, 1958.

Budd, Philip. *Numbers*. WBC 4. Waco, TX: Word, 1984.

Bulkeley, Tim. "Amos 7,1—8,3: Cohesion and Generic Dissonance." *ZAW* 121 (2009) 515–28.

Button, Graham, and Neil Casey. "Topic Nomination and Topic Pursuit." *Human Studies* 8 (1985) 3–55.

Campos, Martha. "Structure and Meaning in the Third Vision of Amos (7:7–17)." *JHS* 11 (2011). https://jhsonline.org/index.php/jhs/article/view/11518.

Carroll, Robert P. *Jeremiah: A Commentary*. OTL. Philadelphia: Westminster, 1986.

Chepey, Stuart. "Samson the 'Holy One': A Suggestion Regarding the Reviser's Use of αγιος in Judg 13,7: 16,17 LXX Vaticanus." *Biblica* 83 (2002) 97–99.

Childs, Brevard. *The Book of Exodus: A Critical, Theological Commentary*. OTL. Philadelphia: Westminster, 1974.

Claassens, Julianna. "Just Emotions: Reading the Sarah and Hagar Narrative (Genesis 16, 21) through the Lens of Human Dignity." *Verbum et Ecclesia* 34 (2013) 1–6.

Clayman, S. E. "Sequence and Solidarity." In *Advances in Group Processes: Group Cohesion, Trust and Solidarity*, edited by E. J. Lawler and S. R. Thye, 229–53. Oxford: Elsevier, 2002.

———. "Turn-Constructional Units and the Transition-Relevance Place." In *The Handbook of Conversational Analysis*, edited by Jack Sidnell and Tanya Stivers, 150–66. Blackwell Handbooks in Linguistics. Oxford: Wiley-Blackwell, 2013.

Clements, Ronald. "Achan's Sin: Warfare and Holiness." In *Shall not the Judge of All the Earth Do What Is Right? Studies on the Nature of God in Tribute to James L. Crenshaw*, edited by David Penchansky and Paul Redditt, 113–26. Winona Lake, IN: Eisenbrauns, 2000.

Clift, Rebecca. *Conversation Analysis*. Cambridge Textbooks in Linguistics. Cambridge: Cambridge University Press, 2016.
Cogan, Mordechai. *1 Kings*. AB 10. New York: Doubleday, 2001.
Coggins, R. J. *The First and Second Books of Chronicles*. Cambridge Bible Commentary. Cambridge: Cambridge University Press, 1976.
Cooke, G. A. *A Critical and Exegetical Commentary on the Book of Ezekiel*. ICC. Edinburgh: T. & T. Clark, 1936.
Corvin, Jack W. "A Stylistic and Functional Study of the Prose Prayers in the Historical Narratives of the Old Testament." PhD. diss., Emory University, 1972.
Curtis, Edward Lewis, and Albert Madsen. *A Critical and Exegetical Commentary on the Book of Chronicles*. ICC. Edinburgh: T. & T. Clark, 1976.
Davidson, Judy. "Subsequent Versions of Invitations, Offers, Requests, and Proposals Dealing with Potential or Actual Rejection." In *Structures of Social Action: Studies in Conversational Analysis*, edited by J. Maxwell Atkinson and John Heritage, 102–28. Studies in Emotion and Social Interaction. Cambridge: Cambridge University Press, 1984.
Davis, Andrew. "Rereading 1 Kings 17:21 in Light of Ancient Medical Texts." *JBL* 135 (2016) 465–81.
De Vries, Simon. *1 and 2 Chronicles*. FOTL 11. Grand Rapids: Eerdmans, 1989.
———. *1 Kings*. WBC 12. Nashville: Nelson, 2003.
Dion, Paul. "The Angel with the Drawn Sword (1 Chr 21:16): An Exorcise in Restoring the Balance of Text Criticism and Attention to Context." *ZAW* 97 (1985) 114–17.
Douglas, Mary. *In the Wilderness: The Doctrine of Defilement in the Book of Numbers*. JSOTSup 158. Sheffield: Sheffield Academic, 1993.
Dozeman, Thomas. *Joshua 1–12*. AYB 6B. New Haven: Yale University Press, 2015.
Dozeman, Thomas, et al., eds. *The Pentateuch: International Perspectives on Current Research*. Forschungen zum Alten Testament 78. Tübingen: Mohr/Siebeck, 2019.
Driver, S. R. *A Critical and Exegetical Commentary on Deuteronomy*. ICC. Edinburgh: T. & T. Clark, 1895.
———. *Notes on the Hebrew Text and the Topography of the Books of Samuel*. 1913. Reprint, Eugene, OR: Wipf & Stock, 2004.
Duke, Rodney. *The Persuasive Appeal of the Chronicler: A Rhetorical Analysis*. JSOTSup 88. Sheffield: Almond, 1990.
Durham, John I. *Exodus*. WBC 3. Waco, TX: Word, 1987.
Eckart, Otto. "Deuteronomiumstudien I: Die Literaturgeschichte von Deuteronomium 1–3." *Zeitschrift für altorientalische und biblische Rechgeschichte* 14 (2008) 86–236.
Edenburg, Cynthia. "2 Sam 21–24: Haphazard Miscellany or Deliberate Revision?" In *Insights into Editing in the Hebrew Bible and the Ancient Near East*, edited by Reinhard Müller and Juhu Pakkala, 189–222. Contributions to Biblical Exegesis and Theology 84. Leuven: Peeters, 2017.
Evans, Paul. "Let the Crime Fit the Punishment: The Chronicler's Explication of David's 'Sin' in 1 Chronicles 21." In *Chronicling the Chronicler: The Book of Chronicles and the Early Temple Historiography*, edited by Paul Evans and Tyler Williams, 65–80. Winona Lake, IN: Eisenbrauns, 2013.
Fahrenthold, David. "Trump Recorded Having Extremely Lewd Conversation about Women in 2005." *Washington Post*, October 8, 2016.
Feldman, Ariel. *The Dead Sea Scrolls Rewriting Samuel and Kings: Texts and Commentary*. BZAW 469. Berlin: de Gruyter, 2015.

Fetherolf, Christina. "Elijah's Mantle: A Sign of Prophecy Gone Awry." *JSOT* 42 (2017) 199–212.
Fishbane, Michael. "Composition and Structure in the Jacob Cycle (Gen 25:19—35:22)." *Journal of Jewish Studies* 26 (1975) 15–38.
Ford, Cecilia E., and Sandra A. Thompson. "Interactional Units in Conversation: Syntactic, Intonational, and Pragmatic Resources for the Management of Turns." In *Interaction and Grammar*, edited by Elinor Ochs et al., 134–84. Studies in Interactional Sociolinguistics 13. Cambridge: Cambridge University Press, 1996.
Forsling, Josef. *Composite Artistry in the Book of Numbers: A Study in Biblical Narrative Conventions*. Studia Theologica Homiensia 22. Åbo, Finland: Åbo Akademi University Press, 2013.
Freedman, David Noel. "The Name of the God of Moses." *JBL* 79 (1960) 151–56.
Freedman, H., and Maurice Simon, eds. *Midrash Rabbah*. Vol. 1, *Genesis*. New York: Soncino, 1983.
Fretheim, Terrence E. *Exodus*. Interpretation. Louisville: John Knox, 1991.
Friedman, Richard Elliott. "Foreword." In *Empirical Models for Biblical Criticism*, edited by Jeffrey H. Tigay, 1–10. 1985. Reprint, Dove Studies in Bible, Language, and History. Eugene, OR: Wipf & Stock, 2005.
Frisch, Amos. "The Story of Balaam's She-Ass (Numbers 22:21–35): A New Literary Insight." *Hebrew Studies* 56 (2015) 103–13.
Gajanan, Mahita. "Melania Trump Says Donald's Comments in Leaked Video Were 'Boy Talk.'" *Time*, October 17, 2016. https://time.com/4534216/melania-donald-trump-billy-bush-boy-talk/.
Geoffrey, Raymond, and John Heritage. "The Epistemics of Social Relationships: Owning Grandchildren." *Language in Society* 35 (2006) 677–705.
Gesenius, Wilhelm. *Gesenius' Hebrew Grammar*. Edited and enlarged by E. Kautzsche. Revised by A. E. Cowley. Oxford: Clarendon, 1910.
Giles, Terry. "God Talk." In *Reading Scripture, Learning Wisdom: Essays in Honour of David G. Barker*, edited by Michael A. G. Haykin and Barry Howson, 113–36. Peterborough ON: Joshua, 2021.
Giles Terry, and William J. Doan. *Twice Used Songs: Performance Criticism of the Songs of Ancient Israel*. Peabody, MA: Hendrickson, 2009.
Goffman, Erving. "Alienation from Interaction." *Human Relations* 10 (1957) 47–60.
Goodwin, Charles. "The Interactive Construction of a Sentence in Natural Conversation." In *Everyday Language: Studies in Ethnomethodology*, edited by George Psathas, 97–121. New York: Irvington, 1979.
Gordis, Robert. "The Composition and Structure of Amos." In *Poets, Prophets, and Sages: Essays in Biblical Interpretation*, 217–29. Bloomington: Indiana University Press, 1971.
Goswell, Greg. "The Literary Logic and Meaning of Isaiah 38." *JSOT* 39 (2014) 165–86.
Gottlieb, Isaac. "Mashal Le-Melekh: The Search for Solomon." *Hebrew Studies* 51 (2010) 107–27.
Gowan, Donald E. *Theology in Exodus: Biblical Theology in the Form of a Commentary*. Louisville: Westminster John Knox, 1994.
Gray, George Buchanan. *A Critical and Exegetical Commentary on Numbers*. ICC. Edinburgh: T. & T. Clark, 1903.
Gray, John. *I and II Kings: A Commentary*. OTL. Philadelphia: Westminster, 1970.

Greenberg, Moshe. *Biblical Prose Prayer as a Window to the Popular Religion of Ancient Israel*. Berkeley: University of California Press, 1983.

———. *Ezekiel 1–20*. AB 22. Garden City, NY: Doubleday, 1983.

———. *Understanding Exodus*. 2nd ed. Eugene, OR: Cascade, 2013.

Greenstein, Edward. "The Riddle of Samson." *Prooftexts* 1 (1981) 237–60.

Gunkel, Hermann. *Genesis*. Translated by Mark Biddle. Mercer Library of Biblical Studies. Macon, GA: Mercer University Press, 1997.

Hackett, J. A. *The Balaam Text from Deir 'Alla*. Harvard Semitic Monographs 31. Chico, CA: Scholars, 1984.

Hadjiev, Tchavdar. "Elijah's Alleged Megalomania: Reading Strategies for Composite Texts, with 1 Kings as an Example." *JSOT* 39 (2015) 433–49.

Harrison, R. K. *Numbers*. Wycliffe Exegetical Commentary. Chicago: Moody, 1990.

Hayano, Kaoru. "Question Design in Conversation." In *The Handbook of Conversation Analysis*, edited by Jack Sidnell and Tanya Stivers, 395–414. Blackwell Handbooks in Linguistics. Oxford: Wiley-Blackwell, 2013.

Hayashi, Makoto, et al., eds. *Conversational Repair and Human Understanding*. Cambridge: Cambridge University Press, 2013.

———. "Conversational Repair and Human Understanding: An Introduction." In *Conversational Repair and Human Understanding*, edited by Makoto Hayashi et al., 1–40. Cambridge: Cambridge University Press, 2013.

Hayes, Christine. "Golden Calf Stories: The Relationship of Exodus 32 and Deuteronomy 9–10." In *The Idea of Biblical Interpretation: Essays in Honor of James L. Kugel*, edited by Hindy Najman and Judith Newman, 45–93. JSJSup 83. Leiden: Brill, 2004.

Heard, R. Christopher. "Echoes of Genesis in 1 Chronicles 4:9–10: An Intertextual and Contextual Reading of Jabez' Prayer." *JHS* 4 (2002) 1–26.

Heath, Christian. "Talk and Recipiency: Sequential Organization in Speech and Body Movement." In *Structures in Social Action: Studies in Conversation Analysis*, edited by J. Maxwell Atkinson and John Heritage, 247–65. Cambridge: Cambridge University Press, 1984.

Heckl, Raik. "Balaam: Numbers 22–24 as a Parody of the Tradition about the Strange Divinator." Paper presented at the annual meeting of the Society of Biblical Literature International, St. Andrews, Scotland, 2013.

Heiler, Friedrich. *Das Gebet: Eine Religionsgeschichtliche und Religionspsychologische Untersuchung*. Munich: Reinhardt, 1918.

———. *Prayer: A Study in the History and Psychology of Religion*. Translated and edited by Samuel McComb with the assistance of J. Edgar Park. Oxford: Oxford University Press, 1932.

Hendrix, Ralph. "A Literary Structural Overview of Exodus 25–40." *Andrews University Seminary Studies* 30 (1992) 123–38.

Heritage, John. "Conversation Analysis as Social Theory." In *The New Blackwell Companion to Social Theory*, edited by Brian S. Turner, 300–320. Blackwell Companions to Sociology. Oxford: Blackwell, 2008.

———. "Current Developments in Conversation Analysis." In *Conversation: An Interdisciplinary Perspective*, edited by Derek Roger and Peter Bull, 21–47. Intercommunication 3. Clevedon, UK: Multilingual Matters, 1989.

———. "Epistemics in Conversation." In *The Handbook of Conversation Analysis*, edited by Jack Sidnell and Tanya Stivers, 370–94. Blackwell Handbooks in Linguistics. Oxford: Wiley-Blackwell, 2013.

Heschel, Abraham. *The Prophets*. Vol. 2. San Francisco: Harper & Row, 1962.

Hodossy-Takács, Előd. "On the Battlefield and Beyond: The Reinterpretation of the Moabite-Israelite Encounters in 2 Chronicles 20." In *Rewritten Bible after Fifty Years: Texts, Terms, or Techniques?*, edited by József Zsengellér, 167–80. JSJSup 168. Leiden: Brill, 2014.

Holladay, John S. "The Day(s) the Moon Stood Still." *JBL* 88 (1968) 166–78.

Holladay, William L. *Jeremiah 1: Commentary on the Book of the Prophet Jeremiah: Chapters 1–25*. Hermeneia. Philadelphia: Fortress, 1986.

Hossfeld, Frank-Lothar. "Die Tempelvision Ez 8–11 im Licht unterschiedlicher methodischer Zugänge." In *Ezekiel and His Book: Textual and Literary Criticism and Their Interrelation*, edited by J. Lust, 151–65. Bibliotheca Ephemeridum theologicarum Lovaniensium 74. Leuven: Leuven University Press, 1986.

Hurvitz, Avi. "The Recent Debate on Late Biblical Data: Solid Data, Experts' Opinions, and Inconclusive Arguments." *Hebrew Studies* 47 (2006) 191–210.

Hutchby, Ian, and Robin Wooffitt. *Conversation Analysis*. 2nd ed. Cambridge: Polity, 2008.

Imschoot, Paul van. *Theologie de l'Ancien Testament*. Bibliotheque de Theologie Serie 3. Tournai: Desclee, 1956.

Japhet, Sara. *1 and 2 Chronicles: A Commentary*. OTL. Louisville: Westminster John Knox, 1993.

———. *The Ideology of the Book of Chronicles and Its Place in Biblical Thought*. Beiträge zur Erforschung des Alten Testaments und des antiken Judentums 9. Bern: Lang, 1989.

Jenkins, A. K. "Hezekiah's Fourteenth Year: A New Interpretation of 2 Kings xviii 13—xix 37." *VT* 26 (1976) 284–98.

Jeon, Jaeyoung. *The Call of Moses and the Exodus Story: A Redactional-Critical Study in Exodus 3–4 and 5–13*. Forschungen zum Alten Testament 2/60. Tübingen: Mohr/Siebeck, 2013.

———. "The Zadokites in the Wilderness: The Rebellion of Korach (Num 16) and the Zadokite Redaction." *ZAW* 127 (2015) 381–411.

Jeremias, Jörg. *The Book of Amos: A Commentary*. Translated by Douglas W. Stott. OTL. Louisville: Westminster John Knox, 1998.

Josephus. *Jewish Antiquities*. Translated by William Whiston. Grand Rapids: Kregel, 1960.

Joüon, Paul, and T. Muraoka. *A Grammar of Biblical Hebrew*. 2nd ed. Subsidia Biblica 27. Rome: Pontifical Biblical Institute, 2006.

Kalimi, Isaac. *The Reshaping of Ancient Israelite History in Chronicles*. Winona Lake, IN: Eisenbrauns, 2005.

Kalmanofsky, Amy. "Women of God: Maternal Grief and Religious Response in 1 Kings 17 and 2 Kings 4." *JSOT* 36 (2011) 55–74.

Kaminsky, Joel. *Corporate Responsibility in the Hebrew Bible*. JSOTSup 196. Sheffield: Sheffield Academic, 1995.

Kendrick, Kobin H., and Francisco Torreira. "The Timing and Construction of Preference: A Quantitative Study." *Discourse Processes* 52 (2014) 255–89.

Kimelman, Reuven. "Prophecy as Arguing with God and the Ideal of Justice." *Interpretation* 68 (2014) 17–27.
Kislev, Itamar. "The Investiture of Joshua (Numbers 27:12–23) and the Dispute on the Form of the Leadership in Yehud." *VT* 59 (2009) 429–45.
Knierim, Rolf P., and George W. Coats. *Numbers*. FOTL 4. Grand Rapids: Eerdmans, 2005.
Knoppers, Gary. *1 Chronicles 1–9*. AB 12. New York: Doubleday, 2003.
———. "Images of David in Early Judaism: David as Repentant Sinner in Chronicles." *Biblica* 76 (1995) 449–70.
———. "Prayer and Propaganda: Solomon's Dedication of the Temple and the Deuteronomist's Program." *CBQ* 57 (1995) 229–54.
Kratz, Reinhard G. *The Composition of the Narrative Books of the Old Testament*. Translated by John Bowden. London: T. & T. Clark, 2005.
Krüger, Thomas. "Where Is God?—And If So, Which One? Some Reflections on Genesis 28:10–22 and 35:1–15." In *Nächstenliebe und Gottesfurcht: Beiträge aus alttestamentlicher, semitistischer und altorientalistischer Wissenschaft für Hans-Peter Mathys zum 65*, edited by Jenni von Hanna et al., translated by Margaret Hiley, 245–58. Alter Orient und Altes Testament 439. Münster: Ugarit, 2016.
Lee, Chee-Chiew. "גים in Genesis 35:11 and the Abrahamic Promise of Blessing for the Nations." *Journal of the Evangelical Theological Society* 52 (2009) 467–82.
Lee, Seung-Hee. "Response Design in Conversation." In *The Handbook of Conversation Analysis*, edited by Jack Sidnell and Tanya Stivers, 415–32. Blackwell Handbooks in Linguistics. Oxford: Wiley-Blackwell, 2013.
Lehming, Sigo. "Versuch zu Ex XXXII." *VT* 10 (1960) 16–50.
Leonard-Fleckman, Mahri. "Stones from Heaven and Celestial Tricks: The Battle at Gibeon in Joshua 10." *CBQ* 79 (2017) 385–401.
Levine, Baruch. *Numbers 1–20*. AB 4. New York: Doubleday, 1993.
Levinson, Stephen C. "On the Human Interactional Engine." In *Roots of Human Sociality: Culture, Cognition and Interaction*, edited by N. J. Enfield and Stephen C. Levinson, 39–69. Wenner-Gren International Symposium Series. Oxford: Berg, 2006.
———. *Pragmatics*. Cambridge Textbooks in Linguistics. Cambridge: Cambridge University Press, 1983.
Lindstöm, Anna, and Marja-Leena Sorjonen. "Affiliation in Conversation." In *The Handbook of Conversation Analysis*, edited by Jack Sidnell and Tanya Stivers, 350–69. Blackwell Handbooks in Linguistics. Oxford: Wiley-Blackwell, 2013.
Long, Burke O. *1 Kings: With an Introduction to Historical Literature*. FOTL 9. Grand Rapids: Eerdmans, 1984.
Luckenbill, Daniel David. *The Annals of Sennacharib*. 1924. Reprint, Ancient Texts and Translations. Eugene, OR: Wipf & Stock, 2005.
Lust, J. "A Gentle Breeze or a Roaring Thunderous Sound? Elijah at Horeb: 1 Kings XIX 12." *VT* 25 (1975) 110–15.
Lyons, John. *Semantics*. 2 vols. Cambridge: Cambridge University Press, 1977.
MacDonald, Nathan. "Anticipations of Horeb: Exodus 17 as Inner-Biblical Commentary." In *Studies on the Text and Versions of the Hebrew Bible in Honour of Robert Gordon*, edited by Geoffrey Khan and Diana Lipton, 7–19. VTSup 149. Leiden: Brill, 2012.

———. "Listening to Abraham—Listening to Yhwh: Divine Justice and Mercy in Genesis 18:16–33." *CBQ* 66 (2004) 25–43.

———. "The Literary Criticism and Rhetorical Logic of Deuteronomy I–IV." *VT* 56 (2006) 203–24.

Mali, Uziel. "The Language of Conversation in the Former Prophets." PhD diss., Hebrew University, 1983.

Mandolfo, Carleen. *God in the Dock: Dialogic Tension in the Psalms of Lament*. JSOTSup 357. London: Sheffield Academic, 2002.

Martin, Lee. "The Narrative Function of the Nameless Prophet in Judges 6." *Journal for Semitics* 16 (2007) 113–40.

Matthews, Victor H. *More than Meets the Ears: Discovering the Hidden Contexts of Old Testament Conversations*. Grand Rapids: Eerdmans, 2008.

Mays, James L. *Amos: A Commentary*. OTL. Philadelphia: Westminster, 1969.

McCarter, P. Kyle, Jr. *2 Samuel*. AB 9. New York: Doubleday, 1984.

Merrill, Eugene. "The Chronicler: What Kind of Historian Was He Anyway?" *Bibliotheca Sacra* 165 (2008) 397–412.

Mettinger, Tryggve N. D. "YHWH SABAOTH—The Heavenly King on the Cherubim Throne." In *Studies in the Period of David and Solomon and Other Essays*, edited by Tomoo Ishida, 108–38. Winona Lake, IN: Eisenbrauns, 1982.

Middlemas, Jill. "Exodus 3 and the Call of Moses: Rereading the Signs." In *The Centre and the Periphery: A European Tribute to Walter Brueggemann*, edited by Jill Middlemas et al., 131–44. Hebrew Bible Monographs 27. Sheffield: Sheffield Phoenix, 2010.

Milgrom, Jacob. *Numbers*. JPS Torah Commentary. Philadelphia: Jewish Publication Society, 1989.

Miller, Cynthia. *The Representation of Speech in Biblical Hebrew Narrative: A Linguistic Analysis*. 1996. Reprinted with an afterword, Winona Lake, IN: Eisenbrauns, 2003.

———. "Silence as a Response in Biblical Hebrew Narrative: Strategies of Speakers and Narrators." *Journal of Northwest Semitic Languages* 32 (2006) 23–43.

Miller, Patrick D. *They Cried to the Lord: The Form and Theology of Biblical Prayer*. Minneapolis: Fortress, 1994.

Milstein, Sara. "Delusions of Grandeur: Revision through Introduction in Judges 6–9." In *A Life in Parables and Poetry: Mishael Maswari Caspi, Essays in Memory of a Pedagogue, Poet, and Scholar*, edited by John Greene, 210–39. Berlin: Schwarz, 2014.

Mittmann, Siegfried. *Deuteronomium 1:1—6:3*. BZAW 139. Berlin: de Gruyter, 1975.

Moberly, R. W. L. *At the Mountain of God: Story and Theology in Exodus 32–34*. JSOTSup 22. Sheffield: Sheffield Academic, 1983.

———. "Learning to Be a True Prophet: The Story of Balaam and His Ass." In *New Heaven and New Earth: Prophecy and the Millennium: Essays in Honour of Anthony Gelston*, edited by P. J. Harland and C. T. R. Hayward, 1–17. VTSup 77. Leiden: Brill, 1999.

Mobley, Gregory. *Samson and the Liminal Hero in the Ancient Near East*. Library of Hebrew Bible / Old Testament Studies 453. New York: T. & T. Clark, 2006.

Moerman, Michael. *Talking Culture: Ethnography and Conversation Analysis*. Philadelphia: University of Pennsylvania Press, 1988.

Montgomery, James. *The Books of Kings*. ICC. Edinburgh: T. & T. Clark, 1976.

Moshavi, Adina. "Biblical Dialogue in the Light of Conversation Analysis: An Analysis of Responses to Yes-No Questions." Paper presented at the Annual Meeting of the Society of Biblical Literature, Boston, November 19, 2017.

———. "Conversation Analysis." In *Linguistics for Hebraists and Biblical Scholars*, edited by J. Cook and R. D. Holmstedt. University Park, PA: Eisenbrauns, forthcoming.

Moyer, Clinton. "Who Is the Prophet, and Who the Ass? Role-Reversing Interludes and the Unity of the Balaam Narrative (Numbers 22–24)." *JSOT* 37 (2012) 167–83.

Muraoka, T. *Emphatic Words and Structures in Biblical Hebrew*. Jerusalem: Magnes, 1985.

Myers, Jacob. *1 Chronicles*. AB 12. Garden City, NY: Doubleday, 1983.

———. *2 Chronicles*. AB 13. Garden City, NY: Doubleday, 1965.

Na'aman, Nadav. "Prophetic Stories as Sources for the Histories of Jehoshaphat and the Omrides." *Biblica* 78 (1997) 153–73.

———. "The Temple Library of Jerusalem and the Composition of the Book of Kings." In *Congress Volume, Leiden 2004*, edited by Andre Lemairé, 129–52. VTSup 109. Brill: Leiden, 2006.

Nelson, Richard. *Deuteronomy: A Commentary*. OTL. Louisville: Westminster John Knox, 2002.

———. *Joshua: A Commentary*. OTL. Louisville: Westminster John Knox, 1997.

Nöldeke, Theodor. "Die s.g. Grundschrift des Pentateuchs." In *Untersuchungen zur Kritik des Alten Testaments*, 1–144. Kiel: Schwers, 1869.

Noort, Ed. "Joshua and Copernicus: Josh 10:12–15 and the History of Reception." In *Flores Florentino: Dead Sea Scrolls and Other Early Jewish Studies in Honour of Florentino Garcia Martinez*, edited by Anthony Hilhorst et al., 387–401. JSJSup 122. Leiden: Brill, 2007.

Noth, Martin. *The Deuteronomistic History*. JSOTSup 15. Sheffield: Sheffield University Press, 1981.

———. *A History of Pentateuchal Traditions*. Translated by Bernhard W. Anderson. Englewood Cliffs, NJ: Prentice-Hall, 1972.

———. *Numbers: A Commentary*. Translated by James D. Martin. OTL. Philadelphia: Westminster, 1968.

Oancea, Constantin. "Die Witwe und Israel: Die Tornerweckungssszene (1 Kön 17, 17–24) als Präludiom für die Karmelerzählung (1 Kön 18, 20–24)." *Sacra Scripta* 5 (2007) 130–41.

Ochs, Elinor. "Introduction: What Child Language Can Contribute to Pragmatics." In *Developmental Pragmatics*, edited by Elinor Ochs and Bambi B. Schieffelin, 1–17. New York: Academic Press, 1979.

O'Connell, K. G. "The List of Seven Peoples in Canaan: A Fresh Analysis." In *The Answers Lie Below: Essays in Honor of Lawrence Edmond Toombs*, edited by Henry O. Thompson, 221–42. Lanham, MD: University Press of America, 1984.

Overholt, Thomas W. *The Threat of Falsehood: A Study in the Theology of the Book of Jeremiah*. Studies in Biblical Theology 2/16. London: SCM, 1970.

Paul, Shalom M. *Amos: A Commentary on the Book of Amos*. Hermeneia. Minneapolis: Fortress, 1991.

Person, Raymond F., Jr. *The Deuteronomic History and the Book of Chronicles: Scribal Works in an Oral World*. Ancient Israel and Its Literature 6. Atlanta: Society of Biblical Literature, 2010.

———. *From Conversation to Oral Tradition: A Simplest Systematics for Oral Traditions.* Routledge Studies in Rhetoric and Stylistics 10. New York: Routledge, 2016.

———. *In Conversation with Jonah: Conversation Analysis, Literary Criticism, and the Book of Jonah.* JSOTSup 220. Sheffield: Sheffield Academic, 1996.

———. "The Problem of 'Literary Unity' from the Perspective of the Study of Oral Traditions." In *Empirical Models Challenging Biblical Criticism*, edited by Raymond Person and Robert Rezetko, 217–37. Ancient Israel and Its Literature 25. Atlanta: Society of Biblical Literature, 2016.

———. "Text Criticism as a Lens for Understanding the Transmission of Ancient Texts in their Oral Environments." In *Contextualizing Israel's Sacred Writings: Ancient Literacy, Orality, and Literary Production*, edited by Brian Schmidt, 197–215. Ancient Israel and Its Literature 22. Atlanta: Society of Biblical Literature, 2015.

Peursen, Wido van, and Eep Talstra. "Computer-Assisted Analysis of Parallel Texts in the Bible: The Case of 2 Kings xviii–xix and Its Parallels in Isaiah and Chronicles." *VT* 57 (2007) 45–72.

Pinker, Aron. "The Expulsion of Hagar and Ishmael (Gen 21:9–21)." *Women in Judaism* 6 (2009) 1–24.

Polak, Frank. "Oral Platform and Language Usage in the Abraham Narrative." In *The Formation of the Pentateuch: Bridging the Academic Cultures of Europe, Israel, and North America*, edited by Jan Gertz et al., 405–41. Forschungen zum Alten Testament 111. Tübingen: Mohr/Siebeck, 2016.

———. "Oral Substratum, Language Usage, and Thematic Flow in the Abraham-Jacob Narrative." In *Contextualizing Israel's Sacred Writings*, edited by Brian Schmidt, 217–38. Ancient Israel and Its Literature 22. Atlanta: Society of Biblical Literature, 2015.

———. "Storytelling and Redaction: Varieties of Language Usage in the Exodus Narrative." In *The Formation of the Pentateuch: Bridging the Academic Cultures of Europe, Israel, and North America*, edited by Jan Gertz et al., 443–75. Tübingen: Mohr/Siebeck, 2016.

Pomerantz Anita, and John Heritage. "Preference." In *The Handbook of Conversation Analysis*, edited by Jack Sidnell and Tanya Stivers, 210–28. Blackwell Handbooks in Linguistics. Oxford: Wiley-Blackwell, 2013.

Propp, William. *Exodus 1–18.* AB 2. New York: Doubleday, 1999.

Rad, Gerhard von. *Genesis: A Commentary.* Translated by John Marks. OTL. Philadelphia: Westminster, 1972.

Reinhartz, Adele. "Samson's Mother: An Unnamed Protagonist." *JSOT* 17 (1992) 25–37.

Rezetko, Robert. "Dating Biblical Hebrew: Evidence from Samuel-Kings and Chronicles." In *Biblical Hebrew: Studies in Chronology and Typology*, edited by I. Young, 215–50. JSOTSup 369. London: T. & T. Clark, 2003.

Ristau, Kenneth. "Breaking Down Unity: An Analysis of 1 Chronicles 21.1—22.1." *JSOT* 30 (2005) 201–21.

Robinson, Bernard. "Elijah at Horeb, 1 Kings 19:1–18: A Coherent Narrative?" *Revue Biblique* 98 (1991) 513–36.

Robinson, Jeffrey. "Overall Structural Organization." In *The Handbook of Conversation Analysis*, edited by Jack Sidnell and Tanya Stivers, 257–80. Blackwell Handbooks in Linguistics. Oxford: Wiley-Blackwell, 2013.

Rofé, Alexander. "Lo studio testo biblico alla luce della critica storico-litteraria. La reprimanda dell'uomo-profeta (*'îš nabi'*) in Gde 6, 7–10." *Henoch* 27 (2005) 137–48.

———. "Writing, Interpolating, and Editing: 2 Samuel 24 and 1 Chronicles 21 as a Case Study." *Hebrew Bible and Ancient Israel* 3 (2014) 317–26.

Rogland, Max. "Abram's Persistent Faith: Hebrew Verb Semantics in Genesis 15:6." *Westminster Theological Journal* 70 (2008) 239–44.

Roi, Mica. "1 Kings 19: A 'Departure on a Journey' Story." *JSOT* 37 (2012) 25–44.

Römer, T. C. "Exodus 3–4 und die aktuelle Pentateuchdiskussion." In *The Interpretation of Exodus: Studies in Honour of Cornelis Houtman*, edited by Riemer Roukema, 65–79. Contributions to Biblical Exegesis and Theology 44. Leuven, 2006.

Rosenblum, Karen. "When Is a Question an Accusation?" *Semiotica* 65 (1987) 143–56.

Rudolph, Wilhelm. *Chronikbücher*. Handbuch zum Alten Testament. Tübingen: Mohr/Siebeck, 1955.

Russo, Joseph. "Oral Theory: It's Development in Homeric Studies and Applicability to Other Literatures." In *Mesopotamian Epic Literature: Oral or Aural?*, edited by Marianna E. Vogelzang and Herman Vanstiphout, 7–22. Lewiston, NY: Mellen, 1992.

Ruusuvuori, Johanna. "Emotion, Affect, and Conversation." In *The Handbook of Conversation Analysis*, edited by Jack Sidnell and Tanya Stivers, 330–49. Blackwell Handbooks in Linguistics. Oxford: Wiley-Blackwell, 2013.

Sacks, Harvey. *Lectures on Conversation*. 2 vols. Edited by Gail Jefferson. Oxford: Blackwell, 1992.

Sacks, Harvey, and E. A. Schegloff. "Opening up Closings." *Semiotica* 8 (1973) 289–327.

Sacks, Harvey, et al. "A Simplest Systematics for the Organization of Turn-Taking in Conversation." *Language* 50 (1974) 696–735.

Sasson, Jack. *Jonah*. AB 24B. New York: Doubleday, 1990.

Schegloff, E. A. "Introduction." In *Harvey Sacks: Lectures on Conversation*, edited by Gail Jefferson, ix–lxii. Oxford: Blackwell, 1992.

———. "On Complainability." *Social Problems* 52 (2005) 449–76.

———. "On the Organization of Sequences as a Source of "Coherence in Talk-in-Interaction." In *Conversational Organization and Its Development*, edited by Bruce Dorval, 51–77. Advances in Discourse Processes 38. Norwood, NJ: Ablex, 1990.

———. "Reflections on Talk and Social Structure." In *Talk and Social Structure*, edited by Deirdre Boden and Don H. Zimmerman, 44–70. Berkeley: University of California Press, 1991.

———. "Repair after Next Turn: The Last Structurally Provided Place for the Defense of Intersubjectivity in Conversation." *American Journal of Sociology* 95 (1992) 1295–345.

———. *Sequence Organization in Interaction: A Primer in Conversation Analysis*. Cambridge: Cambridge University Press, 2007.

———. "Ten Operations in Self-Initiated, Same Turn Repair." In *Conversational Repair and Human Understanding*, edited by Makoto Hayashi et al., 41–70. Studies in Interactional Sociolinguistics 30. Cambridge: Cambridge University Press, 2013.

Schegloff, E. A., et al. "The Preference for Self-Correction in the Organization of Repair in Conversation." *Language* 53 (1977) 361–82.

Scherer, Andreas. "Gideon—Ein Anti-Held? Ein Beitrag zur Auseinandersetzung mit dem Sog. 'Flawed-Hero Approach' Am Beispiel von Jdc. VI 36–40." *VT* 55 (2005) 269–73.
Schmid, Konrad. "Genesis in the Pentateuch." In *The Book of Genesis: Composition, Reception, and Interpretation*, edited by Craig Evans, 27–50. VTSup 152. Leiden: Brill, 2012.
Selting, M. "The Construction of Units in Conversational Talk." *Language in Society* 29 (2000) 477–517.
Sidnell, Jack. *Conversation Analysis: An Introduction*. Language in Society 37. Oxford: Wiley-Blackwell, 2010.
Smelik, K. A. D. "Distortion of Old Testament Prophecy: The Purpose of Isaiah xxxvi and xxxvii." In *Crises and Perspectives: Studies in Ancient Near Eastern Polytheism, Biblical Theology, Palestinian Archaeology and Intertestamental Literature*, edited by J. C. de Moor, 70–93. Old Testament Studies 34. Leiden: Brill, 1986.
Soggin, J. Alberto. *Joshua: A Commentary*. R. A. Wilson. OTL. Philadelphia: Westminster, 1972.
———. *Judges: A Commentary*. John Bowden. OTL. Philadelphia: Westminster, 1981.
Speiser, E. A. *Genesis*. AB 1. Garden City, NY: Doubleday, 1964.
Staudt, Edwin E. "Prayer and the People in the Deuteronomist." PhD diss., Vanderbilt University, 1989.
Steck, O. H. *Überlieferung und Zeitgeschichte in den Elia-Erzählungen*. Wissenschaftliche Monographien zum Alten und Neuen Testament 26. Neukirchen-Vluyn: Neukirchener, 1968.
Steinmetz, Devora. *From Father to Son: Kinship, Conflict and Continuity in Genesis*. Literary Currents in Biblical Interpretation. Louisville: Westminster John Knox, 1991.
Stevanovic, Melisa, and Anssi Peräkylä. "Deontic Authority in Interaction: The Right to Announce, Propose, and Decide." *Research on Language and Social Interaction* 45 (2014) 297–321.
———. "Three Orders in the Organization of Human Action: On the Interface between Knowledge, Power, and Emotion in Interaction and Social Relations." *Language in Society* 43 (2014) 185–207.
Stivers, Tanya, et al. "Question-Response Sequences in Conversation across Ten Languages." *Journal of Pragmatics* 42 (2010) 2615–19.
Stivers, Tanya, et al. "Universals and Cultural Variation in Turn-Taking in Conversation." *Proceedings of the National Academy of Sciences* 106 (2009) 10587–92.
Stokes, Ryan. "The Devil Made David Do It . . . Or *Did* He? The Nature, Identity, and Literary Origins of the *Satan* in 1 Chronicles 21:1." *JBL* 128 (2009) 91–106.
———. "Satan, YHWH's Executioner." *JBL* 133 (2014) 251–70.
Stulman, Louis. *Jeremiah*. Abingdon Old Testament Commentaries. Nashville: Abingdon, 2005.
Suomala, Karla. *Moses and God in Dialogue: Exodus 32–34 in Postbiblical Literature*. Studies in Biblical Literature 61. New York: Lang, 2004.
Sweeney, Marvin A. *1 and 2 Kings: A Commentary*. OTL. Louisville: Westminster John Knox, 2007.
Tanaka, Hiroko. "Prosody for Marking Transition Relevance Places in Japanese Conversation: The Case of Turns Unmarked by Utterance—Final Objects." In *Sound Patterns in Interaction: Cross-Linguistic Studies from Conversation*, edited by Elizabeth Couper-Kuhlen and Cecilia E. Ford, 63–96. Amsterdam: Benjamins, 2004.

Thiessen, Matthew. "The Text of Genesis 17:14." *JBL* 128 (2009) 625–42.
Thompson, John. *The Book of Jeremiah*. Grand Rapids: Eerdmans, 1980.
Throntveit, Mark A. *When Kings Speak: Royal Speech and Royal Prayer in Chronicles*. SBL Dissertation Series 93. Atlanta: Scholars, 1987.
Timmer, Daniel. "Small Lexemes, Large Semantics: Prepositions and Theology in the Golden Calf Episode (Exodus 32–34)." *Biblica* 88 (2007) 92–99.
Trebolle, Julio. "Division Markers as Empirical Evidence for the Editorial Growth of Biblical Books." In *Empirical Models Challenging Biblical Criticism*, edited by Raymond Person and Robert Rezetko, 165–215. Ancient Israel and Its Literature 25. Atlanta: Society of Biblical Literature, 2016.
———. "Samuel/Kings and Chronicles: Book Divisions and Textual Composition." In *Studies in the Hebrew Bible, Qumran, and the Septuagint Presented to Eugene Ulrich*, edited by Peter Flint et al., 96–108. VTSup 101. Leiden: Brill, 2006.
Van Seters, John. *The Life of Moses: The Yahwist as Historian in Exodus-Numbers*. Louisville: Westminster John Knox, 1994.
Vainstub, Daniel. "The Miracle of the Sun and Moon in Joshua 10 as a Solar Eclipse." *VT* 69 (2019) 1–30.
Vanoni, Gottfried. *Das Buch Jona: Literar- und formkritische Untersuchungen*. Münchener Universitätsschriften: Fachbereich Katholische Theologie. St. Ottilien: Eos, 1978.
Vaulx, J. de. *Les Nombres*. Sources bibliques. Paris: Gabalda, 1972.
Wagner, Thomas. "From Salvation to Doom: Isaiah's Message in the Hezekiah Story." In *Prophecy and Prophets in Stories: Papers Read at the Fifth Meeting of the Edinburgh Prophecy Network, Utrecht, October 2013*, edited by Bob Becking and Hans Barstad, 92–103. Old Testament Studies 65. Leiden: Brill, 2015.
Waltke, Bruce, and M. O'Conner. *An Introduction to Biblical Hebrew Syntax*. Winona Lake, IN: Eisenbrauns, 1990.
Wendland, E. R. "Two Dumb Donkeys Declare the Word of the LORD: A Literary-Structural Analysis of Numbers 22–24." *Journal for Semitics* 21 (2012) 167–99.
Weimer, Peter. *Die Berufung des Mose: Literaturwissenschaftliche Analyse von Exodus 2,23—5,5*. Orbis biblicus et orientalis 32. Göttingen: Vandenhoeck & Ruprecht, 1980.
Wendel, Adolf. *Das freie Laiengebet im vorexilischen Israel*. Ex Oriente Lux 5/6. Leipzig: Pfeiffer, 1931.
Werline, Rodney. "Prayer, Politics, and Power in the Hebrew Bible." *Interpretation* 68 (2014) 5–16.
Wessels, Willie. "The Blame Game: Prophetic Rhetoric and Ideology in Jeremiah 14:10–16." *Old Testament Essays* 26 (2013) 864–81.
Westermann, Claus. *Genesis 12–36: A Commentary*. Translated by John Scullion. Continental Commentaries. Minneapolis: Augsburg, 1985.
Wieringen, Archibald van. "Notes on Isaiah 38–39." *Biblische Notizen* 102 (2000) 28–32.
Williams, D. T. "The Dial and the Boil: Some Remarks on the Healing of Hezekiah." *Old Testament Essays* 2 (1989) 29–45.
Willis, John. "Dialogue between Prophet and Audience as Rhetorical Device in the Book of Jeremiah." *JSOT* 33 (1985) 63–82.
Wolde, Ellen van. "A Stairway to Heaven? Jacob's Dream in Genesis 28:10–22." *VT* 69 (2019) 722–35.
Wolf, H. W. *Joel and Amos: A Commentary on the Books of the Prophets Joel and Amos*. Translated by Waldemar Janzen et al. Hermeneia. Philadelphia: Fortress, 1977.
Yoo, Philip. "The Four Moses Death Accounts." *JBL* 131 (2012) 423–41.

———. "Hagar the Egyptian: Wife, Handmaid, and Concubine." *CBQ* 78 (2016) 215–35.

———. "He Married a Cushite Woman! On the Text of Numbers 12:1." In *To Gaul, to Greece, and into Noah's Ark: Essays in Honour of Kevin J. Cathcart on the Occasion of His Eightieth Birthday*, edited by Laura Quick et al., 37–48. Oxford: Oxford University Press, 2019.

Yudkowsky, Rachel. "Chaos or Chiasm? The Structure of Abraham's Life." *Jewish Bible Quarterly* 35 (2007) 110–14.

Zalevski, Saul. "The Revelation of God to Solomon in Gibeon." *Tarbiz* 42 (1972/3) 255–58.

Zimmerli, Walther. *Ezekiel: A Commentary on the Book of the Prophet Ezekiel*. 2 vols. Translated by Ronald Clements. Hermeneia. Philadelphia: Fortress, 1979.

Subject Index

adjacency pairs, 3, 4, 16–17, 20, 39,88, 130, 207, 265
agency, 26–27, 39–40, 60, 81, 90, 99, 104, 136, 144–45,166, 169, 180, 222, 250, 257

Buber, Martin, 10–12

closing, 28–29, 37, 40, 43, 50n25, 53, 57, 69, 74, 79, 81, 96, 252
context, 3, 31–32, 47–48, 50, 54, 58, 64, 67, 70, 75, 86, 93, 98
conversation analysis, 1–3
conversational prayer (defined), 4–8
consequential action, 5, 7, 16, 18, 23, 34, 54, 58, 60, 66, 67, 69, 70, 72–73, 79, 90, 100, 124–26, 131, 151, 162, 164, 185–86, 203, 208, 212, 222, 224–25, 232, 243, 256
cultural transfer, 3–4

dream, 54, 55, 71, 142, 186

expansion, 19–20, 31, 56, 124, 125126
 insert expansion, 21, 131
 pre-expansion, 20–21, 87, 117, 123, 131, 165
 post-expansion, 23, 126, 131, 164, 167

infinitive; saying, 37–38, 44, 93, 98n35, 130–32, 180n29, 207, 225, 238, 249

intersubjectivity, 13, 23, 46, 150, 161, 163, 217, 222, 247, 256–57, 261

notation, 34

opening, 27–28, 37–38, 42, 44, 65, 67, 71, 76, 81, 154

preference, 17, 87
 dispreferred, 18–19, 21, 23, 26, 45, 55–56, 77, 87–91, 95, 102, 105, 118, 134, 137, 145, 155, 156, 161, 167, 206, 218, 241, 243, 249, 267
 preferred, 17–18, 19, 28, 52, 55, 56, 57, 69, 77, 87, 90, 105, 135, 162, 165, 169, 195, 211, 217, 222, 228, 249, 265, 267

question, 19, 22, 49, 89, 99, 117, 118, 167, 169, 210, 218, 250, 265–69
question, reverse polarity, 118–20, 143, 169

recipient design, 29–30, 37, 62, 68, 88, 99, 121, 161, 175, 202, 203, 224, 227
repair, 21, 30–31, 52, 82, 89, 149, 219
round, 20, 40

silence, 4, 18, 26, 29, 75, 77, 169, 189, 211, 218, 267

standing, 27, 37, 39, 43, 49–52, 76, 77, 80–81, 89, 105, 115, 120, 138, 140, 145–46, 166, 168, 174, 182–83, 203, 206, 214, 217, 231, 269
storytelling, 32–33, 154, 204

topic, 33, 46, 49, 87, 103, 105, 128, 156
turn allocation, 25
turn construction, 24, 88n11
turn-taking, 3, 23–26, 90

Author Index

Alter, Robert, 30n48
Anderson, A. A., 171n2, 173n8, 174n11, 175n13, 176n18
Arnold, Bill, 42n14, 42n15, 44n18
Assis, Elie, 170n61
Atkinson, J. M., 231n26
Auld, Graeme, 175n14

Balentine, Samuel, 2, 2n5, 5, 5n22, 6, 7, 12n47, 26n35, 30n48, 31n57, 211n9, 212n12
Baruchi-Unna, Amitai, 203n73
Beer, G., 103n46
Begg, Christopher, 103n46
Berman, Joshua, 136n108, 147n12, 149n22, 149n23
Blidstein, Gerald, 121n68
Blenkinsopp, Joseph, 202n68, 207n79
Blum, Erhard, 62n1, 78n39
Boase, Elizabeth, 63n5, 64n7, 64n9, 66n11, 68n17
Boda, Mark, 241n6
Boling, Robert, 150n26, 151n28, 153n36, 155, 155n39, 156n41, 167n55
Braun, Roddy, 229n20
Broida, Marian, 168n57
Brueggemann, Walter, 50n26, 175n15
Buber, Martin, 9, 10, 10n44, 11n45, 12, 12n48
Budd, Philip, 98n36, 117n60, 142n2
Bulkeley, Tim, 248n30, 249n31

Button, Graham, 33n65

Campos, Martha, 248n30
Carroll, Robert, 240n3
Casey, Neil, 33n65
Chepey, Stuart, 169n58
Childs, Brevard, 95n28, 96n31, 100n43, 103n46, 107n52
Claassens, Julianna, 61n40
Clayman, S. E., 88n11, 247n29
Clements, Ronald, 147n13, 149n23
Clift, Rebecca, 3n9, 3n12, 3n13, 3n14, 16n6, 18n14, 20n20, 20n21, 20n24, 25n33, 34n67, 60n35, 77n37, 87n2, 89n13, 89n16, 143n4, 187n44, 218n22, 218n25, 265n2
Coats, George, 99n36, 121n68
Cogan, Mordechai, 211n6, 213n14
Coggins, R. J., 186n41
Cooke, G., 245n22
Corvin, J., 5, 5n23, 5n24, 6, 6n29, 8n38, 13, 13n2, 14n3
Curtis, Edward, 224n4, 230n24

Davidson, Judy, 218n27
Davis, Andrew, 211n7
De Vries, Simon, 175n14, 194n56, 210n5, 213n14
Dion, Paul, 182n34
Doan William J., 150n27
Douglas, Mary, 127n85

AUTHOR INDEX

Dozeman, Thomas, 35n3, 151n30
Driver, S. R., 137n112, 172n5
Duke, Rodney, 223n1
Durham, John, 100n42

Eckart, Otto, 137n109
Edenburg, Cynthia, 181n30

Feldman, Ariel, 181n31
Fetherolf, Christina, 213n13, 218n26
Fishbane, Michael, 62n1
Ford, C. E., 24n29
Forsling, Josef, 121n69
Freedman, David Noel, 61n38, 153n36
Fretheim, Terrence, 95n29, 99n39
Friedman, Richard Elliott, 35n2
Frisch, Amos, 144n6

Giles, Terry, 10n43, 150n27
Goffman, Erving, 3, 3n10
Goodwin, C., 25n32
Gordis, Robert, 248n30
Goswell, Greg, 207n81
Gottlieb, Isaac, 196n60
Gowan, D., 90n17
Greenburg, Moshe, 1, 1n2, 1n3, 5, 6, 96n33, 176n20, 245n21
Greenstein, Edward, 170n61
Gray, George, 107n53, 117n70, 122n70, 123n76, 127n86, 129n92
Gray, John, 175n14
Gunkel, Hermann, 75n30

Hackett, J. A., 145n8
Hadjiev, Tchavdar, 214n17, 216n21
Harrison, R. K., 98n36
Hayano, Kaoru, 118n63, 143n4, 169n59, 250n33
Hayashi, Makoto, 29n47, 30n51
Hayes, Christine, 103n46, 107n52
Heard, R. Christopher, 224n3, 224n5, 224n7, 225, 226n13, 226n14
Heath, Christian, 62n3
Heckl, Raik, 145n8
Heiler, Friedrich, 4
Hendrix, Ralph, 103n46

Heritage, John, 2n7, 18n13, 58n33, 77n35, 87n5, 250n33, 252n36, 270n5
Heschel, Abraham, 12n49
Hodossy-Takács, Előd, 235n32, 236n34
Holladay, John, 151n28
Holladay, William, 240n3
Hossfeld, F. L., 245n21
Hurvitz, Avi, 175n14, 181n292
Hutchby, Ian, 15n4, 25n31, 30n53, 246n25

Imschoot, P. van, 6n29

Jeon, Jaeyoung, 86n1, 127n86, 127n87, 127n89
Japhet, Sara, 175n13, 175n14, 176n19, 177n22, 182n35, 187n43, 192n55, 195n58, 224n4, 227n16, 231n27, 233n30, 234n31, 235n32, 238n37, 238n40, 238n41, 255n3
Jenkins, A., 203n73
Jeremias, J., 248n30
Josephus, 210n5
Joüon, P., 245n19

Kalimi, Isaac, 175n14, 176n16, 183n36, 186n40, 188n47, 213n15, 224n5, 233n30
Kalmanofsky, Amy, 211n6
Kaminsky, Joel, 147n13
Kendrick, K., 19n17
Kimelman, Reuven, 49n24
Kislev, Itamar, 133n99, 135n106, 135n107
Knierim, Rolf, 99n36, 121n68
Knoppers, Gary, 171n3, 175n14, 181n30, 194n56, 195n59
Kratz, Reinhard, 151n30
Krüger, Thomas, 71n21, 74n29, 79n39

Lee, Chee-Chiew, 81n46
Lee, Seung-Hee, 222n35
Lehming, S., 103n46
Leonard-Fleckman, Mahri, 150n25, 152n32

AUTHOR INDEX

Levine, Baruch, 99n36, 107n53, 114n58, 120n66, 121n69, 122n72, 127n86
Levinson, S. C., 3n10, 7n34, 16n7, 18n13, 19, 19n18, 23n27, 29n46, 31n56, 40n12, 62n2, 90n20, 210n4, 270n5
Lindstöm, Anna, 247n28
Long, Burke, 6n29
Luckenbill, Daniel David, 204n75
Lust, J., 218n24
Lyons, J., 48, 48n23

MacDonald, Nathan, 51n27, 98n34, 139n114
Madsen, Albert, 224n4, 230n24
Mali, U., 4n17
Mandolfo, Carleen, 2n6
Martin, Lee, 152n35
Matthews, Victor, 2n6, 27n38
Mays, James, 248n30
McCarter, P. Kyle, 172n5, 176n17
Merrill, Eugene, 175n14
Mettinger, T., 177n21
Middlemas, Jill, 88n9
Milgrom, Jacob, 117n62, 122n71
Miller, Cynthia, 4n17, 38n9, 98n35, 130n94, 130n95, 130n96, 207n80, 238n38
Miller, Patrick, 5n20, 6n29, 26n35
Milstein, Sara, 152n35
Mittmann, S., 135n105
Moberly, R., 103n46, 142n2
Mobley, Gregory, 165n52, 170n61
Moerman, M., 3n9
Montgomery, James, 203n72, 211n6
Moshavi, Adina, 4n17
Moyer, Clinton, 144n7
Muraoka, T., 245n19
Myers, Jacob, 225n9, 230n24

Na'aman, Nadav, 233n30
Nelson, Richard, 137n111, 148n20
Nöldeke, Theodor, 78n39
Noort, Ed, 151n29
Noth, Martin, 103n46, 135n106, 171n4

Oancea, Constantin, 210n3
Ochs, E., 48, 48n21
O'Connell, K., 88n10
O'Conner, M., 72n22, 80n44
Overholt, Thomas, 243n11

Paul, Shalom M., 248n30
Peräkylä, A., 26n37, 55n30
Person, Raymond, 2n6, 2n8, 175n14, 252n37
Peursen, Wido van, 202n68
Pinker, Aron, 60n37
Polak, Frank, 39n10, 86n1, 95n28, 102n45
Pomerantz Anita, 77n35, 252n36
Propp, William, 89n12, 96n32, 96n33, 100n41

Rad, Gerhard von, 76n32
Raymond, G., 270n5
Reinhartz, Adele, 165n52
Rezetko, Robert, 181n33
Ristau, Kenneth, 180n28, 181n32, 184n39
Robinson, Bernard, 216n18, 216n21
Robinson, Jeffrey, 188n48
Rofé, Alexander, 155n37, 181n30
Rogland, Max, 39n11
Roi, Mica, 216n21
Römer, T. C., 86n1
Rosenblum, Karen, 218n23
Rudolph, W., 238n41
Ruusuvuori, Johanna, 138n113, 247n27

Sacks, Harvey, 2n8, 3n11, 4n16, 28n45, 29n46, 29n47, 33n63, 33n66, 37n6, 37n7
Sasson, Jack, 251n34
Schegloff, E. A., 4n16, 7n33, 17n9, 17n11, 20n23, 21n26, 28n45, 29n46, 30n49, 32, 32n59, 33n64, 77n38, 87n3, 89n14, 89n15, 219n29
Scherer, Andreas, 157n42
Schmid, Konrad, 35n3
Selting, M., 24n29

Sidnell, Jack, 1n1, 2n4, 3, 3n10, 3n15, 5n21, 9n42, 15, 15n4, 15n5, 16n7, 17n10, 18n14, 20n21, 20n22, 23, 24n28, 27n39, 27n41, 28n42, 28n43, 28n44, 30n49, 30n50, 30n52, 31n54, 31n55, 31n56, 33n62, 33n65, 37n8, 40n12, 48n22, 64n8, 76n34, 87n4, 88n6, 206n78, 216n19, 219n28, 228n19
Smelik, K. A. D., 202n68
Soggin, Alberto, 148n18, 155n37, 155n39
Sorjonen, Marja-Leena, 247n28
Speiser, E.A., 50n26
Staudt, E., 6, 6n25, 6n27, 8, 8n40, 9n41
Steck, O. H., 210n3
Steinmetz, Devora, 63n4
Stevanovic, M., 26n37, 55n30
Stivers, T., 3n9, 17n12
Stokes, Ryan, 180n28
Stulman, Louis, 241n7, 242n9, 242n10, 243n16, 243n17
Suomala, Karla, 2n6
Sweeney, Marvin, 187n45, 210n5

Talstra, Eep, 202n62
Tanaka, H., 24n29
Thiessen, Matthew, 44n17
Thompson, John, 242n9
Thompson, S.S., 24n29
Timmer, Daniel, 101n44
Torreira, F., 19n17

Trebolle, Julio, 151n29, 175n14

Van Seters, John, 86n1
van Wolde, Ellen, 71n19
Vainstub, Daniel, 152n33
Vanoni, G., 251n35
Vaulx, J. de, 133n100

Wagner, Thomas, 208n83, 208n84
Waltke, Bruce, 72n22, 80n44, 181n33, 221n32
Wendland, E. R., 145n9, 145n10
Weimer, P., 89n12
Wendel, A., 6n28
Werline, Rodney, 26n35
Wessels, Willie, 240n3
Westermann, Claus, 35n1, 42n14, 71n21, 73n25
Wieringen, Archibald van, 207n82
Williams, D. T., 206n77
Willis, John, 240n4
Wolf, H. W., 248n30
Wooffitt, Robin, 15n4, 25n31, 30n53, 246n25
Wright, G. Ernest, 150n26, 151n28

Yoo, Philip, 60n36, 121n67, 127n87, 137n109
Yudkowsky, Rachel, 269n4

Zalevski, S., 187n43
Zimmerli, Walther, 245, 245n23

Ancient Document Index

Old Testament/Hebrew Bible

Genesis

1	45
3–4	7
3	6, 94n26, 99, 267
3:1–3	269n3
3:9–20	6
3:9–19	267
3:13	59n34
4	6
4:9–15	6
4:9	7
4:14	45
14:14–15	7
12–25a	62
12–14	37
12	65 69
12:1–3	65, 256
12:1	66
12:2	68n14
12:3	54
12:7	159n45, 262n10
12:10–20	64, 257
13	69
13:16	68n14
15	37, 40, 42n14, 49
15:1–21	42n14
15:1–10	36
15:1–6	37
15:1–2	6
15:1	49, 57n31, 65, 68n14, 94n22, 96
15:2	14
15:5	68n14
15:9–21	37
15:16	40n13
15:19–21	88
15:20	45
16	40
16:7–14	6
16:7–12	59n34
16:7	65
16:17–14	59
16:13–14	168n58
17	27n40, 42n14, 44, 49, 80, 81
17:1–21	7, 41
17:1–8	78
17:1	65, 94n22, 97
17:3	80
17:13	54
17:19	54
17:22	80, 173n9
18	22, 31, 32, 57
18:1	65
18:3	122n73
18:4–8	164
18:12–15	46
18:15	59n34
18:18–19	54
18:18	54
18:22	100, 100n41
18:23–32	47

Genesis (continued)

18:23	14
19	71
19:18–19	274
20	21, 64, 66
20:3–8	53
20:3	65, 132n101
21	60n37, 76
21:6–7	46
21:16–19	58
21:17–19	59n34
21:20	61
22	64, 65, 66
22:12	61
22:16–18	64
22:17–18	64
22:17	68n14
24:11	274
24:12–24	5n19
24:26–27	274
25b-36	62
25:1–6	61n38
25:21	273
26	57n32, 62n1, 63, 64, 65, 66
26:1–5	63
26:2–5	64
26:24–25	66
26:24	65, 88n8
27:27	96
28	71, 73, 80n42, 81
28:3	43n16, 97
28:13–22	70
28:13–17	79n39
28:13	65, 88n8, 96
28:14	77
28:15	44n18, 68n14
28:17	73n24
28:18	79
28:22	80, 159n45
30:6	273
30:17	151n31
30:22	273
31:3	68n14, 76
31:13	74n28
31:29	88n8
32:8	75
32:9–12	73
32:9	75n30
32:10	68n15
32:13	75
32:22–32	63n6
32:28	75n30, 79
32:10–13	75n31
32:12	77
32:24–31	164
33:20	79, 80n41
35	73, 78, 80, 81
35:1	159n45
35:7	73n24
35:9–15	78, 79n39, 81, 97
35:9	65, 81
35:13	80, 81
35:14	159n45
43:14	43n16
48:3	43n16
49:25	43n16

Exodus

1–13	91
1:7	45n20
2:23–24	271
2:24	117
3–4	7, 87
3	6, 7, 27
3:2	94n22, 117n62
3:4—4:17	83, 86
3:7–8	120
3:12	157
3:13	167
4:19	94n23
4:21	94n23
4:24	94n27
4:27	94n23
5	258n5
5:22—6:13	92
6	96
6:2–6	120
6:2–8	97
6:5	117
12:42	104n49
12:51	104n49
13:16	104n49

14:10	271	34:6–7	107n53, 109, 113n55, 251n35
14:15	271		
16:4	6		
16:7–8	117n62	Leviticus	
16:28	6		
17	98n36, 99, 99n36, 100	7:19–21	237
		9:24	271
17:1	98	10:2	117n62
17:4–7	97	11:45	104n49
17:5–6	99	13:4	123n74
17:5	100	14:3	123n74
17:7	101	16:21	271
17:14	6	19:36	104n49
19:18	117n62	21:21–23	123n77
19:21	168n56	22:33	104n49
20:2	104n47	23:43	104n49
20:5–6	109	25:38, 42, 55	104n49
22:23	271	26:40	271
24:9–11	168n56	26:45	104n49
29	79		
31:18	102	Numbers	
32–34	101n44		
32	36, 101, 102, 103n46, 105, 107, 107n52, 109, 110, 111, 112, 137, 148, 258n2	3:23–28	133
		6:6	169
		9:10–11	237
		11	7n35, 116, 122
		11:1	116
32:7–10, 15	111	11:2	271
32:7–14	101	11:11–24	115, 118, 169, 256
32:7–8	103, 113, 113n56, 114	11:11	117
		11:23	120
32:9–14	103	11:29	260
32:9	113	12	137
32:10	113, 114n57	12:1	121n67
32:10b	114n58	12:2	117n61
32:11–14	111, 249n32	12:7–8	68n16
32:11–13	112	12:7	260
32:11	13, 83, 113	12:8	36n5, 254n1
32:11b	113n56	12:13–14	120, 121
32:12	107n53, 113	12:13	148n19, 221n31, 221n34, 256
32:13	68n15, 113, 114n57, 120, 120, 213		
		12:28	123n78
		13:12	114n57
32:31–34	101, 102, 103, 114	14	109, 110, 112, 113, 122, 148
33:11	36n5, 254n1, 260		
33:20	168n56	14:11–35	107
34	113n55	14:11–25	107n53

Numbers (continued)

14:11–20	107
14:11–15	101
14:11	110
14:12	113, 114n58
14:13–16	112
14:13	113
14:16	113, 113n56, 114n58
14:18	11n46, 109, 113, 251n35
14:23	120
14:30	120
15	79
15:41	104n49
16	137
16:1–50	94n24, 123
16:2	123n79
16:15	126
16:16	124n81
16:20–24	126
16:22	132n97, 134
20	99, 169
20:6–9	97, 98
20:9–11	100
20:10	99
20:12	100, 134
20:13	100n43, 101
20:16	104n49
20:22–29	133n100
21:3	151n31
21:4	163n49
21:5	104n49
21:7	271
22	7n36, 180
22:9–35	140
23–24	145
23:22	104n49
24:8	104n49
27	135
27:12–23	132, 133, 136, 138
27:14	139
27:16–17	138
27:16	125n82
27:20	139
28	79
31:2	134n102

Deuteronomy

1–4	137, 138
1:16	136
1:27	104n49
1:34	117n61
3	8, 136, 137, 139
3:23–28	136
3:25	138
3:27	136
4:1	139
4:37	104n49
5:6	104n47
5:9–10	109
6:12	104n49
6:16	100n43
6:21	104n49
7:9–10	109
8:14	104n49
9	101, 103n46, 110, 111, 112, 114, 120, 240n5
9:11–14	101
9:12–15	111
9:12–14	110
9:12	104n49, 113, 113n56, 114
9:13	113
9:14	113, 114n57, 114n58, 115
9:19	271
9:22–24	114
9:22	100n43
9:25–29	101, 103n46, 220n30
9:26–29	107, 110, 112
9:26	104n49, 113, 113n56
9:27	68n15, 113, 114n57
9:28	113, 113n56, 114n57
10:1	112
10:10	151n31
12	73
13:5	104n49
16:1	104n49
20:1	104n49

25:9	123n75	10	8, 160
26:5–10	73	10:10–16	160, 162
26:8	104n49	10:15	162n48
29:25	104n49	11:35	148n17
31:7	133	13	259n7
31:1–8	133	13:3–7	59n34
31:14–23	133	13:8–23	163
31:15	133	13:8–20	164
32	139	13:9	151n31
32:48–52	133, 136	13:19	167n54
32:51–52	134	13:25	168
32:51	100n43, 139	14:6	168
33:8	100n43	14:19	168
33:24	137	15:14	168
34:1–4	136	15:18–20	168
34:4	136	15:18–19	168, 258
34:10	94n25, 254n1	16:16	163n49
		16:17	169n58
		16:23–24	272
Joshua		16:28–30	5, 272
4	73	16:28	168
7	149	21:2–3	272
7:3	147n12	21:3	5
7:6–16	146		
7:7	148, 159n44, 247n26	Ruth	
7:10–15	148	1:8–9	272
10	149, 151	2:4	272
10:12–14	150	2:12	272
24:6	104n49	4:11	272
24:10	146n11	4:14	272
24:17	104n49		
24:32	104n49	1 Samuel	
		1:10	271
Judges		1:11–12	5n19
2:12	104n49	1:11	272
3:9	271	1:12–15	271
6	152n35, 165n52, 165n53, 261	7:5–8	249n32
		7:5	271
6:8	104n49	7:6	5n19
6:12—7:11	152	7:8–9	271
6:12–24	152	7:16	272
6:13	104n49	8:6	271
6:19–21	167n54	8:8	104n49
6:20–21	164	8:18	271
6:22	148n17, 247n26	10:18	104n49

1 Samuel (continued)

12:6	104n49
12:8	104n49
12:10–11	5n19
12:10	162n48, 272
12:17–18	271
12:19	271
12:23	271
15:11	271

2 Samuel

6:17	176n17
6:18	271
7	177, 197, 229
7:6	104n49
7:18–29	171, 228
7:18	173, 228
7:19	176
7:23	172n6, 175
7:25	174
7:26	175, 176
7:27	174, 176, 176n16
7:28	177
8:1	175
12:16	271
15:31	5, 272
21:1	271
24	181n33
24:1	180
24:10–17	6, 177, 184, 202, 206
24:10	183
24:11	178, 180, 180n29
24:12	177, 180
24:13	182
24:16	179n27
24:10–17	178
24:17	182, 184
24:20	183
24:28	180

1 Kings

3	197
3:5–14	184, 187
3:5	186
3:6–9	198
3:6	186
3:7	186
3:9	186
3:10	186, 188
3:11	187
3:13	187
3:14	187
3:15	186, 188, 189
4–10	187
8	8, 171n3, 197, 197n64, 234, 236
8:16	104n49
8:21	104n49
8:22–54	189
8:22–53	242n8
8:22	192n53, 194
8:23–26	195
8:25	195
8:26	174
8:28	196, 196n32
8:30	190n49, 196
8:31–32	196
8:33–34	196
8:37–40	196
8:37–39	236
8:38	195, 196n62
8:41–43	196
8:44–45	196
8:46–50	196
8:50–53	11n46, 195
8:50	195n57
8:51	104n49
8:52	196n62
8:53	104n49
8:54	194
9:3–9	236
9:9	104n49
11:9–10	187
11:11	188n46
12:28	104n49
13:2–32	210n2
13:6	271
13:38	117n62
17–18	214
17	212, 213, 257n4, 260n8
17:20–22	209

17:24	210	20:3	221n31
18:27–28	210n2	20:4	206, 207
18:36–38	212	20:5	88n8
18:36	106n51, 213	20:6	207
18:37	213	20:8–9	207
18:42	271	20:11	210n2
19	26n34, 32, 165n53, 217, 261, 265n1	22:41–50	233
		22:45	233
19:4–18	214, 252n38		
19:9	211n10		

1 Chronicles

1–9	235n33
4	226
4:10	223, 255
4:39–43	224n3
5:9–10	224n3
5:20	272
16:34	237
17	181n33, 183, 229
17:2	176n17
17:16–27	171, 172, 228
17:16	173, 176n19, 197, 228
17:17–18	174
17:17	176, 176n19, 177
17:18	176, 177
17:19	174
17:21	172n6, 176
17:24	175, 176, 177
17:25	174, 176n16, 177
17:27	177
18:1	175
21	178n24, 178n26, 181, 181n33, 182
21:1–22	183n37
21:1	143n3
21:8–17	177, 179, 202, 206
21:8	183
21:9	177, 180, 180n29
21:12	182
21:15	179n27
21:17	184, 184n38
21:21	180, 183
21:26	180, 272
22:1	197n66
22:19	197n66
28	229

19:13	211n10
22:41–50	233n30

2 Kings

1:10	117n62
3	209n1
3:10	148n17
4:32–37	211n8
4:33	220n30, 266n2, 271
6:6	148n17
6;15	148n17
6:17–21	206n76
6:17–21	203n74
6:17–20	220
6:17	254n2
11:14	210n2
13:4	151n31
17:7	104n49
17:36	104n49
18:28	210n2
19	202
19:12–13	203
19:15–34	177n23, 198, 206
19:15	220n30, 254n2
19:19	203, 221n31
19:20	6n30, 254n2
19:29	203
19:34	203
19:35–37	203
20:1–7	6n30, 177n23, 202, 204
20:2–3	238
20:2	207, 220n30, 254n2

1 Chronicles (continued)

28:9	88n8
28:20	197n66
29	235
29:1	197n66
29:10–19	223, 227
29:10–13	228
29:10	227n16
29:18	106n51, 213
29:20–22	229
29:22–25	229
29:25	229n21

2 Chronicles

1–9	188
1:1	188
1:7–12	184
1:7	186, 189
1:9	197
1:10	186
1:11	187
4	230
5:13	237
6	8, 195, 196, 197, 234, 236
6:5	104n49
6:12–7:1	192
6:12	192n53, 194
6:13	194
6:14–7:1	189, 242n8
6:14–17	195
6:16	195
6:18	192n55
6:19	196, 196n62
6:21	190n49, 196
6:27	196
6:29	195
6:30	190n51, 196n62
6:32	197
6:36–40	213
6:40–42	11n46
6:40	195
7	234
7:1	195, 198, 229, 236
7:12–22	236
7:22	104n49
13:14	272
14	235, 236
14:2	230n25
14:9	230, 231
14:10–11	230n22
14:11–12	227n16, 230
14:11	227n16, 228n17, 255
16:7–10	230n25
20	234, 235
20:1	233
20:5–19	232
20:5–17	223, 227n16, 228n18, 233
20:5–12	233
20:6	227n16
20:7	35, 254
20:9	236
20:15	6n30
20:31–37	233n30
20:34	233
21:11–15	209n1
21:12	88n8
29	235
30:6	106n51, 213
30:9	195
30:18–19	238, 255
30:18	254n2
30:19–20	237
30:30	151n31
32:16	197n66
32:20	203, 203n72
33:12–13	272

Ezra

8:21–23	272
9:6–15	5, 272

Nehemiah

1:4–11	5n19
4:4–11	5n19
5:19	5n19
9:17	109, 251n35

Job

1:16	117n62

Psalms

69:28	106n50
81:8	100n43
81:10	104n48
86:15	109, 251n35
89:7–9	137
95:8	100n43
103:8	109, 251n35
106:16–18	127n89
106:32	100n43
111:4	251n35
113:5–6	137
132:8–10	195, 197n64
139:16	106n50
145:8	109

Isaiah

1:6	242
1:12–17	260n8
1:15	242n8
4:4	106n50
33:14	117n62
37	202
37:12–13	203
37:14–35	177n23, 198, 200, 206
37:20	203, 221n31
37:21	6n30
37:30	203, 221n31
37:35	203
37:36–38	203
38	208
38:1–8	205
38:3–8	6n30, 177n23, 202, 204
38:3	207, 221n31
38:4	206, 207
38:6	207
38:7–8	207
38:10–20	207
41:8	35, 254n1
42:2–4	271
50:6	123n75
56:7	271

Jeremiah

1:11	7n31
3:22–25	272
4:10	5n19, 148n17, 159, 247n26, 272
7:16	240, 272
11:1—17:27	240
11:14	240, 249n32, 272
12:16	243n12
14:7–9	272
14:11–14	239, 240, 243
14:11–12	242
14:11	5n19, 272
14:13	159n44, 242, 247n26
14:14	6n30, 240, 243
14:15–22	243
14:15–16	242, 243n15
14:16	243
14:19–22	272
15:15–18	272
16:19	272
17:14–18	272
17:16	249n32
18:19–23	272
20:7–13	272
21:2	271
21:7	240n2
21:9	240n2
23:16	243n14
23:25–32	186
23:25	243n12
23:26	243n13
23:32	243
24:10	240n2
27:8	240n2
27:13	240n2
27:15	243n12
29:9	243n12
29:17–18	240n2
29:21	243n12
29:23	243n12
32:16–25	5n19
32:17	148n17, 159n44, 242, 247n26
32:24	240n2
32:36	240n2

Jeremiah (continued)

34:17	240n2
38:2	240n2
42:17	240n2
42:22	240n2
44	79n40
44:13	240n2

Lamentations

3:8	271
3:44	271

Ezekiel

1:3	7n31
8–11	245
8:1	244
8:5	244, 245
8:6	244
8:8	244
8:12	244, 245, 246
8:13	244
8:15	244, 245
8:17	244, 245, 246
8:18	246
9	247, 259n6, 260
9:8–10	244, 245
9:8	148n17, 159n44, 246, 256
9:9	246
9:10	246
10:5	43n16
11:13	246
13:9	106n50
20	107n53
22:30	271

Daniel

2:18	271
2:19–23	272
2:20–23	5n19
6:11	271
9:4–19	7n32, 272
9:4–11	5n19
9:21–27	7n32

Amos

7	248
7:1–9	247
7:2–3	249
7:5–6	249
7:8	249
7:10–17	250

Jonah

1:14	5n19, 272
2:10	253
3:5	251
3:8	251
3:10	251
4	258, 260, 261n9
4:1	238n39, 251
4:1–11	250
4:2–11	216n20
4:2–3	251
4:2	109, 251
4:3	252
4:8	252

Haggai

2:20	7n31

Zechariah

4:8	7n31

Malachi

3:2	117n62

New Testament

James

2:23	35n4

Apocrypha

2 Maccabees

3:24	134n103
14:46	134n103

Jubilees

10:3	134n103

Greco-Roman Writings

Josephus

Jewish Antiquities

3.13.3	210n5